WILLIAM APPLEMAN WILLIAMS

AMERICAN RADICALS
A SERIES EDITED BY HARVEY J. KAYE
AND ELLIOTT J. GORN

Also available in this Routledge series:

MICHAEL HARRINGTON
SPEAKING AMERICAN
by Robert A. Gorman

WILLIAM APPLEMAN WILLIAMS

The Tragedy of Empire

PAUL M. BUHLE
and
EDWARD RICE-MAXIMIN

ROUTLEDGE
New York and London

Published in 1995 by

Routledge
29 West 35th Street
New York, NY 10001

Published in Great Britain in 1995 by

Routledge
11 New Fetter Lane
London EC4P 4EE

Copyright © 1995 by Routledge
Series design by Annie West
Printed in the United States of America on acid-free paper

Buhle, Paul, 1944–
    William Appleman Williams—the tragedy of empire / Paul M. Buhle,
Edward Rice-Maximin.
    p.   cm. —(American Radicals)
    Includes bibliographical references (p. 297) and index.
    ISBN 0-415-91130-3 (hb : acid-free paper). — ISBN 0-415-9113-1
(pb : acid-free paper)
    1. WIlliams, William Appleman. 2. Historians—United States—
Biography. I. Rice-Maximin, Edward Francis, 1941- II. Title.
III. Series
E175.5.w55b84 1995
973.92 092—dc20
[B]   95-19420
                                                                          CIP

Contents

To our days in Madison

ACKNOWLEDGEMENTS

We gratefully acknowledge Harvey J. Kaye for his initiative in suggesting this project, and for seeing it through (with the collaboration of Elliott J. Gorn) a change of publishers in midstream. We wish to give our deepest thanks to those Williams family members who gave us their recollections and encouragement in interviews and family documents: Jeannie Williams, Corrinne Williams, Wendy Williams, and Kyenne Williams. Our critics and close readers, who gave us enormously helpful comments, include Alfred Young, Leonard Liggio, David Krikun, Michael Meeropol, Carl Marzani, Michael Sprinker, Jonathan Wiener, Harvey J. Kaye, Allen Ruff, George Mosse, Larry Gara, Elliott J. Gorn, Jim Lorence, Lloyd Gardner, and Bruce Cumings. Mari Jo Buhle's contributions significantly reshaped the manuscript. Interviewees especially eager to help us included, in addition to Williams family members, Merle Curti, the late Fred Harvey Harrington, Gerda Lerner, Alan Bogue, Lloyd Gardner, Theodore Hamerow, Thomas McCormick, Peggy Morley, and Peter Weiss. Hans Jakob Werlen supplied us with translations from German scholarly journals. The staff at the Pauling Papers, Kerr Library, Oregon State University, was helpful beyond the call of duty in many ways, but especially in making available all the Williams Papers most expeditiously. Likewise, the staffs at the State Historical Society of Wisconsin; Columbia University, Special Collections; the Nimitz Library; the history department at Oregon State University; and the Jeffries Archive of the U.S. Naval Academy extended every measure of assistance. We received extensive documents, otherwise unavailable, via Brian D. Fors, Mary Rose Catalfamo, Bea Susman, William Preston, Ed Crapol, Scott McLemee, Neil Basen, Henry W. Berger, Lloyd Gardner, Martin Sherwin, Walter LaFeber, William Preston, Karla Robbins, Gerald McCauley, and above all, William Robbins. (Many of these documents, with the permission of the holders, have been subsequently turned over to the OSU collection). Letters and phone calls exchanged with David Noble, John Higham, David Montgomery, Nando Fasce, Peter Wiley, James O'Connor, Howard Zinn, Staughton Lynd, Volker Berghahn, Paul Ringenbach, Martin Sherwin, James P. O'Brien, Mike Wallace, Paul Richards, Lee Baxandall, James B. Gilbert, James Weinstein, Paul Breines, and Charles Vevier, to name only a few, illuminated many dark reaches of Williams's past. And Christine Cipriani at Routledge polished off the production process. We are grateful to them all, and we hope that our book justifies their faith in our effort.

INTRODUCTION

"I PREFER TO DIE AS A FREE MAN struggling to create a human community than as a pawn of Empire," wrote historian William Appleman Williams in 1976.[1] Annapolis graduate and decorated Naval officer, civil rights activist and president of the Organization of American Historians, Williams (1921-1990) is remembered as the preeminent historian and critic of Empire in the second half of the "American Century." More than any other scholar, he anticipated, encouraged, and explained the attack of conscience suffered by the nation during the 1960s. Radicals have hailed him as a supreme anti-imperialist, while libertarian conservatives have seen him as the "second Charles Beard," renewing the perspectives of the nation's foremost historian. Fellow historians consider him a great figure in American thought, one who looked for large patterns and asked the right questions. A physically small man with large hands and a wide smile, he seemed indifferent to the abuse heaped upon him from the political mainstream and to most of the praise he earned as well, choosing simply to walk alone.

His *Tragedy of American Diplomacy*, first published in 1959 and then expanded in subsequent paperback editions destined to reach tens of thousands of readers during the 1960s and 1970s, is probably the most important book ever to appear on the history of U.S. foreign policy. For more than thirty years, scholars have vigorously debated Williams's challenge to the prevailing assumptions. As a key source of dissenting wisdom cribbed by antiwar authors and orators, *Tragedy* helped frame the public discussion of the U.S. role in Southeast Asia. Williams explained this moral catastrophe as neither misguided idealism nor elite conspiracy but instead as the inevitable consequence of deeply rooted, bipartisan assumptions. Williams's *Contours of American History* (1961), one of the most influential scholarly books of the age, traced the roots of American expansionism to the nation's origins and attributed the rise of the security state with its planned deception of the public to the impossibility of managing a world empire. In these and other volumes, Williams also pleaded for a democratic renewal, a revived citizenship based upon the activities and decisions of local communities rather than upon the demands of a distant welfare-and-warfare state.

Williams's unique insights could be traced to his penetrating economic perspectives and to his long view of modern history. One of his best recent interpreters, Asia scholar Bruce Cumings, describes a twofold process of reading America "from the outside in," as those abroad have felt the effects of U.S. policy; and conversely, re-reading the historic documents of U.S. diplomacy for American leaders' understanding of the larger world developments at work.[2] Williams framed these insights with his own interpretation of the ways in which distinct social and economic systems evolved, from the rise of modern class society in the seventeenth and eighteenth centuries to the present. This dual or threefold approach is *sui generis,* and his development of it will shortly be seen through a close examination of his life. But its significance can be grasped preliminarily in several large ways.

Williams first of all inverted the dominant assumptions of American intellectuals by viewing conventional liberalism not as a great liberating force but as a suffocating ideology that has preempted both solid radicalism and thoughtful conservatism. In doing so, he drew upon long-neglected Anglo-American traditions of communitarianism and misunderstood traditions of what might be called a judicious paternalism. A Christian socialist and an undoubted patriot, he sympathized with writers as varied as John Ruskin, Brooks Adams, Lewis Mumford, and G. D. H. Cole, who all felt that too much had been lost with the collapse of the pre-modern order. He found in the politics of Tory radicals like Lord Shaftesbury and cautious statesmen like John Quincy Adams and Herbert Hoover the sense of equipoise and the pursuit of commonwealth missing in war leaders Abraham Lincoln, Woodrow Wilson, and Franklin Roosevelt.

For Williams the true antithesis of Empire was the heterogeneous tradition of community spiritedness, rather than the socialization of labor envisioned by Karl Marx and the Marxists. He therefore shared the dismay of those at various points across the political map who gauged the recklessness of modern government. Moderates and conservatives found in Williams what they could not find elsewhere in radical thought: the understanding that Empire had its roots not only in State Department and corporate aims but also in the expansionist assumptions of ordinary Americans that social problems could be successfully externalized and postponed through a constantly moving frontier. As he wrote a few years before his death, "America is the kind of culture that wakes you in the night. The kind of nightmare that may [yet] possibly lead us closer to the truth."[3] This was Greek tragedy in a modern setting, with the audience sharing the stage. Williams nevertheless stubbornly held to his own ideal vision of a *possible* America, running like a golden thread from the historic tragedy of self-deception toward a better future for America and the world.[4]

Seen from other quarters, Williams's message has had a profoundly international and cultural significance that might have surprised the confirmed Middle American. One of the most controversial critics of recent decades, Edward Said, has attributed to Williams the fundamental insight that Empire, more than an economic or political or cultural system, has organized modern thought and encompassed all else within it.[5] On the same note, the editors of the recent and perhaps definitive *Cultures of American Imperialism* suggest that their 672-page volume, with its many distinguished contributors, essentially "aims to explore more fully Williams's . . . understanding."[6] William Appleman Williams's contribution, by these related assessments, cannot be rendered obsolete by the passage of events. His value grows as we approach the twenty-first century.

Williams rarely wrote about culture as such. Yet in his final work, condensing the wisdom of a lifetime, he defined a myriad of words and phrases to explain how the empire operated at the level of internalized (or what theorist Sylvia Winter would call "auto-instituted"[7]) logic. Thus, for instance: dynamic=aggressive, enterprise=overtake, modernize=outstrip, order=regulate, discipline=surveillance, secure=patronize, and benevolent= lord-it-over, or in the most benign redefinitions, innocence=grant-a-favor and tolerance=reform. In each case, Americans took control of the land and its inhabitants. In the process, they transformed each term's meaning *for themselves*, often benefitting materially, but rarely understanding the full consequences. The various historic developments that Williams interpreted as a consequence of the "open" (or forcibly opened) space available to Americans, the almost unlimited resources and the commercial success they experienced in the colonial days and afterward, can also be seen as the shaping influence in the dominant cultural sensibility of the nation.

Amy Kaplan, co-editor of *Cultures of American Imperialism*, carries this dialogue between Williams and cultural studies a step further. She finds in his early work a "major challenge to what might be called the paradigm of denial," the absence of Empire from a scholarly or popular self-understanding of American history.[8] Privileging economics, Kaplan insists, the Williams of *Tragedy of American Diplomacy* insisted upon the strict economic rationality of Americans' expansionism. *Empire as a Way of Life* transcended these limitations, and in so doing, reached out to the future of international experience, Coke bottled in Russia and McDonald's opening shop in Beijing.[9] Williams, with his roots in the small-town America of the Depression, had managed to see these massive, world-changing developments from the inside.

William Appleman Williams passed from the scene just as the collapse of the Eastern Bloc had reached a crucial stage. Those who had vigorously opposed him in life quickly proclaimed their self-vindication: the cold war, with all its deleterious side effects from nuclear terror to environmental damage, had been a noble crusade or at least a necessary strategy after all. The long challenge to free enterprise was over, and the world's only surviving superpower could face the future relatively confident of its own status. Indeed, according to the frequently heard optimistic projections of the early 1990s, liberal democracy faced a golden future.

Not everyone was so optimistic, of course. George F. Kennan, who might rightly be called the father of cold-war strategy, wondered aloud whether the terrifying cost of the crusade had not long since outweighed its benefits.[10] Within a few years and a dozen or more continuing or impending disasters, from civil war and extreme economic uncertainty in Eastern Europe to the accelerating extermination of the planet's biological storehouse in its surviving rainforests, things did not look so good after all. Closer to home, regional issues such as the Haitian crisis recalled the ugly legacy of U.S. support (and CIA guidance) for almost incomprehensibly brutal, light-skinned elites. Doubts continued to plague Americans about many domestic issues as well, including their cities, their children, and their health.

Perhaps most revealing was an absence of any fresh solutions. Growth was finally, as it had always been before, seen as the key mechanism to create a happier society. "Liberal democracy" as a world plan or ideal for success and security outside the United States actually promoted a drastically sharpening division of social classes, growing petrochemical stress upon the environment through the explosion of automobile use, and a popular disillusionment that threatened ominously. No wonder personal detachment, mean-spiritedness, and cynicism remained the intellectual order of the day. The encompassing hate-love fascination of celebrity, from murder trials to the radio talk shows to Congress, seemingly filled the gap left by an exhausted political dialogue. The newer New Right rode to political triumph promising to finish off failed liberalism with the uncompromised rule of the market and the unabashed Pax Americana. Its leaders, as Williams would have predicted, claimed the legacy of Roosevelt and Truman for themselves.[11]

Williams had called the America of the later 1980s a "tired and nostalgic" society, at once weary of politicians' double-talk and terribly hungry in a spiritual sense for the reassurance that manipulated historical images offered to the gullible. He offered his readers, and Americans at large, a profoundly different possibility—but not a painless one. To dialogue seriously with their past, they had to wrestle with truths about themselves that politicians would never acknowledge, let alone face boldly. He never asked them to succumb to paralyzing guilt, or to repudiate their self-identity. Everyone, he believed, could learn from history. Decoding the empire, freeing its subjects at home and abroad from the tyrannical logic of the system, was for Williams the final, grand task of the citizen and the civilization.

A Little Boy from Iowa

William Appleman Williams began his days as he would end them, far from the centers of metropolitan culture. He often claimed that his origins explained his insight into U.S. history and had undergirded his moral strength to sustain himself through political hard times. Seen more objectively, the issues of his life look very different, far more contradictory and more pathos-ridden than he could admit. And yet something about his self-evaluation rings true. As he grappled to interpret his experiences through his historical studies but also in personal interviews, a private family memoir, and an unpublished novel, he could not possibly escape the stamp of the small-town Midwest, the Depression, and the fatherless family. But he had also spent his life literally discovering a wider world and trying to make sense of it in his own highly personal terms.

Attacked frequently as an America-hater, Williams cared about the nation passionately, even obsessively, as if from a sense of family responsibility. He believed that his family background and his life as a Naval officer reflected the economic development and the imperial mission that gave the modern nation its shape. But he also believed that the same resources and initiative could make possible a society organized along very different lines. His fondest political hopes were doomed to disappointment. But his capacity to marshall intense scholarship within a large philosophical framework permitted him a very unique insight into America as a civilization. Few others could have framed such insight in a sustained historical narrative, and Williams himself had enormous difficulty in doing so.

A Midwestern literary regionalist, some modern-day Hamlin Garland, might be able to capture through fiction the emotional toll exacted on the historian's life as he struggled to make sense of society and of himself. The novelist would have to contend, as well, with Williams's own fictionalizing. In attempting to explain or to interpret the sources of his immanent critique of American society, Williams created through screened memory a vividly nostalgic, heavily stylized childhood and native setting.[1] Decades after penning an appendix to his master's thesis, which described closely and without sentimentality the elite rule of his little hometown, he thus reinterpreted the same place in near-idyllic terms. It had become, quite remarkably, a site of approximate social equality and deep-felt community where citizens learned the importance of both public participation and individual restraint.

Here lay the source of the rending tension which might also be seen as the driving contradiction of Williams's life. The locale of community, for him the modern-day version of the Greek city-state, is likewise the source of Empire. Its ethos is successful in its own terms—and tragic as well. He projected this historical experience in all directions, from his idiosyncratic interpretation of agrarian history to his strained views of feminism and the family to his understanding of what a socialist movement might be and do. He also internalized the tension, as he sought to control the story of his life and give it a unified meaning.

Examined carefully and without his blinders, Williams's life and life's work express again and again the same contradictions of individualism and community, Empire and anti-Empire. Woven in and around the saga of boyhood, military academies, war, graduate school, scholarship and political engagement, the tensions reveal themselves.

Williams's own late-shifting version of the past reflected his growing disillusionment with the direction of the country and likewise his despair with the radical left. But he had another purpose, which he pursued through a last burst of non-history writing.[2] He had a large personal debt to acknowledge and, if possible, to repay. He later wrote repeatedly of various individuals and groups who had "honored" their "traditions" in one way or another.[3] They had done rightly, earning his praise and support, unlike those who fecklessly cast off the past without considering its consequences for the present and future. He blessed his childhood home, the mother and grandparents who raised the boy without a father.

Between the lines of the memoir, he asked himself why it had been William Appleman Williams, the most unlikely intellectual, who finally wrote controversial and influential books. He continued to set down his responses to the riddle even as his life drained away; he never finished. No wonder a high-school classmate, asked at the time of Williams's death about his classmate's notorious Marxism, answered matter-of-factly that no one could have anticipated anything like it. The sweetheart of his high-school years and wife of his youth agreed with this judgment.[4] The personally secretive Midwesterner and unabashed romantic eluded even his intimates' efforts to understand the sources of radicalism in his background.

Nor would they have been able to explain his rise into the nation's most important historian. To do so would be to unravel what Williams himself never could fully or candidly analyze: the complex chain of events leading him from childhood and adolescent years to Naval officership to civil rights activist and historian-in-training, or from Depression-era Iowa to wartime Annapolis to post–World War II Corpus Christi and late-1940s Madison, Wisconsin. Full understanding would require deep insight into a character fragmented by childhood tragedy, rebuilt through personal determination, challenged by world events, and settled as firmly as it could be settled through the self-identification of the citizen-scholar.

Some of his more perceptive friends found him looking perpetually for a community like the one he believed he had left behind. Others would say that the later Marxist internationalist, jazz buff, and intimate friend of gay intellectuals—during the days of hiding and persecution—had become a bohemian, if not necessarily an outsider, precisely in response to the claustrophobia of small-town life. Perhaps these two alternatives are not so contradictory after all.[5]

I

William Appleman Williams, during his days as a radical graduate student, carefully depicted his native Atlantic in commercial terms. Shipping center for crops, poultry, and livestock, this town of several thousand residents was also a commercial-retail locus of fertile southwestern Iowa in the later nineteenth century. Among the mostly German and Danish descendents, a small group of extended families dominated manufacturing, financing, merchandising, the judiciary, and political clout. If Atlantic nurtured one resident's radicalism and historical perspective, it most likely did so by fostering a boy's sense of contrast, perhaps the contrast between the small community's day-to-day social life on the one hand and the real power-wielding on the other. But this begins the story too late; Williams the memoirist insisted that his legacy be traced back several generations at least.

Williams's mother, Mildrede, who deserves to be called the most enduring influence on his life, traced her family back through the Appleman line to a Welsh-born Redcoat who deserted General Howe to join George Washington's forces. This Welshman's Philadelphia wife had ancestors in America long before the Revolutionary war. Williams's father, William Carlton Williams, could find still another revolutionary soldier in his family tree, a New Hampshire militiaman blinded in combat.[6] In short, Williams's family had been more than present at the primal act of national independence: he was self-conscious heir to the great tradition.

If Williams often felt "that American History is a pot of imperial porridge . . . of who fought where for what conquest," he could nevertheless find a family exception here and there. His mother's great-grandfather, Zopher Hammond, bought his son's way out of service in the Civil War and insisted that the North should have seceded first or simply let the South go its own way. Born in Patchogue, New York, in 1804, Zopher may have been the original "Little America" believer in the family, unwilling to pay the price for Empire. Zopher's son, Joseph, Williams's great-grandfather, attended Hillsdale College in Michigan and resettled in Marshall County, Iowa, in 1866. His Iowa-born wife, Amanda Louis Havens, was reputedly the first "strong-minded" woman of several generations of them to come. The couple moved by wagon to Iowa's southwest, claiming through the Homestead Act some of the richest farmland anywhere on earth.[7]

Williams neglected to mention the less rational, helter-skelter qualities of settlement and the troubled memories left behind. A naturally beautiful region of the Nishnabotna River Valley and the main drainage basin of southwestern Iowa, it had once been home to the Ioway, the Oto, the Omaha, and other tribes. Before its settling, James Audubon had praised the beauty of its trees, native wildflowers, and fabulously beautiful birds (a county was subsequently named after him), which were mostly destined like the Indians themselves to disappear for productive agriculture and commerce. The Mormons had crossed en route to the West in 1846, and a generation of later settlers debated the name of a nascent municipality. Thinking mistakenly that they were exactly halfway between the two oceans, they tossed a coin to decide whether to call their new place by one or the other. "Pacific" won, but another town had already been given that name, so they christened it "Atlantic."[8]

Williams's ancestors had made a shrewd economic choice. The farmer of the 1860s was no primitive pioneer but a modern agrarian. He needed mechanical mowers, hay rakes, reapers, corn planters, seeders, along with improved plows and decent weather, to realize a profit on his considerable investment. Still, corn, wheat, oats, rye, and other crops afforded abundant yields, while hogs, cattle, and (in southern Iowa particularly) even sheep production raced ahead. Decades later, the entire region would be known as the "Corn Belt," an oversimplified appellation that signified rich soil, adequate rain, and a summer heat which could make daily life extremely uncomfortable (not to speak of the bitter winters with their savage plains winds), but which also made possible a good living.

Iowa community life naturally reflected the intense self-consciousness of its businessmen-farmers. The local and regional newspapers described in detail the agricultural and market developments which made one line or another profitable or unprofitable. Farmers and their journalists put special emphasis on improvement of stock and a range of other innovations such as veterinary sciences (including rudimentary pesticides).[9] Williams took great pride in the solid business sense of his ancestors and their communities. A major investor in Atlantic had convinced the Rock Island Line to build its main trunk system for the region through the town and to stop every train there. As he wrote in the introduction to *Roots of the Modern American Empire*, the fathers of Atlantic then "plotted the town by plowing a furrow straight south from the spot they selected for the depot."[10]

Grids went up in the 1870s for the development of wide streets suited to civic affairs, while Joseph and Amanda Hammond established themselves outside town on a spread not far from the future golf course of the well-to-do. In Williams's imaginative recreation, they regularly joined perhaps five hundred neighbors on market days to sell surplus, take shaves or haircuts, buy calico, and gossip. Historians' accounts, indeed, describe this period as the "golden age" of the county fair, a market day writ large with exhibitions of machinery and seminars on scientific husbandry along with various competitions, including "female equestrianism."[11]

Williams's predecessors surely played their part in the rituals that he regarded with admiration. They raised churches with stained-glass windows, created schools, founded a public library, scheduled a lecture series and musical events. He viewed it as a "marvelous mix of town and country," much the way that Lewis Mumford had described the early nineteenth-century New England village. If considerably less picturesque than the rocky hills that many Yankee residents had left behind, Atlantic was at once human scale and connected by its visiting trains to New York, Chicago, Omaha, and San Francisco. Thus the great anti-imperialist Williams could write, without a hint of irony, that "Atlantic was part of the empire."[12] And not an insignificant part: according to his own account, Atlantic made itself the major agricultural-merchandizing center between Des Moines and Omaha. With less than six thousand residents, it reputedly maintained the nation's highest rate in turnover of retail goods for many years, off and on, until the Depression.

Atlantic and the surrounding region also entertained its share of dissidents and even radicals for at least an occasional moment in the nineteenth century. John Brown had briefly made his headquarters in Tabor—itself named for the legendary Czech city of communal resistance against king and clergy—during the 1840s. Never a major center of agrarian agitation like nearby Kansas or Nebraska, Iowa saw its Greenbackers and Populists mount third-party challenges during the 1870-80s. The major weekly of agrarian movement during the middle 1880s, *Industrial West* (later, the *Farmers' Tribune)* was published in Atlantic. One of its editors, Knights of Labor activist J. R. Sovereign, used the Atlantic base to project himself into Grand Master Workman of that fading organization a few years later.[13] After these unsettled days, modestly successful agrarian reforms and the rise of a world market for local commodities prompted Atlantic to become staunchly conservative, in politics and moral alike.

Given worldly success and social homogeneity, its citizens seemingly had no more pressing reason to doubt or to wonder. Less sympathetic observers might have described them as indifferent or hostile to the dramatic rise of the Socialist Party with its many small-town locals in Kansas or Oklahoma, likewise toward the Industrial Workers of the World headquartered in nearby Chicago. The great hopes and the savage repression of radicals made little impression on them because they evidently had other things on their minds. Indeed, during the war, a local manufacturer of folding stoves and Army cots produced nearly five million dollars of goods for the government. Afterwards, the large Atlantic Canning Company plant added sweet pumpkins to its profitable line of corn, converting the globes into pulp and sending the seeds as far away as China. From the perspective of the Atlantic Legion Memorial Building, which served as a community center, life was no doubt good.[14]

Writing about Atlantic during his graduate student days, Williams dissected the *mentalité* of the elite. Their way of seeing the world, he claimed, was based on parroting the ultraconservative *Chicago Tribune* positions on national and international issues. Local newspaper editorials—as Williams related from his own personal experiences—were hammered out at a breakfast club composed of the elite's second string. Their view of the world, notably of foreign affairs (and especially revolutions abroad, i.e., threats to continued U.S. economic expansion) lacked any element of enlightened conservatism let alone liberal acceptance. Perhaps this had been manipulation of small-town democracy from the metropolis, but it was not one that local elites resisted. They had chosen to respond to events in strictly business terms. It did not make them mediocre minds, or mediocre stylists. Indeed, the paper's savant Edwin Percy Chase won a Pulitzer Prize for the best editorial of 1934. But it limited their capacity to see other possibilities.[15]

But through the rose-colored glasses of the later Williams, the flourishing life of the county seat had been, if perhaps a "disorienting distortion of the reality of America," nevertheless "the best that *could* happen." He proved it with that most elusive evidence—memories of his childhood and the recollections of neighborliness which mattered to him most. Thus, for instance, he recalled Jewish and black families perfectly integrated into the community, when in reality so few existed that segregation would have been all but impossible.

Williams had his own version of the dark side of Atlantic social life. The town's proprietors sold medicinal whiskey and laudanum over the counter of the nominally dry town, and thousands of gallons of moonshine liquor mysteriously found their way into waiting hands. Railroad workers, farmhands, traveling businessmen, and prostitutes ("soiled doves" in the police blotter of the local press) drank and carried on beneath the averted eyes of the authorities. When law-breaking occasionally turned violent through the misdeeds of a frontier-style gang of criminals, citizens acted in concert to crush it. Williams's own great-grandmother died with a gun still under her pillow. She never used it, but presumably would not have hesitated had the need arisen.

The degraded and sometimes dangerous lower classes existed only at the margins of Atlantic life, certainly never becoming likely protagonists of social change. Hired agricultural workers were no more than "bummers," transients hired for harvest but expected to be gone soon. Railroad laborers, more stable but still fewer in number, kept to themselves.[16] To all this we might easily trace Williams's later aversion to class models of socialism, and his hopes for the "ordinary" middle class as the agency of redemption.

Williams's ancestors experienced troubles of their own, but rather than economic or social ones, these were more likely to be personal difficulties or perhaps a restlessness prompted by the psychological narrowness of small-town life. Great-grandfather Ed Hammond made a good living and belonged to the founding circles of local fraternal organizations like the Odd Fellows and the Masons. He emerged as an impressive local figure, probably too much so for his strong-willed mate, who sought more for her life than a comfortable home and an absentee husband. Their beloved first child had, as a teen, given birth to a baby out of wedlock, a grave embarrassment to a respectable family at that place and time. Their second child, Maude, always feeling ignored by the family, distanced herself from them through mental self-cultivation (eventually she would become a Christian Scientist). She also sought a marriage of acknowledged equals. Her choice, Porter Ikeler Appleman, would be the grandfather who played a central role in young Bill Williams's life. Four inches shorter than his wife, he was a man too playful to grow up entirely.

"Tossie," as the acrobatic figure was fondly called (Porter could, reputedly, leap over a handkerchief held out toward him), had attended a "normal" or teachers college in Shenadoah, Iowa, after his family moved west from Pennsylvania, and had opened a business office for loans, insurance, and real estate. An independent-minded Congregationalist and charter member of the local Elks, he was also a skilled shot and above all "magic with dogs." He won top prizes and trained the dogs for shipping across the U.S., Europe, and even Asia. Prone, however, to impractical investments and speculation, and self-indulgent about cars and clothes, Porter spent too much time with his friends in the bars and too little time at home. In doing so, he attained the negative virtue of removing himself from the business-minded Puritanism of his parents' generation. The community, of course, never took him seriously.[17]

For all his weaknesses, which would grow worse in time, he raised his one daughter as a sort of free soul. A young woman who could not only name birds and flowers but could shoot a gun accurately and became one of the first women in the county to drive a car, Mildrede (she added a final "e" to distinguish herself in grade school from two other Mildreds) was intelligent and musical, playing leading roles in school plays and opera. She was also, reputedly, part of a modest sexual revolution in early twentieth-century small-town life. She enjoyed being alluring on the dance floor with the Charleston or Black Bottom, yet she restrained herself from the increasingly common practice of "going into the bushes" with potential lovers.[18] In her son's retrospective view, she could be at once sexy and personally responsible: she had "pizzazz." Less sympathetic observers saw the same impulses as evidence of her fundamentally cold and domineering character.

She fell in love with only one man, the original "Billy" Williams. His parents and grandparents had made themselves prosperous around De Kalb, Illinois, with their prize cattle and hogs. They had also showed some interest in politics (as northern Democrats opposed to Republican support of railroads and banks). Billy's father, when they came west, was to become the first Democratic postmaster of Atlantic, and his mother became an amateur painter.

Billy went off to college and then joined the fledgling air force in World War I, while Mildrede attended the Indianapolis Conservatory of Music, with special work to qualify her to teach part-time in Iowa grade schools. Her beau, hopeful of becoming a flying ace and war hero, was so skilled with the experimental equipment that the service made him a demonstration pilot to prepare others. His marriage with Mildrede, although the result of a "Grand Passion" (in their son's eyes), began in physical separation and never achieved a long-run stability. When the war ended in 1919, Billy found himself unwilling to return to the mundane life of Iowa.

He had real adventures as a barnstormer. The best, no doubt, was running nitroglycerin across the border to Mexicans consolidating their revolution against the Church and against the U.S. State Department's wishes. Billy had little interest in the revolutionaries' politics as such. But he had the instincts of a small-town iconoclast mistrustful of contemporary America's business culture. From that standpoint, he appreciated his Mexican clients' romantic quest for freedom and their hostility toward the rich. Short on cash, the revolutionaries gave him classic Mexican pottery which remained the one art collection of the Williams household, redolent of faraway places and exotic history. When the work gave out, Billy turned to safer private jobs hauling wealthy clients. Still later he became a car salesman while Mildrede substitute-taught school, devoted his leisure to bridge and golf, and seemed to spend a lot of his time gazing into the sky.[19]

William Appleman Williams was born in 1921, after a labor so frightening that the parents determined to have no more children. Billy the father might have settled down for that reason alone, until the spectacular flight of Charles Lindbergh, Jr. (whom he knew slightly) across the Atlantic Ocean. Lindy's subsequent publicity tour through America led him near Atlantic, and at his fellow flyer's request he passed overhead, waggling his wings in recognition as the whole family sat in the front yard and waved. Most remarkably, the son later reinterpreted Lindbergh, Jr., as personifying the imaginary escape from corporate bureaucracy, a "last national hero from the past" preserving the "nineteenth century dream that the individual could become one with his tools and his work."[20] This observation hints at Williams casting his father as a man who also had one last chance to elude twentieth-century depersonalization and took it desperately, knowing the risks.

It would not be hard to imagine a more distant scientist–father figure for the boy: that favorite son of Iowa, Herbert Hoover. Solidly Republican, Atlantic shared a particular fondness for the engineer-president born in West Branch, whose political and intellectual reputation Williams the scholar would continually seek to rehabilitate. Until the Depression, Hoover represented the proud contribution of Iowan ways to Washington, the mixture of know-how, moralism, and resistance to centralization.

Within a year of Lindy's aerial visit, at any rate, Billy had joined the Army Air Corps to return to flight duty. His son, who claimed to have had such an active childhood libido that he kissed the girl next to him on the first day of kindergarten, poured greater love and energy into model airplanes, styling many versions of Lindy's "Spirit of St. Louis." In old age the famed historian returned to making the Lindbergh model as if recovering a piece of himself lost somewhere along the way.[21]

Lt. Williams seemed to love his new life of male camaraderie and mechanized excitement. Mildrede and their son shared his excitement vicariously. The airman was scheduled to be given a permanent commission to Captain after the major war games of March 1929, although he still had private reservations about a military future. Mother and son made a special visit to him in Texas as he prepared to take part in the war games. One early morning of the games, he executed a dive and his plane failed mechanically. He crashed, mortally wounded with multiple skull fractures. It was unquestionably the worst moment of the boy's life. Many times later, Williams would return to the painful memory of seeing his father go off in the morning, cheerfully assuring the boy of his return— only to disappear forever.

Mother and son returned home to a funeral attended by much of Atlantic, and to a flood of sympathetic mail that continued for weeks. Nothing could console the two, abandoned in the world by a figure they had already learned to idolize at a distance. Young Bill had recurring nightmares which were so horrible that, decades later, he could still not bring himself to describe their contents even to his family.[22] Every child has dark moments, of course. But these anxieties may have not really passed, only gone into abeyance and taken other forms. Perhaps his later secretiveness, the inwardness masked by stern self-reliance, had its origins as much here as in Midwestern Protestantism.

Too stricken ever to marry again, Mildrede raised her boy with the help of her mother and father. Her in-laws, and the farm life outside Atlantic that they might have offered, never figured in her projection of the boy's future career track. He would visit his paternal grandparents from time to time and maintain a nodding friendship with an uncle who worked as a garage mechanic in Atlantic, but Mildrede's family had claimed him. He would become what she wanted, even if she could not be on the scene personally to supervise his rearing.

After her son's eighth birthday party she enrolled at Iowa State Teachers College in Cedar Falls, placing Billy (scarcely aware of any other name, he was uniformly called "Billy" throughout his youth) in a sort of parental limbo with her as an occasional visitor. His grandfather, Tossie, and his grandmother, Maude, would be Mildrede's surrogates.

Bill nevertheless thrived. As he looked back on this time, he could recount an early-twentieth-century Midwestern pattern of life slipping away even then. Caring for the root cellar, learning the mysteries of the ice box, using hand tools to make a soap-box racer, shooting a BB gun (he recalled that he had killed a sparrow and on the spot lost his love for gunning down living creatures), playing the piano, and vegetable gardening occupied much of his time and attention. He claimed in an autobiographical sketch to have been "reared in an extended family consisting of literally countless people" related by kinship or friendship, a "joyful and illuminating experience."[23] One can be skeptical of these claims without disputing the best of his small-town experiences. He spent little time with paternal grandparents or cousins, but neighbors and friends of the family were almost certainly sympathetic to the fatherless child.

A bright boy too active to be unusually studious, he later considered himself very fortunate to be situated in a town that believed staunchly in education. With his playmates, he often returned Saturday mornings from a film matinee to the public library, only later moving on to the ball field. At home, he poked through a stock of free thought–oriented family books unusual in Atlantic, from *The Well of Loneliness* by Radclyffe Hall, the first widely-distributed lesbian novel, to Margaret Sanger's birth-control volumes and Hemingway novels, to the standard of Poe or Tom Swift available in many Atlantic households. Probably the more avant-garde volumes had been bought by his father. At any rate, the family bookshelves were open with no prohibitions on what he might choose to read. Like so many future intellectuals, he browsed and absorbed what interested him.

Still, as his mother grew more deeply involved in school (so much so that an association of women enrolled in primary education at Iowa State made her their president), young Billy suffered another round of severe nightmares about abandonment. He imagined himself terrifyingly alone, missing the father who had rarely been present for long. He concluded later that Mildrede, driven by her need for a profession, had deprived herself and obviously him as well of the intimacy of a normal mother-child relationship. She, too, he now admired mostly from a physical distance. He must have felt, from early years, a need to be emotionally self-reliant and, more than that, to be strong for her.

Despite her career successes Mildrede suffered serious depression, and suggested unwisely in her letters to the boy that she believed her good life was over. During a mother-son driving trip undertaken to restore their relationship, Billy found her crying uncontrollably in a country outhouse, and he ran screaming to get help. Emotionally, the two recovered together, traveling all the way to California and enjoying each other's company. Meeting old flyers along the way, they had adventures memorable for the boy. A stranger in a hotel apartment in Long Beach, California, where they stayed for a few weeks, initiated him in the game of billiards. "The joy of being treated as an equal taught the boy to understand the true sense of skill and sport," he remembered.[24] One might as well call this experience the source of his later passion for the pool table and the pool hall atmosphere of male camaraderie, alcohol, stogies, and bloodless combat. At any rate he was growing emotionally, preparing for life without his mother again.

These episodes invite further psychological exploration, if only because Williams himself was so taken with the psychological theories of personality development in a later era. Williams strictly avoided Freudian theories with their inevitable Oedipal component. One of his favorite alternative prophets, Abraham Maslow, proposed the self-creation of the personality through "peak experiences," energizing moments which can reshape approaches to life. In Maslow, the instinct for creativeness and for meaningful existence possesses an importance at least equal to subconscious sexual desires. This species of existential psychology, a variant on the existentialism of such contemporary philosophers as Jean Paul Sartre and Albert Camus, permitted Williams to recast his youthful traumas as forced opportunities for personal growth. Gestalt psychology, another of Williams's preferred theories, viewed the surrounding environment and the subject's current situation as critical to development and reorientation. The "life-space" of mental and physical factors was decisive to life possibilities, helping to frame a self-actualization, the individual's growth toward what he (or she) might potentially be.[25]

There are other hints along the same lines. Little in the boy's family background suggested the self-conscious, sentimental Welshman that Williams's close friends claimed to perceive so clearly later. Any memories of the old country were generations back. Only his stature, which levelled off at under 5'10", and his sometimes almost maudlin manner evoked images of the popular sentimental film, *How Green Was My Valley*, with its singing coal miners—surely a nonexistent species in Iowa. If young William Appleman Williams needed to create a persona, he obviously drew upon and probably improvised resources deep inside himself. He wanted urgently to be *different*, to be special, as his first wife emphasized. To do so, he would assume *sui generis* identities sometimes quite charming and sometimes troublesome to those around him.

2

The next period in his life demanded all his psychic creativity for somewhat different reasons. By the time he and his mother recovered from their mutual crisis, the Depression of the thirties had struck. Like so many other American towns and cities, Atlantic was soon prostrate. The corn-canning factory, for decades the largest such enterprise in the world, went bankrupt. The fertilizer plant managed to stay open only by switching to synthetic fertilizer and drastically trimming its personnel. Atlantic rebounded slowly through a shift to growing cereals for feed cattle and other future meat animals. But Williams remembered best the rural desperation at the close of the day, when through the wild shadows flung across the barnyard by a swinging kerosene lamp, [one saw] the desperate fear and fatigue in the very soul of an uncle as he scuffed his shoes clean with a worn corn cob. And, sometimes, to see his deep frustration at not having the corn to feed the pigs, erupt in an angry outburst during a conversation with his wife or children—or myself.[26]

Williams's immediate family was only a little better off. Grandfather Porter lost everything, a terrible defeat that wiped out his various investments and left him mulling over his dog trophies and drinking to kill the disappointment. A tiny government pension, along with some military and civilian insurance, helped Mildrede pay for her own continuing education, and she made Billy's clothes with her foot-powered sewing machine.

In Williams's recapitulation of the period, these were also times of sharing and intensified community sentiment. No doubt he captured the best of Atlantic in his images of judges handing down suspended sentences for theft of food, theater managers looking away when kids opened the back door for their poorer friends, and storekeepers keeping a "tab" that they rightly suspected would never be repaid. As he also observed, "women were at the center of the community during the depression years" around America. Later feminists, he reflected, might see such women's lives as "limited, demeaning and destructive," but "the issue was survival."[27] He was proud of Atlantic's women (obviously including his mother and grandmother) *because* they used their strength to hold the family together, and not to assert their independence from it.

His memoirs were more frank. Grandmother Maude wearied of it all, falling into a deep personal depression. "So much for the claims of capitalism to provide opportunities for everyone to realize their full potential," Williams remarked with a rare suggestion of bitterness about his younger days. His grandparents, like hundreds of thousands of Protestant Midwesterners, left Republican ranks for the first time in their lives, if only temporarily. Crisis drove them into the arms of Roosevelt and the New Deal. The terrible price of economic recovery, when it finally came, would not be learned until later.[28]

Mildrede got a regular job teaching third grade in Atlantic. At that stressful time, more and more children appeared in class undernourished and sullen, their parents unable to understand what value an education might hold in a jobless future. She could only offer them hope of better times and more opportunities, for which education would serve them well. For her pains, she earned less than $800 per year. The family cut expenses to the bone. Any luxuries, such as athletic equipment, Saturday movies, a new model airplane kit, or music lessons were reserved for Billy. She took a better job across the state, bringing Billy along with her. But neither of them could adapt to the stress of single parenthood in an unfamiliar scene. He found himself alone and lonely in their apartment after school, waiting for her, imagining that his father was actually alive and destined to return.

The two came back to Atlantic, Mildrede reluctantly accepting a pay cut in order to see the boy through high school. Williams views this sacrifice as a mark of her personal maturity. But he adds that for himself, "life in the slow lane with Maude was more interesting and meaningful than life in the fast lane with Mildrede." He missed the quiet diversions of a relaxed home setting. His grandmother, with all her troubles, had been more of a mother to him than his own mother. In her struggles, Mildrede made an uncomfortably intense partner for a child who preferred security above all.

Strange memories rise up here, in this extended family reunion. Grandfather Porter, who had abandoned his customary drinking en route to home, now limited himself to a single tumbler of whiskey which he drank while playing cribbage and talking with the boy: he would fill a pitcher with water and then replace the imbibed whiskey, sip by sip. It was surely a discipline to drink in measured fashion. But to down a quarter pint in this rigorous fashion was at once self-justifying and self-deceiving in a deeply Protestant way, as if his grandmother had gone through liquor-tinged patent medicine by the case. Decades later, Williams confided (or rationalized) to a close friend, in the same vein, that alcohol taken at specific periods perfectly balanced his body's respiration; a scientific explanation that only a heavy drinker could take seriously.[29]

Intense adolescent family conflicts emerged, pitting mother against son over William's playing varsity basketball and drumming, rather than singing in the glee club and chorus. Grandmother mediated, and Williams emerged a small-town sports star, even an idol to younger boys—quite an accomplishment for a youngster of rather small stature. With sheer determination, fast hands, and the acquisition of good shooting skills, he made himself into the hero he had hoped to become. He acquired from his father's reputation the awesome importance of performing not just well but brilliantly if possible. And like many a lower-class or minority youngster successful in sports, he quelled inner demons if he could not eradicate them. Meanwhile, he excelled in English, Math, Physics, Biology, History, and Citizenship.[30]

Williams had also become a lifetime sports fan, however much he would later complain about the commercialization of athletics and control of play from the bench. Like so many youngsters, he admired the irrepressible Babe Ruth. But Red Grange, the "Galloping Ghost" from neighboring Illinois, also naturally caught his attention. Indeed, Grange was the first star of professional football, quickly putting the Chicago-area team on the map. A later Williams clearly appreciated athletic dexterity, but he especially liked to imagine himself in the leadership status of the coach or manager, quarterback or the captain of a basketball team.[31]

Jazz offered yet another dimension. By the middle thirties, dynamic developments in radio and record distribution had reshaped popular music, bringing in waves of black musicians and singers including Louis Armstrong, Mary Lou Williams, Bessie Smith, Count Basie, and above all, Duke Ellington, whom a later Williams considered "a master of the age." For a young Williams, jazz accommodated black contributions to American culture, even in little Atlantic.[32] Playing the drums was a way to literally tap into the excitement of American popular culture at its best.

Williams had thus gained an important measure of self-confidence all around, enough to be a winning personality comfortable with his recent success. Mildrede could feel satisfied that her boy acquired a good high-school education, even if he were considered popular rather than brilliant. He was regularly elected a class officer. Now and then he could shine academically, as when he wrote a prize-winning essay for the Daughters of the American Revolution–sponsored contest on "Citizenship." For his own part, he had begun to make plans. An Eagle Scout, he was selected for the Iowa delegation to the International Scout Jamboree at the Chicago World's Fair of 1933 with his way paid by philanthropic Atlantic businessmen.

There he fell in love with the buildings of Louis Sullivan, an architect he would later criticize for creating exquisite physical structures which symbolized centralized power and the triumph of the corporation over the individual. He almost certainly also glimpsed the work of Frank Lloyd Wright. One of the great and also typical intellects of the Midwest, Wright built on a human scale and, when he retreated, did so by embracing the organicism of the family and community that Williams held sacred.[33] The boy dreamed of going to Iowa State in Ames to study architecture.

He also began to earn his own first pocket money. A newspaper route was one of the few ways then for a boy in school to acquire an income. Desperate to get the job, he haunted the outgoing delivery boy until it was passed along to him. Williams later claimed that, while delivering the paper, he learned sociology and psychology by closely examining the daily life of his customers across the social spectrum and interacting withe them.

During his junior year, he struck up a serious romantic flirtation, his first, with Jeannie (or Emma Jean) Preston. Bright and spirited, small of stature like him, she was the daughter of the town's barbershop owner, a hard-working and kind-hearted businessman who dreamed of seeing his children acquire a college education. In a typical high-school romance, as he recalled later, the two could "make an ice cream soda last an hour."[34]

Ties went deep in small-town social life. Her mother and his mother, with birthdays on the same day, had once, in childhood, had a party together. Later, Bill's father had taken Jeannie's mother to the high-school prom, and still later Bill and Jeannie had shared music teachers and both attended meetings of the Bach Juvenile Society. Attending separate public grade schools, they lost touch; a year ahead of him, she had no classes with him and little contact at all afterward. But teenaged Bill, full of life and often dating several girls simultaneously, dared Jeannie to sit with him in a balcony of a movie theatre; then they began seeing each other regularly.

They shared many interests, from books to music, but especially Jeannie's writing for the school paper, *The Needle*, a year before Billy would be eligible as a senior to follow her as a cub journalist. The two naturally attended all social functions together. Her younger brother, Sam, became Bill's devoted follower, shadowing the older boy's trajectory from high-school sports to later military-school training. Perhaps by then Bill Williams had acquired at last the larger family that he had yearned for; he seemed more emotionally secure than ever before. He and Jeannie envisioned a married life together. Mildrede, more than protective, subtly and not-so-subtly resisted anyone threatening to take her Billy away. She suspected, as parents often do, that her son was well on his way to sexual adventures. She tried, without success, to limit his participation in dances and outings.[35]

In the most extraordinary passages of his memoir, Williams describes his mother ("a full-bodied, handsome woman") overinterpreting the courtship as a threat to chaste youth. Calling him to her room as she dressed, she put on her bra and her silky step-ins trimmed with lace, then the rest of her clothes in front of him. She warned him not to "play" with the sensitive part of a woman's body, and through sobs urged him to hold the line at some modest petting. "How she did it," he reflects, her son "will never quite understand. It was surely one of her bravest, most magnificent moments." A different interpretation would see a woman so desperate that she engaged unconsciously in borderline seductive behavior toward him. A half-century later, he claimed to hear the sound of her rustling silk in the rush of the Oregon tides.

She nevertheless readied him, and also herself, for the wider world. In the summer of 1938, Jeannie Preston prepared to leave Atlantic for Simpson College, a small coeducational liberal arts school in Indianola, Iowa, and Mildrede attended a summer session at Columbia Teachers College, taking an exuberant son along for the New York World's Fair. He heard Duke Ellington live and also Mildrede's own favorite, the debonair Cab Calloway. They were small-town bohemians at home in the metropolis.

Mother and son seemed, at last, to have put their troubles behind them as he passed from boy to man and she finished her degree, moving from Atlantic to a job at Central State Teachers College in Stevens Point, in central Wisconsin. Williams later took immense pride in her favorable graduate teaching evaluations as a tough but fair instructor who would go on to head the local American Association of University Women chapter. She was surprised but deeply gratified to hear that he had won a basketball scholarship in 1939 to Kemper Military Academy in Booneville, Missouri, grasping the only possible financial opening for a college education. Like his mother, he was leaving Iowa for good, returning only for family visits.

His grandparents lived on in Atlantic, the last of them dying in 1962, and his mother remained in Wisconsin until she died of cancer in 1978. Williams remained emotionally close to them and proud of them. But he had set his life on a wider course than Atlantic or Iowa or even the Midwest would allow. Many middle-class children from similarly small and generally prosperous towns had been prepared to leave home for wider opportunities. But few would spend so much of their lives intellectualizing the significance of it all.

There was another childhood issue which returned to him repeatedly in later life: his mother's struggle to bear the responsibility of the family and also to become her own person. He recalled that a friend of his mother's told him shortly after her death that "independence for a woman of [her] generation was a two-edged sword. We thought about it as members of a community, and [then] that [possibility] kind of disappeared."[36] This memory may have well been shaded by Williams's predilections, for Mildrede *was* an independent woman. But if she, the exceptional person, had won out, she had also been worn out by the fight. And so one can see the great themes of Williams's life: community and the individual, the achievements of the independent-minded American and the immense price imposed upon those who also yearn for peace and security.

William Appleman Williams later made much of the mixture of community and individualism that he had known in Atlantic. He believed that the country needed a specifically American brand of communal and regional socialism created by the kind of independent-minded, diligent, and determined "ordinary" citizens with whom he had grown up. How that vision related to his real home scene that Jeannie remembered as strikingly cold, where a youngster growing up read the newspaper at dinner to avoid conversation with the adults, remained to be seen. He pushed the frontiers of historical scholarship further than any other American of his time, but Williams always—at least in his own mind—remained rooted, spiritually, politically and philosophically, in his own idealized heartland. The great Pan-African historian C. L. R. James, like Williams an astute critic of Empire, once observed that the average American, while achieving an unprecedented degree of individual autonomy, for that very reason craved an elusive fellowship and community with others.[37] The Williams family could have been James's proof positive.

The fall of 1939 brought Williams into a happy moment of his life. He enjoyed the mixture of quasi-military discipline, rigorous scholarship, and competition at Kemper and did well. It exemplified, in many respects, what he admired most in Middle-American institutions. It had a good national reputation for academic standards among military academies, and its administrators and teachers encouraged students, as he recalled, to "play it straight," with "no crap" of the usual cliquish school kind or the artificial discipline that many military academies offered for troubled youngsters shipped off by their uncoping parents. A literature teacher might assign students to read pulp novels for weeks so that they could appreciate Shakespeare as a follow-up assignment; a math teacher had students read Descartes, Leibnitz, Spinoza, Russell, and Whitehead while learning calculus, spherical trigonometry, and differentials. Williams did especially well in Physics, English Literature, and various art courses, and almost as well in Composition and Calculus. Administrators treated the likeable Bill as a "fair-haired boy," Jeannie recalled from her visits for school dances.[38]

Williams found it a real pleasure to be trained and tested rigorously, to "do the best you could and then accept the losses, defeats, along with victories." A "very good" athlete by his own account, he quickly lost interest in organized sports, but had to continue in order to keep his scholarship. His interests had drifted elsewhere—to music, and above all, to reading books new and exciting to him. In this environment of limited distractions, where boys met girls only on specified weekends, his intellectual life blossomed for the first time.[39]

According to Williams's recollections, Spinoza meant the most to him, as the philosopher determined to see the relationship of the part to the whole, to grasp in each "ostensibly positivistic fact" the hidden pattern of connections which gave it meaning. It was during this period, Williams believed, that he became predisposed to something like Marxism, without grasping in the least any alternatives (or even the need for alternatives) to the social system as it existed.

The threat of war inevitably occupied the attention of military preparatory schools.[40] But as Williams mulled over his life ahead, corresponding on a daily basis with Jeannie, he managed to believe with millions of others that the U.S. might somehow stay out of the conflict. At the end of his two years at Kemper, he still inclined instead toward becoming an architect.

Fate intervened. Among the Annapolis appointments made available to each state's congressional delegation, one position opened up for Iowa. A Republican congressman, Ben J. Jensen, looked to Bill not only as the son of a late military veteran (and well-liked public figure), but also a young man obviously suited for officership. According to one version, his mother—now in Stevens Point—and his grandmother insisted that he accept the offer. He could not refuse such an opportunity. And he did not refuse. In September 1941, he entered the Naval Academy.

Looking back many years later, he had a reason to think that a larger inevitability had spoken. His great-uncle—a former apprentice seaman and later Captain Guy Kramer, with more than thirty long voyages under his belt—had told his story to youngster Bill Williams. Laying half-paralyzed in bed, carving an exact model of the final ship he had commanded, he conveyed "that eerie combination of exhilaration, dream and consummate fatigue" of ocean life to the "impressionable child" who also grew into a sailor.[41]

But Billy's first approach to the Navy was uneasy at best. For two years he suffered through classes and routines he hated. According to Navy records, he had especially deficient averages in Electrical Engineering and Foreign Languages, and these low grades meant that he eventually graduated 706th out of 915 class members.[42] Decades later, thinking aloud about how a renown scholar-to-be might have scraped by with mediocre grades, Williams reflected that he had learned so much about military discipline and taken so many similar courses at Kemper, he felt initially that he was only passing time. Classmates recall him as quiet, serious, completely uninterested in the routines of hazing and public hoopla, and intensely missing Iowa and his sweetheart. The couple wrote every day, and according to Jeannie's recollection, Williams had twin bracelets inscribed, "I BELONG TO BILL WILLIAMS" and "I BELONG TO JEANNIE PRESTON." A few years later, twin wedding rings read similarly, "NO ONE ELSE EVER."

He was also likely depressed at the prospect of active warfare, which some of his classmates anticipated with naive enthusiasm. Annapolis self-consciously prepared its plebes for active combat by this time. Instructors frankly described the preparatory stages taking shape in the Atlantic, American ships supplying the English and inevitably inviting German response. Mental escape seemed better to Williams than brooding about a grim future. "So," he recalls, "I laughed at it all and went off to read novels, economics, history, and in general, do my other things." Most memorably, he had fun as a jazz drummer, sitting in with the visiting bands of Benny Goodman and Artie Shaw (who he especially admired as a musician-intellectual), and serving in a warm-up band for Gene Krupa, who sauntered on stage with his characteristic Coca-Cola bottle in hand, complimenting the young man on his drumming skills.[43]

Gradually things changed, for reasons that Williams himself never made entirely clear. Certainly the courses got more interesting, the opportunities for real hands-on maritime training more frequent. He served as an assistant editor for the Academy's *Trident Magazine* in his final year and even wrote twice for the cadets' rather amateurish magazine: a short story which, according to its heading, would "prove once and for all, that midshipmen can write good fiction" on a wartime marriage and a naval war encounter; and an essay on the defeat of the Nazis by the Red Army. In the first, a flyer remembers his romance and hopes for a happy life together with his new bride while he makes a heroic, doomed bombing run on a Nazi munitions factory.[44] In the second—"A scholarly and interestingly written article giving valuable background on our little known ally"—he sees the "crimson flag of the Soviet Union . . . now maturing in . . . the blood of its men and women." Williams reflected on the background for the victory at Stalingrad in the rebuilding of factories amid wartime conditions, the breakdown of Nazi logistical lines inside Russia, and above all the heroism of the ordinary Red infantrymen. They had simply won the war, more than any other single force. "Thanks to them," Williams concluded, "we shall read of the Nazi Fashion rather than living as its slaves."[45]

With the passage of time, he also adjusted better to being away from Iowa. A close friendship might well have been decisive. Billy Bonwit, a rare Jew at Annapolis—not so much abused by that time as simply pushed aside from the military camaraderie—needed a roommate and Williams made himself available. They were a perfect match. One, from an economically privileged but emotionally damaged Jewish home, had been heavily exposed to artistic ideas including the art photographs that his late father had taken. The other, instinctively egalitarian, had plenty to teach his new friend in the worlds of jazz and sports. Novelistically, Williams described their relationship as a marriage of roommates who could each think the other partner was a bit crazy but also revel in activities together.

Williams had by now accepted the inevitability of participation in the war, and he assumed his prospective commanding role with the utmost resolve. He and his fellow future officers were "taken very damn seriously" by the instructors and, increasingly, by each other as well. They studied together, reciting on history, political theory, and English and American literature every weekday, writing small essays on sections of the blackboard—a great training in prose, Williams claimed later. They also trained together and above all "learned about power," including the moral necessity of accounting for one's actions. These leadership questions recalled Williams's sports days and seemed to bring out the best in his often steely character.

He thereby experienced a remarkable 180-degree turn in his attitude toward being at the Academy. He remembered his last three semesters as "exciting academically and otherwise," the basis for a lifelong pride in his Annapolis experience. Remarkably, the old-fashioned virtues of being "an officer and a gentleman," with emphasis on both parts of the equation, had become all-important. He improved his grades, but even more he changed his attitude. The yearbook described "Will" as notable for his straightforwardness and for "his hatred of poor organization and his determination to finish a job."[46] He might be forgiven for making a fictional version of himself the best hands-on ship's officer of the class. He probably came close in real life.

The Navy had for generations wanted its officers to receive a well-rounded training and a sense for the culture of the military and diplomatic elites with whom they would interact. At least from the Victorian days of Alfred Thayer Mahan, founder of the Naval War College and himself a talented historian, the Academy also aspired to make its graduates ready for global politics. Specialization would fragment the liberal arts tradition at Annapolis within a decade, but during the middle 1940s it remained strong. Having so doubted a vocation not of his own choosing, Williams determined to be the kind of officer who exemplified the Academy graduate in the world of high politics and culture as well as war. He immediately bought "miniatures" (replicas) of his Academy class ring for the two most important women in his life, his mother and his fiancée. They married just before he shipped out, but Jeannie had to claim Bill's grandmother's ring, which had not been sent on to her by Mildrede. Williams wore his own Annapolis ring the rest of his life, unconsciously twirling or tapping it while making an important intellectual point, sometimes consciously fingering it to unnerve his left-wing graduate students.[47]

The sheer nautical aspect played a considerable role in his deep feelings for the Navy. As an executive, he learned to love the "beauty and the terror" of the sea from his very first cruises. He also formulated the vital environmental lesson, so important to him in the last decades of his life, "that man can survive only by treating nature as a senior partner in life." In a day when so many battle-wounded ships went down with their crews, he had no thoughts of conquering the elements, but instead set himself to learn how to live within them. Tactically or strategically, he absorbed yet another lesson that many fellow cadets somehow missed: it was militarily impossible for one nation to dominate the globe without making a mess of the attempt.

Williams broadened his intellectual horizons in remarkable ways. Having absorbed Spinoza, he now turned with growing curiosity to Marx and Freud. This choice of intellectual giants had a definite relation, he later recalled, to his classroom training in the science of engineering. He pressed scientific inquiry to the broad questions of society and the human mind. At a moment when Marx's star was soon to fall considerably in the West and Freud's to rise sharply, many intellectuals looked for a kind of synthesis or dialogue between the two. Thus Erich Fromm's *Escape From Freedom*, published in 1941, pointed the way by arguing that alienation from the soil and community of feudalism to modern capitalist relations had increased mass insecurity and fear. Socialism, in Fromm's perspective, would cure the alienation. Whether or not Williams read Fromm, this kind of thinking had begun to take hold in contemporary intellectual circles.

Williams also recalled first reading the English "guild socialist" G. D. H. Cole, who outlined a possible peaceful transition to a decentralized economic and social system based in autonomous communities. Cole's own inspiration had been William Morris, the famed designer, poet, and utopian novelist who led a wing of the British socialist movement during the 1880s. For Morris as for many late nineteenth-century socialists, capitalism was best seen as an interruption in the historical communities that advanced human society. The medieval era, with all its inequalities, its spiritual corruption, and its resistance to scientific advance, still had the important qualities of community feeling, pride of workmanship, and spiritual aspiration (no matter how cynically the ruling cliques regarded it all) toward a more worthy goal than the self-pride and possessions of this world.

Morris, Cole, and other such thinkers were never entirely welcome in formal Marxist circles, suspected of romanticism and similar heresies by communists and reform socialists alike. Yet they continued for Williams as a personal influence and as a style of thinking, a British counterpart in some important ways to the democratic and ecological regionalism of Lewis Mumford and other American enthusiasts of the Tennessee Valley Authority, as a model for social reorganization. Williams hints that he may have been grappling, this early, for a socialism influenced but not overwhelmed by Marxist ideas or Marxist organizations.

He had unquestionably come to a personal sense of the decisive importance of future relations between the United States and the Soviet Union. No far-thinking prospective military officer could fail to see the outline of possibilities. Indeed, millions of ordinary Americans but especially radicals and self-conscious antifascists felt an admiration and awe which decades later Williams described as the utter "dependence of the Western powers upon the courage of the Red Army."[48] The "worldly-minded" Williams, as the Annapolis yearbook called him, inevitably grew more emotionally involved in such quasi-political deliberations as his time for active service drew near.[49]

Annapolis graduated Williams's entire class a year early in 1944 to put them into the war. He later recalled that his classmates informally voted him most likely to reach the Joint Chiefs of Staff. He was someone they saw as possessing administrative skills and an unrelenting focus on detail.[50] Like his fellow graduates, he was immediately commissioned. He volunteered for the Amphibious Corps to avoid becoming an executive "errand boy" on a large ship and to be allowed a command of his own, however minor. He thus served the last fifteen months of the Pacific War as an

Executive Officer on board what he regarded as a mere splinter of a boat, a so-called Landing Ship Medium. His task was to ferry infantrymen toward battle while the Japanese tried to sink the ship from under him.

He never wrote at length about this period; nor did he recollect old war stories in the fashion of so many former military participants, nor mention the Purple Heart that he was awarded. He often commented, more generally, that with the military brass hard at work, the outcome nevertheless "all depended upon the men who went into combat," who "bled and died" and finally won the war against fascism.[51] Even his quasi-autobiographical novel about a Navy man said surprisingly little about the actual conflict. He had been chosen in the first wave of invasions, his protagonist claimed, because his task was like "tossing newspapers right on the mark while flirting with the girl three porches down the block." He had learned, through application of instinct, how to "handle a ship like it was flying a model airplane," letting the ship itself do most of the work. Alternatively, "reading" a ship was a Spinozan project, a model in political-scientific economy in understanding how the engine room and deck provide the base that supports the superstructure of guns and bridge, which in turn affects the function of deck and engine room.[52]

Williams offered no insights into the inevitable moments of terror, except to say, in a passage of *Contours of American History*, that modern war increasingly made targets into mere blips on the radar screen, and to add, in many private letters, that no novel yet written had been equal to the complexity of the World War's battle scene. Some of the most iconoclastic accounts, however, clearly appealed to him: Joseph Heller's *Catch 22*, Kurt Vonnegut's *Slaughterhouse Five,* and Norman Mailer's *The Naked and the Dead* all captured the "dehumanizing and undemocratic character of war and the armed forces."[53] Part of him wanted to remember, but part of him sought to suppress detailed recollections of battle gore.

Williams concluded several times later that an officer on a ship could create either an atmosphere of subservience or the framework for an "honest community." By self-consciously choosing the latter, he was clearly underlining a key value of his own life. He also said that life on shipboard was "not so much a chain of command as it is an interlocking network of mutually known and accepted responsibilities."[54] He admired those under his command, and by reading their letters as military censor for fifteen months, appreciated their clarity and insight as they struggled to explain their experiences to loved ones stateside. He also continued to read his favorite authors deeply, including Marx, and now also Kant and Faulkner. He claimed to have read Ernest Hemingway's own war drama, *For Whom the Bell Tolls*, at just the perfect moment in his life, when it gave him the political push he had been waiting for.[55] The fatalism, the romanticism, and the rugged antifascism with a leftward political tilt no doubt hit the right note in the captain's quarters.

As "Captain of the Line" in the secondary invasions intended to advance from the Philippines to Japan, he was thrown against a bulkhead in heavy seas during the closing months of the war, severely injuring his spine. Despite a determination to keep fit, he suffered discomfort and increasing pain for most of the rest of his life. Old age found him reliving the injury in nightmares, seeing himself as a helpless cripple. Had he not been injured and the atom bombs not been dropped, he might well have been part of the landing force on the Japanese mainland.

Williams nevertheless built parts of two novelistic chapters around bitter disagreement with his Annapolis roommate and a later Commanding Officer about the morality of using the bomb. He insisted decades later that "it is possible to be grateful that oneself and comrades were not killed in an assault on the Japanese home islands and yet have regret and remorse about how we were saved—and the consequences of being saved in that particular fashion."[56] The quest beyond victory had been Empire. He could not hate the Japanese, and unlike many who served in the Pacific, he could never justify to himself the use of the bomb to end the war. Like Lewis Mumford, the dedicated antifascist whose only son had died in the war but who nevertheless issued a manifesto against the use of atomic weapons ("Gentlemen, You Are Mad"), Williams felt the horror of the deed. There are some things, he often said later, that a right-thinking officer and a gentleman will *not* do. War crime was high on the list.

The war ended but Williams was still in service. Like so many other officers, he considered a military career. Self-consciously in his father's footsteps, he found the prospect of flying "very exciting and demanding," with the aircraft "unforgiving" to human error. He did not expect to be as good a flyer as the senior Billy Williams, but Naval flight school would let him see how far he could go. Corpus Christi was the nation's largest air naval training base, and there Williams's fortunes took several decisive turns.[57]

The first was marriage. After several missed trains and typical wartime confusion compounded by bad weather, Jeannie Preston joined him in December 1945. Williams probably captured his own mood accurately in the protagonist of his later, unpublished novel. Like so many other young men recently released from armed conflict, the fictional Williams was erotically inclined to an extreme degree ("the *second* thing I want to do when I get home" began a standard joke of the time) and very much in love with his wife. But he also loved flying, jazz, and alcohol. The couple made friends quickly and might have gone on together in any number of different career and personal directions.

Civil Rights and an accompanying radicalism made a sudden appearance, however, so sudden that Williams could never satisfactorily explain his remarkable shift of attention. Although race seemingly played no role in Atlantic as any kind of issue, he prided his grandmother on describing the dignity of Indian peoples, telling him that he needed to "walk a mile in their moccasins" to understand their unique and tragic experience. He would later tell students that the racial caste system of Annapolis and the surrounding area, with African Americans practically restricted to the servant class, had disturbed him. But he had no way to act upon inequity. Jeannie Williams recalled a burning sense of unfairness that she felt, too, because of the straightforward values of equal play she had learned, and because she felt a need for improving the world. She, rather than he, had been the aggressive leader of local and college clubs, the activist of the family, and now she urged him forward. She had not been politically active but was not to be frightened off, either. Henry Wallace's family had been patron saints of Iowa's farmers, and Jeannie's college roommate was the granddaughter of Milo Reno, the leader of 1930s "Farm Holiday" agrarian radicalism.

The antifascist and antiracist mood of the nation also played a large role. Williams novelistically reflected on the warmth of feeling by GIs who imagined an America with blacks, Indians, Jews, and others as equals. At this moment, *The House I Live In*, a short film feature starring Williams's (and the rest of the nation's) favorite crooner, Frank Sinatra, toured movie houses nationally, urging multiracial democracy and picking up awards. This marked a clear opening for racial change, almost a sanction for idealistic action.[58]

At any rate, a fractious local political campaign impelled Corpus Christi's black community leaders to seize the moment. They looked to the Supreme Court's *Smith v. Allwright* decision of 1944 to demand the opening of the voting process to all races on a non-prejudicial basis, and they followed in the wake of organizing by Corpus Christi's large minority population, the Mexican Americans. The potential advance in elections carried a hidden contradiction, the future use of black votes as leverage for payoffs by candidates to various ward leaders. But the local NAACP, headed by a respected black dentist and supported by a noted veteran southern white lawyer, spearheaded an effort to press the momentary advantage, raising a variety of social issues around segregation and employment.

Williams, now in his mid-twenties, had absolutely no experience in protest politics, even if his reading seemed to point him in that direction. But he had a new friend of the greatest importance to him. Air Safety Officer Herb Gilmor, an earlier Annapolis graduate from an abolitionist family background, was one of thousands of instinctive or simply unaffiliated American radicals. He had considered joining the American volunteers in the Spanish Civil War, with its Abraham Lincoln Batallion so clearly dominated by fearless left-wing (mostly Jewish), working-class youths. Gilmor had instead bided his time and served in the big war. At Corpus Christi he saw his latest chance to make a difference. The local African American community was small, certainly less than five percent of the total population. But black workers especially wanted access to jobs in the flight line as mechanics. Gilmor and his wife, Charlotte, threw themselves into the task of supporting integration just as they became the newlywed Williamses' most intimate friends.[59]

Williams later sought, in his unpublished novel, to capture the scene that he had lived. The fictionalized eye of the storm was a local Abyssinian Baptist Church, built by freed slaves with the assistance of whites in 1869. Serving as the nerve center of a community striving to transform race relations and in that sense the trajectory of the nation, it had been cheated of a historic opportunity. Populism, a quarter century later, raised prospects again, only to have them crushed by lynch law and the indifference of national business and political leaders. When another half century had rolled by, the struggle was joined here once more.

In chapters devoted to the eloquence of sermons and the excitement of political meetings there, Williams sought to recall and elaborate the historical lessons that he had been privileged to learn firsthand. In a rough but marvelously concrete way, black leaders understood the burden of American history. They also looked beyond their immediate suffering. They saw, for instance, the necessity to link their own fate to the "white niggers," however difficult poor whites had made that task. They could even appreciate that reformers firmly situated within the political system, like a young Lyndon Johnson, could play a positive role over time if given a big enough push from constituents back home. Williams thus grasped, or projected, a complex view of democratic transformation; it depended upon elites quite as much as grassroots action.

In the short run, black residents properly demanded elementary decency from the city. They insisted that buses run at night so that domestic servants could return home safely, and that at least a few of the local white merchants begin to hire them at decent wages. They also wanted an end to the climate of terror conducted intermittently by the Ku Klux Klan. Taken together, these changes along with similar ones for Mexican Americans would have transformed the racial climate of Corpus Christi. Racists, but not only racists, determinedly resisted.

Williams believed that a combination of giant interests had set themselves against major racial readjustments. The Navy brass and local officials of the immensely influential Catholic Church simply wanted no possible threats to their established hierarchies and rules. These were formidable foes, indeed. Meanwhile, General Motors and the King Ranch, two economic giants of the region, had hatched a long-range plan to pipe gas to Mexico and make steel there, barging it back up the Mississippi. Not only would this facilitate a "New South" economic initiative from the standpoint of regional elites, it would also undercut union-made steel for automobiles, weakening key union forces then considered a threat to capitalism's stability and its future. Indeed, it would not be hard to see in retrospect the emerging framework of a heavily populated, conservative Southwest dependent on oil dollars and on military subsidies. Racial minorities could not be permitted to upset the plan with too many early demands for civil equality—or, far worse, to pose any serious challenge to the power structure.

In the cold-war political climate, charges of "Communism" could be readily launched against anyone mobilizing African Americans for social change. Nationally, the FBI mounted a major campaign against "red" union leaders, by no coincidence the most aggressive supporters of racial minorities within the labor movement. Political conservatives and some liberals, again greatly assisted by the FBI, denounced and investigated civil rights groups guilty of left-wing associations. Across the South during 1945-50, pressure increased against organizations like the Southern Negro Youth Congress and the League of Young Southerners, whose activists would one day lead many local campaigns for integration. Corpus Christi was no exception. The local Catholic hierarchy reputedly favored modest and gradual improvements in the conditions of African Americans. But it sought to demonize those who organized for more dramatic and egalitarian shifts. According to Williams's own account, the regional FBI office was predictably reactionary on racial matters and unfriendly towards the most elementary demands for integration.

This set the dour political climate for Williams's first public political role. Using journalistic tools learned at their high-school paper and during Williams's days with *The Trident*, the newly married couple boldly produced a newsletter for the NAACP chapter, *CORPUS CRISIS*. Williams actually wrote most of the copy and Jeannie typed the stencils, with the shades of their apartment carefully drawn to prevent observation. In its scant pages, the newsletter mostly carried news items of the civil rights struggle that local newspapers were likely to ignore or distort. But by the second issue of the *CRISIS*, a contributor also warned that "baiting, whether race, labor, or red-baiting is distasteful to the more intelligent segment of our population," and it accomplished nothing positive. Very possibly Williams wrote this column himself, under a *nom de plume*. In any case, the author was careful enough to couch his remarks within the standard liberal argument that once justice truly reigned in America, "we shall see that Communism is fading away."[60] Catholic notables including a local monsignor and a prominent layman responded savagely. Criticisms of the Catholic Church and its behavior, they made clear, would not be acceptable in Corpus Christi in any form or for any reason whatever. A local integrationist who considered herself otherwise a social conservative wrote to the NAACP leader, "I [have] warned you that the person who is now publishing your bulletin . . . [has] expressed antagonism toward the Church." One of a "few transient Anglos who will frankly admit that they are here of short duration, have been allowed to take over the NAACP." The unnamed Williams, obviously a troublemaker and perhaps a red, obviously preferred "temporary zeal to slow but sure progress."[61]

Williams carefully suggested in the newsletter that the issues at stake were rather different than the empowered Catholics and other conservative integrationists imagined. He did not editorialize, but the *CORPUS CRISIS* urged major economic and social changes. A minimum-wage bill in Congress, acceptance of African Americans at all levels of professional life, and government adjustments of prices to the rising cost of living and an end to the arbitrary executions of African American prisoners constituted the primary demands.[62] This was a program considerably beyond mere racial integration.

The Gilmors, a handful of Quakers, and other white sympathizers backed these and local demands. Jeannie remembers drop-off points for the newsletter in small black businesses and churches, and the NAACP meetings in which copy for the next issue would be discussed at length. Looking back with pride, Williams felt that he had been initiated then and there into "the strategy and tactics of radical politics," building a community among otherwise ordinary, but extremely brave, people.[63] By his own estimate, the mimeographed publication was, within the limits of the medium, a grand success. Its appearance and continuation confirmed the growing sense of resolve in the black community.

Inevitably, at that place and time, intimidation and threats swiftly increased. The FBI, which probably warned the Williamses' landlord about harboring a dangerous radical tenant under his roof, harassed the young Naval officer at work by having his commanding officer call him in for a warning. He also recalled being pushed around a few times by local toughs and threatened with worse. The NAACP's local leader was assassinated a few years after the Williamses left town. "Yes, sir," Williams told an interviewer decades later about the ferocity of response to a modest campaign for equality, "that will make a socialist out of you. Unless you're dead."[64]

Williams almost certainly considered himself a socialist by this time. But he had to walk a careful line in public statements. He brushed off the red-baiting charges in the *CORPUS CRISIS*, for instance, insisting the newsletter was not in the least anti-Catholic or taking any political position about the world at large, but only for racial harmony, free speech, and dialogue on all sides. Any close reader could spot a modest socialistic slant, however. Williams published (and possibly wrote, under a pseudonym) a quite favorable review of James S. Allen's 1937 volume, *Reconstruction—the Battle for Democracy*, written by a former southern activist and published by the Communists' International Publishers. Critics charged that the National Maritime Union, at the time led by communists and active in the port city of Corpus Christi, infiltrated the NAACP via the national CIO's Political Action Committee and attached itself precisely to integration campaigns like the one around Williams.[65]

Williams, for his part, decades later unembarrassedly recalled having "enormous respect" for the handful of local communists who had bravely joined activities and had moreover "been down there a lot longer than I had."[66] They risked more, and went on risking their careers and their lives. Although he never became a member of any interracial Party-oriented organization, he intuited logically that subsequent FBI spying and harassment probably began in Corpus Christi. "Jeez," he reflected in a 1980 interview, "*did* I join the Communist Party? I mean it sounds strange, but [the local Left] had never been that formal an operation. Well, could anybody construct anything I'd done as proving that I'd joined the Party? Weird experience. You really get a sense of Kafka." There may possibly have been nothing local *to* join, in which case mere friendship and common political reform work were *prima facie* —proof of guilt.[67]

Williams was already apparently politically sophisticated enough to reject the national Communist position on race in 1945. Amidst an internal upheaval of their own, American Communist leaders that year dethroned Popular Front symbol Earl Browder and reintroduced a smattering of earlier "class struggle" themes (in many cases, mere symbolic slogans). For a decade, the Communists had stressed racial integration, winning over many black elites as well as white liberals to their programs. Now they returned to a partial version of an early 1930s plan for independent "black belt" states in the South where nonwhites constituted a majority of the population. Advocacy of this view was meant to stimulate an incipient black nationalism, but the real-life framework of political repression and rising individual opportunity made a shambles of the policy. "The party line in the South in '45 made about as much sense to me as . . . bah, humbug. That's not what these people needed, they were already an isolated community," reflected Williams decades later.[68]

And yet this rejection of communist views had nothing in common with either the anticommunism of local conservatives or with the emerging positions of prominent liberals in the newly founded Americans For Democratic Action (ADA). Indeed, just at the time Williams wrote against red-baiting, leaders of the ADA had opened a blistering propaganda campaign for blanket exclusion of all communists (and by extension, all opponents of anticommunist actions) from unions, political movements, and the entertainment industry, high and low culture alike.[69]

It was not the blunders of the Communists, in any case, that doomed the Corpus Christi campaign. Williams later described its best efforts as having been blunted by "prejudice, violence, and indifference."[70] Aided by both red-baiting and the indifference of the new Truman regime in Washington, local authorities foiled the prospect of any sustained African American social movement. Williams would probably have found himself on the outside if he had managed to stay in Corpus Christi any longer. He seems already to have been caught in the NAACP's own blacklist, which local or regional leaders often used to eliminate Communists and near-Communists. Indeed, over the next year he appealed repeatedly to national headquarters for formal membership and apparently got no satisfaction.[71]

Meanwhile, the Navy brass fully intended to send Williams upon the most unpleasant postwar mission they could imagine: to the little Pacific island of Bikini. There, he and others would personally test the viability (and safety) of post–atomic bomb land invasions through amphibious warfare games. Had they managed to order him to that location, Williams would almost certainly have been placed under an extended death sentence of radiation poisoning.

The recurrence of his spinal injury ruled out that plan for him. Dropping him from flight-training entirely because of the pain he suffered while in the cockpit, the Navy directed him to San Francisco's Treasure Island hospital for extensive treatment. There, doctors discovered he had been born with an extra vertebra. Evidently unnoticed at the time of his induction, the deformity should have ruled him out of Naval service in the first place, and might have made his injury grounds for litigation.

Navy doctors wanted Williams to undergo fusion surgery that had, however, left others he knew crippled for life. Refusing that treatment, he was covered in a cast from the shoulders down to the thighs for several months. As he wrote his mother (quoting from a letter he sent, and decades later rediscovered among her things), the pain during his worst days in the hospital was sometimes so severe that he wanted to "go elsewhere," i.e., to die. Instead, he brought himself back to life with thought, books, and Jeannie, who joined him after returning temporarily to Iowa to teach shorthand and business skills in high school while he was overseas. By the spring months of 1947 he had applied for and received a tentative medical discharge.[72]

Williams often said that the entire Naval experience had driven home to him the modern version of a classical adage, "Don't let bastards grind you down." In its good and bad features, it taught him the importance of unshakeable self-confidence. The Corpus Christi incident had given him a sense of mission, not necessarily to renew acvitity in the integration movement elsewhere but to do *something*. Ordered out of Corpus Christi, his novelistic protagonist tells a black Navy friend who has been through the civil rights efforts with him, "I keep thinking there are things to do down that lonesome road."[73] Elsewhere he noted that those who went to war hoping for a better world continued to do their best under difficult circumstances. "Some gave it up as a hopeless effort" but "others continued the struggle." He obviously considered himself one of the latter.[74]

But how could he act upon his newfound ideals? His mother, without necessarily advising him, helped him to decide what to do with himself. Then a teacher with a third-grade class at Stevens Point, she had for years put her visiting son in front of the classroom and walked out, saying something like, "I want you to give children a sense of what it is to be at the Naval Academy (or whatever) and what a commitment to quality involves." The experience, and her example, drew him to teaching. It was also his only immediate family role model in the world of wage labor.[75]

MADISON AND HISTORY

SOMETIME IN THE EARLY 1940S, Williams considered becoming a mathematician but discarded the idea. He was not, a teacher informed him, destined to be an Einstein.[1] Neither did he take up a career in electrical engineering or thermodynamics, his majors at Annapolis, although he remembered being offered good jobs in several corporations.[2] He and some of his radical shipmates had clearly chosen Marx over (Alfred) Mahan, as he joked later. But how could he figure out what was really wrong with society? He had concluded that the nation needed "structural change as opposed to secondary reform," and the study of history increasingly seemed to thim the best means to "make sense out of what the hell was going on in the war and the way the world was going" with "the bomb and all that."[3] It may also have been the one discipline other than the social sciences where he could conduct the Spinozan search for interrelations or organic connections among apparently disparate elements. Surely, a study of history would make sense of his experiences in Corpus Christi. The key problems of

American democracy, becoming more urgent as the cold war intensified, were not new but deeply rooted in the national past.

Harry Truman's surprising victory in 1948, a year after Williams arrived in Madison, established the political and even the socioeconomic framework for decades to come. Portraying himself as heir to the New Deal's entitlement acts, the Missouri backroom politician effectively quieted his opponents by raising the twin threats of entitlement rollbacks and the Soviet menace. If his first administration proved the most publicly reviled since Herbert Hoover's Depression doldrums, Truman's second administration enjoyed a paradoxical success of expanding trade and rising productivity against a background of international tensions and unprecedented weapons spending. Truman had, in effect, discovered the formula for the consumer society. Muting the New Deal rhetoric of social equality, his Fair Deal simultaneously enshrined individual initiative and unprecedented growth at taxpayer expense. It also put the domestic impact of foreign policy on the national agenda.

Williams's graduate work and his life in the Madison, Wisconsin, of the late 1940s helped him locate the source of these developments more precisely, and prepared him to deliver his own unique responses to them. Williams, according to all reports, went his own way in almost everything. He was no professor's disciple, and no single thinker or writer could be credited with a decisive influence on his work. Still, the particular mixture of Beardian-American and Marxist-European professors, radical graduate students, free speech, and free thought offered the milieu in which Williams could consider and vigorously debate the various possibilities. A remarkable place at a remarkable time offered him lifelong friends, sponsors, and intellectual influences. He would bear the stamp of his graduate school days throughout his career, so much so that time away from Madison could be considered the exile periods of his life.

Later, Williams would look back and compare professors and students around the University of Wisconsin's history and sociology departments of the late 1940s to the Frankfurt School.[4] Circumstances did not permit the ideas discussed in Madison to come together in the way that those of Theodor Adorno, Max Horkheimer, Herbert Marcuse, and others did, he admitted. But the pessimism of the Wisconsin intellectuals about the prospects of radical change from below, and the consequent task of analyzing society through a radical perspective on the inner logic of the ruling system had important elements in common with the German Marxist (or post-Marxist) effort. So did the search for the reasons why ordinary Americans might passively accept that logic or even adopt it as their own.

Like the Frankfurt School, but with a much closer view of U.S. history, Madison intellectuals faced the exhaustion of traditional perspectives. The always schematic American Marxist notions of contemporary class conflict had already disappeared for all practical purposes into frantic and unrealistic hopes for another benign central administration, similar to patrician Franklin Roosevelt's, but improved. Applied to earlier history, American Marxism had referred to occasional heroic insurgencies and the misery of the oppressed (especially African Americans), but could not explain the sheer stability of the social system, let alone the economic recovery of capitalism after the war.

Williams's Madison intellectual circle came to grips with history's surprises in the best ways that it could manage. No Walter Benjamin was to be found here, with the dextrous dialectics to turn despair into utopian observations, and there was no Adorno to find solace in experimental modernism. But Williams, with his own disciples in the decades ahead, would almost be a school in himself.

I

Frustrated at receiving no satisfactory response from a series of letters to the University of Wisconsin registrar requesting permission to enter graduate school, Williams got through to longtime history chair Paul Knaplund. Williams lacked the necessary credentials, but his sense of determination struck Knaplund, who was then building up a departmental faculty and graduate student body. Knaplund's successor, Chester Easum, like Knaplund a political conservative, rapidly took the young man under his wing in a preliminary "undergraduate" seminar to make up coursework, and later wrote him sterling recommendations. So far as they understood Williams's political views, they had no sympathy for them, and simply admired his abilities. If Williams already considered himself a socialist— and he held his cards too close to his sleeve for any public reputation—he also had good reasons to take a distanced and scholarly approach.[5]

Madison, Wisconsin, proved the perfect place for him to study, at any rate. An isthmus situated among several lakes that had been praised by a visiting Henry Wadsworth Longfellow as jeweled diadems, the city was spectacularly beautiful if also bitterly cold for months at a time. During the late nineteenth century, the land-grant University of Wisconsin and its accompanying state institutions had become a center of social history and great scholarly influence. Frederick Jackson Turner, himself from rural Wisconsin, had transformed historical thought with his Frontier Thesis that the American character had been formed through continual westward movement.

Generations of historians debated the implications, but they uneasily joked that their entire profession was a "Turnerverein," a word play upon the *Turnverein*, the fraternal associations whose combination of gymnastics and free thought made them a center of nineteenth-century German-American social and intellectual life. From popular thought to the highest ivory towers, Turner's influence went forth. One of Turner's students, Algernon Simons from little Baraboo, Wisconsin, had gone on from 1890s Madison student days to edit the premier American socialist theoretical journal and to write a popular socialist history—arguably the most influential until Williams's work—of the nation, based conceptually on the virtue of the farming class.[6] Another of Turner's students, Merle Curti, had in turn spawned at Columbia some of the outstanding historians of the 1940s-50s, notably Richard Hofstadter, and had taught Williams's own mentor, Fred Harvey Harrington. With these giants on hand, physically in the classroom rather than perpetually on leave as in typical Ivy League schools, Madison's attractions proved irresistible. Besides, Mildrede was only a few hours away by car and wanted her son close to her.

The other notable feature of Madison's Americanists was their notorious loyalty to Charles Austin Beard, the great successor to Turner and to Madison's earlier Progressive scholarly tradition. Beard and his wife, Mary Ritter Beard, had written in 1927 *The Rise of American Civilization*, easily the most influential history of the nation ever published. Scarcely a home of educated Americans lacked it, a claim that could be made for no single scholarly or popular historical volume that has followed. It would be surprising, indeed, if the Williams home in Atlantic had not also possessed a copy. From the 1910s to the 1930s Charles Beard held forth on a wide array of political and social issues, in hundreds of newspaper essays, radio talks, and pamphlets. Never a socialist (although a definite ally of socialists on specific issues), Beard managed to appear somehow above all the particular controversies of the day. In the public perception, historical understanding had given him deep insights into the national mentality.

Beard's reputation suffered a monumental decline after the 1930s. Disillusioned with World War I, like so many fellow historians he had grown increasingly suspicious of the rise of the leviathan state apparatus. Taken up temporarily by archconservatives (like those at the *Chicago Tribune*) who had long attacked him, Beard argued against America's drift toward involvement in a second world war. The nation would be better served, he believed, by reliance upon its own resources. After Pearl Harbor, he accused Roosevelt of disingenuousness, a failure to place the issues before the public and to draw their approval for crucial war decisions. Thereafter, Beard's adversaries, notably in the Eastern schools and media, went on the attack. Once-eager publications and radio shows shunned him, and younger liberal historians, attaching themselves to Truman's policies, slashed at him furiously. He died in 1947 after a *Walpurgisnacht*—a burning of his private papers.[7]

But Beard retained the respect of many Madisonians, intellectually and politically. During the 1930s-40s, the History Department at Madison had become especially well known for its scholarly elaboration of Populist-Progressive themes close to both Turner and Beard. John D. Hicks, the foremost historian of Populism and himself a graduate of the University of Wisconsin, had returned to Madison at the height of the Depression. There, he wrote one of the most successful progressive-oriented U.S. history survey textbooks for generations. Beardian economic historian and colonial specialist Curtis Nettels, a former editorial associate of the Marxist journal *Science & Society* and later a campus leader of the 1948 Henry Wallace presidential campaign, was also on hand. Merle Curti arrived in 1942, the year that he won the Pulitzer Prize for the *Growth of American Thought*, and immediately expressed his deep sympathies for Beard. These scholars and others felt the continuing inspiration of Beard's emphasis on economic and social history, an outlook endangered along with Beard's own reputation. All a Wisconsin history student had to do for preliminary examinations, one graduate alumnus suggested jocularly, was to read Beard carefully.[8]

This generalization did little justice to the independent character of Williams's mentors, known by some as the "Murderer's Row" (after the Yankee batting lineup) of the history profession. Fred Harvey Harrington, a native of upstate New York, had arrived at Madison in 1937 after completing his doctoral studies at New York University under Henry Steele Commager. He concentrated his interests on the domestic sources of U.S. foreign policy, unlike the standard diplomatic historians of the time. His broad notion of foreign relations sought out a wide variety of influences and particular economic ones behind government policies, and not just the usual study of official diplomatic records. Harrington found himself inevitably at odds with the East Coast "court historians" who not only took a narrow methodological view of diplomatic history but seemed dogmatically determined to defend the State Department's record. Like other Americanists at Madison, Harrington took pride in challenging the well-funded and even better connected Ivy League establishment. His own history of late-nineteenth-century U.S.-Korean relations, written in 1940 but not published until 1944, focused upon the American imperial experience and the inevitability of competition from the Japanese. His biography of Nathaniel P. Banks, sponsored by the American Historical Association's Albert J. Beveridge Memorial Fund and published in 1948, was a study in political and military power.[9]

Harrington's scheme of graduate training shuttled some of his outstanding prospects into a preliminary year with William Best Hesseltine, a political historian who also rejected cold war imperatives (a decade later he would appear among "Sponsors" on the board of the pacifist magazine *Liberation*). A sympathetic soul who had also attended military school and whose father had died when he was two, Hesseltine trained a handful of the more distinguished historical scholars and popular history writers of the 1950s-60s, including Kenneth Stampp, Richard Current, Stephen Ambrose, and Gordon Parks.[10] Even more than Harrington, Hesseltine was a "scoffer" who liked to "say outrageous things and have people combat him"—a model for Williams's later style of scholarly-political provocations. In later years, when Williams joined the Madison faculty, he and Hesseltine spent many social evenings together; indeed, they were drinking and talking only a few hours before Hesseltine suffered a fatal heart attack in 1963.

During Williams's second year, Harrington invited the bright student to join his own more select crew of graduate advisees. He taught them, as might be expected, the nuts and bolts of research and publishing. But more notably, he had a ruthless way about his criticism of student papers, sitting across his old-fashioned green bridge table going over his comments, or slicing up an entire seminar with harsh criticisms of students for not having worked hard enough. Thus in seminar he would "dissect any decision, event, or movement into its constituent parts with a subtle, loving ruthlessness," qualities that earned him nicknames like "Mr. Cold" and "Fish Eye." This was not meant to be destructive except, perhaps, to the hopelessly thin-skinned youngster. Harrington conveyed through all his gruffness, as Williams later put it, "a great ability to let you consider his criticisms and then do it your way *and take the consequences*." Warren Susman would later observe shrewdly that Harrington thereby offered an incentive to Williams's inclination to engage in his own methods of historical exploration, making discoveries all the time and "discovering America like Columbus."[11]

Harrington also had, Williams later recalled, a "genius for integrating biography and policy in a way that implicitly transcended interest-group analysis." He could analyze Theodore Roosevelt and other early eager architects of the diplomatic "Open Door" without falling back into vulgar materialism. Had he not chosen an administrative career, he might well have gone beyond Beard in the attribution of a worldview or *Weltanschauung* to America's elite, a speculation Williams frequently entertained in private letters. But perhaps Harrington had precisely coached Williams to do what he himself could not do or simply did not want to pursue further. The multitude of ways in which Harrington guided Williams's career and took enormous pride in its development gives good grounds for this conclusion.[12]

Finally, Harrington spent rare social time with the bright and ambitious Navy veteran, dropping by the Williams's apartment with his wife, Nancy, to talk about culture and history or sports or some other favorite topic. A future president of the University of Wisconsin who considered himself (according to persistent rumor) a serious prospect for a future Cabinet post, Harrington clearly had questions of power on his mind. That approach, as admiring young student and future American Studies notable David Noble has observed, was rare among scholars and especially radical ones. Williams, who freely remarked that he would one day have been an admiral if he had remained in the Navy, listened carefully.[13]

Hesseltine and Harrington had ample help in guiding Williams through the Progressive legacy toward new vistas. Colonialist Merrill Jensen created a school of young historians—the last Progressive historian to do so—sharing his view of the Articles of Confederation as the true democratic document, tragically overthrown by the centralizing Constitutional Convention. (Jensen's most noted protégé, Turner's grandson Jackson Turner Main, was another classmate of Williams's and yet another link to the historiographical legacy of the frontier.) Howard K. Beale, still another mentor, was a militant civil libertarian known to dramatize his cause by offering the Declaration of Independence *sans* title to passersby around the State House in downtown Madison to see if they would be willing to sign such an inflammatory document. Not by accident, Beale would soon be at work as editor of a memorial volume on Charles Beard, a most distinguished collection of essays by Richard Hofstadter, Max Lerner, Harold Laski, George S. Counts, and others. Another famous-to-be radical historian, Herbert G. Gutman, was Beale's research assistant.

These mentors all shared a penchant to see history as did Beard, a study of elites more than of social classes, and a study of "useable" history applicable to the need of the moment—from their viewpoint—to avoid another world war. At a methodological level, they also shared a deep commitment to the importance of the primary document. They felt a sort of aesthetic attraction to the *feel* of the document, examined with the belief that if properly viewed, it would yield up its secrets; and a firm confidence that great history could be built, brick by brick, from such documentation. These progressive-tradition Americanists gave Williams a framework or perhaps reinforced the one he had already intuited.

Williams also learned much from scholars indifferent to the Progressive tradition and conceptually far from the History Department. Economic historian Paul Knaplund, who had done so much to build the department, was a sympathetic scholar of the British Empire and gave Williams a framework for thinking about Empire in general. A later Williams called him "Madison's John Quincy Adams." English professor Fredrick Hoffman taught the novel, especially the radical novel. Paul Farmer, a brilliant but disillusioned former Marxist turned slightly cynical taught French history, did the basic historiography course, and imparted a sophisticated view of European ideologies such as Marxism and Freudianism, which few Americanists could then claim to grasp well.[14] Despite his formal politics, Farmer amply illustrated the appeal of European studies. Williams had actually considered, for a short time, a career in Russian history. He lacked the language skills, but more important, the doctrinaire cold-warrior Russianist at the University rejected out-of-hand Williams's skeptical intuitions about U.S. motives and U.S. responsibilities for world unrest. He would be a U.S. historian and a radical one at that. Yet Williams prided his graduate education as being marked by a dialogue with conservatives, the Socratic road to learning.

To Williams, more important by far than all the other non-Americanists was Hans Gerth. Harrington had advised Williams to minor outside history, and that may have been decisive in the young man's responding to the perceived theoretical deficiency. Williams chose the historical or dialectical sociologist, a brilliant but melancholy figure who had been repeatedly held back from promotion by the American-style empiricist sociologists around him and driven into a kind of internal exile. A German emigre and once a lesser-known member of the Frankfurt School, Gerth surveyed the totality of the social system's weight against free thought and activity. More than anyone else, he lent Williams an idiosyncratic Marxist social psychology and almost certainly a Weberian overview of system paralleling Williams's own admiration for Spinoza. Max Weber's influence, however indirect, offered additional clues to understanding the framework of a large and complex process. In later years, Williams simply described it as "the point of view of totality."[15]

Gerth directed the young man towards what Williams later called "a broad knowledge of the methodology of *Weltanschauung* (including serious study of Marx)" and helped him to apply it to foreign relations. Recuperating his Spinoza and reaching out for more, he responded to Marx as "a genius in social history and political economy," able to see "in one piece of evidence a set of relationships" at once economic, ideological, social, and political, at the root of "our alienation from our Humanity under capitalism." With this Marx, rather than the figure whose iron doctrines were purported to be guiding the Soviet Union, Gerth "took me by the hand . . . teased and pushed me into a confrontation with the central theory of reality into a manageable intellectual tool."[16]

Through Gerth, Williams became "deeply involved" with Hegel, Theodor Adorno, Max Horkheimer, Georg Lukacs, and philosopher William Dilthey, whose work actually explicated the notion of a worldview, or *Weltanschauung*. Sharing a bus bound for school, Williams sometimes saw Gerth reading a newspaper and then appearing with questions, based on his clippings, that he demanded his students solve by reading six or seven books in a single day. The sessions that followed were intense enough to be fresh in memory four decades later. So were the self-immersions in texts which posed "dialectical interacting world views" and the "tension" of an idea or concept "coming apart at the seams at midnight," practically demanding Williams stitch it back together in the wee hours of the morning.[17] According to Harrington, Gerth sent Williams soaring, while the job of the Americanists was to bring him back down to earth.[18]

It is more than likely that Gerth or Farmer directed Williams towards two important thinkers whose current works commanded considerable attention among those interested in large views of the world. Joseph Schumpeter, known in some circles as the "bourgeois Marx," was a sophisticated and somewhat cynical Austrian economist who found in the *Communist Manifesto* much that he could admire. Capitalism's impetus of "creative destruction," as Schumpeter wrote in *Capitalism, Socialism and Democracy* (1943), meant the replacement of the network of previous religious and secular, extra-familial ties with market rationality, when by any standard the "stock exchange is a poor substitute for the Holy Grail." In a political conclusion that Schumpeter would share with modern liberals and that Williams disdained, the Austrian insisted that ordinary people could never be trusted with the initiative that great leadership of nations and world society required. Schumpeter took no pleasure in the inability of capitalism to meet the test of pervasive social crisis; he simply expected some authoritarian form of socialism to triumph. Despite these differences, Williams often said that he found in Schumpeter someone he could admire.[19]

The other current thinker would very likely have been Karl Polyani, whose massively influential volume, *The Great Transformation*, appeared in 1944. The Polish economist elaborated a *sui generis* "organic rationality" to explain the evolution of capitalism from feudalism, and thus to explain the modern state and economy. Capitalism was not simply the latest social system but, as Schumpeter would have said, one completely unique in its social effects. "Modernity" signified disintegration of face-to-face working relations with a web of government systems and atomistic economic actors, together making a moral society increasingly difficult to maintain.

The sixteenth-century English "enclosures" which pushed the poor off the land for sheepherding prompted Tudor and Stuart kings to create labor regulations, church responsibilities for paupers, and other accommodations previewing the modern welfare state. People who felt themselves owed a living, however miserable, lost the conceptual means to grasp their own social significance and the role of labor in creating value. As mechanization continued, the historic traditions of guilds and of self-sufficient classes of farmers almost disappeared from memory. A society demoralized at its lower levels could hardly resist the completely commodified economy. The masses acquiesced helplessly or shared the dream of the emerging middle class in a market utopianism where competition of all against all would somehow become the happy route to freedom and prosperity.

Polyani could readily accept the Marxist view of twentieth-century irrationality, highlighted by horrifyingly destructive nationalism. But Marxism isolated the economic factor, in his view, when economics and culture had to be analyzed together. Classes might be seen better as functional groups distributing responsibilities. At their most productive, they struggled not for all-out class victory but to preserve and transform an increasingly self-destructive social order. Polyani looked, personally, to the promise of a moral tradition blending Christianity and socialism.[20]

Thinkers like Schumpeter and Polyani spoke to the felt need of Williams and his fellow graduate students for more theory than the Progressive historians could supply. As Warren Susman observed, they also had a gnawing sensation that the framework of political Progressivism was hopelessly outdated. These two gaps had much in common with each other. The frontier, which had supplied the key mechanism for the interpretation of American civilization by Turner and Beard, had rapidly faded into the historical distance. Neither the New Deal (regarded by liberal intellectuals as the culmination of national political evolution) nor the war, nor America's newly predominant place in the world could be satisfactorily and comprehensively explained from the older view.[21]

Grappling for a better methodological handle, they needed a larger view of culture, of modernization, and of social psychology. Their beloved U.S. history teachers could not offer much of this. But these professors were interested in such subjects themselves and eager for dialogue arising out of their students' challenges. Williams once described his fellow students (including the likes of future notables John Higham, David Shannon, Harvey Goldberg, and Wayne Cole, as well as a handful of eager intellectuals who never found a place in academic life) as "uncommonly intelligent and intellectually daring," enthusiastic about discussing historical questions inside the classroom and out, and especially hungry for fresh perspectives. No wonder that Harrington, Williams's faculty role model, remembered the graduate students as being the *most* influential on Williams's young intellectual development.[22]

They had an emotional support for this activity that they might not have had anywhere else in the country. The university and the Madison community together had also remained, in some ways, within a curious Beardian time warp. Defenders of free thought and of resistance against the national juggernaut state, Madisonians seemed at once quaintly outdated and yet almost recklessly courageous in the face of cold-war pressures. University administrations generally tolerated and even mildly encouraged the presence of left-wing dissenters. Otherwise conservative legislators had often agreed, despite recurrent grumbling, that the spirit of free opinion was a proven incentive to attract top figures in sciences and the liberal arts. Selective repression, such as the intimidation of controversial faculty and denial of facilities to controversial speakers, had taken place in times of national stress such as the 1919-21 Red Scare, but was considerably less severe than at most schools. And it always tapered off after a mood of national calm returned.

Williams often reminded younger generations of radicals that the teachers he admired and the colleagues he later embraced had not been so much radical or even political as simply the best in their fields. But the progressive, radical, and bohemian elements also had an unquestionable leavening effect. University President John Bascom, one of the nineteenth-century founders of the campus free-thought tradition, had embraced the Knights of Labor and woman suffrage before being cashiered by the Regents for opposing the state's liquor ring. Labor economist Richard T. Ely, fired by Johns Hopkins for his radicalism, espoused Christian Socialism in the Gilded Age. Twenty years later, "Fighting Bob" LaFollette built his brain trust here, a decade before he led the doomed Congressional resistance to U.S. entry into World War I. Close by, the daily *Madison Capitol Times* was launched in 1917 around an upsurge of popular antiwar sentiment. *LaFollette's Magazine* (later, the *Progressive*) kept the faith alive in hard times for the resisters against the monopolies and the big state that served corporate interests.[23]

Documenting the life and labor of ordinary people, the State Historical Society (practically an extension of the History Department) meanwhile rapidly outpaced the Ivy Leagues in the amassing of socioeconomic data. And this was not merely compulsive gathering. The first University of Wisconsin historian of note, Henry S. Allen, had himself collected slave songs in the Reconstruction South, in what might be described as early ethnographic or oral-history fieldwork. A succession of scholars, including labor economics giant John R. Commons, arranged for the Historical Society to gather an unprecedented volume of labor and radical materials. The democratic intent could not be misunderstood: the lives of ordinary people were *worth* studying.

Campus life was also unorthodox from the bottom upward. By the late 1920s, out-of-state Jewish undergraduates made their presence evident at Alexander Meikeljohn's Experimental College, where they imparted a distinctly bohemian and sometimes politically radical undertone to the usual Big Ten spirit. Student strikes might have rocked the 1930s campus but University President Glenn Frank personally greeted the strikers and declared the demonstrations a "peace assembly." The *Daily Cardinal*, the student newspaper, traditionally tended to be the voice of the avant-garde, liberal, and even radical students. A handful of well-liked professors, themselves bohemians or at least libertarians, encouraged the radical youngsters and drew the fire of perpetually enraged conservatives in the state legislature. By the late 1940s all this was a hallowed but also a living tradition, like the student dining cooperatives where left-wingers and other youngsters with small incomes gathered to share meals and talk about politics and culture.[24]

Williams the small-town Iowan with radical and modest bohemian leanings fit in easily here, even as he focused his energies upon his studies. Admitted for 1947, with his way partially paid by the GI Bill, Williams had to take extra undergraduate history courses to complete his preparation. Recalled to California in mid-semester for a last Navy physical and release, he left Jeannie behind to attend his classes and take notes. She loyally withdrew from the classroom once he was firmly enrolled, although she had been urged to continue her own studies. By spring 1948, Williams was extremely proud to be part of a great institution. It stimulated him, and it also gave him a sense of security.

He and Jeannie moved to an apartment next to one of the giant fraternity houses on campus, living just above another future campus legend, football star and later athletic director Elroy "Crazy Legs" Hirsh. Jeannie supported both herself and Williams by working full-time as a secretary in the extension school and later in the YMCA. Apart from an occasional play or concert they could share, the scant luxuries—notably the books he purchased for his own studies and separate interests—went to him just as they had at his boyhood home. They both pushed hard for him to race through his courses and his dissertation, graduating early to make up for time lost and in order to enjoy a post-military, post-college life together. He took his degree in a remarkable three years, en route impressing his professors with a seriousness toward his teaching, but even more with his ability to convey to undergraduates his enthusiasm about ideas.[25]

In the little time they had for extra activities, they made a small circle of friends, Bill's fellow history graduate students along with the Harringtons. They also went to church. Having been active in Presbyterian youth circles in Atlantic, Jeannie succeeded in interesting Bill during a wartime visit home, thanks to a dynamic young minister. Williams had himself baptized, and thereafter attended Sunday services irregularly. He evidently considered himself a sort of Christian socialist. During a summer visit to Madison in the early 1950s, he even gave a sermon at the new Unitarian Center, in a building designed by Frank Lloyd Wright.

They could not entirely avoid the glare of campus political life and its various cultural by-products. McCarthyism (not yet named) had begun to settle over American life. Hollywood moguls declared their unwillingness to hire anyone who refused to sign a loyalty oath. President Harry Truman moved somewhat hesitantly at first, then with increasing speed towards a massively coordinated attack upon suspected communists, homosexuals, radical dissenters, and potential dissenters in government jobs, labor, and public life. Colleges and universities, as purported centers of interracialism, homosexuality, and communist sympathies, received special scrutiny from the FBI and various other investigative agencies.

The local effects were oddly muted in part because Senator Joseph McCarthy was reluctant to attack an institution so close to home: such action could cost him votes and financial support. But several visiting scholars, including the famed German exile composer Hanns Eisler, found themselves barred from speaking in university facilities. A handful of young professors were also denied tenure on clearly political grounds. In many other places, opponents of such actions were intimidated into silence. Not infrequently, the FBI actually set up an office on campus and worked hand-in-hand with the administration to stalk and eliminate suspected dissenters. In Madison, however, even as state legislators sniffed and growled at purportedly subversive professors misleading youth, any hints of actual censorship and retribution met a volley of protests. Distinguished scholars on the faculty, including historians Merle Curti and Howard Beale, rushed into print to protect civil liberties. College administrators made mollifying noises, while trying to hold off the hotheads in the legislature. Student letters in the *Cardinal* warned that "we may kiss our liberties goodbye," and openly ridiculed the campus redhunters for sniffing out borscht and vodka (i.e., Russian agents) on every side.[26]

The crackdown intensified on other campuses across the country, but avowed Marxist discussion groups still met openly in University of Wisconsin facilities. Leftwing folksingers made regular appearances, and *Golden Boy*, leftist Clifford Odets's sardonically anticommercial drama, was staged amid great fanfare (the Williamses, too, enjoyed Odets enormously). Vintage antifascist European and American cinema, in an only slightly subtextual response to threatened fascism at home, played regularly at the student union. Like the 1948 election of socialist Frank Zeidler to the mayorality of Milwaukee, this was part of a definite anomaly in American life, but for the participants a happy one.[27]

Campus antiwar sentiment, which aroused the vitriolic denunciation of conservatives and cold war liberals alike, was pushed toward the margins at Wisconsin, but not quite beyond them. Visiting candidate Harry Truman, claiming to represent the New Deal tradition against the impending Republican backlash, met overflow crowds shortly before the fall elections. Yet Socialist Party presidential candidate Norman Thomas (introduced by

William Hesseltine) could still fill a good-sized hall, as could guitar-playing Idaho Senator Glen Taylor, running mate of Progressive Party candidate Henry Wallace. Compulsory ROTC was vigorously debated and rejected in a student straw poll. Most important, teachers who fled repression elsewhere, in Europe and New Hampshire alike, found a home in Madison and, especially if tenured, kept their voice. Gerth, who had coached the radical sociologist C. Wright Mills during the early 1940s, stressed in campus talks the desirability of planned economies in a democratically socialist postwar Europe.[28]

The intellectually curious and sympathetic Williams, notably absent from any such activities, made a crucial distinction between active politics and teaching so early, and so easily, that he hardly seemed to realize for decades that it had been final. Fellow graduate students and mentors remembered him in these years as a "gentle sort among the extroverts competing for the attention of the faculty," as Harrington put it. He opened up, if at all, only among close friends. Drawn to undergraduate students, he spent his public passions teaching. Merle Curti remembered him talking in private often and easily about Russia, but not about any real or potential American radical movement. David Noble recalls him blistering John Dewey and the tradition of Pragmatism as capable only of leading to superficial reform—as if Williams were seeking his own, more radical tradition. Williams still had no apparent particular interest in the history of U.S. diplomacy, but it seems clear that he would be drawn to a field which allowed a political slant but also some personal distance.[30]

There was still another reason, more idiosyncratic, for Williams's political inactivity. He and Jeannie had remained registered Republicans from their Iowa days, absentee voters still plugged into their home state's issues. From that unique perspective, they could appreciate Henry Wallace, whose family's magazine, *Wallace's Farmer*, had played a major role in Iowa life for generations and who personally visited Simpson College often. But such Midwestern sentimentalism played poorly alongside the issues surrounding the Wallace campaign of 1948. Conducting a fierce red-baiting campaign, Truman and his allies successfully drowned out what Wallace had to say about American life, making him into a mere stalking horse for Russian tyranny. Madison's own cold war liberals jumped on the Truman bandwagon, while a few professors joined Hesseltine in registering their affection for the Norman Thomas campaign, an acknowledged lost cause. The debacle of the elections rendered the progressive political tradition a memory which neither Republicans nor Democrats would now acknowledge. Thousands of other former GIs, many of them with young children, were like the Williamses, spending little time in campus political activities so that they could get through their courses and on to careers as quickly as possible. That said, they were still probably the most democratic and aggressive undergraduate body in history to that point and long after. Coming from virtually all social classes and groups, they had acquired a collective self-confidence during the war, and also a certain skeptical disrespect for authority. They—or at least most of them—doubted that they could stop the express train of history. Williams concluded later that they had ambivalently accepted the privatization of life that middle-class consumerism offered them. But they sincerely wanted to know what had brought the world from victory over fascism to the precipice of another and potentially more catastrophic war.[31]

If the hopeful elements in the intellectual radicalism sustained since the 1930s were faltering badly in the face of the cold war and postwar military-backed prosperity, if old versions of socialism seemed discredited as capitalism offered consumer pleasures galore, the prospects for a radical critique remained very much alive. Nowhere was this more true than in diplomatic history. At the historical moment when communist sympathies had become taboo and liberals celebrated the cultural pluralism of American society, Williams chose to focus on the power of corporations to control the perceptions and realities of international policies.[32]

2

Williams's master's essay and dissertation, his first two sustained pieces of writing, bore out the richness of his observations. He attempted to understand how the corporate-owned press limited the flow of available information on foreign affairs and reshaped data according to its own editors' interpretations; he also sought to interpret how perceptive and brave individuals could break through the web of disinformation, offering challenges to reigning diplomatic policies.

"McCormick Reports on Russia: A Study of News and Opinion on Russia in the *Chicago Tribune* from 1917-1921" (1948), grew out of his experience at newspaper work and his interest in responses to American views of revolutionary events abroad. Not surprisingly, he found the *Tribune* so editorially biased that it "ignored facts which would have modified this extreme hostility," contributing "both to the ignorance and error of American opinion and . . . exerci[sing] a negative influence on the possibility of the peaceful co-existence of the United States and Russia."

Tracing the controlling influences on the *Tribune*, Williams pointed to the internal "revolution of 1914" which placed Colonel McCormick at the helm. The *Tribune* had not been staunchly pro-war before 1914, but once committed, beat the drum for "virile" patriotism and declared, as early as 1915, the central conflict in American life as one "between individualism and communism." By 1917 the paper sharpened its knives against Bolshevism, and thereafter engaged in wild exaggeration and the dissemination of outright falsehoods about Russia and the Russian revolutionaries. Soon, the Industrial Workers of the World, incongruously became, by the words of *Tribune* writers, agents of Lenin within the U.S.; all manner of political repression was justified as patriotic duty. Havoc in Russia was attributed entirely to Marxist ideas, as revolutionary turmoil would be so often in the twentieth century. Finally, in 1919, the *Tribune* editors trained their hopes upon armed intervention in Russia, under whatever excuse could be mustered. As Williams might have added, the paper had established a prime motive for all future U.S. interventions.[33]

Much of the rest of the master's thesis documented the campaigns of distortion and falsification—Williams called the final chapter "The Poverty of Philosophy," after a manuscript by the young Marx—which took an increasingly racial character. Thus Bolsheviks became "hordes of barbarians, semi-Asiatic, pressing toward central Europe" aiming to "destroy . . . western civilization of Christianity, nationalism and property, the fountain of life as we live it." The *Tribune* editors thereby deprived their readers of any unbiased opportunity to learn about communism, or Marxism. They insisted that human behavior could not be based upon any motive but private gain. In the end, the paper identified as "red" any protest against its own particular interpretation of "nationalism, religion, political faith, and economics."[34]

In seeking a foil for the *Tribune's* disinformation campaign, Williams identified a protagonist for his dissertation and a twentieth-century radical after his own heart. "Raymond Robins and Russian-American Relations 1917-1938" (1950) told the story of a Midwestern progressive politician who devoted his life to Russian-American rapprochement. A descendent of early settlers, Robins grew up poor, became a coal miner and struggled to organize a union, and later caught gold-rush fever in Alaska and became a successful executive. Discovering rampant corruption in American business and political life, he shifted his goals from personal success to municipal reform. Relocating to Chicago, he emerged as a prominent reformer, close to Jane Addams and several leading philanthropists. He also quietly bankrolled socialist journalism. But his strongest sentiments ran to the social gospel, and he became one of Theodore Roosevelt's staunch supporters in the Progressive Party campaign of 1912.

But the war marked a turning point for Robins. From inside the philanthropic quarter of the elite, he worked to ease suffering as best he could. Part of the Red Cross Commission to revolutionary Russia, he felt at first an intuitive revulsion to the Bolsheviks and resolved to assist Alexander Kerensky. But he was impressed with Trotsky and eventually came to see the Bolsheviks as the only possible force for a stable government that could feed the people. The fact that Alexander Gumberg, Robins's translator and assistant, was the brother of a devoted Bolshevik hardly damaged the case.

Robins thus worked squarely against the Wilson administration and its furious efforts to mount a counterrevolutionary international crusade. But Robins also placed himself in close cooperation with major Wall Street figures who wanted to do business with the new government. By the 1920s, advising isolationist senator William Borah and sustaining close relations with Warren Harding and Calvin Coolidge, Robins sought to effect Russian–U.S. cooperation against Japanese expansionism in the Far East and against the rise of a resurgent German nationalism. Repeatedly stymied, he nonetheless influenced the Roosevelt administration's recognition of Russia in 1933. However he could not bring about a sufficient American desire for reconciliation in time to stave off Stalin's retreat into isolation and a desperate nonaggression pact with Hitler in 1939. Perhaps no force on earth, except a Franklin Roosevelt willing to confront prejudices and risk supportive alliances at home and abroad, could have accomplished this goal. But Robins was uniquely placed among world observers, American political figures, and businessmen to see how the world had again and again lost opportunities for peace.[35]

To get the full story, Williams made contact with Robins and interviewed him at length in 1949. Robins was, not surprisingly, eager to talk to a rare sympathetic graduate student in a society where any openness toward Russian experience had become inherently suspicious. He was also ready to turn over large quantities of his own documents. Williams buttressed his arguments with a thick folder of evidence—materials from the State Department papers of Wilson's Secretary of State, Robert Lansing; and the papers of William Borah, Woodrow Wilson, and others. Following Robins's logic, Williams insisted that even at the onset of the cold war, "the fact of German aggression and Russia's fear of Japanese encroachment provided a significant opportunity for Allied representatives to conclude an agreement with the Soviets." Tragically, "pride, fear, personal and official antagonism" had intervened.[36] Reexamining the intrigues of diplomatic history, Williams convinced himself that detente had nearly been achieved at a crucial moment in world history. The Munich agreement of Hitler and Chamberlain, and the appeasement of fascism by the antirevolutionary Western governments which opened the road to a second world war, had not been an inevitable consequence of the 1910s-30s. In a larger sense, the American twentieth century did not *have* to be one long antirevolutionary crusade.

Anticommunism had its way of course, and catastrophic events ensued. Williams's scholarship challenged the confrontational mood of the late 1940s. Eastern Europe had slipped into the Soviet orbit, and the last piece in the postwar puzzle was about to fall into place. Harry Truman had more than honored Republican Senator Vandenberg's advice to "scare hell out of" the American public to prepare them for unprecedented military expenditures and perhaps World War III. Between the superpowers, virtually all other possibilities had been excluded.

It was a moment for anyone, let alone someone of Williams's inclinations, to feel like a reluctant civilian combatant in an unwanted clash of titans. One part of the world still seemed, however, to be moving toward a higher form of society. The British Labour Party, taking over from war hero but dislikeable peace leader Winston Churchill, promised massive social reconstruction. The Labourites finally accomplished little more than an advanced welfare state. But they genuinely frightened the English wealthy class (and U.S. leaders) by threatening to go further. They also encouraged British workers and left-leaning intellectuals throughout the English-speaking world with the hope that they might expand their agenda. Britain was, then, easily the most exciting place for a socialist in the English-speaking world. Williams urgently wanted to go and learn, if only for a few months.

He applied for and accepted a scholarship to join a ten-week seminar at the University of Leeds on the Labour government's economics. The scholarship did not include all travel or living expenses, however, and an ever-dutiful Jeannie remained behind to supply the necessary funds. Williams, unburdened by any sense of guilt, had a wonderful time. Most of the Labour cabinet came up at some point during his stay, to lecture to and discuss programs with the seminar. A. J. Brown, an economist who ran the class, pointed toward decentralization as an alternative model to the nationalization of "sick" industries, like coal, then underway in Britain (and saddling Labour with impossible responsibilities).

Here in Leeds, Williams also received in person another dose of the non-Marxist but Marxist-influenced, non-Communist but also anti–cold war logic that had earlier reached him in G. D. H. Cole's work. Facing the cold war world, Cole repeatedly stressed, in ethical terms, how the Socialist movement *should* conduct itself and how the world *should* be. Freedom, individuality, equality, democracy, and fellowship created a continuity and web of values between them, antithetical to the perniciously individualistic values of capitalism. Cole's avowed Utopianism (calming, he insisted, the "Bolshevik soul" with the "Fabian muzzle") would realize itself in the "making of good societies."[37] Cole also stressed the importance of decentralization, or "devolution," as a step toward a more functional division of government's responsibilities so as to reduce the control over the citizen's life. He echoed Karl Polyani's plea to strip the class mysticism from Marxian pronouncements and to find an ethical antidote for capitalism's destruction of the common spirit.

Cole, a lesser minister in the British Labour government, had precious little opportunity to explore these possibilities in action. The other and more dominant impulse of Fabianism, toward a paternalistic State overseeing the welfare of the middle classes and the poor, fed into the worst of Labour's experiment with power. A watchful U.S. State Department, feeding Europe with the Marshall Plan and simultaneously warning against any move toward a much discussed "third force" of democratic anticapitalism, would not have permitted the Europeans anything more radical in any case. And yet Cole remained, for a certain type of Anglo-American socialist, a reminder of what might have been. Socialism *could* be based upon voluntary mixtures of collectivism and individualism, decentralized and cautious of state impositions. Thirty years later, the kindest compliment that Williams could hand out to a libertarian, anti-state think tank in Washington was that it represented the historical legacy of guild socialism.[38]

Williams had reportedly told Fred Harrington that he was going to England to "study Schumpeter," and that raises yet another intriguing possibility for the trip. Schumpeter, apart from his other theoretical inclinations, proposed that imperialism had relatively little to do with economics. Rather, he believed that it reflected the determination of conservative elites to find outlets abroad for domestic tensions. Schumpeter's thesis, pursued by several generations of German scholars, actually had an influence on Beard, and in turn, Beard's influence went through Williams to the younger Germans.[39] By refuting Lenin but offering a different and no less charitable description of the imperialist impulse, Schumpeter had helped make possible Williams's later perspective on the "open door" as capitalism's pseudo-solution to the threat of its demise.

As in other matters, the Labour Party was not about to adopt this or any critique of imperialism. The formal British Empire, like its French counterpart, was dissolving as nationalist movements grew. But the West's control over much of Africa and Asia would simply pass from London to Wall Street and the White House, maintained by financial aid or CIA operations. Russian sponsorship of anti-imperialist national movements projected the cold war around the globe in an endless waste of resources and ideals.[40]

Foreshadowing the heroic efforts of his later friend and fellow historian E. P. Thompson to break through the divisions still separating Eastern and Western Europe during the 1970s-80s, Williams took part in the last international peace conference of students from all of Europe. Meeting together in Paris at the end of summer 1949, they expressed a hope for amity that had been denied in both camps of cold war mobilization. As he must have guessed, his participation as a delegate (arranged from Leeds) invited just the kind of suspicion that fell upon so many other professors and graduate students at the time. Undaunted, Williams returned to Wisconsin in the face of the cold war, determined to apply the lessons he had learned.

3

Harrington arranged Williams's first major appearance at an academic gathering: the American Historical Association meeting of 1950, for a symposium on foreign policy. Williams's denunciation of American aggressiveness seemed to stun the audience. At such a moment, with the cold war turning hot in Korea, Williams seemed to many listeners either a spokesman for a hated national enemy or, more likely, a young man foolish enough to throw away his career on the most unpopular ideas imaginable.

Just a year earlier, AHA president Conyers Read had warned in his presidential address against historians thinking of themselves as "free agents." They should, rather, "accept and endorse such controls as are essential for the preservation of our way of life." Merle Curti, against whom this blast had been mainly directed, and Howard Beale, against whom it might as well have been aimed, answered with a stinging defense of historians' right and duty to write what they saw as the truth.[41] Madison professors and the British experience together gave Williams something more, or reinforced a determination deep within himself.

He had reasons for his self-confidence that his views might be taken seriously. His essay, "A Second Look at Mr. X," rebutted the theory of containment anonymously set out by George F. Kennan in a famed *Foreign Affairs* essay of 1947. Submitted to *Foreign Affairs* through a third party, Williams's rebuttal was much discussed by the editors at that journal until finally rejected as too sharp a criticism of the distinguished diplomat's views. Ironically, Kennan himself had meanwhile backed off from his "Mr. X" conclusions, convinced that a permanent threat of military confrontation with the Soviet Union was a terrible error.

The essay had been submitted, without his knowledge, by the editors at Rinehart, publishers of his first book, *American–Russian Relations, 1781-1947* (1952), for which it was originally written as a coda. An incisive and, for the time, extremely bold work, it practically invented the field of "cold war revisionism." During the early 1950s only a few other serious writers contested prevailing cold-war scholarship. Carl Marzani's *We Can Be Friends* (1952) was written behind bars by a victim of McCarthyism jailed on Contempt of Congress charges for refusal to testify. I. F. Stone's *Hidden History of the Korean War* (1953) actually inspired the establishment of Monthly Review Press because no other publisher would touch Stone's questioning of the war's causes and its course.[42] It is safe to say that Walter Lippmann's *The Cold War* (1947) was the only widely available critique challenging the

Truman administration claim that diplomacy with the Soviet Union had become impossible. "Cold War" studies tended otherwise to be left to the field of international relations, a field dominated by refugees and "Sovietologists" professionally hostile toward the Soviet Union, as well as by those close to the foreign services and to the current views of containment. Save for Williams, U.S. historians hardly played a role yet.

American-Russian Relations, a cautiously phrased but distinct challenge to accepted orthodoxy, was written with the undertone of a scholar who wished to focus the reader's attention on the historical backdrop of controversial current political questions. Compared to the style of Williams's later works or even his MA and PhD theses, its measured prose bespoke the dangers of the times. He could put across a message very similar to that of his dissertation, he seemed to suggest, only by stressing the lesser-known details of the subject.

It was above all else a remarkable performance in research strategies. *American-Russian Relations* drew upon a wealth of new material from official government documents and extensive private collections of the papers (some key sources gathered himself, from Robins and Gumberg) and personal interviews with such formerly high-ranking State Department figures and diplomats as Cordell Hull, William C. Bullitt, and Henry L. Stimson. Fred Harvey Harrington had helped make the necessary appointments with former State Department notables. But putting himself forward as a decorated Naval veteran and curious young scholar, Williams successfully drew out these men in the fashion of a skilled oral historian.

Williams thus detailed the opinions and activities of U.S. politicians, businessmen, and private individuals as well as diplomats involved in Russian affairs between 1900 and 1939. Less than fifty pages concerned events before 1904, and only seventy dealt with events following the Russian Revolution. Fully half of *American–Russian Relations* focused on World War I and the Bolshevik Revolution, i.e., the decisive moment when change might have taken place but did not. He stopped in 1939 because of the national security regulations placed on documents from World War II and the cold war. But within his scope, he wrote as if he had met the men as equals.

From the days of Secretary of State John Hay to the present, American policies toward Russia had remained remarkably consistent, notwithstanding the state form or the particular personalities of the two regimes. The influence of U.S. financial and industrial interests had been at all key points central. Expounding for the first time on Frederick Jackson Turner's "Frontier Thesis" and the expansionist ideas of Brooks Adams, Williams articulated his notion of an "Open Door" imperialism: the strong belief among policymakers and many other Americans that without ever-expanding markets and places for investment, the economy and society at large would surely collapse.

Thus, Williams found that after a long period of "loose and informal entente" with the Czarist empire, American economic interests seemingly collided with Russian interests. Such magnates as E. H. Harrington and strategists as Willard Straight aimed to build railroads in Manchuria, a challenge to the aims of Russia in northeast Asia after 1895. Presidents Theodore Roosevelt and William Howard Taft refused Russian offers of cooperation against Japanese expansion in Asia in order to play the two off against each other. A short-sighted strategy at the time, it foreshadowed later U.S. unwillingness to combine with the Russians against the Japanese forays of the 1930s and thus to forestall the terrible price paid in the Pacific (not to speak of the Korean peninsula and Chinese and Japanese mainland) during World War II. Williams did not say so, but he obviously spoke with the memory of his own battle days fresh in mind. Other veterans who became historians had by and large accepted the inevitability of the war; Williams had not.

The Russian Revolution understandably exacerbated anxieties on all sides, but American leaders had never seriously considered cooperation with the new regime as a way to relieve their worries. Indeed, Williams dated the cold war precisely to Woodrow Wilson's decision for military intervention in support of the dreaded White armies, intimate allies of royalists and anti-Semites. Most officials, especially at the State Department, had been staunchly, even unreasonably anti-Bolshevik from the beginning. But a number of well-informed observers, most notably Robins, had clearly pointed out that the Bolsheviks could not be driven from power, enjoyed great popular support, and were flexible enough to accept amicable relations with the West.

Williams retold the sad story of Robins's failures to persuade Wilson's successors, who, like Wilson, expected or vainly hoped that Bolshevism would somehow collapse. He recast from his dissertation the images of business groups and individuals eager to participate in Russian economic reconstruction and urging early recognition. Here, too, Williams recalled Robins's Republican allies, Senators William Borah and Hiram Johnson, who argued for a similar course on security as well as economic grounds.

The coda, "A Second Look at Mr. X.," spelled out the major conclusions and took risks avoided in the rest of the book. Kennan's unwillingness to credit the Russians' desire and need for security from 1917 onward (or even their attempt, through much of this period, to woo Washington) fatally undercut his logic. He could not perceive that Japanese and German activities could pose threats to Soviet security but insisted that Moscow threatened an America armed with the only atomic weapons in the world.

Kennan, at his most level-headed, advised a waiting game. But "freedom is not nurtured by nations preparing for war." Such a waiting game, Williams insisted, was the real treason to the ordinary people of the planet.

In pursuing Kennan's formulation of containment, Williams insisted, American leaders had conceded that Marx had been right: capitalism could not live with a specter of competition, even peaceful competition. By offers of cooperation and of encouragement to modify the Communist system into a political democracy, we might still prove the German master to be wrong.[43]

The reception of *American-Russian Relations* from the scholarly journals to the *New York Times* confirmed the value of Williams's first book. Almost all the critics praised his extensive research, although some felt that he had concentrated too much on economic interests. His political judgments also proved disturbing. Reviewers questioned, for example, whether an alliance with the Russians would have worked out better than closer cooperation with the Japanese in East Asia. Many other scholars, then and later, simply denied that Wilson intervened in Russia to crush the Bolsheviks, insisting that the actual reasons were more complex (but offering no convincing counter-theory). Few could accept Williams's plea for closer relations with the Soviet Union either before or after World War II. In their eyes, he had too easily overlooked the nefarious character of the Soviet regime and its aggressive designs. Hugh Seton-Watson, the first of many British scholars to take Williams very seriously, complained that he seemed for all his research to be "extraordinarily innocent of the way that foreign policy is made." Williams was not so much victim of the "illusions of Marxism," Seton-Watson suggested, as reflecting the American "anti-tycoon" tradition of blaming irresponsible millionaires for their national dilemmas.[44]

Writing in the *New York Times*, Dexter Perkins valued the book's detailed treatment of economic interests and admitted it "useful to know" that certain State Department interests had been ideologically fixed against Bolshevism from the beginning. He considered most of Williams's other conclusions debatable, especially the "dependency" of Russians as allies and associates. Those American leaders who actually wanted to get along, he argued, had been thwarted by "Russian obstructionism."[45] In the same vein, the *American Historical Review* found the book "decidedly uneven," with "infinite detail on numerous relatively unimportant items" but "not the answer to the need for a survey of relations between the two countries." The *Pacific Historical Review*, admitting that Williams's "many sweeping and undocumented statements" might possibly be true, nevertheless required "more adequate proof." The *Mississippi Valley Historical Review* praised the author's skillful tracing of economic rivalries in Asia, while not losing sight of many other factors, such as anti-Semitism in Czarist Russia. If

Williams's tone was at times "petulant and abusive," his interpretations nevertheless remained "within the bounds of scholarly comment." The *Indiana Magazine of History*, more typically cold war in its response, found the book "turbid and tendentious," an attempt "to present *Othello* without Iago," i.e., the protagonist United States without the villain, Russia.[46]

Catholic historians, at the time heavily under the sway of McCarthyism, were probably the most distressed. A Georgetown scholar pronounced the book a "failure" in every important respect. Williams had ignored or slighted "the innumerable Soviet violations of . . . legal and moral principles." For a Boston College professor, likewise, the "philosophy of communism, the imperatives of the third international," and the eagerness for "conversion by revolution" rendered amicable relations utterly impossible. St. Louis University's William A. Nolan conceded that the *Daily Worker*'s praise for the book did not necessarily make Williams a "party member [or] international sympathizer," but did "cast suspicion upon [his] objectivity." School libraries would "do well not to clutter up their shelves with books of this sort."[47]

Conversely, left-wing scholars, along with the effusive communist press, eagerly endorsed the volume. Richard Van Alstyne, another rare precursor of revisionist diplomatic history, called Williams a "forthright and penetrating" scholar, both "honest and courageous." He had, however, ignored the degree of "sentimentalism, missionary zeal and sheer naivete" involved in making policy, overemphasizing the economic content. British socialist E. H. Carr had likewise "nothing but praise" for the "real and original contribution" that Williams made.[48] The *Daily Worker*, the major public expression of a heavily persecuted Communist Party, USA, headlined its literary page "Crisis Laid to Anti-Soviet Policy by Oregon University Professor's Book." A stirring review described Williams as "one who faces facts with both courage and honesty," and proposed that "many more Americans" would "be able to struggle against a new war by making known the facts in Professor Williams's book—the facts which will destroy the Big Lie of 'Soviet Aggression.'"[49]

While few scholars could accept Williams's major suggestion that the U.S. should have established a closer relationship with the Soviet Union, few treated *American-Russian Relations* as Communist propaganda. Very likely many more professors, like Berkeley political scientist Ernest Haas, found it "refreshing and reassuring" to discover an author "willing to state the true implications of his source material" at a time of "rapidly vanishing tolerance" for research that did "not happen to fit the ideological needs" of the society.[50] Many others probably lacked the opportunity or the self-confidence to put forward such views themselves, but admired Williams's doing so.

Compared to his later and far more controversial works, *American-*

MADISON AND HISTORY

Russian Relations foregrounded the author's research. Williams complained in a letter several years afterward that he took little pleasure in writing monographs, already felt he had done his share, and wanted to turn to the extended essay as his favored form. Only once more, in the *Roots of the Modern American Empire* (1969), did he engage in similarly extensive archival work, and this book too was widely praised for its scholarship.

Other critics of the cold war pleaded for peace. But only Williams offered this peculiar "What If?" twist (also the most characteristically Williamsesque stroke of the book). While cold-war liberal writers drew a line, as he would say later, from Marx to Lenin to Stalin, Williams tried to encourage his readers to think the matter through in reverse, back to the origins of the conflict. Americans, regardless of economic station, who had real confidence in their system, he suggested, could only welcome an intellectual challenge offered in lieu of the arms race, proxy wars, and a potential thermonuclear disaster. Williams could not have expected to have his views adopted on Wall Street or in the White House. But he had struck upon the sort of appeal that American radicals had nearly forgotten, a way of speaking to conservative and patriotic instincts outside the adversarial framework of a common foreign enemy.

In the long run of two or three decades, *American-Russian Relations* practically invented the field of "cold-war revisionism." An area of scholarship that would eventually blossom into the central academic challenge of American politics during the 1960s-70s, it "revised" the orthodoxy of the cold-war specialists and with them the assumptions maintained from Truman (or perhaps from Woodrow Wilson) onward. Revisionism would also, from another viewpoint, become a major academic industry, with hundreds of monograph writers in various disciplines and thousands of teachers offering it to students of the 1970s-90s as the truth behind the national fictions.

The Williams of *American-Russian Relations* had established himself as the author of a well-researched and controversial scholarly volume, but nothing resembling the major figure he would become. He had hidden, or simply saw no reason to expose, the philosophical underpinnings of his study, or to reveal more of himself to the reader. In 1953, it is fair to say, he was just another promising young professor.

4

Looking back on the late 1940s, a crucial decade for a new generation of intellectuals, David Noble opines that the triumph of corporate capitalism as a national American ideology was not then nearly so secure as it would be a decade hence. "Marxism" in the communist sense had never really escaped marginalization in academic life. Just as a significant number of Marxist-influenced graduate students moved toward careers, cold-war pressures prompted them to camouflage their work; many of them abandoned it altogether. But the major liberal alternative to the Marxist view, the pluralist-universal model of consumer society, remained still inchoate. Grasping for a method to explain society and pursue their own research, most students found the remnants of the republican or Beardian tradition too contradictory and limiting to permit any reformulation of them as radical articles of faith. But most students were not William Appleman Williams.[51]

If Williams was strangely placed to improvise on socialist ideas, he was uniquely placed to revise radical notions of American democracy. A young man with a strong sense of leadership and a fascination with those in power, he had developed, he admitted later, remarkably little interest in such popular subjects for radical young scholars as "the negro in American society," or untarnished heroes like William Lloyd Garrison and Eugene V. Debs. Instead, Williams cultivated a strong and enduring interest in a certain type of dissonant, aristocratic mind which could consider the various options open to society on their merits. This was the discussion that Williams desperately wished to join, if it ever convened again.[52]

Writing a paper in William Hesseltine's seminar—the first piece of scholarship in which he took enduring pride—the young intellectual discovered for himself the immensely alluring observations of Brooks Adams. Scion of an American dynasty who in the nineteenth-century *fin de siècle* brilliantly grasped the *mentalité* of the time, Adams had squarely faced the available choices of the age. Bitterly disappointed by the unabashed materialism of the labor movement, Adams turned away from socialism, his first inclination, toward the promise of imperialism as a solution to the nation's political instability and recurrent depressions. Only something better—more exalted and more strongly suited to American idealism than Samuel Gompers's demand for a share of the pie—would have won over thinkers as vigorous as Adams. The intellectual who engaged in long talks in Cambridge with Frederick Jackson Turner after Turner's shift from Madison to Harvard happened to choose wrongly, but he was nevertheless a romantic melancholiac after Williams's own heart. Adams fortified himself against bad times and low morals with an exquisitely developed sense of irony. That might be the best option that American society offered.

Adams, seen perhaps through the lens of an imaginary radical Schumpeter, provided a model for the William Appleman Williams who all his life had believed in the "exceptional" or superior figure. He envisioned not sudden uprisings from below, but instead divisions among the ruling classes which would allow personal interventions and make possible grand political strategies at crucial moments. He could prepare the way for himself and for others by taking the elite at its word, judging its members fairly on their accomplishments within the existing system, and pointing out errors of logic and temperament. Their more intelligent members would listen to such a voice warning them against common disaster, if only in the collective self-interest of their class.[53]

Behind this quasi-aristocratic pose something else lay hidden, something more deeply personal and more enigmatic. Merle Curti, who had known the greatest U.S. historians of the age and not a few of the leading intellectuals, described Williams as heir to the "minor romantics," those who had carried on the dreams of the early nineteenth century in the face of diminished reality.[54] An important student of his, Thomas McCormick, describes Williams himself as an "incurable romantic."[55] Curti and others remember him evincing a wistful look, as if reality might not be at all that it seemed. Other friends said that specific issues appeared to assume a symbolic significance to Williams, just beyond explication. He was holding back something so securely that not even his wife Jeannie, an exceptionally intelligent and politically alert partner, could fathom it.[56]

Any number of reasons could restrain professor-to-be Williams from wearing his political heart on his sleeve. Perhaps this was a necessary guise for any radical during such a bleak moment of the century. No doubt it also reflected his personal experiences in Corpus Christi and in Madison: the dangers of open political activity and the rewards of finding a niche suitable to personal predilections. But Williams's small-town Protestant idealism and his background of childhood emotional insecurity, reshaped successively by the rigors of Annapolis, the horrors of war, and the driving need to make something special of his own life, could account for the energetic intellectualism and the personal elusiveness of the young man. Approaching his thirtieth birthday, he was still in the process of becoming the psychic offspring of that little boy from Iowa. He correctly anticipated glory, but he had a long, hard push ahead.

3

A RADICAL PROFESSOR IN THE COLD WAR

BETWEEN 1950 AND 1957, William Appleman Williams gradually approached the *cause célèbre* status he would acquire in the following decade. In relative obscurity, he moved from job to job until he found a secure station from which he could issue manifestos, shaped as essays and reviews, well before his return to Madison in 1957. He worked at his teaching as he did at his writing, and raised the hackles of cold-war zealots in both liberal and conservative camps. He began to develop his celebrated persona, expressing positive and negative sides alike in his romantic, competitive character. He cultivated the *sui generis* literary style that later fascinated and puzzled readers, underpinning a typically Williamsesque analysis with an equally Williamsesque phraseology at once quaint, poignant, and as deeply American as the writer himself. Finally, and least obviously, he continued to work out his long view of societal development, the historical periodization and genetic examination of objective and subjective factors which would characterize *The Contours of American History*.

Williams's intellectual accomplishments were both remarkable and in some ways deceptive. He personally broadened diplomatic history in two ways: methodology and message. His extensive use of primary documents encouraged scholars to offer them to the scrutiny of nonspecialists in an age when foreign-policy elites (with their pet scholars) considered such materials unsuited for anyone outside a reliable coterie. Second, he deployed evidence and his own ruminations to pose large and troubling questions about deep continuities of U.S. policies over several centuries. Reigning foreign-policy specialists, assuming that American leaders were virtuous even in their Realpolitik, seemed stunned as well as outraged by William A. Williams's critical stance. These contributions, as much as the particular interpretations Williams set forth, made enemies aplenty in the academic world and the federal government. His presentation and their reception of his ideas threatened to disguise deeper purposes that transcended, in ways even his close readers often missed, the particular political divisions and parochial quarrels at hand.

The historical setting went a long way toward explaining the sources of Williams's complex analysis and also the possibilities of diplomatic history as a prestigious scholarly subject. Foreign news, as never before in peacetime, filled the daily press. While Americans stepped into the vacuum left behind by British and French spheres of influence from the Middle East to Africa and Asia, the success of the Marshall Plan in Western Europe seemed to presage the golden American future ahead. Even the Berlin crisis, threatening a third world war, provided Truman the welcome opportunity for a symbolic confrontation with the Soviet Union and the rationale to assume unchallenged leadership of the European allies under the new NATO banner.

Truman's own presidency did not experience the full benefit of his various cold-war moves, in large part because the Chinese Revolution and the Korean War unleashed forces that America could not control. By 1951 he had become a phenomenally disliked president for the second time in a few years, and yet he had launched (or perhaps merely propelled) apparently irreversible changes. Like the British Conservative government returning to office in 1953 after an era of welfare-state Labourism, the resurgent Republicans under Dwight Eisenhower accepted the broad outlines of Trumanism. Corporations ruled the economy virtually unchallenged, and business values ruled society. By the 1950s, however, they ruled at unprecedented levels of public funding and government participation.

The history of foreign policy, long considered the record of a mere exchange of diplomatic notes, now inevitably acquired a wider significance. International affairs had always been connected with domestic concerns, but never before had the connections been so dramatically outlined by events. In arguing that the battle against communism encompassed a conflict between ways of life, Truman had repeatedly warned against the loss of markets—just as his State Department promised assistance to governments which chose the American way over the competition. Despite some subtle differences of approach, Eisenhower's State Department continued this strategy and the accompanying rhetoric. As the old European-based empires continued to dissolve and superpowers assumed the reins on both sides, the globe had also become dramatically smaller.

Williams's "life of the mind," both his understanding of events and his personal experience, made remarkable sense of the bipolar world and America's prevailing intellectual currents. From a political angle, he could be seen as an outcast or underdog courageously locating himself among a relatively small constituency of anti-cold warriors. But from a methodological and, even more, a personal angle, he followed contemporary trends closely, in philosophy or psychology even more than in history. Alienation, the fragmentation of community, and the complex connections of social mobility with economic growth had hardly affected the historians of Charles Beard's generation. These issues quickly became central to the intellectual concerns of the 1950s as the threat of Armageddon receded into the long perspective of an extended arms race and cold-war prosperity.

Williams also reacted, in regard to the internal development of the nation, as forcefully against the prevailing myths of left scholarship as against those of the dominant right and center. He asked questions very different from the ones asked by the radical historians of the 1910s-20s or 1930s-40s. They had normally assumed as deep sources of progress what he reformulated as problems: the rise of the labor movement and the state regulation of the economy. If the New Deal seemed to swallow up the radical tradition, Williams sought to untangle a new radical conception from Roosevelt's legacy. Left-liberals and socialists had embraced the leviathan state and persistently held out the faith that a resurgent coalition of liberals and labor would someday, somehow outbid the Establishment in promising (and delivering) material benefits for another New Deal, a final happy ending. He had never thought so, and he began in this era decades of ruminating on alternative scenarios.

Williams protected himself through alliance and friendship, establishing the cooperation destined to make his later work possible and to broadcast its importance among a widening circle of devotees. More than that, politically, could hardly be done in the high cold-war years. But in another way, the context of limited political forms of protest suited him perfectly. Jeopardized by the undercurrent of repression, freedom of speech on the campus seemed more precious than it did later. In an age of cold-war sexual politics, with a rampant homophobia among liberals as well as conservatives, Williams was also a secret sharer of personal sympathies and deep friendship. The collegiality of administration, professors, and students, along with the interest generated by his writings, complemented his sense of himself as a public intellectual with private time for study, rumination, and family life.

I

Williams was above all determined to be a good teacher, and after several false starts he gained the kind of opportunity which would allow him a maximum of freedom in the lecture hall and seminar rooms. These experiences stirred him, and in some ways set the foundation for his engagement as a unique scholarly writer. He pushed himself to develop original approaches to problems, and he responded to students' eclectic interests by continually broadening his own intellectual horizons.

These were remarkably conventional aspirations, because Williams differed little from his generational cohorts who also entered academic life. The rapid growth of universities and the college town, the emergence of the suburbs for young faculty members, the tennis courts and golf courses had as much appeal for him as for thousands of other similar young men and a smaller number of women professors. His self-confidence soared as he reached for the good life that had eluded his Iowa family—even as he had increasing doubts about the price to be paid for it all.

Fred Harvey Harrington, in the best academic fashion of the time, found Williams his first position in 1950 at Washington and Jefferson College. Living about forty miles outside Pittsburgh, Williams seemed to have settled beyond any immediate political controversies, happy to do so at a time when McCarthyism rapidly intensified in academic life. He later remembered this year as a very happy one; his first marriage was still in bloom and he found, as he recalled later, "the happiest integration of academia and community I have ever known."[1]

The all-male college attracted many keenly motivated sons of working-class families whose members were employed by the local Corning Glass factory. Washington and Jefferson's young professors, whose own educations had been made possible by the GI Bill, vitalized various departments, from literature to economics and psychology to sociology. Williams made friends easily in a town-and-gown lecture series. Each Wednesday night a faculty member would read a paper and then the group would adjourn to a colleague's house for liquor and conversation. Here Williams's knowledgeability and charm found an ideal setting. Cautious on some current political issues, he was voluble on the larger subjects of American history.

Meanwhile, nothing could dampen the enthusiasm of a young couple surrounded by beautiful countryside. On weekends they loaded up their Crosley station wagon—America's version of the VW bug—with picnic materials and drove toward Wheeling, West Virginia, to shop and walk around. Or they headed to Pittsburgh for Pirates home games in slugger Ralph Kiner's heyday. Free of military and graduate school rigors, on their own at last, they simply and deliriously enjoyed each other's company: a fulfillment of expectations from the time of their teenage courting a dozen years earlier. Following in his father's footsteps, Williams took up golf seriously, a game he considered (as he wrote later) the utmost test of combined skills and dexterity and in which he repeatedly sought to instruct hapless protégés. With a little luck, Williams might have spent some years at Washington and Jefferson. But the cold war had turned hot.

The outbreak of military conflict in Korea had already shocked the quiet community a few months before the Williamses' arrival. The expectation of a renewed universal draft, threatening to deprive the school of its students, prompted the administration to give faculty newcomers their notice. A group of students wanted to stage a protest against the firing of their favorite professor, but Williams politely resisted. By the end of a post-midnight session, he convinced their leaders not to risk any student's status at the college for the benefit of his welfare.

The couple nevertheless spent a happy summer living close to Bard College in Annandale-on-Hudson, New York, where Williams taught in a seminar preparing Japanese and German scholars to teach in U.S. colleges—once again, thanks to Fred Harvey Harrington. On weekends, they would often travel to New York City and occasionally to Washington, D.C. Together, they sorted the personal papers of trade representative and unofficial diplomat Alexander Gumberg in the sub-basement of the Russian American Institute. These archives would be shipped to the State Historical Society of Wisconsin, like the papers of Raymond Robins that Williams gathered in Florida two significant caches of documents from important figures who opposed the cold war. Williams received a small but badly needed fee of several hundred dollars for his and Jeannie's efforts on the Gumberg materials, and he rightly thought of himself as being part of a Madison network of research efforts.[2] He even thought about returning to Madison to work in a bookstore, asking friends to find an apartment for the two to occupy if his academic career fell through completely. Jeannie, unaware of any such plans, remained confident of her husband's future success. They also tried, unsuccessfully, to begin a family.

By August, Harrington had come through again. He landed Williams a job at Ohio State teaching Western Civilization and Latin American history. This mix was not terribly close to Williams's specialty and only a nontenured instructorship at that, but warmly appreciated anyway. The couple moved into a made-over coach house in a small town ten miles from campus, and Williams cheerfully used his childhood-acquired skills to make furniture for them.

Williams renewed and deepened his friendship at Ohio State with a casual friend from his graduate-student days, French historian Harvey Goldberg. Brilliant, chain-smoking, animated, and affectionately gay, Goldberg seemed immediately to Williams "a great intellect, radical and teacher." Grandson of a rabbi and a native of Orange, New Jersey, Goldberg had spent three years after graduate school at Oberlin College and moved on to Ohio State. An outspoken professorial radical, utterly dedicated to undergraduate teaching, he shared more of Williams's intellectual enthusiasms than anyone except perhaps Warren Susman.[3] In Columbus, the odd couple set in place a foundation for decades of academic-political collaboration and comradeship, outlasting virtually all of their other personal relationships. For Goldberg in particular, it became the most important emotional relationship of a lifetime.

Friends of both men suggest that Williams possessed an open-minded appreciation of the gay intellectual rare outside bohemia (and uncommon enough within it) during those days. Like many other men, Williams adored women and needed them but felt intellectually drawn mainly to men. Unlike most other men, he was relaxed enough to extend this sentiment to his emotions: he could intuitively appreciate the gender-bending minority so quietly influential in the arts because he felt so drawn to a few of them. Strikingly unlike many leading liberal intellectuals of the age, he had no need to engage in homophobic attacks upon the "effeminate" traditions of caring reform and historic peace movements. Then again, politics and personality apart, Goldberg was to Williams an extended version of what his former professor Paul Farmer had been: the mentor in European ideologies like Marxism and Freudianism that an inveterate Midwesterner urgently wanted to understand.[4]

Williams thus characteristically recalled, after Goldberg's death, one "beautiful autumn day" in his and Jeannie's converted Ohio barn. "Off in the distance," as he sardonically put it, "we heard the primitive sounds of 85,000 men and women breaking wind about a football game," clearly the dominating spectacle of the day. Meanwhile, the three sipped bourbon and talked about virtue and history. Williams introduced Goldberg to a near namesake of his own, William Carlos Williams, reading him passages aloud of *In The American Grain*, on Aaron Burr and history. Decades later, Williams would similarly break bread and share wide interests in Aaron Burr with another friend and historically-minded gay intellectual of note, Gore Vidal, a more Henry Adams–type personality.

The communion of spirits demonstrated to the two junior historians the necessity and the possibility of devotion to historical discipline, as scholar and teacher, even in the face of overwhelming odds. "One way or another," Williams commented across a life to follow, "we were always seeking to free that Left hand that is history."[5] Real history, as Goldberg wrote in a sort of self-memorium before his death in 1987, could "destroy passivity" as few other intellectual acts, making a different future possible.[6] That was the faith they shared. Together they would offer a remarkable congruence, Williams teaching large classes and seminars through documents and Socratic dialogue, Goldberg through breathless detail and exhortation to revolutionary possibility.

Williams was not destined to stay at Ohio State in any case, but he refused to back off from his own notions of academic integrity. Football coach Woody Hayes, the most popular and arguably the most important figure on campus, had made himself widely known as both a Civil War buff and an extreme political conservative. In neither case was he likely to appreciate Williams. But the young professor did the unforgivable, assigning a dull-witted star halfback unacceptably low grades in successive semesters of Western Civilization. According to Williams's later account, Hayes came to see him personally, warning "*instructor* Williams" that Hayes's football team paid the faculty's salary and that the instructor would change the grade if he wanted to keep the job.

Many professors would have given in to the all-powerful Hayes. At that moment across the country, hundreds or thousands of former radicals bowed low to hold onto positions, and a large handful of beaten or opportunistic ones testified against former friends and mentors. Williams had too much integrity. He often said that he had already faced during military days far more frightening circumstances than joblessness. Heading for the nearest bar, he stoked himself with liquid consolation. Once again, Fred Harvey Harrington soon came through, this time with Williams's first sustaining position, at the University of Oregon in picturesque Eugene.

This was a fortunate development. Sparsely populated and heavily Yankee, Oregon had a strong reputation for libertarian acceptance of oddball types, Wobblies in the wheatfields and lumber camps, and a regional political radicalism that had flowered into a third-party movement of the 1930s. The Willamette Valley, including Eugene and Portland, had even known its "red" unions in various trades. From a less historical standpoint (and as Williams liked to call it), Oregon remained the "last frontier" of the American small businessman fending off high costs and franchise-domination. Statewide, liberal Republicans were often more critical of foreign policy than were Democrats. Eugene, along with Madison one of the most lovely of the nation's medium-sized towns, hosted a university once known best for its fraternity and sorority atmosphere but becoming steadily more diverse. Here, "radical" professors might be attacked and known Communists threatened with loss of positions, but outspoken dissenters were also widely admired, especially by the former GIs of Williams's generation. Like the University of Wisconsin if in a smaller way, the University of Oregon's freedom of intellect had value as a marketable commodity understood by moderates and even many conservatives of the state.

Williams spent five years there as an assistant professor (with an interim year of funded research in Madison), ultimately gaining tenure. Jeannie remembered these first few Eugene years as once more happy for the two of them together, pocket-poor but savoring the new experiences big and small. Williams found the most congenial physical surroundings that he could imagine. He loved the state's natural beauty, including the varied mountains, woodlands, and particularly its spectacular coast. "The sound and drive of the surf" inspired an almost unquenchable appetite for experience. The seacoast, as yet little touched by modern vacation housing and retail development, enthralled the couple, and they drove and walked their way along the ocean during many weekends. A Midwestern meat-and-potatoes man forever seeking something unique to say about himself, Williams now responded to a familiar question about his favorite food with the phrase "grilled swordfish"—his wife had just added it to her repertoire.

He ran his own large classrooms in "a truly *fine* small liberal arts environment." Frantically busy with his own work, he acquired no real protégés during this period, but many casual devotees. He also relished meeting outstanding people in various other departments, from the hard sciences to math. Like him, they felt certain they were making new discoveries. At first, living close to campus in a prefabricated housing development with small apartments but a large common space, he and Jeannie quickly made good friends. Several young historians not so different from himself, and even lower-level administrators destined to rise to considerable influence at the university, also drew close. The couple and their friends played bridge or golf, drank, and talked, enjoying each others' company enormously. "We were young, hot and rolling . . . having the time of our lives," notwithstanding the political hurricane outside.[7]

The two experienced the same difficulties as millions of other middle Americans. It had already become obvious that the couple could not bear children. Perhaps because of Williams's background as an only child and desire for his own flesh and blood, adoption would not do. As he created a campus charisma for himself, the great mind and the great radical, he claimed privately to have turned down numerous invitations for sexual liaisons. It is not difficult to read between the lines of this boasting. After a few years, Williams had likely begun the not unusual half-life of the young male professor, turning on the charm to women who attracted him. For the first time in his life, he had the self-confidence to do so. The couple meanwhile moved out to the foothills, enjoying a richer material existence. But they were headed for a marital crackup; none of his old friends doubted whom to blame.[8]

He was also en route to a controversial writer's life. For several years, he could not get his essays published in the two major journals, the AHA's *American Historical Review* or its Americanist cousin, the *Mississippi Valley Historical Review*. About one submission in particular to the *MVHR*, he recalled a "thirty page essay on American policy in Latin America from 1917 to 1933, with every single footnote from a primary source, and all but five footnotes . . . from archival materials," held by the editors for six weeks and returned as "insufficiently researched."[9] In another case, a noted conservative figure in foreign relations serving as referee had rejected Williams's submission to the *American Historical Review* on the basis that the young scholar had cited documents not ordinarily used, i.e., had called upon something beyond the characteristically self-apologetic State Department records to explain American policies.[10] Rather than belabor his effort or change his style, he went elsewhere with his extended historical essays, to *William & Mary Quarterly* and *Pacific Historical Review*. But these open-minded journals were clearly the exception.

Williams had ample reasons to complain of political prejudice, at a time when some of the highest awards went to shallow monographs proving the inapplicability to U.S. society of purportedly "Marxist" categories such as class conflict. The study of history was subjected to an unprecedented ideological assault even as notable historians rose to denounce ideologies in general. It was a high season of pseudo-objectivity.[11]

2

An attack upon historical relativism lay behind the overt politics of coldwar historiography. From Frederick Jackson Turner onward (and however much various historians might disagree with his particular conclusions), the utility of history was widely assumed to be discovered by testing the past against the questions facing the present. The ideological and personal enrollment of historians in World War II once again prompted commitments which seemed to render relativism suspect, if not actually treasonous. Important historians, conservative and liberal alike, determined that no return to "frame of reference" relativism should follow this war.[12]

These scholars had rising prestige on their side, and a popular press which readily accepted them as the ablest chroniclers of the American past. They also appealed to many historians who had wearied of one or another element in the Progressive synthesis epitomized by Turner, Beard, and V. L. Parrington. As economics-based history had riveted the Depression generation, intellectual history and a new stress upon the psychology or "myths and symbols" of society naturally attracted readers in an age of material comfort and mass anxiety. These factors alone might not have been sufficient to ensure a long-term hegemony. The emerging giants also had the cold war and McCarthyism strongly on their side.

Speaking to his fellow graduate students in 1953, Williams's friend Warren Susman described the war on relativism as a war against all scholarship which faced hard questions without ideological blinders. Shibboleths had become the marching orders of the day. Cold-war historians posing the history and fate of "Western civilization" against communism somehow managed to encompass "the teaching of a Nazarene who lived out his life in the Near East" and yet completely exclude "the teaching of a German PhD who wrote his monumental work in the British Museum"—Jesus but not Marx. Such monumental oversights typified a larger approach. As Susman warned,

> These vague notions of civilization have not helped us to more clearly define our position in the world. They have not given us any sharp insights that will enable us to overcome the many problems we face in dealing with people and nations, East and West. What they have made possible is . . . the obscuring of America and her internal problems. They have given us a perspective so high above and so far away from our own shores that we can no longer see our important section and economic divisions and problems; we can no longer see our nation with people of different races and national origins, different religious views derived from different cultures. By assuming the sameness of men, by refusing to examine the basic differences between cultures, it has allowed us to fall under the spell of Toynbeen mysticism and therefore to believe we—as part of some vaguely defined civilization—are citing correctly [whenever] we "respond" to the "challenge" of communism.[13]

In short, historians enrolled as cold-war soldiers could no longer act like citizen-scholars.

Susman, Williams's devoted correspondent over the decades to follow and a near companion in Oregon (he had helped secure Susman a position at Reed College, and the two couples spent many weekends together, where Williams and Susman loaned books to each other), keenly perceived what later historiographical scholars would detail. The political campaign within the world of scholars was shaded with an odd blend of conservative theology and dime-store Freudianism. Not many decades before, Social Gospel progressives and the moral avant-garde had made their own uses of religion and psychology to emphasize an openness to non-Western societies and a faith in the perfectibility of man; on the political backspin, these themes had become twin philosophical bulwarks of order.

The war of ideas that Susman described certainly commanded obeisance on foreign-policy issues, but it also commanded a parallel acquiescence toward a reverential view of American business history. Samuel Eliot Morison, in his 1950 American Historical Association Presidential address, savaged Charles Beard's "scornful attitude" toward American accomplishments and called for history to be rewritten "from a sanely conservative point of view" honoring the appropriate leaders.[14] Not only were the financial and industrial giants of the past to be seen as more virtuous than historians had often allowed; they were also admirably *manly*. Thus Columbia University's Allan Nevins repudiated in *Fortune Magazine* the "feminine idealism" of Progressive historians and called for a major reevaluation of the American past in which, for example, the "Robber Barons" of the late nineteenth century would be revalued as the virile "builders of an indispensable might."[15]

Nevins saw McCarthy-era America as glowing with the radiance "of the Periclean era," and this extraordinary myopia was freely adopted by other prominent historians to cast doubt about any and all excessive idealism of the past. If capitalism had brought capitalist America (in the encompassing vision of Henry Steele Commager) to its rightful place dominating world society, then the same America had been (as Daniel Boorstin put it) a "disproving ground for utopias" with any drastically different America or even a different world in mind. Boorstin, who zealously identified former friends and teachers as subversives at hearings of the House Committee on UnAmerican Activities, dismissed colonial Quakers as holding "bizarre" beliefs, their resistance to Indian-killing based upon "false premises about human nature." In the eyes of similar writers, agitator Tom Paine had become a "fanatic," the Transcendentalists "men without responsibility," and so forth.[16]

These judgments had a particularly coercive force because historians, like other professors, were often suspected as corrupters of innocent youth, possible subversives, or defenders of suspect activities including communism and homosexuality. To be guilty of a dangerous view of the past raised questions about one's trustworthiness in the present.

If not quite as glum as in many occupations, the situation for historians and especially young historians out of step therefore looked bad in the early 1950s. Untenured teachers identified as having left-wing organizational pasts often did not gain permanent places in the university. Hundreds more, including every scholar and graduate-student teaching assistant in the state systems of California, had to sign humiliating and conscience-searing loyalty oaths. The FBI also sought to interrogate privately and publicly, and often to engage students to investigate and report upon their fellow students, friends and professors. According to a recent study, an unknown number including undergraduate William F. Buckley, Jr., and graduate student Henry Kissinger, did so voluntarily.[17]

Prominent and ostensibly liberal historians as well as conservatives and ferociously anticommunist academics such as Sidney Hook demanded the firing of all identifiably left-wing professors. Arthur Schlesinger, Jr., among others, proposed what was then widely considered a moderate approach: only those teachers whose Communistic ideas had actually *influenced their teaching* should be eliminated.[18] The integrity of the profession thus suffered unprecedented blows, despite many instances of courageous resistance and an occasional outright victory for civil liberties, like the election of Merle Curti to the presidency of the Mississippi Valley Historical Association in 1953.

Hundreds of professors who did not lose their positions spent their time dodging red-hunters or only slowly gained the standing that would have allowed them to publicize controversial views aggressively. Campus life at large remained under the gun. Young Marxists felt they dared not speak the name of their doctrine, even as methodology.[19] Among Williams's fellow Wisconsin graduates, for instance, Herbert Gutman was singled out for his long-past teenaged activities as a counselor in a progressive summer camp and was interrogated by the House Committee on UnAmerican Activities. Others like William Preston had fled repressive environments by enrolling at Madison. At traditional centers of presumed academic freedom, such as Harvard and Yale, university administrations worked voluntarily with the FBI, combing faculty and student records, employing spies from classrooms to dormitories, and warning of severe sanctions against public dissent.[20] Even in civil-libertarian Madison, FBI agents closely monitored campus radicals and offered administrators details about current suspects. The administrators in turn informed department heads, who apparently made their own courageous or cowardly decisions.[21]

But perhaps most revealing, from Williams's standpoint, was the parallel delegitimation of a traditional conservative or libertarian perspective along with radical scholarship. During the 1920s-30s, as Gerald Nye's Congressional hearings exposed war-profiteering to public light, a small army of popular scholars such as Harry Elmer Barnes had reached great audiences on all sides of the political spectrum with accusations of abuse of power in the World War. Libertarians of the "Old Right" became after World War II the main supporters of Beard's and Barnes's heritage, while communists lined up to defend Roosevelt's pre-war actions. A "New Right" headed by young William F. Buckley, Jr., and his *National Review* quickly abandoned the Midwestern or isolationist Republican tradition, registering zealous approval of a massively enlarged military-industrial state with internal security forces working overtime at public expense. Scholarly supporters of the cold war described libertarian muckraking of the recent war effort as psychopathic and warned that revisionism could not be allowed a place in the sun again. Mired in charges of anti-Semitism both deserved and undeserved, the Old Right drifted into isolation and the atavism of the John Birch Society.[22]

No political issue was more crucial for the merger of centrist ideological forces across old boundaries than the preemptive powers of the Executive. Henry Steele Commager, in other days a noted civil libertarian, passionately defended Harry Truman's actions during the Korean War and argued that Congressional attempts like that of "Mr. Republican" Senator Robert Taft to limit presidential seizure of authority "had no support in law or in history." Thomas A. Bailey, senior authority on U.S. foreign-policy history, insisted in 1948 that Roosevelt had proved "because the masses are shortsighted, and generally cannot see danger until it is at their throats, our statesmen are forced to deceive them," and would indeed perforce have to deceive them more and more "unless we are willing to give our leaders in Washington a freer hand."[23] Williams would find himself decades later tilting at forces across the ideological spectrum, from Arthur Schlesinger, Jr., to Oliver North, for deceiving Congress and subverting the Constitution on the premise that only through such deception could a necessary freedom of presidential prerogative be retained.

This drift or concerted campaign had further philosophical implications for the legacy of Progressive historians. Charles Beard, it might be remembered, had based his vastly influential intellectual contribution on the premise that monopolistic capitalism was a foreign species and that Progressive American democracy had fought repeated battles to fend off a parasitic Europeanization. The intellectual revolution (or counterrevolution) of 1945-50, aimed at overthrowing and discrediting Beard, was devoted to interpret the American tradition as both democratic and capitalist, indeed democratic *because* it was capitalist in a special, productive, and individualistic sense.

Beard's chief antagonist of the 1940s-50s was Reinhold Niebuhr. Popular theologian and former Christian Socialist notable, Niebuhr argued in massively influential essays that innocent America, with no inherent expansionist or imperialist interests of its own, had been forced to respond to totalitarian Germany and Imperial Japan. Now it was likewise compelled to respond to totalitarian Russia. The United States had little choice but to defend both its own freedom and world progress through the particular program of massive militarization and foreign-policy strategies that

Truman, the State Department, and the CIA had chosen. Depicting communism uniformly as a "demonic religion" (in the phrase of his biographer), Reinhold Niebuhr generally neglected to account for the troubling details of massive human rights abuses and other dubious means taken by the U.S. for its own ends. Sometimes criticizing one or another facet of various U.S. policies, he used even his criticisms to defend the whole package. No wonder conservatives could hardly believe their luck at the defection of a leading left-liberal to many of their long-held theological and political positions. They were just as surprised to see liberals praising the very same conservative qualities of Niebuhr's vision.[24]

Niebuhr, as critics charged, was more than a little disingenuous. He not only refused to see the historic role of the U.S. in Latin America, for example, as that of a bullying power long before communism came onto the scene; he baldly denied that any such thing as American imperialism existed or even *could* exist. Niebuhr suggested repeatedly during these years that the historic extermination of Indians, the dispossession of Mexicans, the use of the slave system in continental America, and the massive overkill in a rebellious Philippines at the turn of the century, among other uncounted symptoms, were "honest" failures of morality in a young, expansive society, possibly to be regretted but certainly not to be used to judge American society or American capitalism.[25]

Nor would Niebuhr criticize in any fundamental way the theological implications of an unprecedented military-industrial complex at the center of the U.S. economy. Backpedaling furiously from his Christian Socialist days, Niebuhr had resolved that original sin could not be overcome through historical acts, nor a perfect society reached. Even the idea of "*potentially innocent men*" was best seen as "an absurd notion" in a world where "nothing that is worth doing can be achieved in our lifetime." Spiritual conviction required identification of the dark side of human nature (oddly enough not including business morality), and severe controls upon it. Niebuhr's remarkably one-sided moral views, adopted enthusiastically by many thinkers but especially by Arthur Schlesinger, Jr., offered a key trope to cold war liberalism.[26]

So did the marked gender tilt of Niebuhr's narrative. As conservative scholar James Nuechterline later grandly summarized, "it would be impossible to find a less feminized imagination" than Niebuhr's, less polluted by the "soft" and effeminate progressivism of the past.[27] Niebuhr's rhetorical hyper-masculinity captured the self-image of the 1950s pen-pushing intellectuals who fretted about the reputed omnipresence of homosexuals in the national life of the mind and sought to demonstrate their own political virility through muscular prose.

From the viewpoint of historical scholarship, as Susman put it, by defining reality in terms of the single great conflict with communism, Niebuhr calls the intellectual back into the fold of pessimistic, deterministic Christianity, which offers hope in a future world and no solution in this one . . . Niebuhr raises an impressive bulwark of Christian pessimism against the spectre of communism and in place of traditional history. For history, as we know it, has utilized the optimism, the rationalism, and the pretentious social studies that [Niebuhr] has discovered to be useless in Man's attempt to answer the problems that face him . . .[28]

Unable to see that Christianity, too, had a history (and that the great histories of the ancient world had been written before its appearance), Niebuhr negated many centuries of historical sensibility. The effect of his teaching, Susman concluded, would not simply be to damage any sensible view of the world but to destroy "the study of history itself."[29] Susman might have added the same for American democracy, because without perspective, ideology ruled all.

Arthur Schlesinger, Jr., was curiously positioned in all this. Destined for decades of intense conflict with Williams, he often seemed to represent the great radical's *doppelgänger* (as to many of Schlesinger's sympathizers, Williams was Schlesinger, Jr.'s *doppelgänger*). Schlesinger, too, had early in life sought to remake his own identity—but in the extraordinarily unique way of changing his middle name to *become* a "Jr." to Arthur Schlesinger, Sr., who was perhaps the most prominent U.S. historian after Beard. A precocious scholar and bestselling author of the *Age of Jackson* (1945), Schlesinger, Jr., quickly (and without any particular credentials in studies of the twentieth-century U.S. Left) took on the journalistic status of an authority on American communism. During the next decade or so, he used the popular press and the upper chambers of Americans for Democratic Action to urge the expulsion of pro-communists (or non-anticommunists) from public life and to warn against the return to respectability of noted Blacklistees. *The Vital Center* (1950) confirmed that role in the eyes of many observers. Some liberal critics, no less anti-communist than he, wondered why Schlesinger, Jr., had so very little to offer in values or vision beyond anticommunism. Perhaps, like so many others of his generation, he never found a replacement for youthful semi-socialist beliefs.[30]

The Schlesinger, Jr., of *The Vital Center* had undergone a swift deradicalization directly parallel, one might say, to Williams's radicalization. Schlesinger, Jr., had as late as 1947 declared socialism "quite practicable" in the United States. A "series of New Deals" decisively expanding government ownership and control could create a postcapitalist state administered largely by intellectuals. Capitalists themselves offered little prospect of resistance, Schlesinger, Jr., insisted. In his mind's eye, Republican businessmen who lined up behind old-style conservatives like Robert Taft were so gripped by a death wish as to be foolishly eager to lower the U.S. military profile merely to balance the budget. They might indeed welcome a socialism which relieved them of their wearisome obligations. But liberals unwilling to confront the Soviet Union, men and women who seemed to Schlesinger amazingly influential in American life, could throw off this entire promising socialism-by-government scenario.[31]

If a young Williams looked to a sort of Social Gospel theology of redemption and perfectibility with an unacknowledged bow to homosexual friendship, Schlesinger, Jr., borrowed heavily from Niebuhr (borrowing heavily, in turn, from the current fascination with Freud and psychoanalysis) to demonstrate his main opposing points. The pro-communist liberals' moral softness had led them to credulously believe "man to be essentially good" and to offer incessant rationalizations of "why he does not always behave that way." Their consequent "addiction to myth," such as the Marxist or Populist myth of ordinary working people taking over society, was based in

> the intellectual's sense of guilt over living pleasantly by his wits instead of unpleasantly by his hands, the somewhat feminine fascination with the rude and muscular power of the proletariat, partly in the intellectual's desire to compensate for his own sense of alienation by immersing himself in the broad maternal expanse of the masses . . . [32]

The heavily gendered accusations of intellectuals' homosexual urges and childishness had arisen in wartime and powered a postwar drive to return women to the home or at least to the psychiatrist to recover their true roles. A large contemporary literature, led by Ferdinand Lundberg and Marnya Farnham's bestseller, *The Lost Sex*, blamed women for the sexual uncertainty of sons and directed a return to more proper behavior. Schlesinger, Jr., built upon the same basic analysis to create an edifice of larger political-historical points.

If man's *nature* was dark, depraved, and sinister, then a new equilibrium or control was the best that humanity could hope to see—even under a future democratic form of socialism. For the present, containment demanded measures that might at other times have been considered morally doubtful or undesirable, such as a willingness to "bribe the labor movement" by creating the military-industrial jobs of a "permanent war economy."[33] Ideological objections whether conservative or radical revealed an unpatriotic unwillingness to accept the basic framework achieved. Above all a strong national leadership was required, and ensuring popular support for foreign policy had become a first obligation of intellectuals.

Read back into history, this perspective became one of strong leaders and citizens loyal to the main thrust of the society, exemplified neatly by the expansionist policies of the nineteenth century. To question them raised doubts about loyalty, and possibly also sexual orientation. Tough cold warriors like Harry Truman added a "new virility" to government. Liberal supporters of Henry Wallace, by contrast, were likened to homosexuals in a boy's school enjoying the naughty secret of their shared support for Russia. Historians condemning the expropriation of Indians or Mexicans were guilty in a related way, childishly unwilling to accept at face value the material bounty that modern American society offered them.[34] Mature minds, realistic and firmly heterosexual, evidently saw their responsibilities better. They did not flinch at the use of force against those standing in the way of American progress.

Schlesinger, Jr., and his mentor Niebuhr also fretted, however, about an excessive or hysterical American response to the world situation. Niebuhr's *Irony of American History* (1952) thus remained somewhat troubled by the equation of the U.S. with Christianity (in the other half of the dyad, communism with deviltry), even while he argued that the threat of nuclear war and the economic tyranny of a permanent war economy were risks altogether consistent with Christian commitment. Late in his life Niebuhr, like Schlesinger, Jr., even turned against Vietnam War strategies that the two had earlier defended, admitting that American "innocence" in world politics might have led to Empire—but scarcely repudiating the various degrees of exploitation and human rights violations earlier rationalized or quietly endorsed as a necessary evil. The partial about-face also came decades too late to compensate for the treatment given to the Beardian legacy among a 1950s generation of influential intellectuals terribly eager to discount the virtues of past dissenters' ideals.[35]

Only when this darkest of scholarly eras had closed, and perhaps not even then, could the full measure be taken of the delayed or abandoned scholarship, broken lives, and the swift advancement of hardened cold-war ideologues into many positions of continuing professional authority and public prestige. Those seeking the threads of a future, more critical or reflexive historical study would find them scattered and very often at the margins of professional expression. In those margins, Williams found eager editors and his own public voice.

3

The glorious era of Progressive history had finished and could not be resurrected, Warren Susman concluded in 1952. Despite its many virtues, Beardian relativism could neither explain the key historical questions that its descendents wrestled with, nor even their own experiences in a growingly complex America. It consequently left behind "little but faith" in the possible uses of scholarship. The historian seeking to be of value today had to chart new courses boldly, improve his intellectual tools, and "do what he can . . . to aid man in passing from reality to even more meaningful reality."[36]

In this spirit, Williams took the first large risks of his intellectual career: he offered his controversial political essays to those few radical and left-liberal magazines willing to publish such challenges. When "A Second Look at Mr. X," the coda to *American-Russian Relations*, was refused by *Foreign Affairs*, he redirected it to the *Monthly Review*. Edited by former Harvard and New Deal economist Paul Sweezy and former labor educator and historical popularist Leo Huberman, the *Monthly Review* was the most notable independent Marxist journal published in the U.S. since the 1930s. It was also most notably the intellectual locus of a sustained economic, historical, and sociological critique of American imperialism.

Founded in the aftermath of the 1948 Henry Wallace presidential campaign, the *Monthly Review* located a "progressive" readership outside the ranks of the Communist Party and other left political groups. Cerebral but not academic, the monthly insisted on the continuing vitality of Marxism to explain capitalism's deep contradictions as well as the new problems posed by the cold war. To the discomfort of many Marxists, it refused to treat the labor movement as the potential savior of society, and increasingly focused its interest upon the African, Asian, and Latin American societies seeking to throw off the historic weight of colonialism and post-colonial controls. With the early optimism of growing nationalist forces, the Bandung Conference of 1956, and the creation of the "Non-Aligned Movement," a wing of American socialists had another star to steer by. For all their knowledgeability about Marxism, the *Monthly Review* following most resembled the Abolitionists and Christian antiimperialists of earlier days, passionate in their commitment to end white domination as the main principle of world order.

Monthly Review was eclectic, within limits. Welcoming into its pages Williams's favorite British intellectuals, the non-Marxist socialists G. D. H. Cole and E. H. Carr, it could also endorse Lenin's critique of imperialism and embrace the principle of state control of the economy while offering somewhat (many would say not nearly enough) critical descriptions of Russian or Chinese society. Never failing to assess the prospects for socialist transformation, it did not foresee any dramatic changes in that direction in America, at least not in the short run. This attitude matched Williams's own "cautious socialism." On the key question of the day, however, *Monthly Review* refused to support the West in its struggles with the Soviet Union and was therefore seen by liberals as worse than suspect. Communist leaders for their part regarded the journal as heretical. Still, anyone who contributed to its pages, emphatically including the young professor from Oregon, would certainly be tainted as an intellectual "fellow traveler."[37]

Williams saw in Paul Sweezy, by this time practically the only noted Marxist economist in the U.S., a kindred soul for correspondence and long conversations, which they held during Williams's rare trips to New York City and Sweezy's equally rare ventures to Madison. Genteel, handsome, and soft-spoken, Sweezy was every part the gentleman. Although Williams conspicuously failed to convince him of the virtues of American political aristocrats like John Quincy Adams, as Williams observed wryly later, and they had nearly opposite assessments of the New Deal, the two rebels nevertheless complemented each other's strengths.

Here at any rate Williams found a secure harbor and an outlet of last resort for some of his speculative essays. The magazine's own press, initially created to publish I. F. Stone's iconoclastic *The Truth about Korea*, put in print one topical volume of Williams's and an anthology with which he assisted his friend Harvey Goldberg. Among Monthly Review Press's small handful of other authors, Williams found himself placed with the likes of muckraker Stone, economist Paul Baran, and British historian E. P. Thompson—easily three of the most distinguished and intellectually heterodox critics of Empire anywhere.

The magazine's several thousand readers, academics and nonacademics from all walks of life, in turn constituted the first wave of devoted non-campus Williams followers. Veterans of older movements, but especially the scattered young radicals in the 1950s, found their way through *Monthly Review* to the future New Left's favorite historian.[38] Toward the end of the 1950s, as a small revival of intellectual radicalism began, Williams shipped off political essays and briefly served as an editorial board sponsor for a sister political journal, the *American Socialist*.[39]

The theoretically dense quarterly of the 1930s Left, *Science & Society* likewise welcomed Williams's contributions. Founded by a Harvard group close to the Communist Party, *Science & Society* drew in its early years upon such Marxist historians as W. E. B. DuBois, Broadus Mitchell, and Herbert Aptheker; also Turner students (and prominent U.S. historians) Curtis Nettels and Fulmer Mood, among others including Williams's future teacher Merrill Jensen. During the 1940s it had become politically isolated, many of its editors and writers blacklisted. But by the early 1950s major changes in its loyalties coincided with Williams's appearance. A break with the pseudo-scientific rationale for current purges of Soviet intellectuals led the journal toward the *Monthly Review*-style independent Left. Unlike most of the academic or professional journals, *Science & Society* editors also seemed eager to engage Williams privately in give-and-take—exactly the opposite of their supposedly "dogmatic Marxist" reputations. Williams appeared to them all the more welcome because he represented the rare Middle-American radical. He validated them, in short, as they validated him. For Marxists leaving the Communist Party milieu without abandoning their hostility to capitalism, he offered an open sesame to U.S. history.[40]

The *Nation*, organ of crusading Left liberals, afforded Williams's most public outlet. Having broken with the Communist camp in 1948 after many years of cautious support and occasional criticism of Russian policies, the *Nation* remained determinedly against U.S. military mobilization and the spirit as well as the practice of foreign intervention. For that, the magazine and its editor, Freda Kirchway, won the enmity of the other liberal weeklies such as the *New Leader* and the *Reporter* (both showing close allegiances to U.S. intelligence policies and at times a credulity bordering on complicity) and the undying support of anti-cold warriors. Kirchway happily published Williams's initial contribution in 1953 on the Russian "peace offensive," and Williams followed with four essays and six reviews for the *Nation* during the next five years.[41]

Carey McWilliams, taking over the historic magazine as editor in 1955, was himself a noted reporter on California's agricultural workers' lives and a talented popular historian. The academic historian had found a good friend as well as a serious and probing editor here, too. Writing widely on the cold war and on the major works currently appearing in U.S. diplomatic history and foreign policy, Williams rapidly emerged via the *Nation* as a major voice of foreign-policy dissent. In his middle thirties, he had thus identified himself with the Left as it began to piece itself together intellectually in the years of Communist disgrace, de-Stalinization, Third World independence movements, and unremitting U.S. interventions.

His favorite subject in nonacademic essays was the practical failure and the moral catastrophe of Containment. Following the death of Stalin in March 1953, many intellectuals in the western world argued that the subsequent mellowing of Soviet internal and foreign policies meant the vindication of U.S. assumptions. But for Williams, Stalin had been a reluctant revolutionist. He had proved himself most willing to cooperate with the West (for example, forsaking Greek revolutionaries by denying them material support in their civil war of 1946-47) in return for guarantees of stable frontiers in Eastern Europe, a six billion dollar reconstruction loan from the United States, and the major part of reparations from Germany. American leaders balked on each of these points, determined to isolate the Soviet Union politically and economically, evoking in turn an increasingly hard-line Russian response. Hence in Williams's view, Containment had actually tightened Stalinist control over Eastern Europe when a different policy would have brought an easing of pressures.[42]

Winston Churchill, whose evocation of the "Iron Curtain" in 1946 had been one of the principal manifestos of the cold war, inadvertently admitted in 1956 that Containment had boomeranged. The embittered Russians threw down the gauntlet of anticolonialism to a West ill-prepared to pick it up. The "narrow and militant anti-Soviet policy" had thus worked powerfully indeed, but mainly to "increase the power, influence and prestige of the Soviet Union throughout the world" as well as to reinforce the ideological and nationalistic forces within Russia. No doubt, Williams reflected, sounder results could be attained by reversing course.

Even better would have been never to have adopted Containment in the first place. By 1947, the United States clearly possessed superiority over the Soviet Union militarily, economically, and in every other way. Democrats and Republicans alike had nevertheless reviled both progressive Henry A. Wallace and conservative Robert Taft for pointing out this disparity. "Instead of long-term credits and candid negotiations" which together might well have moderated Soviet behavior, "the Russians got Kennan's Containment, Truman's doctrine and Dulles's liberation." The result was enormously costly and hardly "sublime," for Americans or Russians or the rest of the world. Perhaps Thucydides saw it best, Williams concluded, in analyzing an earlier war that also had catastrophic consequences: "'The greatest exercise of power lies in its restraint.'" Or at least it should.[43]

The hidden costs of the cold war to American society, Williams took pains to demonstrate, were far greater than they seemed. Despite liberal assertions that the nation had developed "beyond socialism," and Schlesinger, Jr.'s belief that everyone but "the nobodies on the Right and Left" had become part of the "vital center," the deep truth was that Americans enjoyed a modestly higher standard of living at the price of an eroded democracy. The cold war had served to "sustain, rationalize and tighten [the] corporate system," favoring certain large corporations (mainly those with military or military-related contracts) at the expense of many others. It threatened the delicate balance between labor and capital, and it glutted agricultural markets, forcing many farmers off the land. It also possessed its own crazed logic, to the point where key players in the American economy fiercely resisted detente with the Russians despite all the obvious benefits of reducing world tensions. It thereby contributed greatly to the widely lamented psychological malaise and apathy, especially among workers, minorities, the poor, and the young.[44]

These tendencies reinforced an especially dark side of the American past. Since the 1890s, a corporate industrial model had been set into place, adopting from feudalism the idea of the organic model of society with interlocking freedoms and responsibilities, the principle of *noblesse oblige*, and the inspiration of a universal ideal (including "crusades" against nonbelievers). Despite its claims to success, the new system could not prevent the "recurring crises that plagued the supposed harmony of interests" and worked best only in wartime or under the threat of war.[45]

The internal dilemmas of corporatism had been compounded by those of imperialism as embodied in the ideology of the "American Century," enunciated in 1941 by *Time* magazine founder Henry Luce. This magnum figure of corporate journalism had urged Americans to "accept wholeheartedly our duty and our opportunity . . . to exert upon the world the full impact of our influence, for such purposes as we see fit, and by such means as we see fit." Such an intent or *Weltanschauung*, "shared by big corporation executives, labor leaders and politicians of every ideological bent," Williams noted, thoroughly dominated national thinking. Foreign-policy debates did not question the validity of Containment but only whether it "went far enough fast enough," while military debates concerned "which war should be fought [where] and at what time." Looking across the modern history of foreign policy, Truman's Doctrine had only paraphrased Theodore Roosevelt's "Corollary to the Monroe Doctrine," while Republican John Foster Dulles essentially renewed Woodrow Wilson's crusade. Williams later acutely observed that Luce and his "American Century" had successfully "contained" the discussion of American democracy within a very narrow range because the elites agreed with him: that was the deepest truth about Containment.

The bipartisan abandonment of any real difference between corporate and political ideologies increasingly limited American politics to the expression of mere rhetorical differences. Thus a "deeply conservative corporation director" such as Averell Harriman could campaign for the Democratic nomination "with the rhetoric of left-wing liberals," while highly touted liberal intellectual Adlai Stevenson (many of whose speeches were reputedly drafted by Arthur Schlesinger, Jr.) repeatedly reassured the corporations of their permanent leading role in U.S. society.

It was high time, Williams argued, to "abandon . . . bipartisan imperialism," to recognize that America was "neither the last best hope of the world nor the agent of civilization destined to destroy the barbarians. We have much to offer, but also much to learn."[46] A wise and far-sighted policy would create something like a small but progressive World Civilization Tax, to be turned over to U.N. programs for economic and cultural development of the undeveloped world without any strings attached. In turn, Washington would cease any unilateral economic and technical missions of its own. Hundreds of billions of dollars would no longer be directed toward right-wing dictators, and the U.S. could intelligently increase trade with the Communist countries. But Williams did not really expect this kind of enlightened development. He hinted at a more probable consequence, the historical axiom that imperialism, over the long run, destroys republican institutions.[47] These contributions in the *Nation* set the path, in a variety of ways, for *Tragedy of American Diplomacy* (1959).

Behind the journalistic thrusts informed by scholarship, a certain personal turn of mind could also be detected. This revealed itself best in an occasional shift of style, increasingly important to his self-expression by the early 1960s but present as early as his master's thesis. It might be described as his literary equivalent to John Dos Passos' famed historic montage novel, *U.S.A.* Thus his highly personalized view of the *Chicago Tribune* in the period of Joseph Medill's reign:

> Tribune Tower has withstood both rotten eggs and explosive verbiage. It is not the Tower of Babel.
>
> A detailed examination of the paper's history is not the present aim, and interested parties are herewith referred to the bibliography. It is necessary, however, to consider the structural skeleton if the outer form is to be understood.
>
> The shock of amazement upon entering the concourse at 435 North Madison Avenue is great. Size, scampering couriers, and indifference beget apprehension. An armed guard glares his challenge: "Are you on our side?"
>
> Once recovered, the visitor realizes that the walls are covered with various bits of information. Wind velocity and direction indicators, a barometer repeater, and a plastic weather map prepare one for his exit. On the north wall, however, is a more important indicator. In firm hard characters is engraved the testament of Joseph Medill . . . Perhaps it is the god Aelous keeping a date with the lake front, but a chill sweeps through the reader. Those are the words of a powerful personality calling for a high code of ethics. The glaring headline of a nearby *Tribune* underscores the apparent disparity between command and execution. Or perhaps the ethics were of a peculiar character. This heritage is important.[48]

Neither Charles Beard, nor Charles Francis Adams, nor any other obvious sources of inspiration for Williams contain this particular kind of counterposition, although the rhetorical strategy of a sudden turnabout was a popular nineteenth-century literary comedy device from Heinrich Heine to Mark Twain. Williams uses it often to speak to power and to the effects of misused power, a condensed stylistic metaphor of his view of American society's self-made tragedy.

Writing in the *Nation* with a freewheeling style, Williams whimsically synthesized his theories of corporate imperialism through a witty tale about the four personae of various *Weltanschauungen*: the crusading, moralistic, Puritan (most recently exemplified by John Foster Dulles); the paternalistic, aristocratic Planter (whose chief recent archetype was Franklin Delano Roosevelt); the conservative, mercantilist, industrialist Hamiltonian (the likes of Herbert Hoover, Dean Acheson, and George

Frost Kennan); and the liberal, populist, revivalist, expansionist Homesteader (both Harry S. Truman and Henry A. Wallace). They all had similarly covetous intentions, but carried out their plans in very different ways, with differing rhetorics. Williams's imaginary drama also included Virgins (land, markets) and a plethora of Devils (from Native Americans to Stalin). Through historical interplay, the collective cold warrior had gained a life of his own. So far, only a few of "Clio's own courtiers" had taken "a searching look into the mirror of history," and still fewer policymakers (mostly Hamiltonian conservatives) had come to the logical conclusion that "even the best foreign policy cannot convert all the *Heathens*."[49]

Published at a time and in a place destined to draw controversy, Williams's *Nation* essays marked something more than his personal courage or willingness to take the risks of exposing himself to McCarthyite persecutions in academic life. Williams was becoming a "public intellectual" in the last substantial generation of public intellectuals. He was also very different from virtually all the rest of them.[50]

The McCarthy Era and the coincidental rise of television dramatized the drastic narrowing of the public intellectual domain during the 1950s. With television sales booming, general magazines had become less numerous and less important. Meanwhile, economic and social issues discussed during the 1930s-40s as evidence of capitalism's gloomy future had been virtually banished from sight or turned miraculously into proofs of American superiority. The vast expansion of colleges and universities for the returning GIs foreshadowed further bursts of institutional growth for the approaching baby-boom generation, providing intellectuals the employment that the world of magazine culture and popular books no longer offered. A swiftly expanding class of professional thinkers, in other words, ironically had more political restraints and ever fewer means to reach people outside the classroom and the academic journals.

This sea change in intellectual life was disguised in important ways. If challenging either U.S. foreign policy or American capitalism in any fundamental way had been all but precluded, discussions continued and even accelerated during the 1950s on other issues related to the overall quality of life. A vital circle of urban critics (including Paul and Percival Goodman, Lewis Mumford, and William H. Whyte), for instance, struggled to defend urban culture from destruction by the expansive highway system and resulting inner-city decay.

A second set of more political-minded writers, including Irving Howe and Dwight Macdonald among others, conducted themselves carefully within cold-war political bounds but grew increasingly critical of many elements within the culture. They wrote for the flourishing paperback market and for such middlebrow magazines as the *New Yorker, Harper's,* and *Saturday Review,* directing sometimes bitter sarcasm toward mass society and "conformism." Fervent avant-garde literary radicalism also made an important *sub rosa* appearance, as in the surprisingly widely read poetry of Allen Ginsberg and Lawrence Ferlinghetti and in the work of a few of the Beat novelists. For the most part, however, those with a large continuing role in public discussion had moved rightward from earlier sharp criticism of capitalism and adeptly relocated themselves within liberal respectability. African American figures who had once been widely hailed, Paul Robeson and W. E. B. DuBois, were practically banned from print and public appearances because they disagreed with basic cold-war premises.

One exception to this large picture was most meaningful for William Appleman Williams: Madison-trained C. Wright Mills. Son of a Texas insurance salesman and the grandson of a rancher killed in a gunfight, Mills made his way via Madison and training by Hans Gerth during the early 1940s to New York City and Columbia University. His *New Men of Power* (1950) took apart the myth of idealistic labor leaders, one of the cherished notions of the 1930s-40s Left and a section of 1950s liberals. *White Collar* (1951) did the same for corporate employees and professors, pointing to their eager submission to the authority of hierarchies. *The Power Elite* (1956) paralleled Williams's critique of capitalism's corporate-military authorities; his studies within his own field of sociology had, for a time, the same kind of explosive impact that Williams's works would have among historians during the 1960s-80s. Finally, and on a personal level, Mills loved to play the Texas Wobbly among Eastern intellectuals, a motorcycle-riding bohemian who flaunted his differences from them. Williams often found himself, although less cheerfully, playing a similar down-home-American-radical role amidst New York intellectuals.

Williams the public intellectual was already, in some important ways, closer to the 1960s intellectual rebellion that Mills did so much to launch. As the political gatekeepers' influence eroded and dependable views on international issues were no longer assured, many would rush in behind him. But he had precious few outlets beyond the *Nation* to get his message across. And if he thought much about the ways that a citizen-scholar acted upon the processes of public discussion, he was more likely to see Charles Beard than Dwight Macdonald or Lionel Trilling as his model. He sometimes did well in the essay form, he had a great private interest in literature and music, and he studied the psychological theories of the time. But the close study of the historical document rather than the literary work was his home ground, and the epochal view of historical development his philosophical forte.

Looking back from a distance of almost twenty years, Williams remembered the winter of 1952-53 with several different research options. He could investigate the idea that "capitalism could not sustain itself without an expanding marketplace." That would lead him, eventually, back to questions of foreign policy and to the "problem of the relationship between the frontier thesis and the theory of marketplace expansion under capitalism." Whatever route he took, he would eventually come to the same nexus. But he had to choose whether to begin before the articulation of Turner's frontier in 1893, or afterward. In the short run, encouraged by finding so many references to a sort of frontier thesis in twentieth-century U.S. leaders' private and public documents, he turned mainly to modern history.[51] He sought to pin down the evolution of expansionist thought, and sought also to learn from the mirror image of the expansionist mentality, the dissidents who in taking a stand against the logic of the Open Door developed their own large views of American society.

The Shaping of American Diplomacy (1956), a hefty two-volume documents book with extensive editorial commentary, stayed largely in the areas of foreign relations, as in his earlier monographic volume. But Williams also offered the close reader a study in his own evolution. Published in a Rand-McNally textbook series edited by Fred Harvey Harrington, *Shaping* covered the two centuries after the 1750s, two-thirds of which concerned the twentieth century. Williams wrote over a hundred commentaries along with the two hundred documents, many of which had been previously unknown save to specialists.

Designed initially to train graduate students—he had personally mimeographed reams of documents for his classes at Oregon—the project had grown more or less organically from his own research. He complained later that he had not gained much through the labor-intensive method because royalties had been too low to cover the expense of preparing the volume. But the book played a large role in the classroom for well over a decade, offering sympathetic teachers a tool for engaging students with documents and exposing them to views that might be considered in other contexts to be dangerous propaganda. According to Harrington's testimony, Williams had to be urged to balance the selections with more liberal (and conservative) commentaries, but his basic analytical thrust served him well.[52]

All in all, *The Shaping of American Diplomacy* marked a bold new departure in the study of U.S. foreign relations. Traditional historians had analyzed foreign policy in terms of diplomatic exchanges but contradictorily suggested that democratic "public opinion" had ultimately determined U.S. policies—even when scholars knew better from the study of elites making the key decisions.[53] Williams stressed, on the contrary, how economics and ideology as much as the familiar political or military considerations affected U.S. decision-making. While the essays and editorial comments of the volumes avoided polemics, no sophisticated reader could miss implications about the baneful implications of imperialism, not excluding an imperialism overwhelmingly supported by the American public.

By the second volume, covering the period since 1898, Williams's essays and documents showed vividly how the pursuit of the Open Door led to military interventions abroad. Theodore Roosevelt looked like a belligerent bully, but Woodrow Wilson hardly seemed better (only such "isolationist" critics as Senator Borah consistently looked good). Basic U.S. policies had made involvement in both world wars deliberate and inevitable. Right down to the Eisenhower era, Williams suggested how very hard it was for diplomats and presidents to unshackle themselves from their own assumptions even when they could have benefitted personally and saved their nation from peril by doing so.

Especially impressive, because so little known elsewhere in academic or public life, was Williams's treatment of the U.S. and the Third World. Document after document revealed the continuity of Gunboat Diplomacy in Latin America from the 1850s to the 1950s. An evenhanded treatment of the Korean War, with the North no more guilty than the South, was especially daring for the time. The criticism of U.S. China policy that he reprinted similarly suggested how foolish had been the refusal to deal with the nationalism of the Chinese Communists. In all this, he declined the easy (and familiar Marxist, especially Communist) path of charging U.S. policy-makers with venality. A tragic shortsightedness, he indicated, had made their actions inevitable.

Beneath and behind all this, Williams's assumptions were disguised in plain sight, so to speak, in the volumes' introduction. "Human beings decide what will be done with the available resources," he wrote in italics, and added that "letters from American citizens to the State Department are just as important as the official diplomatic cables to another country," because finally, foreign policy stems from "domestic conflicts over what *should* be done and what *can* be done." These were ethical questions, he might have added—but did not.[54] Williams chose to be indirect throughout the volumes, from the bland title to the anonymous dedication ("For a friend who was very courageous," i.e., Harrington).

The reviews were few in number, as is usually the case with textbooks. On the Left, Charles Madison described in *Science & Society* a "rich and rewarding collection . . . pertinent and perceptive." A reviewer in the *Southwestern Social Science Quarterly* found it "very judicious," as did the many professors who assigned it in foreign-policy courses.[55] His Ohio

State friend and colleague Paul A. Varg was the most perceptive critic. Williams's introductory essays he considered "highly interpretative and controversial . . . provocative and imaginative . . . [containing] highly interesting analyses [and] enriching hypotheses." Although Williams might sometimes be charged with "reducing history to too schematic a basis," he was raising questions "which ought long ago to have been considered . . . [and which] provide "a healthy irritant conducive to the re-examination of stereotypes."[56] As a New Left commentator would write decades later, he had a knack for opening up "questions to which historians have generally paid little heed."[57]

Williams could not be pinned down easily, any more than the solidity of his source materials could be readily impeached. As the young professor's devoted new readership might say, Williams was busy shaking off orthodoxies of all kinds. He had borrowed enough from the current drift of historiographical debate to see the foreign-policy elite suffering its own crises of conscience or confidence, enough from the shifting history of expansionism to understand that motive to be rooted as much in what DuBois had called the "American Assumption" of endless land and business growth as the logic of any fixed capitalist class.

Williams collaborated in much that spirit with his friend Harvey Goldberg on *American Radicals: Some Problems and Personalities* (1957), published by Monthly Review Press; the book was one of a relative few new radical titles to appear in an era when publishers fled from dangerous ideas. It was, in many ways, the invocation of radical traditions in tough times. Close to a dozen of the standard Left or Left-leaning figures, such as Robert M. LaFollette, Eugene Debs, Big Bill Haywood, and even John Brown (considered in the conservative 1950s official scholarship and many college texts to have been a madman), found their place here.

But it was also very far from what a book on American radicalism might have been in other hands or other times. None of the standard Abolitionist intellectuals appeared, no African Americans, no women, no Communists, and few Socialists, and most obviously *American Radicals* lacked the sentimental evocation of the American Revolution so common to the Left of the later 1930s and the war years. Defenders of free speech, like newspaperman Heywood Broun and Illinois governor John Peter Altgeld, figured heavily here. A whole section was devoted to repression, to ex-left renegades and liberals who chose Empire and sought to coopt dissent for their own purposes. The most incisive section by far treated the deep thinkers, Thorstein Veblen and Charles Beard, who had little personal hope for American radicalism but described with an acid pen the civilization's destructive course. In short, *American Radicals* would not be considered the kind of text that a detached and distanced critic like Richard Hofstadter could call his own, but it was probably closer to that sort of position than it was to the familiar Communist-style celebration of Thomas Jefferson and Sam Adams, Populism and the New Deal.

Williams inevitably found his own version of the intelligent patrician in Beard, fellow Midwesterner of similar Protestant upbringing. In *American Radicals*, he wrote the nearest thing to a biographical treatment that he would deliver on the man he obviously admired most. Born in Spiceland, Indiana, to a family of conservative farmers and agricultural businessmen, Beard observed the hellish labor conditions of Chicago Stockyard workers and the degradation of politics by city machines. Somewhat like Williams, Beard spent three years traveling and studying in Europe, becoming particularly acquainted with the British labor movement and some Fabian Socialists. A graduate of DePauw University, he received his PhD from Columbia in 1904 and immediately joined the faculty there. Resigning from Columbia in 1917 after Nicholas Murray Butler had fired three faculty members for allegedly associating with subversives (i.e., opponents of the world war), Beard thereafter became the independent, public historian that Williams imagined as the ideal intellectual.

Williams had earlier come to know Beard's writing as an admiring graduate student, probably more than he realized, by way of osmosis through his favorite professors. He revisited the master a second and decisive time, in the mid-fifties, while crafting his mature methods of historical analysis. Here, Williams showed his fascination with the intellect which could balance radical insights with conservative caution, the historian who stressed the interconnectedness of economics to the rest of human behavior and who sought a general theory of causation. In each of these respects, Williams emulated the great man.

Williams wrote that Beard was a radical who went "to the heart of the matter," who insisted that "economics and morality [were] respectively the cornerstone and the keystone of a good life." While economic maladjustment would certainly undermine morality, "the lack of ethical integrity [would] corrupt the best economic system." This, according to Williams, was Beard's enduring legacy to American radicalism. Moreover, in all of this, Beard had not embraced an alien philosophy; he had been a quintessential American, showing the "Indiana common sense" which the prairie radical Williams could appreciate. Beard also refused to separate his intellectual from his political activity. For him, the ivory tower was "a refuge for the intellectual and moral coward—or scoundrel."[58]

While Goldberg edited the volume (no doubt with advice from Williams), the two collaborated on the introduction, a sober and not very optimistic account. American radicalism had failed, they opined, to meet the challenge of American expansionism. The deeply held assumption "that there was enough at hand, or within reach, to meet and satisfy the needs and desires of all segments of the nation" seriously circumscribed any "radical analysis of society." Radicals—and non-imperialist conservatives, they might easily have added— would first have "to wrench themselves [out of the expansionist] tradition before they could grapple with the central crises at hand." The self-proclaimed national mission of "carrying civilization and liberty to the benighted masses of the world" had only compounded the problems of democracy.[59]

So, ironically, did the Russian Revolution, an admission that no Communist or philosophical Leninist could ever have made. Although the Russian Revolution had greatly inspired American radicals, it had provided an extremely inappropriate model for the U.S. Left, while the unsavory aspects of Soviet rule had given reactionaries and liberals powerful sources for antisocialist propaganda. The ensuing repression of democratic traditions and of pleas for alternatives at home meant that radicals often had to establish their own freedom before they could begin to work out "a coherent and integrated radical program for America."

This presented a thoroughly daunting prospect. The "European radical, consistently sensitive to the difficulties of challenging a class system, could be broken and yet rise again." But the American dissenter, surrounded by those who shared the illusions of living in a near-perfect society, had a far harder row to hoe. Some "toughened their hides," while others "fell away when the reality replaced the dream." Not nearly enough had remained for a consistent tradition.[60]

The "unprecedented power of vested interests" and the "calculated manipulation of public opinion through the mass-communications media" frequently left radicals feeling so futile, afraid, and frustrated that they groped wildly for alternatives. Some knowing better but unable to find an alternative path accepted the liberal version of Empire. Others shared the alienation pervasive in society, demobilizing themselves from any useful action. Failing a proper reorientation, defeated radicals abandoned the field entirely to the hope for reformed Russian or Chinese Communists, or to "the new breed of men which will arise as a phoenix from a nuclear holocaust."

Perhaps most damning was the charge that American intellectuals had as a group grabbed the opportunity for personal advance in the prosperous society, trading their critical talents for unworthy ends. "The cutting edge of criticism can be easily dulled by the soft center of personal gain," Williams and Goldberg charged, and the "compromisers and hairsplitters . . . adorn themselves" with self-congratulation for their reasonableness. The authors were evidently describing former radicals who now dominated literary criticism and heavily influenced academic life through their prestige, connections, and their firm embrace of cold-war policies.[61]

Hidden in the text, well away from the concluding paragraphs, lurked another implication that had little to do with Goldberg's personal vision but much to do with Williams's. Perennially lacking solid "long-term popular support," the Left's programs paled in comparison with the "rational corporatism" of such enlightened conservatives as Herbert Hoover. A quarter century later, it had taken a "West Pointer and a General Motors executive [i.e., Eisenhower] to begin America's disengagement from the cold war."[62] One could almost say that the fascination of a critic like Lionel Trilling for the literature of the elite found its match here, albeit at the other end of the political spectrum. Or again, as a wing of former radicals turned to Adlai Stevenson as the best hope of the age, Williams (if not Goldberg) "liked Ike" with a similar mixture of fatalism and admiration.

5

In the less-read academic journals and in the free commentary of reviews, Williams experimented with theories of *Weltanschauung*, or worldview, to explain U.S. history and foreign policy. His classroom discussions with Oregon undergraduates, and his conversations with fellow Oregon historian Orde Pinckney and economist Robert Campbell, gave him a sense of historical background that made expansionism an epochal phenomenon. Williams was already thinking in large, long-range terms, utilizing "modernization" or periodization as ways to examine the stages of political economy and society at large.[63] Here and there he staked out a major position in foreign-policy research. For the most part, the conceptual experiments or trial balloons served as a basis for larger conceptualizations in his later works. Returning often to the writings of the classic historians, he prepared to challenge the dominant liberal historiography.

The prime American *Weltanschauung* of the twentieth century, according to Williams, was that of "Open Door imperialism," the right of the U.S. to enter all markets on formal terms of equality, in a relationship naturally favoring the stronger party. Reflecting on the development of this concept many years later, he insisted that it belonged to no particular school of thought, but had been advanced since the 1890s "by a disparate group of policy-makers and politicians, bureaucrats, nonacademic intellectuals, and university and college teachers."[64] Nearly all of them, it is fair to say, were elements of the ruling strata.

Scholars had been aware of the importance of the Open Door policy almost from its beginnings. Marxist Rosa Luxemburg had previewed the economic basis of it in *The Accumulation of Capital—an Anticritique* (1913), which argued that capitalism sustained itself only by extending its grasp of accumulation outward, absorbing lesser economies.[65] Several of the keenest interpretations of Open Door strategy as such, from liberal Englishman John A. Hobson's *Towards a Lasting Peace* (1916) to the Williams-influenced German scholar Hans-Ulrich Wehler's *Der Aufsteig des amerikanischen Imperialismus* (1974), were also penned from outside the U.S. An assortment of American historians appreciated the importance of the subject but failed to see it as anything resembling a comprehensive worldview, and the Marxist economists (including those around *Monthly Review* magazine) were preoccupied with the economic details of imperialism. Charles Beard and Mary Ritter Beard, along with Fred Harvey Harrington, possibly came closest to abandoning atomistic, interest group–based theories to identify a modern imperialist *Weltanschauung* as such.

In Williams's perception, the chain reaction that ignited his interpretation of Open Door imperialism took place in the History Department at Wisconsin shortly following World War II. Intellectual cross-fertilization helped, Americanists interacting with Europeanists and with scholars from other fields including sociology and literature. So did the ideas of the Frankfurt School, which seemed to be in the air at the time. The "particular genius of Harrington" had been to bring these people together.[66] It was also interesting that Williams should think of the milieu in these terms, especially because as successor to Harrington he would guide the work of a later and much enlarged generation of radical scholars. Williams's own work was the key link between the two generations, and his preparations went far to make that extended process possible.

His efforts in the 1950s and on American-Russian relations in particular, Williams admitted later, had only tested his new methodology. He was so far "not fully in command of the approach." He tried out the concept in specialized studies—Frederick Jackson Turner's Frontier Thesis and Henry Luce's articulation of an "American Century"— before analyzing the historical context and crucial consequences of Secretary of State John Hay's "Open Door Notes" of 1899-1900. Williams conceptualized these particular documents as the "basic formulation" of a general outlook leading to "a vast network of internal relations" that, taken together, integrated "economic theory and practice, abstract ideas, past and future politics, anticipations of Utopia, messianic idealism, social-psychological imperatives, historical consciousness, and military strategy." Guiding both "elitist *and* popular thinking (and responses)," the Open Door finally became "an ideology (even theology) and ultimately a reification of reality." Williams found little difficulty in delineating the development of this ideology with most of Hay's successors. Indeed, he remarked that one grew weary of repeated references to Open Door policies in published State Department documents alone.[67]

Charles Beard had doubtless understood best for his time that "empires are not built in states of absent mindedness . . . and expansion does not in and of itself solve problems but often complicates them." But he could never "pull the personal and group world views into one national *weltanschauung* for the United States," and develop a comprehensive analysis of the mainsprings of American foreign policy. He moved in that direction during the 1930s, until the approach of World War II diverted him entirely.[68] The historical giant had nevertheless crystallized a philosophical framework that allowed Williams to develop further what his fellow Madisonians had so ardently discussed. Less concerned with raw economic motives than with hypothesizing about interests and ideas, Beard offered a working theory of causation.

Williams also admired and drew upon Thorstein Veblen, widely considered along with Beard one of the three leading intellectual influences of the 1930s (the third was Freud). Another fellow Midwesterner, born in Wisconsin and educated in Minnesota, Veblen had never been well accepted by the academic establishment. Although he read and admired Marx and became very sympathetic to the Bolshevik Revolution, he also remained outside Left party circles. And yet he was an anticapitalist and antinationalist who believed in fundamental structural changes and not merely reforms of the existing system. Williams particularly appreciated how Veblen connected foreign and domestic policies, and specifically how he understood the ways in which the U.S. could be ardently pro-imperial while generally anticolonial. Perhaps most of all, Williams appreciated Veblen's temperament: brilliantly iconoclastic, yet an idealist beneath it all.

With this timely return to Beard and Veblen, Williams plunged further into the synthetic interpretation of U.S. foreign policy outlined in *The Shaping of American Diplomacy*, but with a more keenly sharpened edge. In the *Nation* and a variety of scholarly journals, he directed his comments consistently and openly, for the first time, against the accepted wisdom of liberalism. He critiqued the existing historiography and in the process sketched out the alternatives he would detail in his masterworks, *Tragedy of American Diplomacy* and *Contours of American History*.

During the last decade of the nineteenth century, Americans had developed a set of ideas that had later become hardened into a worldview. Derived partly from Frederick Jackson Turner's theory that "America's unique and true democracy was a product of an expanding frontier," and partly from Brooks Adams's theses in his *Law of Civilization and Decay* that the struggle against entropy demanded a combination of Empire and corporatist coordination, this set of ideas passed on to John Hay and Theodore Roosevelt to subsequent presidents, secretaries of state, and assorted policymakers.[69] Turner's thesis achieved, meanwhile, great popularity with the general public. Writing during the 1890s, a time of serious socioeconomic crises, he gave Americans "a nationalistic world view that eased their doubts, settled their confusions, and justified their aggressiveness." Expansion would not only improve business but also extend white Protestant democracy. Far from a Republican or conservative project, it was evidently a bipartisan and even a consensual program.[70]

The liberal Woodrow Wilson seeking to "fit his conservative sense of noblesse oblige to an industrial society," thus articulated a "fundamental identity between the economic supremacy of American capitalism and [his] image of the good world." Contrary to the liberal orthodoxy of historians like Arthur S. Link, this Wilson was anything but an innocent idealist.[71] His ideological and military offensive against the new Soviet Union had been instinctive, as doctrinaire and unyielding as U.S. policy would be toward any society or ideology perceived as an obstacle to the Open Door.[72]

Williams decisively challenged the familiar notion that Americans had retreated into isolationism after World War I only to return to international responsibility as fascism threatened to overtake Europe. In a historical note and in a major convention paper (read to the Pacific Historical Association) that became the most reprinted essay of Williams's work during the 1950s, he sought to show that the prevalent historiography disguised deeper complexities. All the way back to the 1790s, Alexander Hamilton had proposed "no entangling alliances," but actually intended "a de facto affiliation with the British" rather than disengagement. If concerted opposition to U.S. entry to the League of Nations had been motivated not by isolationism but by the desire for unilateral options, and if the purported isolationism of 1920s Progressives like Senator William Borah of Idaho had included the very internationalist aim of the U.S. recognizing Russia, then mainstream interpretations of American leaders' international aims explained little.[73]

Liberal historians had, in fact, been stacking the deck by portraying a stagnant (i.e., Republican) 1920s against a dynamic (i.e., mostly Democratic) 1910s and 1930s. The contrast of Hoover and Roosevelt that would later earn Williams scholarly notoriety (and friends in ostensibly strange places, among conservatives and liberal Republicans) began properly here. The ruling group around Herbert Hoover, heirs to a wing of the Progressive Party, embraced shrewd capitalists, financiers, and labor leaders in a comprehensive corporatism aimed at "internationalization through the avoidance of conflict."[74] As a community of interests building upon the mechanisms established in the Wilson reign, they would guide the abandonment of the old territorial imperialism for a new economic Pax Americana.

This interpretation so thoroughly sliced through the liberal faith that it left the domestic economic interpretations as well as foreign policy in tatters. Bearing down on Arthur Schlesinger, Jr.'s *Crisis of the Old Order, 1919-1933* in the *Nation*, Williams argued that Schlesinger had not only fundamentally misunderstood Hoover but blunderingly misinterpreted the crisis of 1929 and its underlying causes. No nineteenth century–style, individualist capitalism had still existed to collapse. Schlesinger threw the blame on Hoover because to accept Hoover's rationalization of the system would be tantamount to admitting that corporate capitalism and not its predecessor had failed in 1929. Schlesinger had better described the crisis of the 1890s or even the Panic of 1873 than he did 1929, so much did he fear coming to grips with the implications that the key problems of the society had remained unresolved except by war and Empire.[75]

If Williams had set his enemies to sharpening their knives for him, he prepared himself for his next great conceptual leap forward. He had also shown some of the idiosyncratic edges which inspired curiosity and amazement from political observers, Left to Right. His rehabilitation of the 1920s in general revealed something about Williams and his Wisconsin milieu. Warren Susman later devoted considerable energies to debunking the 1930s as the supposed "red" or radical decade. Like Williams, he sought to upturn the standard liberal historiography which portrayed the New Deal as the apex or end-goal of political accomplishment; like Williams, Susman found himself working upstream all the way in the existing climate of scholarly sympathies, his task better conceptualized in essays than argued in monographs.[76] Williams's twist of this radical revision, making Hoover a political centerpiece and sentimentalizing the conservative gendered family-centeredness of 1930s life, found him at odds with almost everyone among a liberal and socialist cohort, but not so distant from his Iowa Republican background after all.

6

Suspiciously publishing in "red" journals and almost certainly tracked by the FBI since his Corpus Christi days, Williams was ripe for victimization. In 1954, Arthur Schlesinger, Jr., added an accusatory phrase to an otherwise unrelated letter to the executive secretary of the AHA, attacking Williams as a "pro-communist scholar."[77] At that moment in the profession, such a letter from a distinguished scholar and famed writer could easily have been taken to be an invitation to banish a possibly subversive writer and teacher. Offered very few grants, fewer jobs, and no particularly prestigious ones over the course of his career, and awarded only one honorary degree (by a black community college) despite his later presidency of the Organization of American History, Williams evidently never entirely escaped an informal blacklist.

Whether by coincidence or not, he also faced a modicum of harassment in liberal Oregon. After the departure of a trusted and powerful ally to Berkeley, the senior figure of the history department decided to make life difficult for the young radicals. One day at the water fountain after a day of work, the elder professor demanded, "Are you a Communist?" It was not an innocent question. Williams recalled he replied simply, "I consider the question as an insult," and turned on his heels.[78]

This dour chairman did not and perhaps could not prevent Williams, one of the most intellectually productive members of the department, from gaining tenure. Oregon, moreover, lacked the kind of state legislation which would have allowed a public political hanging. But the issue of his real or possible political connections and inclinations floated around campus and became an obstacle to his further advancement as well as a cloud over his general status in the community. In an academic novel about Oregon by Williams's colleague and friend, Bernard Malamud (who reportedly considered Williams the only one to have correctly interpreted his baseball novel, *The Natural*, as a metaphor of American life), a professor unravels the tale of his predecessor's firing as a confused, heavily personalized, nightmarish mockery of political struggle. Drawn by the beauty of his surroundings despite the almost constantly overcast skies and deep sense of geographic isolation, the protagonist triumphs—but only by leaving. Williams himself moved out of his home, albeit for more personal reasons. The same year, he had been offered an untenured position at the University of Illinois in Champaign-Urbana, which he turned down. It is likely he simply felt little desire for a position no better than the one he had. Perhaps he had other reasons.[79]

From Williams's point of view, his marriage with Jeannie had gone bad, and after a trial separation, the two had decided that they were "doing . . . each other more damage than good."[80] Jeannie could not see matters so nonjudgmentally. From her perspective, he was an adulterous husband who had already made his life decisions without giving her the dignity of a sincere explanation. Between his second and third marriage there would be talk of a reconciliation with Jeannie. He wrote to her in great detail about his further experiences and marital troubles, evidently feeling guilty for wrong done to her.

Drawn into what some later described as "a Great Passion," he had meanwhile struck up a relationship with Corrinne Croft Hammer, an Oregon-raised radical who had returned to graduate school after bearing two children. A decade earlier, fleeing the conservatism of small-town Oregon and of her southern-born parents, the bright and rebellious Corrinne had attended Portland State College and joined the United World Federalists. Later, trapped in an abusive marriage, she set her heart on becoming a social worker with an advanced degree, and had managed to secure a teaching assistantship in Sociology at the University of Oregon. There, Williams swept her off her feet.

Corrinne put aside her aspirations for a love match. The similarly stubborn temperaments of the two should have set off warning bells, many friends concluded later. But they plunged ahead, marrying. She accompanied him to Madison for a Ford Fellowship in research from the fall of 1955 to spring 1956. Having finished *The Shaping of American Diplomacy*, he could seriously begin work on *The Tragedy of American Diplomacy*. They lived in a house overlooking picturesque Lake Mendota, and he renewed his many acquaintances, especially a warm friendship with a noted scientist, the emigre German socialist Karl Paul Link. Williams had enjoyed his life in Oregon, but Madison offered him incomparable intellectual excitement.[81]

The national mood of McCarthyism had also eased significantly, even as generalized blacklisting, roundups of Communists, and the jailing of unwilling witnesses before Congressional committees all continued to chill free speech. Meantime, flagrant U.S. misdeeds abroad began to provoke a skepticism and even a protest unthinkable in the anticommunist liberal press only a few years earlier. Norman Thomas, still "Mr. Socialism" to *New York Times* reporters, would soon be heard denouncing the "New American Imperialism" and omnipresent, unquestioning American support of "corrupt, reactionary cliques so long as they [are] anti-communist."[82] Williams could rightly anticipate in Madison an arena for relatively free, open discussion of America's Empire past and present.

In 1957, Fred Harvey Harrington was elevated to Chair of the History Department in Madison and made no secret of his aspiration to climb higher. Well respected on campus and around the state, he would become university president five years later and preside over the most rapid growth the school had ever known. With his influence looming large, he bypassed the normal controversies of new appointments and asked Williams to replace him as historian of U.S. foreign policy.[83]

Wisconsin policy prevented an immediate tenured appointment, but Harrington made Williams the tentative promise of tenure, promotion, and a significant salary increase at the end of the first year. The younger man might have preferred to stay in Oregon for another year or so. But Wisconsin offered $7,600, four hundred dollars more than his present pay. When he asked Oregon to match the four hundred dollars, his department adversaries made sure the Dean would not budge. Williams seized the moment. By the time he, Corrinne, and her own two children left Eugene permanently for Madison, she was pregnant with their first child. A new life had begun in more ways than one.[84]

4

HIGH TIMES IN MADISON, 1957–1963

THE RETURN TO WISCONSIN HELD PROMISES and hazards that Williams could not have fully anticipated. He had waited as he had worked and lived all along, since the late 1940s, for the revival of a political Left. If he guessed that he might be its chief scholarly avatar, the one who could point to the crucial developments in national life, he betrayed no advanced knowledge of this possibility. His key books, in no way styled for a new generation, resonated with that tone of the 1940s–1950s which brought his powerful intellect to bear upon the large saga of democracy and Empire. More subtly, they also resonated with the memories of the 1930s that encompassed his childhood and the diminished promise of modern times.

The resulting intellectual edifice, in style as well as content, was unlike anything that U.S. historical scholarship had seen before or would likely see again. Idiosyncratic to the core, Williams's *Tragedy of American Diplomacy* and *Contours of American History* overviewed the national saga from the standpoint of a bereaved patriot. He offered at different moments, occasionally within the same paragraphs, grand syntheses of historiography, insights entirely outside existing scholarship, and witty observations about the nation's giants. Unlike those nineteenth-century "comic histories" (the most famous by Eugene Debs's friend Bill Nye), which ridiculed American statesmen for their looks and behavior, Williams reconstructed these giants as leviathans indeed, but not as Americans had ever seen them. In this way among others, Williams the patriot escaped being a mere iconoclast. He challenged not so much the details of the existing canon as the very root assumptions of the liberal-conservative coalition which had held the commanding towers of prestige and influence since the defenestration of Charles Beard.

He did not entirely escape the suspicion, especially among younger historians, that he nevertheless held to some certain very conventional assumptions: a small number of great, white men make history; and the rest of society acquiesces to their rule, not only from powerlessness but from a widespread agreement with their purposes. Nevertheless, he proposed an extremely radical way of viewing that history. In short, he came at his subject from various perspectives that would in others have been merely contradictory or confusing. For all his weaknesses, he dazzled again and again.

For a moment in time Williams also made himself into a major exemplar of Madison, Wisconsin's progressive tradition, as its revived importance in the beginnings of national dissent was reflected in him. Of course, merely a sliver of campus knew much about Williams, took his courses or cared; outside the university only the circles of progressive intellectuals and casual readers of local press articles mentioning him from time to time would likely even have known his name. But history popularized for the common citizen had been a significant claim in the land-grant university and in the much-utilized State Historical Society of Wisconsin with the mural of "Fighting Bob" LaFollette painted on its interior stairwell. Within that tradition, Williams personified progressive Midwestern citizenry self-realized. No better candidate, at any rate, could be found since the death in 1925 of the legendary idealist and third-party Presidential candidate.

In that spirit, Williams trained a legion of future professors. These democratic-spirited youngsters in turn sought to give the nation, beginning with their own students, a more realistic picture of American society, its deep problems, and its vast possibilities. Williams also encouraged the formation of a sort of brain trust, like-minded youngsters brought together around his ideas as a method of approaching the complexities of the Corporate Age. Working in this atmosphere, he developed the crucial insights into "Corporate Liberalism," the historic view popularized by his devotees in conscious preparation for the momentuous social movement arising a few years later.

Behind the bold front, a certain pathos might be detected, but only by the very perceptive observer. Williams disguised the ample private weakness hidden in the strength of many a remarkable public figure. A slap at him in *Time Magazine* and ferocious personal attacks upon him by veteran cold-war operatives like Theodore Draper did not daunt him; nor did the cancellation of book contracts on political grounds, nor even the chilling experience of persistent harassment by the U.S. House Committee on UnAmerican Activities and the Internal Revenue Service. But a certain political and emotional inconsistency, the difficulty of reconciling current hopes with an unsentimental interpretation of American history, cast a shadow over his efforts. Beloved and admired, he frequently seemed in private a radical alone with his own soul.

I

Madison was ready for Williams's return. Ground had been broken for a new library the year he left, across a mall from the Historical Society, with a magnificent collection of volumes opened in 1953 to students and all state residents. The University of Wisconsin's national and international reputation across many departments grew steadily as well. By the late 1950s, it had entered an era of good feelings with a state legislature markedly proud of its rising stature and almost eager to fund its continuing expansion.[1]

In the seven years since Williams had departed, the political atmosphere had changed considerably and almost welcomed the pre-dawn of a new Left. Numerous students and prestigious faculty members would become his natural allies, shielding this public intellectual when necessary and lauding him as their own radical champion *qua* historian.

The dissipation of cold-war gloom had begun, in small ways, just as Williams and his graduate school cohorts left graduate school in 1949-50 to take up their first faculty positions. New graduate students with the experience of Left summer camps or the Henry Wallace campaign behind them arrived with their ideologies battered but their scholarly hopes high. In American history, Warren Susman, David W. Noble, Herbert Gutman, William Preston, and George Rawick, among others, were just beginning their momentuous work of redefining modern cultural studies, working class immigrant and African American history. Some of them were also at the heart of the failed but heroic "Joe Must Go" campaign aimed at defeating Senator McCarthy in his home state. Susman, the speaker-system expert for the campaign, would remain one of Williams's intimates in the decades ahead, and Noble one of his keenest interpreters. Together with a few beloved professors, this intellectual cohort created the "Smoking Room

School of History," an informal but dynamic round table of historical discussions in an alcove of the State Historical Society.[2]

These graduate students, even more than their sympathetic professors, made Madison an increasingly vital locus of historical study outside the political mainstream. Their devotion fostered a small-scale political renaissance that predicted the distinctively cerebral character of Madison radicalism during the 1950s. As teaching assistants for such favorite professors as Howard Beale or Merle Curti, they cultivated the circle of undergraduate students who would form a crucial link between Williams and the New Left.[3]

A dozen or so precocious Jewish undergraduates, mostly from the New York area and deeply interested in history, quickly made themselves an active political group on campus, stirring controversy and driving liberals into action. The communist-linked Labor Youth League (LYL) offered cultural variety to a student body otherwise heavily inclined toward the beer guzzling of the "frat-rats" and the plodding of the upwardly mobile engineering majors. At the very depths of McCarthyism, they and a circle of radical pacifists protested compulsory ROTC and the presence of racial discrimination in campus housing, and they formed support groups for local strikers. Professors like Beale and Curti defended them in print, insisting that even communist views deserved free-speech protection.[4]

Madison thus remained a remarkably lively place during the national nightmare of political paranoia and bomb shelters. Elsewhere in the country, unions were demobilized and purged of suspicious members, thousands of Americans considered either subversive or homosexual lost their jobs, and Hollywood enforced its blacklist of those who refused to testify against their colleagues. But on the University of Wisconsin campus, Marxists like slavery scholar Herbert Aptheker or Shakespeare scholar Annette Rubinstein spoke freely. Meanwhile, the civil rights movement elicited wide local sympathy, with visiting southern activists drawing enthusiastic audiences and volunteers determinedly raising thousands of dollars on Madison street corners. As usual, radicals were among the most active in their sympathy, the most eager to draw the campus into the national integrationist effort. In this odd moment, history had almost caught up with the William A. Williams of 1946.[5]

Dramatic international developments propelled the young University of Wisconsin intellectuals in new directions of their own. The 1956 Hungarian Revolution and the brutal Russian response, along with the Twentieth Congress of the Soviet Union and Nikita Khruschev's revelations of Joseph Stalin's misdeeds (including horrendous anti-Semitism), abruptly ended Communist sympathies on campus. Joining with other campus radicals, former Labor Youth League members created a portentous post-Stalinist entity: the Socialist Club. Heavy with history enthusiasts, the SC would provide Williams's prime forum outside the classroom.[6]

Parallel developments in Britain set the pace for a revived Anglo-American radicalism with its roots in fresh historical interpretations. A group of brilliant young scholars with a shared background in the British Communist Party, including E. P. Thompson, Eric Hobsbawm, Christopher Hill, and George Rudé, founded the journal *Past and Present* in 1953. It aimed to move beyond Marxist generalities and old dogmas to a close investigation of the national past, underpinned with a certain moral reverence for the anticapitalist and antimaterialist sentiment of the English Revolution's Diggers and Levellers. In the following few years, Thompson founded the more political-minded (but scarcely less historical) journal, *The New Reasoner*, and joined others in a massive "Ban the Bomb" movement. Young intellectuals on various British campuses called themselves the "New Left."[7] The initial U.S. response was fairly anemic. Groups actually formed at a handful of colleges or universities, but only Wisconsin's Socialist Club was both scholarly and intently historical-minded.

By the later 1950s, the combined Left of ex-communists, pacifists, and independent radicals began to reach considerable chunks of an apathetic campus majority. The 1959 Anti-Military (shortened to "Anti-Mil") Ball, a counter-spectacle to the ROTC annual event, actually had more participants than the high-heels-stars-and-braids showcase. Talented young impresarios like Marshall Brickman (later collaborator with Woody Allen in several films, including *Annie Hall*) prepared witty left-wing theatricals.[8] In this burgeoning cultural climate, Williams the Midwest bohemian and amateur jazz musician was especially valued as a link between the youngsters and World War II's radical generation.

Williams, in his return to the University of Wisconsin, was thus somewhat larger than life. Inevitably the Socialist Club's favorite speaker on such immediate political subjects as the "test ban" that leading scientists had proposed to halt the proliferating nuclear weaponry, he spoke also on Marxist philosophy as well as foreign policy in general. If conservative undergraduates of the time complained to the *Cardinal* about a dark force throughout the campus, manifested in the denunciation of imperialism inside the classroom and out, it could be traced directly or indirectly to Williams. Student political rallies renouncing U.S. policies in Latin America naturally sounded like popularizations of the ideas pronounced by the speakers' favorite professor.

Williams thereby found himself unexpectedly a public figure. As several of Williams's students openly supported the right of Cubans to make a revolution, the *Chicago Tribune* warned of subversion on campuses. A worried University of Wisconsin Dean of Students added to the atmosphere of intimidation, pointing to the probability of future damaged careers among undergraduates who joined certain left-wing student groups. Williams, for his part, simply defended his students against a former state assemblyman's charges that they were being made "dupes of the Communists." But when the campus Young Democrats—led by Williams student Henry W. Berger—denounced the red-scare atmosphere and boldly passed a resolution calling for the abolition of the House Committee on UnAmerican Activities (HUAC), conservative legislators hungered for revenge.[9]

A judicial-committee hearing of the state legislature summoned in 1961 to urge Congress to continue HUAC inevitably sparked political fireworks. American Legionnaires and liberal undergraduates demonstrated and counter-demonstrated outside the Capitol, adding further drama to some of the best-attended sessions in decades. Called to testify before the committee, Williams charged that HUAC wasted money, usurped legitimate constitutional powers, and provided biased information to leaders. "Proud to be an intellectual" who could dissent, he boldly avowed that "among man's rights is the right to revolution."[10] Asked what he taught his students, he answered, "I teach people to think," bringing down the house in a veritable explosion from the galleries.[11]

Such courageous theatrics could not be staged entirely without cost. Conservatives insisted, just as they had about other campus radicals for generations, that Williams's supporters in the capitol were out-of-staters, mainly from New York—another way of saying that they were radical Jews. A doughty American Legion commander and frequent letter-writer to the local press charged that Williams, known to encourage disloyalty, had rapidly been "amassing a reputation as a fellow traveler."[12] Madison Peace Center pickets holding up signs at a Civil Defense exercise were heckled with shouts of "Jews, go back to New York and the Soviet Union!"[13] The familiar anti-Semitic undertone to local red-baiting only hardened the determination of cold-war critics. Williams, the professor-as-war-veteran and an officer at that, offered his person as evidence that dissent was deeply American.

Williams meanwhile placed himself comfortably among colleagues in the History Department and the university at large. More perhaps even than he expected, he had come home. As veterans of that time recall, the great changes brought by the 1960s had not yet taken place. U.S. history still seemed to be taught here largely "from the view of North Dakota," as one of Williams's colleagues wryly described the continuing Beardian or regionalist outlook. Professors continued to be valued on the basis of their teaching (it was a commonplace to say that each historian had one good book in him) rather than on their literary output. William Hesseltine was still around to say that real historians "eat and drink history," properly devoting much of their leisure conversation to points raised in classes. Williams was unusual in this crowd only because he seemed also to eat and drink research, so enthusiastic about his discoveries that he could hardly stop talking about them off duty.[14]

The close-knit Americanists included Alan Bogue, a Beardian agricultural historian from Iowa, and a small circle of the familiar 1940s Progressive crew, most prominently Merrill Jensen and Merle Curti. Former mentor William Best Hesseltine and university administrator Fred Harvey Harrington were Williams's special colleagues and friends. The European side featured historian George Mosse, destined to be another of Williams's closest colleagues. A gay, Jewish refugee from Germany—the scion of a vanished dynasty of influential newspaper publishers—Mosse synthesized and reinterpreted the modern European cultural legacy for generations of students. Quickly, undergraduates and graduates alike learned that by taking Mosse, Williams, and sociologist Hans Gerth in tandem, they could acquire knowledge that no book held and insight into European and American life that no other university offered. Such students would also have encountered three of the most atypical professors in the American academy.

History students knew little about Williams before he arrived in Madison except the "larger than life stories" that they heard on the grapevine. Some had read *American-Russian Relations* and found its epilogue in particular to be unsettling and exciting. But its author was also supposed to be "crotchety," altogether "difficult and opinionated," a "kind of Socrates as Socialist who habitually got up on the wrong side of the bed," eager for dialogue but also cranky and stubborn. They could not miss the element of distance he demanded to keep his spare time free for research and writing. Few of them could fully appreciate that Williams had been groomed in the stern school of historiographical training and was mainly trying to pass on his own experience.[15]

In the seminar or one-to-one encounter, Williams was quietly charismatic, his presence in one recollection "the irresistible attraction of a commanding, creative intellectual, who possessed such a robust and essentially healthy ego that he would knowingly make himself vulnerable." He commanded respect and yet also invited personal attachment. His syllabus for an undergraduate course thus typically read:

> I teach this course on the assumption that History is a way of learning about how we humans operate: in thinking about what we have done and what have been the consequences; and in thinking about how we can learn from that vicarious experience in making our own history. I look upon the lectures as a way of giving you information that you can use in your own thinking, and as a way of showing-by-example how to

make sense out of the information you gather. If you find that my way of making sense out of the information convinces you, that is fine, but I am not primarily interested in persuading you I am right. The object is to help you make your own sense out of our history.[16]

Williams's lecture style was also fascinating, if not as dramatic as that of some colleagues. "You were seeing a world-class intellectual thinking on his feet; you could see the wheels turn and grind and mesh," according to Thomas McCormick. Williams's graduate assistants found a certain "Thomistic logic" inherent in what he said. His train of argument, once set into motion, had an almost irresistible appeal.

If America were a self-conscious empire rather than the idealistic democracy it claimed to be, angling for power rather than compelled against its collective will to seize world influence, then everything else followed. McCormick, former undergraduate president of the Young Republicans at Cincinnati, remembered fighting "tooth and nail over those first premises for a full year before finally succumbing. But thinking back, I realize that the battle was both shorter and more one-sided."[17]

Almost immediately, three of the more promising graduate students in diplomatic history, Walter LaFeber, Lloyd Gardner, and McCormick invited Williams over to dinner to "decode" him. In the discussion which lasted until the wee hours of the morning, he gave them "a private screening, as it were," of *Contours of American History*. It took weeks "to sort out what had happened," Gardner recalled. But the graduate students had the feeling that the field of foreign-policy studies would never be the same, and for them personally, "life was never going to be the same either."[18]

Williams brought them from foreign-policy issues as such, and the methodological breakthroughs of the time (mainly the process of traveling abroad to use non-U.S. archives) toward something far off in the intellectual horizon. If they studied and learned from Thomas Hobbes and John Locke, understood the counterpart theories of social organization worked out by Thomas Jefferson and James Madison, and grasped how the capitalist market plunged society from one age to another, then they could study with some facility the various internal developments that had traditionally been outside the scope of diplomatic history. Above all, they could understand something about how the society worked organically and evolved as a dynamic unit. In that light, foreign policy became a vantage point to view the past as no one else but Williams had done.[19]

For many graduate students, Williams also offered a model of the way they might strive to conduct their lives. He always seemed to have "a new slant on things" and his open-forum Friday afternoons quickly became "a weekly mecca for ever-growing numbers of students—some coming to praise him, others to bury him."[20] Walter LaFeber recalled that "sitting in that classroom and listening to him lecture, I understood for the first time what a teacher . . . was supposed to do." Williams time and again compelled students toward fresh perspectives, "from a broader perspective and more critical in context" than they could reach by themselves. The capacity to teach in that fashion constituted, for the professorial trainee, "the test of a great historian."[21]

Williams's ability to stimulate unorthodox thought located a particular soft spot in twentieth-century U.S. history. As Lloyd Gardner recalled, the New Deal was then generally seen as the climax of contemporary history. World War II, and then the Truman and Eisenhower presidencies reshaped but also reinforced that legacy as an adopted "Americanism" of government entitlements for citizens and business. A flood of prestigious academic monographs during the 1950s and early 1960s on a variety of subjects, from Teddy Roosevelt to Woodrow Wilson to Franklin Roosevelt, drove home the uniform message and effectively marginalized any alternative, Left or Right.

Williams came at this seeming historical truism from all sides, including among his favorite authorities Marx, Sartre, Herbert Hoover, John Quincy Adams, and science fiction writer Arthur Clarke, and adding random shots from mass-culture genres from jazz to sports. According to him, even those self-consciously elitist and perennial world-champion New York Yankees, showed the excellence that modern liberal bureaucratic mediocrity so palpably lacked. The use of such sources unexpectedly demonstrated, through Williams's unique interpretations, that the New Deal had actually brought forth monsters, and that America could do better.[22]

Conservative undergraduates, who might otherwise have found this line of thought tantalizing, tended to view criticisms of U.S. foreign policies as bordering on treason. (A later generation of young libertarians, bitterly opposed to the Vietnam War, would find in Williams penetrating criticisms of liberalism and the imperial agenda it shared with neoconservatism.) Williams's very command over his teaching assistants appeared to the same suspicious minds as a concerted conspiracy against America. Still others were put off by his high-flow conceptualizations, his occasional abrasiveness, and his toughness toward students he considered lazy.[23]

But Williams found himself mostly admired, and he worked hard to reinforce his influence. In the ethos of the period, the professor who generated the greatest interest among graduate students gained maximum status, and at this project Williams rapidly excelled. On the level of sheer concentration, he scouted graduate school applicants who had less than exemplary undergraduate academic records but who showed signs of promise and determination similar to his own a decade earlier. Through untiring attendance at department meetings, he also usually obtained funding for his favorites. Many of his colleagues indeed felt he pushed too hard in this respect. To the end of his career in teaching graduate students, when he claimed to be bored and exhausted by it all, he remained extraordinarily patient in coaching his charges and then prompting them to go off in their own directions.[24]

He also assiduously promoted his students' postgraduate careers by making sure to find available jobs for them a first and even a second time. In an era before more formal procedures and affirmative action programs, this kind of informal networking practice was normal, although it demanded so much effort that not many professors had the influence or energy to carry through continuously. Within a decade, Williams produced thirty-five PhDs, far more than an average historian, and with considerably more individual attention per student than was usual.[25]

The effort took its toll on his energy and patience. By 1960, he wrote his old friend Warren Susman that he desperately needed more time off, and that the young radicals' demands for less emphasis on elite class consciousness and more on lower class consciousness drove him to distraction.[26] Within a year, he had already begun to look for another job, hoping to find some picturesque and distant place where he could escape graduate students altogether and work out his ideas to his own satisfaction.[27]

Still, he found much of his renewed Madison life very enjoyable, especially in these early years. He worked furiously in his garden, played tennis until his back began troubling him too much, and above all zealously guarded his home life from student interference. He returned home from school by 4:30 p.m. as often as possible and gave himself over to his children (two girls and a boy born in Madison, in addition to Corrinne's boy and girl) until they went to bed, then retreated to the study he had built under the clothesline in the basement. There, puffing steadily on cigars, he would write until 2:00 a.m. or so. Between the pleasures of family life and the atmosphere at school, "I had so much energy [that] I didn't know what to do with it."[28] He had accomplished mightily in the extraordinarily favorable circumstances Madison afforded. The draining unhappiness of marital and family troubles, increased drinking and a deepening sense of urgency to leave Madison were all still years away.

2

Williams formulated the major syntheses of U.S. history that he had been mentally preparing in the 1950s through two book-length studies, *The Tragedy of American Diplomacy*, which first appeared in 1959, and *The Contours of American History*, published two years later. *Tragedy* concerned foreign policy and *Contours* focused on domestic developments leading to the corporate state, but the two books can be read together as Williams's foremost intellectual expression.

Tragedy, his most widely read and certainly most influential work among the general public, traced the development of Open Door imperialism from the 1890s through the early cold war. As a sort of point-counterpoint to the claims of George Kennan's *American Diplomacy* (1950) that expansionism had been a product of State Department naivete fumblingly continued afterward, Williams showed that the notion of Empire arose as a solution to late nineteenth-century social crisis and became the *deus ex machina* for national well-being.

U.S. policy-makers sought initially to halt the ongoing division of the globe by existing imperial powers, encourage an increased international volume of trade and production, and promote development American-style in pre-capitalist societies and cultures. The globalization of American economics, antidote to the domestic clash of farmers and labor with capital, demanded an Open Door. Thus, the U.S. could (with only a few exceptions of its own, such as Hawaii and the Philippines) declare itself anticolonial and still become the leading counterrevolutionary force of the twentieth century. Throughout, Williams stressed the importance of economic factors influencing foreign policies, although he did not ignore politics, culture, or psychology.[29]

Many particulars in *Tragedy* had already been expressed in previous articles, but Williams amplified some areas and added new ones. There was more, for example, on Woodrow Wilson's responses to various revolutions (Mexican and Chinese as well as Bolshevik) and the economic imperatives that led him into World War I. Also new were Williams's discussions of Franklin Delano Roosevelt, the New Deal, and how "the nightmare of depression and visions of omnipotence" had led the United States to engage in a world "war for the American frontier" and then into a cold war to preserve and expand the Open Door. Particularly irksome to critics was his continued insistence that the United States should have better accommodated the Soviet Union during and after World War II.

Behind these particulars, Williams had begun to work out his own version of the Spinozan, Frankfurt School, or Diltheyan wholeness as the notion of inner unity within the events, institutions, and personalities of a historical epoch. He did not yet develop the concept of *Weltanschauung* as he would in *Contours of American History* to express the worldview of a time and place. But in analyzing the rise of American imperialism, he argued that it involved a deeply held philosophy, embraced by almost all sections of the community (politicians, intellectuals, farmers, workers, industrialists, and financiers). National prosperity and freedom, these groups had agreed, depended upon unlimited economic expansion. The creative originality of the Open Door policy, that "brilliant strategic stroke" that he had pioneered earlier, reflected a belief that America's economic might was so great that it could conquer without European-style military occupation. The broad outlines of this policy had been conceived well before the Bolsheviks took power in Russia and required only a shift of ideological strategy. But American leaders were not entirely disingenuous when they contrasted communism with the "American System," rather than capitalism as such. Open Door imperialism *was* modern America's capitalism.[30]

The United States could for the moment avoid Europe's far-flung colonial wars of invasion, conquest and repression. But the premise of the Open Door brought the nation into ever increasing conflict with any and all "closed systems," whether European colonialism, fascist hegemony, or popular revolutionary uprisings (Communist or not) to shut national doors and thus permit autonomous economic development. Herein lay the story of most of the history of recent American foreign relations, including participation in two world wars—one completely unnecessary and the other precipitated by a failure to cooperate with the Russians in joint pursuit of collective security—and a ruthlessly destructive cold one. Americans had in the process vitiated their own values and ideals. The nation could reverse course, bring the world back from the verge of nuclear destruction, and allow other peoples to develop as *they* best saw fit. But this broad change would require detaching American democracy and prosperity from imperial economic expansion, much as Charles Beard had envisioned decades earlier.

A good part of Williams's originality in this by-now-familiar argument lay in his presentation. He began his introduction, "History and the Transcendence of the Tragic," by describing the history of U.S. actions in Cuba leading up to the Bay of Pigs invasion. These policies were "not caused by purposeful malice, callous indifference or ruthless and predatory exploitation," and *for that reason* they "contained the fundamental elements of tragedy," a destruction that the hero or protagonist brings upon himself.[31] In the book's conclusion, he returned to this thought, offering a sharp critique with an unmistakeably moral center:

> The tragedy of American diplomacy is not that it is evil, but that it denies and subverts American ideas and ideals. The result is a most realistic failure, as well as an ideological and a moral one; for in being unable to make the American system function satisfactorily without recourse to open-door expansion (and by no means perfectly, even then), American diplomacy suffers by comparison with its own claims and ideals, as well as with other approaches.[32]

Many younger historians who owed Williams serious debts later complained that he had naively suggested American interference could be anything but manipulative and predatory, or was ever intended to be.[33] But he needed this proposition, and not merely for political reasons. His belief went to the heart of his style, epitomized in his proposal to replace the Open Door with "a program for helping other people that is closer to American ideals and also more effective in practice" in bringing world peace and cooperation out of the current destructive chaos. He thereby offered readers an idealistic challenge to "transform the tragedy into a new opportunity for great achievement."[34]

Near the end of the book, Williams similarly posed a series of questions beginning with the phrase, "Isn't it time?" as in time to "stop saying that all the evil in the world resides in the Soviet Union and other communist countries." He desperately wanted to encourage policies that would help reform communism into the real rather than the merely rhetorical pursuit of utopian possibilities; by the same token, he wanted the U.S. to abandon the cold war so as to come to grips with its own internal dilemmas. If Kennan and Schlesinger, Jr., were elitists and moral cynics, as many students comparing relevant texts easily concluded, Williams the heretic was the true patriot and the democrat.

He offered no primrose path to freedom. Only an "open door for revolutions" could achieve what Williams had in mind, and only by "having achieved maturity" could Americans cope with the complexities and dangers that lay ahead. They had every reason to aspire to a "radical but noncommunist reconstruction of American society." But in the short run they needed to evoke and even to assist the "calm and confident and enlightened conservatives" at the centers of power to see the light and steer the nation away from disaster.[35]

The unusual appeal to a mixture of radical ideals and enlightened conservatism had great possibilities. But in 1959, Williams's ideas were daring indeed. The contracted publisher, Braziller, gave Williams a twenty-five hundred dollar advance for the work. But one of the readers, Max Ascoli, editor of the staunchly anticommunist magazine *The Reporter*, "went through the ceiling." Cowed by political pressures, Braziller cancelled the contract but did not demand return of the cash. "You're damn right I'll keep the money," Williams responded. He turned to an agent who got World Publishers, a lesser but reputable house known mostly for their textbooks, to accept it. A second and expanded edition of the book, released in 1963 by Dell, had great success on campus and off.[36]

Initial reviews by professional historians were surprisingly positive for a book that would elicit so much controversy and hostility. *Tragedy* was not yet associated with a major movement to revise major tropes of U.S. history and hence did not challenge or particularly threaten the historical establishment. Nor had broad student and New Left movements, politically receptive to the findings of *Tragedy*, coalesced as yet.

Foster Rhea Dulles, one of the leading traditional diplomatic historians, wrote in the *American Historical Review* that Williams was "brilliant but perverse," a scholar who despite "extensive knowledge" in other disciplines was "obsessed by an almost exclusively economic interpretation" and who "arrogantly dismisses rather than answers what he considers the mistaken ideas of most of his fellow historians." Nevertheless, the book was "stimulating and provocative," enlightening, and in all a "highly interesting contribution to today's great foreign policy debate."[37] Academic blacklist survivor Armin Rappaport, writing in the *Pacific Historical Review*, saw Williams as an "original and decisive thinker" whose thesis of Open Door imperialism, while "plausible and interesting," nevertheless led to "some tenuous if not bizarre and distorted conclusions." And yet the historical profession could use more such "bold and stimulating analysis."[38] Gordon M. Craig, later a president of the American Historical Association, complained that Williams made too many "flat, unsupported," and ultimately unconvincing statements, but was "on solid ground" in dismissing the accepted explanations of American diplomacy as "superficial and naive."[39] Williams had thereby already earned the sobriquet that the *New York Times*, reluctantly respectful, one day hung upon his obituary: the great gadfly or iconoclast.

At least a few major observers outside the academic mainstream but prominent in public life caught Williams's larger importance. James P. Warburg, veteran critic of foreign-policy issues, argued that Williams deserved "the widest possible reading by those, alas, all too few American citizens who are deeply concerned over the future of their country and the future of mankind." If only Williams had included "the impact of the corporation-dominated machine age upon democratic citizenship . . . the failure of religion to sustain a sense of moral responsibility," and the failure of an educational system that now served only "the needs of a parochial, self-contained" society, his work could have been broader still. This, at least, was a warning that Williams sought to heed.

Tragedy's most important reviewer, former New Deal think tank veteran Adolf A. Berle, saluted Williams in the *New York Times Book Review* section for a "brilliant book," one marked by "provocative insights" and a "courageous and essential" attempt to grapple with a vast problem. He particularly agreed that U.S. foreign policy to its discredit did not "accommodate . . . revolutionary changes elsewhere in the world," and that it should learn to work with "social systems different from our own." At the same time, he thought Williams wrong in assuming that America *could* have developed otherwise. He also regretted Williams's adopting certain words—notably "imperialism" and "colonialism"—so far outside the boundaries of the permitted discourse that they hinted at communist propaganda.[40]

Berle countered Williams in terms that would seem curious to scholars generations later, but had long been assumed by 1960. America did expand earlier, Berle readily admitted, but only "to occupy vacant real estate" (thus neatly cancelling out the centuries-old presence and culture of Native Americans). It did acquire overseas influence at the turn of the century, "when real (not semantic) imperialism was rampant," but did not conquer vast populations (likewise cancelling out the Philippines and the various Latin American societies made victims of Gunboat Diplomacy). Former New Dealer Berle insisted that the New Deal had not been designed to "'rationalize corporate development,'" even if the results had gone in that direction. Finally, Williams's recipe for an "Open Door for revolutions" was and had to be "uncritical nonsense." The U.S. could hardly be expected to keep an Open Door to revolutions which went against its own or the larger human interest. Despite these caveats, Berle "anticipated with lively hope" the "more mature development" of Williams's thinking.[41]

Others would say about *Tragedy* that Williams's ideas had actually reached maturity decades earlier, i.e., in the mind of Charles Beard. There was a degree of truth in this observation, for the Beard of *The Idea of the National Interest* (1934), written with G. H. E. Smith, had carefully articulated the economic interests of American nationals leading to involvement in war and had spelled out that war was in essence "one of the fruits of the system" at large rather than a disruption to the system. *The Devil Theory of War* (1936), a very popular essay, dismissed conspiracy theories so as to treat seriously the "impersonal," economic, and social underlying causes of conflict. Most of all, Beard's essays of the late 1930s asked why the U.S. should "have the effrontery to assume that we can solve the problems of Asia and Europe, encrusted in the blood-rust of fifty centuries?" In short, Americans should not deceive themselves with rhetoric about the power of their own ideals. Leaders and especially presidents, as he urged in his final work, *American Foreign Policy in the Making, 1932-1940*, could lead properly only if they dealt in candor with their citizens about what they intended to do and why.[42]

Williams's responses generally, and *Tragedy* in particular, followed this logic only up to a point. Beard had been more concerned with internal developments than foreign policy until the 1930s. He lacked Williams's psychological approach to the mass support of Empire and he did not foreshadow Williams's analysis of the democratic-imperial contradictions in the dreams and strategies of the Founding Fathers. Beard's general attempt was to assess economic influences and the framework of public history and the citizen-as-historian, far more than the particulars of analysis, carried over to Williams. The younger man still might be seen as Beard *revividus*, but mainly in the matter of personal bearing.

In any case, Berle's response and Williams's sudden prominence in the *New York Times* meant that the scholar, not yet forty, was making serious headway and also making waves. A few months later a *Time Magazine* writer attacked the book in no uncertain terms, describing Williams as an unlikely Annapolis graduate.[43] An occasional rising state politician, like future Milwaukee Congressman Henry Reuce, would now spend hours discussing *Tragedy* with the controversial Madison professor.[44] The *Foreign Policy Bulletin* meanwhile asked him for eight hundred words to respond to an essay by Dean Acheson.[45]

More important than all this was Berle's continuing interest. He had used *Tragedy*, Williams recalled, "to begin to get off the containment bandwagon."[46] So he responded with enthusiasm to Williams's invitation to speak in Madison and the two enjoyed "an absolutely magnificent seminar" with graduate students. Amazingly, a year later Berle invited Williams to be his "personal first assistant" dealing with Latin American Affairs in the new Kennedy administration. He was told that he would also sit on the Council on Foreign Relations.[47]

This was a remarkable proposal for several reasons. Understandably, Williams had enormous mistrust for Kennedy's "New Frontier" as yet another "frontier" to conquer, more so as Kennedy intensified the confrontationist cold-war rhetoric in his presidential election drive. "He scares the hell out of me," Williams reflected privately at the time. In mid-campaign, Williams actually wrote a long note to candidate Richard Nixon about the New Frontier, and received an intelligent reply—obviously not from Nixon himself but from someone who understood Williams's point.[48] In the end, according to George Mosse, Williams himself voted for Nixon as the "lesser evil."[49]

Second and more to the point, Kennedy quickly adopted Arthur Schlesinger, Jr., as a house intellectual (or court jester, as some wags suggested). The new president could hardly have brought to power a more violent opponent of the views set out in *Tragedy*. Perhaps, as Williams suggested privately, Berle was warning him in the *Times* to "mature" (as Williams put it, show himself "ready to 'join the system'") and then rise to the top. Schlesinger, Jr., himself had obviously done the same almost fifteen years earlier, with great personal success.

But with Berle and Schlesinger, Jr., in charge of Latin America, "maturity" would have meant joining the Alliance for Progress team, whose plan aimed at dramatically increasing the rise of a Latin American middle class, expanding these nations' export economies, and accelerating the transfer of subsistence lands, inevitably driving rural families from the countryside and encouraging wider use of chemical pesticides as well as toxic industrial substances. This move neatly predicted the course of future U.S. programs for the region, where "economic growth" and regional integration replaced serious attempts at redivision of the highly concentrated pockets of national wealth.[50] In the immediate future, Williams's tenure would clearly have depended upon his quiet acceptance of the Bay of Pigs adventure and Kennedy's personal sponsoring of an imperial counterrevolutionary strike force, the Green Berets. To stay on the team, Williams would have had to accept U.S.-paid and -guided "counter-terror" methods which previewed in the devastated rural villages of Latin (and especially Central) America the widespread military abuses against civilians during the Vietnam War, and even more galling, to accept the flat-out lying denials of covert wrongdoing.[51]

Williams also hesitated for personal reasons. Fred Harvey Harrington urged him on, promising "if nothing else you'll get to read a lot of stuff you wouldn't get to read for thirty years." But he feared uprooting his family. Above all he did not trust the Kennedy clan: "Don't ask me why, I just don't trust them." In light of the Bay of Pigs fiasco and Schlesinger's ignominious role as scholar-activist summoning his talents to deceive the public, Williams later reflected, "Thank God! I would have had to resign before I'd even found an apartment to live in!"[52]

An ugly political sequel followed this refusal to serve. In 1960-61, the House Committee on UnAmerican Activities demanded to examine the still-unpublished manuscript of Williams's next book. The Committee never revealed its reasons for this extraordinary demand, but some members had apparently been inflamed by Williams's public testimony in front of the Wisconsin legislature. They viewed his grant from the leftish Rabinowitz Foundation as an excuse for an intellectual fishing expedition through the troubled waters of one campus, perhaps to chill once more the warming campus political climate nationally. It was a curious moment, as White House initiatives simultaneously moved out of the dreary fifties moods by encouraging an end to the Hollywood Blacklist (John and Jacqueline Kennedy personally attended a premiere of the film *Spartacus* despite American Legion calls for a boycott).[53]

HUAC was not the all-powerful force it had been during McCarthyism's better days. Leading members had disgraced or exposed themselves by their bitter resistance to racial integration as well as their moral turpitude, and civil libertarians, including some who had made appearances on the Madison campus, boldly urged the Committee's abolition. But in an age when the FBI continued to launch furious plots against civil rights leaders and occasionally made spectacular public "discoveries" of current professors' earlier political identities, HUAC and its allies still successfully engaged in intimidation. They certainly remained capable of creating much personal grief for particular victims. Williams had just cause for concern.

Fred Harvey Harrington, by this time en route to being president of the university, assured Williams that he would not be fired, but suggested that he conduct his own defense. As Williams wrote to his intimates, he personally shunned any orchestrated public campaign as a bad defense tactic. Young radical admirers and their older supporters, eager to dramatize his "martyr" status, would doubtless call national attention to the case and do him more harm than good.[54] Friends in the Law School put him in touch with Paul Porter, a major Washington attorney for the labor movement.

Porter "took me up and down and sideways and backward," trying to figure out the logic of the Committee and the proper response.[55] Porter advised him to refuse to hand over the manuscript. HUAC then played him "like a yo-yo," issuing a summons and then, after he had boarded a train from Madison to Washington, cancelling the order. That way his time had been lost and he could not collect any money for the trip. When he finally did get to Washington, Porter's partner Thurman Arnold handled the case. A former New Dealer of note and author of the iconoclastic 1930s classic, *The Folklore of Capitalism*, Arnold advised Williams to get himself off the hook by "paying his respects" to the Committee. Williams dutifully complied, appearing for about ten minutes privately in a "little tête-à-tête" and offering no information beyond himself and his work. Arnold told him that he had "handled it perfectly."[56] The subpoena for his manuscript was dropped, and he left Washington a free man.

Unlike less fortunate witnesses of an earlier era, Williams had not gone to prison nor had his career been ruined. Still, his treatment during a notably liberal Washington administration warned him that intrusions of the state upon dissenting individuals did not ever really go away. If he needed more warning, his treatment at the hands of the Internal Revenue Service, the auditing of his tax records year after year, showed the government had not finished with him.

Back in Madison, the publicity for *The Tragedy of American Diplomacy* and Williams's treatment by Washington had the converse effect of solidifying a radical, dissenting scholarly climate of opinion around him and probably pulled Williams further to the Left. His work and notoriety convinced scores of graduate students that diplomatic history "could have real meaning for the present and could be a pioneering field," as one put it, and that the story of history could be "a vital part of creating, sustaining, and changing a culture," work which required "serious and consequential labor."[57]

Within the decade, he and his doctoral protégés (including Lloyd Gardner and Walter LaFeber, who actually finished under Harrington) earned a national reputation as the "Wisconsin School of Diplomatic History." In the Anglo-American world of historical studies, only the influence of social historians around E. P. Thompson had a more long-lasting effect in any field; it would also be difficult to imagine any other U.S. school of studies (such as the social histories of labor, or women's histories, or the black history field) which continued to have so much effect on scholarship at large.

The reasons for this are not mysterious. Williams created a scholarly following guaranteed to grow steadily in public prestige as well as intellectual importance when the Vietnam conflict and a series of U.S. misdeeds elsewhere drove Williams's points home.

The year of the publication of *Tragedy* saw the appearance of *Studies on the Left*, the first of the U.S. "new left" publications, engineered principally by Williams devotees in the Socialist Club. *Studies* might properly be seen as the delayed political response to the British New Left and to the U.S. civil rights movement. But *Studies* could also be seen as an expression of wider academic stirrings, a profound break from the claims of scholarly "objectivity" so popular among social scientists of the 1950s.

Studies's opening editorial, "The Radicalism of the Disclosure," could easily have been written out of a Williams seminar. In the current climate, so-called "objectivity" was finally "reducible to the weight of authority, the viewpoint of those who are in a position to enforce standards, the value judgments of a not so metaphorical market place of ideas." The editors mounted no claims of their own for scholarly dispassion. On the contrary, they had entered the "scholarly racket" because they wanted to deal with the problems of the real world, not merely to gain a "means of livelihood and security." Their task was not, however, to change society directly, but to commence an "investigation of the origins, purposes, and limitations of institutions and concepts" along paths where liberals and conservatives alike obviously feared to tread. They determined, in a phrase, to create a real community of intellectuals.[58]

The tone was especially consonant with Williams's own self-distancing from the Old Left. *Studies* did not claim to speak for (or to) the "struggling masses," workers and the poor. It obviously did not identify itself with the Communist Eastern Bloc, even while bitterly criticizing most U.S. intellectuals' supine posture before demands of their own security state. It did not look upon the ultra-Right of the Republican party (active in the Birch Society and other such institutions, but soon triumphant in nominating Barry Goldwater for President in 1964) as the main enemy or describe current liberalism as betraying Franklin Roosevelt's heritage. Instead, it pinpointed "corporate liberalism" as the hegemonic ideology of the cold-war age.

If a future Socialist movement were to play a vital role, it had to "cut itself free from the stifling framework of liberal rhetoric and recognize that at heart the leaders of the United States are committed to the warfare state as the last defense of the largescale corporate system." The task of Socialist intellectuals, formulating a "new system of political ideas . . . capable of serving an effective movement for the good of society," could best be accomplished by acknowledging their special status as intellectuals. Unlike the ideals of previous (and future) radical generations to go "to the people" as organizers of unions, civil rights movements, and the poor, they had to stay in the universities.[59]

Williams later warmly recalled his association with these young intellectuals as one of his most fulfilling moments. The members of the Socialist Club and the editors of the journal *Studies On the Left* had made important contributions to the understanding of important concepts like "corporate liberalism," and to the dialogue about the intellectuals' possible contributions to the civil rights and early anti–Vietnam War movements. As much as anyone, they had been responsible for the intellectual side of the New Left. For the young participants, as Saul Landau noted later, it was Williams himself who created the intellectual excitement, stirred young radicals to serious study, and convinced them of the possibility of a conceptual breakthrough that could have large implications for the world beyond the universities.[60]

Williams could certainly have played a direct role in *Studies*, but he chose very consciously to remain in the background. In part, he wanted to give the new generation its own opportunity to make mistakes and learn. Secondly, he had his work to do, and it kept him hopping. Thirdly, as he wrote privately to Warren Susman, the *Studies* editors had too much of the "left-over nuttiness of the 1930s image that they carry around in their bones," with a built-in proclivity to believe that they had to shock in order to be radical.[61]

Still, he felt he had "calmed them down" on some issues, and that his presence had a special effect upon the magazine's leading figures. Martin J. Sklar, former hod carrier and later major theorist of "corporatism," was a particular Williams favorite and a moving spirit of the publication, raising money and gathering subscriptions on the road. Saul Landau, a national leader of the Fair Play for Cuba Committee, was another fundraiser as well as editor. Nina Serrano, Saul Landau's wife and yet another Williams devotee, worked in the *Studies* office with Gerth student and cultural critic Eleanor Hakim. James Weinstein, destined to be one of the more important older intellectuals of the 1970s-90s Left, had moved to Madison after dropping out of Columbia graduate school, made himself *Studies'* leading editor, and provided his own funds to the magazine. He recalled meeting casually with Williams over coffee to talk about the direction of the journal. Weinstein's well-received monograph, *The Corporate Ideal in the Liberal State, 1900-1918*, like Martin J. Sklar's notable essays on the rise of corporate government, came out of a collective dialogue in which Williams traded ideas and, more than anyone else, reformulated them for an increasingly large intellectual following.[62]

The importance of *Studies on the Left* was far greater than its circulation of a few thousand. *Studies* reached out to encourage the creation of intellectual networks across the more liberal campuses and major cities. Occupying this historical juncture, *Studies* was perfectly placed to shape the intellectual development of the New Left. Indeed, many of the emerging political leaders were connected with it in one way or another, as writers, editorial associates, or full-scale editors. By the early 1960s, Williams had thereby founded a "school" twice over.

The journal also had a more immediate function. Like Williams himself, it first of all attracted respectful interest from a section of liberal academia tired of the stifling intellectual atmosphere of the 1950s. Thus political scientist Andrew Hacker offered a positive, if patronizing, estimate in 1960 for the well-read *Commentary* magazine. Trained at the University of Wisconsin where "the radical tradition runs deep," the editors, "serious about their radicalism," would likely have an "important influence" over American scholarship in the years ahead.[63] *Studies* writers sought not "the abolition of private property or the establishing of human equality by political means" so much as a "rational social order" through better education and knowledge. Hence they remained safely "theoretical" or "utopian" Marxists. These graduate students, Hacker predicted, would soon enough find well-paying positions from which to launch "recognized and acceptable" careers.[64] C. Vann Woodward, highly esteemed author of *The Strange Career of Jim Crow*, similarly welcomed the journal a few years later as a "sign that graduate students are still alive and kicking in spite of all the professors can do to anesthetize them."[65] If only a few years earlier Turnerian historian Lee Benson had feared to articulate his Marxist predilections, *Studies* made radicalism, or at least cerebral radicalism, respectable, allowing many students to discuss and publish in their areas of interest without fear of sanction.[66]

3

A subtly subversive element within historical revisionism of the 1950s meanwhile made possible the boldest moves by Williams and his students beyond the realm of foreign policy. If Arthur Schlesinger, Jr., had shifted from a model of bureaucratic socialism to guided liberalism in the post-Progressive mode, others influenced by Marxism in their youth rebutted Progressivism more definitively and in so doing opened up new conceptual territory.

Political scientist Louis Hartz's *The Liberal Tradition in America* (1954) was seen at the time of its publication as an exemplary text of anti-Progressive thought. By removing from consideration the same historical phenomena that Reinhold Niebuhr had dismissed as irrelevant to American experience—expropriation, exterminism, slavery, and international forms of exploitation—Hartz managed to create the picture of an American social order based almost wholly upon the principles of classical liberalism. American society had been so free of major conflicts (rather amazingly putting aside the Civil War, labor uprisings, and continuing race conflicts as well) that Americans had not even recognized their freedom from European ideologies. Hence, on the conservative side of Hartz's critique, the Populists' strictures against greedy capitalists had indeed necessarily been irrational "demonology."

But if, in Hartz's account, nearly all Americans were white and actually or potentially middle-class, they had nevertheless thrashed about in the psychic threat of personal failure that individualism imposed upon the national mentality. Influenced by a background in Marxism but even more by a detached iconoclasm and the contemporary predilection for psychologizing, Hartz also implied (though he did not state openly) that the seamless "Americanism" prompted international crusades with no clear positive purpose, like Woodrow Wilson's entry into World War I and perhaps even the current crusading anticommunism.[67] This was not at all what Schlesinger, Jr., and Niebuhr had in mind.

Richard Hofstadter had already gone still further in several key respects. Without doubt the most widely read American historian of his generation (although by only a small fraction of Charles Beard's earlier public audience), Hofstadter carried his own sense of high irony into a major new interpretation of history. He later insisted that his *American Political Tradition* (1948), essentially a series of biographical essays, stemmed directly from his earlier Marxist training. In youth he had been a Communist, albeit keeping this secret from his academic advisor and mentor, Merle Curti. From his first published essay, on Charles Beard, he had worked with the tradition of the Progressive historians, raising sharp questions about them and revising their interpretations. He responded more to historiography than to historical evidence.[68]

In the *American Political Tradition* he had, by and large, reversed the Progressive optic. Hofstadter's America was in fact no democracy corrupted by capitalism, but rather a business-minded society from top to bottom—Hofstadter also conveniently ignored the bottom, for the most part—with the elite being the only truly "class-conscious" sector of it. This "democracy in cupidity" need not be admired, but it needed to be understood without the old rose-colored glasses of the Popular Front's historians who had always seemed to see the heroic plain folk rising somewhere in the distance. The real heroes (and he saw a few, notably the abolitionist Wendell Phillips) had worked against the grain. Arguably, they were the real radicals. *The Age of Reform* (1955), however, pushed the conservative edge of this perspective further. As he had earlier praised slavery spokesman John C. Calhoun's shrewdness and intelligence, Hofstadter viewed reformers like William Jennings Bryan altogether unsympathetically as frustrated capitalists, and the Populists as prototypes for anti-Semitism and McCarthyism.[69]

Appealing for an "intelligent conservatism," Hofstadter seemed, like Hartz, also to be warning vaguely against the illusions of liberalism, in suggesting that the perpetual scramble for materialistic advance had not necessarily been worth the effort. But he suffered the defects of his status as the cold-war liberals' favorite historian, so much so that he appeared to accentuate just the aspects of his theory that they endorsed. He gained entrance into their inner circles of influence and prestige, but at a heavy cost. *Their* Hofstadter (an interpretation which he did not at the time resist) looked suspiciously upon the American masses as responsible for the dangerous drifts in national life, and hoped for a far-sighted elite to hold them in check.[70] The rightward-drifting liberals of the opinion magazines were not alone. If some sophisticated graduate students read the *American Political Tradition* and the *Age of Reform* as subtly radical critiques of liberalism, cold-war liberal professors taught them to a generation of undergraduates as clever proofs of America as a business civilization and of radicalism as perhaps interesting but finally irrelevant to the main process.[71]

This perspective had its own internal limits. Hofstadter's work and that of other contemporary revisionists remained essentially a revisionist critique of Progressive history. It therefore never gained the solidity and finality of the Progressives' effort, except as it tended toward vulgar celebration of America in the writings of Daniel Boorstin, for instance, that Hofstadter himself disdained.[72] Few of his readers or even his academic colleagues realized how unstable Hofstadter's ideas were and how greatly they changed over time.

Hofstadter swam for more than a decade in a current of fervently anti-Beardian publicists destined to become key neoconservative operatives, corporate fundraisers for conservative think tanks, and "Reagan Revolution" favorites such as Irving Kristol, S. M. Lipset, and Nathan Glazer.[73] But when he reevaluated his positions on Beard, Turner, and literary historian V. L. Parrington during the later 1960s, he found them far more insightful than he had remembered. They had something extremely important to say, even if their views might be outdated in historical particulars. Always prone to considering himself politically detached, telling friends he had "nowhere to go," Hofstadter suggested late in life that consensus theories failed to explain American life and that radical historians (including some of his own favorite students) were destined to have an important impact on historians of the future.

Unlike his former associates who became steadily more vulgar in their conservative views and rabidly opposed the New Left scholars, he had actually drifted through conservatism, never really recovering from his youthful disillusionment. Yet he had never lost faith in the possibilities of historical scholarship. For Hofstadter, it had always possessed the great virtue, in an age of increasing nihilism and academic positivism, of a potentially humanizing art.[74]

Williams had sharply criticized Hofstadter's *Age of Reform* on its publication. He was too kind to accuse the book of disingenuous rationalizations for Empire-building. But he argued that the so-called "psychic crisis" to which Hofstadter attributed the late nineteenth-century surge of U.S. expansionism could hardly explain the "relationships between a given conception of the world, entertained by individuals and groups with power, and subsequent events." Whether or not Americans of the time had been locked into a "general neurosis," one had to explain specific economic and functional forms taken, and the consequences as well. Hofstadter had clearly failed to do so, a flaw that applied to much of his work.[75]

But Williams shared more space with Hofstadter than seems obvious at first. He dealt with many of the same subjects and treated more than a few from a roughly similar angle, the analysis of *mentalité* in the leading figures of the time. Indeed, as in the case of Abraham Lincoln, who they both criticized harshly, they often stood remarkably close. They created a perspective at equal distance from the cold-war liberal re-reading of history by Arthur Schlesinger, Jr., however much they might carry the implications in different political directions. Williams, far more than Hofstadter, moved beyond critique of historiography and toward synthesis. There was another key difference, however. Hofstadter was the veritable bridge between the New York literary world and the university. Williams was by contrast the outsider, the non-Easterner at large.[76]

Taken from yet another vantage point, the turn of Hofstadter, David Potter, and other noted 1950s historians toward a quasi-psychological view of an American "character," had its origins not only in the abandonment of Beard (or Marxism) but also in the commonplace reading of Freud, as in the influence of "culture and personality" interdisciplinary studies of the 1920s-40s. Influenced by anthropology and psychoanalysis, its practitioners, especially anthropologists and sociologists such as Columbia's Margaret Mead and Yale's John Dollard, sought to understand the origins of group behavior and tradition. During the 1930s the influence of such anthropologists as Mead and Ruth Benedict had been heavily antiracist and relativist, suggesting that America had much to learn from other cultures, especially in regard to gender roles and racial attitudes.

Cold-war intellectuals, placing the United States at the pinnacle of human possibility, of course abandoned and often condemned such relativism, viewing American achievements and even the American character as models for other societies to follow. But they strived to encompass interdisciplinary methods as a major step forward in historical understanding. On the overwhelmingly positive side for optimists such as Potter, the "culture of abundance" had shaped the American character for the better. Although they feared the alienation in contemporary America, and they bemoaned the poverty of African Americans, they regarded both these developments as products of specific cultural and psychological dysfunctions rather than the effects of capitalism.[77]

A younger generation of scholars used the available cultural methodologies for another and very different purpose: to escape the economism of the Progressive historians without lapsing into cold-war ideological assumptions. By the later 1950s and 1960s, the "new social history" sympathetically investigated the lives of the lower classes, minorities, and women. Adopting anthropological methods, it argued for a complexity and a humane nobility of ordinary people, even those ill-placed to transform society from below. Herbert Gutman, who entered the University of Wisconsin graduate school just three years after Williams (and with many of the same mentors), would become the major proponent of this view and for a time the most admired U.S. radical historian after Williams.[78]

Williams, caught between radical generations, retained the economistic frame of the Progressives but styled within it a psychological version of national character and the individuals who epitomized its workings. In this way, Williams depicted expansionism taking shape not as (in the crude Marxist version) the scheme of wicked capitalists but as a common belief of Americans that expansionism would somehow resolve or at least postpone serious social problems.

Still another distinct and seemingly unrelated trend in scholarship also facilitated Williams's personal growth and potential impact. In the unlikely district of Western history, long dominated by perhaps the most triumphalist believers in democratic expansionism, the definite beginnings of a political shift could be felt. Walter Prescott Webb, dean of scholars of the American West and in most of his past interpretations a great devotee of the white settler, cast a remarkable shadow with *The Great Frontier* (1952). After a lifetime assessing U.S. expansionist assumptions beyond the given territorial limits, Webb had quietly and on his own come to the rather staggering conclusion that expansionism had its own inherent logic beyond any economic, or social, or ethical purpose. Americans were hooked.[79] This conclusion implicitly challenged the entire weight of the cold-war liberal enthusiasm for Schlesinger, Jr.'s model Democrat, Andrew Jackson. Perhaps, as a small but significant trickle of "good Indian" Western films seemed to suggest, expansionism had actually undercut the democratic ethos.[80]

The Williams who gave his wife a three-volume set of Freud and who referred repeatedly in later years to psychological symptoms in society and the individual shared many of the same sources as his cold-war liberal intellectual critics. But he saw the issues through different eyes. The deep criticisms of American culture that he and Warren Susman derived from Frankfurt School theorists like Theodor Adorno and Max Horkheimer, whose few translated works they had traded in Oregon in the early 1950s, fell onto rocky soil among most of the intellectual elite. Complaints about the Frankfurt School often followed the view of David Riesman: America was not at all "authoritarian," big business was certainly not "ruthless," and criticisms of the anticapitalist kind made by Adorno and his colleagues were completely outdated, if ever relevant to American society.[81] But what if Williams tied the Frankfurt School to Webb's revised history with a new conceptual knot?

The implications of this for Williams's published work lay years away. But to judge from scattered correspondence, Williams was reading Marx, Thomas Hobbes, John Locke, Emmanuel Kant, and the writings of American leaders like Jefferson and Madison, classical economic theory, sociology of knowledge, and social theory, always searching for his own synthesis. In the future, he would make the argument openly that the market society (to which Richard Hofstadter's circle of future neoconservatives naturally attributed the democratic virtues) was in fact the "Great Heresy" in human history.

4

Williams's *Contours of American History* (1961), his magnum opus, confirmed his status as the controversial and unpredictable leader of the budding corporate critique from the *Studies On the Left* circle, and in doing so applied the insights of *Tragedy of American Diplomacy* to virtually the entirety of American history. But in attempting a major synthesis of historical information and psychological or behavioral insight, *Contours* did still more. Little understood at the time, it set a final note to the critical revisionism of the historical revisionism of the 1950s by recuperating crucial threads of Progressive history and reaching far into the future interpretations of Western history. With all its abundant flaws, it is one of the most remarkable U.S. history books ever written.

Turned down repeatedly by major commercial presses, *Contours* saw light from the same World Publishing of Cleveland that had brought out *Tragedy*. A tiny left-wing press, Prometheus Books, quickly bought up several thousand copies and stamped on its own imprimatur, expanding the book's circulation widely among the existing "progressive" (i.e., Left) circles outside the university.[82]

Contours was Williams's most ambitious work, his most enduring and influential among historians, if too difficult for most of the popular readers of *Tragedy* as well as for many intellectuals in other fields. At a time when observers of historical interpretation began to complain sharply of excessive specialization and lack of synthesis, Williams offered a big-picture approach. Just as newer scholars from all sides commenced to pummel the 1950s consensus history which saw America (in John Higham's words) "coming to seem a much more homogeneous country, more uniform and more stable" and also more cheerful than any previous historian had imagined, Williams confounded critics by embracing aspects of consensus history only to shift the interpretation decisively. Indeed, if Frederick Jackson Turner and Charles Beard had sketched out the major interpretations of U.S. history, Williams was arguably their proper successor, for the good reason that he had them always in the back of his mind.

To change and update the metaphor, no other contemporary radical scholar in any field, not Marcuse and not even Mills, had sought to systematically apply a critique to the national experience.[83] As James Livingston observed, writers as different as Mills, Marcuse, Hannah Arendt, and Norman O. Brown found their various trips through the American mind "only cause for debunking and despair."[84] Williams discovered a useable past, as the Progressive historians used to say, because he knew what he was looking for.

Williams sought to periodize American capitalism in ways that economic historians considered overly bold and to interpret that periodization through the thoughts of the ruling classes as the ruling thoughts of the age (hence taking a page from Marx). He therefore took American thought as a whole seriously, in ways that American historians had rarely done and that the Ivy League intellectual historians in particular had studiously avoided. Writing of "freedom," the Founding Fathers and others had not meant something abstract as the intellectual historians suggested, but something definite, concrete, economic, and social in the ways the age had allowed them to see complex issues.

If U.S. history could be described in that way, without the flagrant use of the Marxist theoretical apparatus so obvious in the hands of the greatest European historians, something large would have been accomplished. Williams did not see, or perhaps could not have recognized, that in the attempt much of the precision of overall coherence might slip away. Readers often had to stumble across large thoughts, as Williams did himself. Many of his students, primed by assignments in Hegel's *Phenomenology of Mind* for George Mosse's European history classes, had learned to move from one page to another hoping for insights rather than expecting to understand every word. Others simply felt befuddled and gave up the effort.

Contours, even at its weakest, possessed another large virtue that disarmed many would-be critics in advance. Placing individuals within an all-encompassing and increasingly destructive system, Williams nevertheless treated them with personal sympathy—at least until the early decades of the twentieth century. Once again as in *Tragedy*, students and others could read Williams as "pro-American," a radical who saw great potential good in his society even when he viewed the outcome of their actions with distress.[85] Williams thereby went far to reinvigorate the history of ideas in U.S. historical scholarship at large by recasting the dialogue about liberalism and conservatism, showing the similarities of the two intellectual systems as no one had earlier. In all this and despite his stress upon *system*, he seemed always to suggest that with sufficient knowledge and sympathy, individual actors *could* have exerted themselves toward better ends—just as the reader might, whatever his or her place in the nation.

If *The Tragedy of American Diplomacy* had drawn heavily on the legacy of Beard, *Contours* was determinedly original. In his sweeping panorama, Williams detected three *Weltanschauungen* informing the national experience, beginning with the colonial and early national periods (1740-1828) and their "mercantilism," the favorite Anglo-American system of economic growth and regulation.[86] This age was succeeded, or subverted, by that of "laissez nous faire" (1819-1896) which led, at the end of the nineteenth century, to the present system of "corporate capitalism" or "corporate syndicalism."[87] As usual strongly iconoclastic, Williams praised certain individuals often criticized in standard liberal historical accounts—such as John Quincy Adams, Henry Clay, Thaddeus Stevens, Charles Evans Hughes, and Herbert Hoover—who despite their limitations saw the American dilemma and appreciated the need for community. Williams consequently looked darkly at those other national heroes, including Jefferson, Jackson, Lincoln, Wilson, and Roosevelt, who avoided the nation's fundamental problems by turning to expansion and/or war.

But one can approach the dense historical details of *Contours* more easily, perhaps, from the ethical or philosophical standpoint that Williams brought to the text. He began with the proposition that market values had to be seen as the "great heresy of human history" rather than (as in the standard Marxist accounts) an unhappy progenitor of the growth that would lead inevitably to a deferred communal gratification. Williams's own perspective would have been most familiar to late nineteenth-century social-ists, especially William Morris, and it permeated the popular perception of capitalism's special cruelties. Memories of the handicraft tradition and the evocation of a vanishing communal warmth filled the iconography of European socialism and overflowed into the various rituals, from choral choices to holiday costumes. Morris's favorite illustrator, Walter Crane, captured this sensibility, and Williams must have seen Crane's illustrations of British and American socialist volumes. The popularity of early anthro-pologist Lewis Henry Morgan's work among socialists, attributing communal values to neolithic societies, deepened the sentiment.[88]

Discredited or displaced by fascination with industrialization and by the accessibility of consumer goods to the Western working classes, the mood passed but never entirely vanished. Humanity, according to an argument renewed by liberation theologians shortly before Williams's death, had required a considerable degree of cooperation throughout its eons of social evolution or it would simply not have survived. Humanity would finally recover its capacity for cooperation or surely destroy itself. Not susceptible to proof or disproof, this sentiment might be called the Christian Socialist kernel of Williams's historical perspective.

But unlike other Christian Socialists, including the Reinhold Niebuhr of younger days, Williams looked sympathetically through the prism of his-toric development at the ways the system had been successively reordered. In *Contours*, mercantilism was seen as the last of the somewhat cooperative systems, compromising its sense of community or common values with nationalist imperatives (such as expropriating the wealth of other nations) and the large-scale African slave trade, but still retaining a notion of com-monweal and a belief that the social elite *could* rule judiciously.

Williams had grappled to comprehend how the American break-through into new dimensions of freedom had also engaged the opposite possibility, conquest beginning with indigenous societies at hand. He had been ruminating on questions of pre-capitalist expansionism since his days in Oregon with his friend, economist Robert Campbell, so the interest he now had in mercantilism was not strictly new. But as he wrote to Warren Susman in 1958, he discovered in an essay by economic historian Curtis Nettles (which he had reprinted in *The Shaping of American Diplomacy)* a suggestion that he had not pursued before, the role of British mercantil-ism in creating an *American* mercantilism. And he added with a sense of difficult accomplishment:

> Well, the fiftieth time I read that[,] it finally got through my skull: this is a key insight to the whole period from 1776 to 1825. [The] Articles of Confederation represent a treaty between 13 bunches of damn fools who think each of them can have their own mercantile

empire; [the] constitution is the mercantile state; and the foreign policy is beautiful, concluding with the War of 1812 as a classical mercantile war for trade and the colonies (see Jefferson's change of heart on land policy, et al.) and the Monroe Administration with John Quincy [Adams] as Sec[retary of] State and the Monroe Doctrine as the document of mature American mercantilism. Then we get the wild spell of laissez faire, and back to corporate capitalism in the 1893-1903 era. Suddenly Madison becomes comprehensible as the American mercantilist philosopher: so ideas and economics come together in a fascinating way in the minds of the characters themselves as well as in ours. And Johnny Locke, of course, suddenly makes sense as the mercantilist natural law philosopher. I am excited about this, as this paragraph indicates . . . [89]

Williams used this shrewd and original interpretation to set the philosophic linchpin or mainspring for *Contours* with the compromise of democracy and Empire. Arriving at the end of the Age of Mercantilism when ideas of national welfare had turned into corruption and special interest, the American Revolution definitely espoused the values of liberty and democracy. It also opened a Pandora's box of individualism's potential effects. In doing so, it recuperated the "modernization" theories proposed by Schumpeter or Karl Polyani, but with a twist. A shadow American socialism lay always, even in the most unexpected places, within the opposition to the imperial option.

Lord Shaftesbury, an aristocrat after Williams's heart, had accepted the framework of British mercantilism but sought to curb its excesses. A political and intellectual Renaissance man with real literary style and a typically Tory Radical verve, he hoped to establish a system of Empire that would ease Britain's internal pressures. He also sought to create a workable relation with the colonists, and on that basis showed a remarkable toleration for religious dissenters, arguing that they made good economic citizens. He demanded the supremacy of elected parliaments even while clinging to the monarchical form. And he rejected firmly the emerging notion that poverty was caused by sin rather than economic maladjustment.

Of course, expansionism and mercantilism had their own deep logic. Shaftesbury's intellectual successor, John Locke, disdained the very notion of corporate responsibility. With Locke (Merle Curti had called him "America's philosopher"), individuality became the highest virtue, even while it rested upon the twin foundation of Empire abroad and conforming citizens at home. This vaunted individuality was, then, defined mainly by a near-absolute control of personal wealth. Pleasure and the avoidance of pain, a sort of working definition of what would become Pragmatism, measured the narrow parameters of secularized Puritanism.

Mercantilism in either guise demanded taking the resources from one nation or empire to enrich another: Britain had to best the competitors for the New World. But the North American colonies that the British created would soon enough consolidate their own system sufficiently to prompt the rise of an independent-minded American mercantilist class with a nationalist Lockean orientation. Until the last historical moment before the Revolution, future leaders of the new nation fervently wished to exercise their colonial prerogatives within a broad, Shaftesbury-like definition of the British empire. When this became impossible, the rhetoric and the experience of the Revolution carried them in a new direction. The determined decentralism of the Confederation pointed away from the national consolidation and expansion that mercantilism demanded. But historic logic dragged the actors, some of them uncertain of their own loyalties, in another direction.

Throughout his narrative, Williams had an almost obsessive determination to overturn the accepted hagiography of American heroes, including many of the traditional favorites of liberals and radicals. Examining their rhetoric and action carefully, he found the impulse for national expansion near the kernel of their political being. He offered interesting asides on the worldview and tactics of the Quakers, of Massachusetts' Puritan descendents, of Benjamin Franklin's Philadelphia milieu, and of the various rebels like Nathaniel Bacon who seemed to threaten stability. In the colonial era, Calvinism's heirs held a special fascination because they "asked the right questions and struggled for the right answers" in their struggle for a kind of community. But in Williams's folksy vernacular, he added that

> like the little girl with the curl in the middle of her forehead, these early Puritans had a kink in their ideology; when they went wrong, they went very, very wrong. Devoted to the ideal of a corporate community guided by a strong moral sense, they developed a great talent for misinterpreting any opposition. From the outside, for example, they were prone to view the Indians as agents of the Devil .... The propensity to place Evil outside their system not only distorted the Puritans' own doctrine, it inclined them toward a solution which involved the extension of their system over others.[90]

This interpretation actually marked a return to the critique of Puritanism by the avant-garde crowd around the *Seven Arts* magazine of the late 1910s, fleshed out by Lewis Mumford during the 1920s and 1930s when a young Williams had been reading omnivorously. The cold-war years saw a revival of the Puritans' reputation by Perry Miller and others. Williams sought to preserve their ideal of community while revealing the dangerous implications in their thought that Mumford's generation had noted.

The Virginia dynasty naturally had a special fascination for Williams as the closest approximation to an American royalty. Thus Thomas Jefferson, long honored by radical scholars as the champion of liberty, came to be seen in this light as the key visionary of Empire. He and James Madison buttressed their plan for the American future with the vision of endless expansion. They created the working ideology that W. E. B. DuBois later named the "American Assumption": with sufficient resources every white man could create his own sphere of freedom. Millions of practical-minded settlers lived out the paradox of possessing the liberty to expropriate at will and, if necessary, to destroy everything in their path that they could not turn to profit.

It would be difficult to overstate the originality or radical quality of this interpretation for the field of U.S. history. Previous radicals' attempts had often reduced great national conflicts like the Revolutionary and Civil Wars to raw class interest, a favorite conclusion of turn-of-the-century socialist classics. Or they had, like Herbert Aptheker and other Communist writers, chosen a pantheon of heroes to cheer onward, insisting that the side of the angels would one day be that of class-conscious socialists and communists.[91] Williams would have none of this. Reading the American saga as Greek tragedy, he once more sought the errors not mainly in venality but in human weakness, reading into the minds of the Founding Fathers a well-nigh irresistible temptation offered by "empty" land and the vast economic productivity of the slave-plantation system.

Williams's view of the Founding Fathers, in particular, was an engaged view of major personalities and their dilemmas. John Jay had promoted the idea of expansionism as the road to prosperity and republicanism, even perhaps temporarily abandoning claims to the Mississippi River and New Orleans in return for access to the Spanish Empire and Asia. He could admit that whites had done wrong to Indians but insisted nevertheless that the mercantilist system worked that way. ("It would seem," Williams observed in an ironic offhand parallel to U.S. policy during World War II, "that the principle of unconditional surrender and total war appeared rather early in American history."[92]) Jefferson evaded the problems while Monroe saw the implications clearly. Jefferson's own steady move toward the imperial solution made him seize, unwontedly, what Jay intended. And Madison recognized that republicanism degenerated into conflict when state grew into Empire, without ceasing his own contribution to the direction of things. The point of postrevolutionary settlements had been to try to square the circle of mercantilism, to bring in the new order with efficient upper-class leadership. As Merrill Jensen might well have taught Williams more than a decade earlier, that was the main point of the Constitutional Convention.[93]

In its own waning days, two generations later, mercantilism yielded to a *laissez nous faire* principle that relied flatly on expansion to resolve internal contradictions and conflicts. Echoing the arguments of Lewis Mumford's almost-forgotten *The Golden Day* (1927) with its apotheosis of small-town New England, Williams insisted that the frontier had mainly offered opportunities for self-barbarization, and that Andrew Jackson epitomized the malignantly burgeoning individualism. Williams thus turned upon its head *The Age of Jackson*, Schlesinger, Jr.'s sentimentalization of the Democratic Party alliance of working people and entrepreneurs. Apart from ignoring Jackson's well-earned reputation as one of the most murderous enemies ever faced by American Indians and his deep personal attachment to the South's "peculiar institution," as many other scholars would point out, Schlesinger, Jr., had willfully refused to see how cupidity had triumphed over commonwealth.[94] The same transparent parallel which led Schlesinger, Jr., to view Franklin Roosevelt (and later in his own writing, Harry Truman) as rightful heir to Jackson's regime obviously propelled Williams toward his own, nearly opposite conclusions.

When he turned to the later nineteenth century, Williams added even more remarkably to the changing currents of historical sympathies. As the contemporary civil rights movement stirred imaginations, the historical reputation of Abolitionism had sharply revived among scholars and the public at large. Passages were quietly withdrawn from reputable textbooks which for decades had portrayed Abolitionists as madmen and southern blacks as happy children. Leading historians' hostile portrayals of Abolitionist leaders as neurotic malcontents likewise fell out of fashion. Williams pointed out what few on either side of the argument about Abolitionists had noticed. No one had so thoroughly glorified individualism as had the Abolitionists. To an unsympathetic eye, they had urgently wanted to free the slaves but did not put equal effort into providing them with the land they needed to ensure their independence.

Williams touched the most sensitive patriotic chords in his portrait of Abraham Lincoln. Hardly anyone but loyal Confederates had pilloried the Great Emancipator, not even those anti-Reconstructionists (such as film-maker D. W. Griffith) who made Lincoln's assassination into the occasion for a supposedly brutal treatment of beleaguered southern whites. From the Left, boy socialist Carl Sandburg had grown into a beloved popular biographer of the Illinois lawyer. And in the liberal-conservative mainstream, Lincoln had been canonized as the spirit behind U.S. entry into two world wars (and the cold war), the veritable father of the Republican Party. Only in the iconoclastic historiography of moderate conservatives like Richard Hofstadter and David Donald had any respectable scholar dared puncture Lincoln's aura.

But in Williams's eyes, the corporate railroad lawyer become president was, mainly, an empire-builder par excellence. Rather than accept the logic of the Declaration of Independence and the Constitution, which all but promised the right of secession, Lincoln had pressed his goal of national unity at any price. He thus set in place two foundation stones for an unceasing world crusade. The corporation would become the mechanism and rationale for that ultimately self-destructive venture.

Williams brilliantly characterized the rise of the corporation as the emergence of a new model for the social compact. He hit his stride with an analysis of overseas Empire, seen through the eyes of the diplomatic elites and political leaders at the end of the nineteenth century. Unlike traditional radicals who saw American leaders solidly in favor of expansion, Williams detected subtle fissures and hesitations. He also hinted at the premise of a later volume, that farmers' own demands quite as much as corporate interests and sheer nationalism had powered the conquest of Hawaii, the Philippines, and Cuba, as well as influence in China and elsewhere. He showed his strongest card in demonstrating the fallacy of the common assumption that the United States had acquired an empire "in a fit of absent mindedness" (according to the popular phrase about England), almost against the national will. No great empire had ever been created with inattention or ease, he observed.

Williams carried this perspective forward in a savage critique of Woodrow Wilson, and of the U.S.'s entry into the First World War as the act of a reckless empire-builder. As much as Harry Truman would be for neoliberals of the 1990s, Wilson had been granted iconic status among 1950s cold-war liberals through discrediting the popular ignominy heaped on him in his last years of office. Wilson biographer Arthur S. Link, a severe antagonist of Williams, portrayed the president as a finely tuned intellect, a magnificent reformer, and a dedicated idealist doomed by a tragic turn in world events. Link made just as little as possible of Wilson's other side, quite apart from the war: his racial policies, the very worst in generations of the presidency; his antienvironmental giveaway, the release of massive federally protected lands to Western states' developers and the consequent drastic reduction in future national parks; his imperial invasion of Mexico; and his direction of the nation's most violent and repressive red scare ever.[95]

Williams saw Wilson as a fellow historian who had, however, early set his sights upon Empire, struck a grand deal with the corporations for a refined profit system, and brought his overweening ego into the catastrophic world scene. Wilson had determined to make the world safe for U.S. economic expansionism, committing vast lives and resources to that goal. Above all, he made the U.S. into a formidable counterrevolutionary world power from Mexico to Russia, meanwhile turning his back on

Chinese nationalists and repeatedly invading the smaller nations of Latin America. Williams used Wilson once again to delve more fully into the theory of corporatism as the major *Weltanschauung* of modern American society.[96] From the end of the nineteenth century, American leaders had drawn drastic conclusions about the change they intended to bring to the society at large. In a drive to rationalize the economy and increase production, a kind of oligarchic rule had encompassed government, big business, labor leaders, and large farmers. Individualism had indeed been subverted by this change, but without creating a genuine community.

The core idea of this perspective was not new to Williams. Herbert Croly had advanced a version of it early in the century, glorifying in its triumph during World War I. A host of *New Republic* writers gleefully greeted Wilson's War because they believed that corporatism consolidated a system of potentially benevolent elites, guided by the best minds (obviously, their own). A few keen-eyed socialist theorists saw the same phenomena of consolidation but from a harshly critical perspective, outlining the passage of private capitalism to a corporate-led state capitalism with the collaboration of craft workers and the petty bourgeoisie. These socialists had even noted the critical connection of state hegemony with the acceleration of postcolonial, economic imperialism, and in that specific sense, they foreshadowed Williams, more than any others.[97]

A school of rather conservative business historians had subsequently, especially since the 1940s, tended to use corporatism as a way to explain the logic of business organization as the proper model for an evolving society.[98] Traditional left-wing scholars less interested in "system," or casting it in familiar Marxist dichotomies of class interests, had been inclined to write off this business history as mere apologism. Williams took it seriously enough to borrow the logic while shifting the interpretation.

Several of Williams's students were to elaborate better than Williams himself some of the main implications of corporatism for the twentieth century. Labor unions, for instance, achieved recognition as part of a corporate system. Their leaders, such European immigrants as Samuel Gompers and Sidney Hillman, could be made an important part of the corporate order.[99] Wise businessmen, from the National Civic Federation to electronics magnate Gerald Swope, had foreseen the process, and even encouraged unionization under certain circumstances.[100] A psychological or ideological penetration of Woodrow Wilson showed how the system came together at its administrative center, with Protestant values merged into the marketplace and expansion as the only possible American system.[101] McCormick and Michael J. Hogan, in particular, later applied corporatism to explain twentieth-century U.S. foreign policy, thus providing a more complete explanation than Williams supplied with his Open Door thesis in the *Tragedy of American Diplomacy*.[102]

Williams himself added the conceptual final touches, in a sense, by portraying Herbert Hoover as the last of the maximum leaders to seek a kind of internal solution to the problem of business's expansive needs, rather than looking to Empire. In that light, Hoover, the goat of the Depression, looked better, while Roosevelt (still seen by liberals as the greatest figure of the century) looked far worse. One could suggest—as Communist historian Herbert Aptheker did—that Williams had in this sense finally come home to Charles Beard; indeed some ironically concluded that Williams was "more Beardian than Beard."[103]

This was not entirely off the mark, but Williams took Beard for the larger thought of an age and a mood discredited by later liberal and conservative thinkers. Lewis Mumford, Van Wyck Brooks, Waldo Frank, and other heterodox radical intellectuals of the 1920s-30s had rejected the Wilsonian solutions and strove in a variety of ways to project images of possible communities. Dreading the prospect of another world war, they had hoped that historic recollections of realized communities or small-scale models of cooperative living (such as the new towns of the Tennessee Valley Authority, or the "garden cities" planned for several states) might provide ways to turn America's best energies inward. Only the pressure of fascism, and the popular support of the New Deal, had reconciled them to Roosevelt's programs.[104]

The last few chapters of *Contours* touched oddly on various aspects of American life reshaped by imperial ends, such as the ways in which labor leaders (including Walter Reuther, often idealized by cold-war liberals) shared basic international objectives with business leaders. Or the mighty moralists of the age, like theologian Reinhold Niebuhr, who had blessed the emerging military-industrial complex as a work of righteousness, concluding that Americans could retain their morality by accepting the logic of business, i.e., endless expansionism. "But Christ, and Marx and Freud as well," wrote Williams in a characteristic passage,

> had insisted that the only important frontier was man in society—not man on a frontier. To them, the frontier was harmful not merely because it offered an escape from difficulties that needed to be faced and resolved; that was but a minor point. To them, the frontier was harmful because it was precisely what Turner called it: an escape from even the chance to become fully human. Hence Christ and Marx and Freud quite understood the vital function of a Utopia. Unlike Dewey and Niebuhr, they put stars in their philosophic sky. Such an ideal was essential if men were to move beyond the enervating and ultimately dehumanizing stalemate of existence.[105]

That passage fairly encapsulated the peculiar writing style and moral vision of Williams, which along with an absence of footnotes puzzled his sympathizers and offered his critics fuel for counterattack on various grounds. Hardly anyone noticed the other oddly significant methodological note in the volume. In his acknowledgments section, alongside credits to Mosse, Gardner, Warren Susman, Harvey Goldberg, Hesseltine, Jensen, and Hans Gerth, among others, Williams offered a paragraph tribute to Marx, adding that a passage in the Socialist giant's correspondence concerning the concept of "feudal socialism" had "probably" moved him toward "the questions and research that produced this interpretation of American history."[106] He did not identify the passage, but he apparently referred to a mention of the concept in Engels's correspondence with Marx, finally published in English in 1955. Here, Engels describes Marx's distinction between different kinds of socialism, essentially feudal, utopian, and "scientific."[107]

But something was decidedly lacking here in Williams's own logic. His "reactionary" statesmen, like John Quincy Adams, earn the highest praise and not only because they identify the ills of the rising bourgeoisie. Marx and Engels (with perhaps the exception of their literary tastes, as for the pronounced French royalist Honoré de Balzac) had relatively few flattering words for Tory radicals or Tories, and then only in contrast to capitalism's apologists. Williams, understandably lacking Marx and Engels's confidence in a future proletarian revolution, by contrast actually identified with "feudal socialism" as superior to the development of anarchic individualism.

One critic suggested, decades later, that Williams had repeatedly missed his best opportunity to clarify his methodology and his philosophical assumptions; his impact upon historical study and especially Marxist-influenced study would suffer as a result.[108] He could be blamed too easily, however. If Williams remained vague, Marx and Engels had been almost as vague in references to the meaning of pre-capitalist collectivism and its significance for the post-capitalist future. At most—and Williams would repeatedly use this insight—Marx had noted that capitalism dissolved the older forms of village life. Yet, the aging Marx struggled in his notebooks with the possibility that capitalism could possibly be overleaped by backward societies in revolution.[109] Williams echoed the popular views of late nineteenth-century socialists like William Morris that capitalism had been a monstrous interruption in human development. But this insight or belief related approximately at best to Marxism or to most of white American experience.

Contours' critics hardly noted these fine points, however. According to Williams's recollections, Henry Steele Commager called Williams and they spoke for some time about the book, but the *New York Times* killed the review that had been commissioned from him.[110] The first noted commentaries came from conservatives, and were characterized by a vituperation rare to scholarly discourse. Williams had plainly made nervous the self-avowed pluralists who celebrated 1950s America and looked uneasily upon the fast-changing scene. If they had earlier failed to demonize him as a pro-communist, they sought now to drum him out of intellectual respectability. "One cannot exclude the possibility that [this book] was intended as an elaborate hoax," declared Oscar Handlin in the *Mississippi Valley Historical Review*, and "that its author has been enjoying himself by ingeniously pulling the legs of his colleagues." Williams's interpretations were simply "perverse," his writing style parodied "the literary striving of unskilled freshmen," and large sections of the book were "altogether farcical." The book, in short, was a "total disaster," permeated by "pervasive wrongheadedness," and inviting "no form of rational discourse." "Enough," Handlin concluded woodenly, "This much can certainly be said for the book: it is original. There has never been anything like it before."[111]

The acceptance of Handlin's polemic at face value by the editors of the *Mississippi Valley Historical Review* suggested how far a wing of the scholarly establishment might go, and how far others would permit them. Critics wondered aloud if Handlin's own maudlin treatments of American history would have been turned over to a radical historian for review, or whether those of various other respectables, Samuel Eliot Morison to Arthur S. Link to Arthur Schlesinger, Jr., would have been allowed to be attacked in such a scurrilous fashion in the leading journal of Americanists. Not likely. Indeed, the subsequent shift of the profession leftward brought nothing like the crudeness of these attacks.

Younger historians in particular considered Handlin to be overstepping the bounds of scholarly propriety. "Cheap ridicule," "bullying," and "a scandalously intemperate polemic" had no place in a professional journal, according to immigration historian John Higham.[112] Williams's fellow graduate student at Madison but also a staunchly anti-Communist liberal, Higham even took to the pages of *Studies On the Left* to celebrate Williams's "patriotic radicalism" and his originality, and to rationalize the "almost vertiginous complexity of application and incident" involved in the writer's unique thought process. If not entirely persuaded—as a self-described liberal, Higham could hardly be persuaded by an "anti-liberal" text—he nevertheless insisted that Williams had the merit of dealing "more extensively and strenuously" with the relations of freedom and community that any previous writer hitherto.[113] In his insightful letter to the *Mississippi Valley Historical Review*, Higham also pointed out Handlin's real intent besides blackening Williams's reputation: he meant to deliver a blow at Charles Beard. Although a student of Beard's own pupil, Arthur Schlesinger, Sr. (a relation fraught with still more ironies), Handlin had as early as 1942 dismissed Beard's influence on subsequent U.S. historical scholarship, as if engaging in scholarly wish fulfillment.[114]

Other conservatives tended to be equally hostile and only slightly less polemical. Williams, according to John Braeman, was simply "naive and wrongheaded." As a historian, he failed by attempting "to force the whole of the American experience into the straitjacket of an economic interpretation of history," making it appear that only "the dollar sign" counted as "a dominant motif force" in American history.[115] James Malin, who had hosted Williams at a Kansas regional history session in 1957 and was himself known as a vituperative critic of big-state liberalism, could not get past his impression that Williams proposed unfair limits upon the American magic of success. The pragmatic national confidence that "both parties to a business transaction may gain, and that there are no known limits to natural resources, except that man's contriving brain may fail him," were clearly missing from Williams. Malin's attack pointed to a deeper difference which passing time (with the ever worsening environmental situation) and future historians would further illuminate.[116] Williams's estimate of limits, his kind of Christian Socialist corporatism, ran up against a liberal conservatism whose central logic was the absence of natural restraints.

And this question in turn raised an important point made decades later by Williams's former fellow graduate student, David Noble. For many of the young radicals of the 1940s, including John Higham and even to a degree Warren Susman, the materialistic cornucopia and the ethnic pluralism of the 1950s had become a rather successful substitute for the socialism they had embraced in their youth. It offered a utopia of sorts if not a cooperative model. The *Tragedy of American Diplomacy* remained ambiguous on the matter: if Americans could abandon their expansionist fixation, they might all enjoy the middle-class ideal that the author embraced in his private life. The Williams of *Contours* was closer by contrast to Noble's own conclusions in *The Eternal Adam and the New World Garden* and to later ecological observations: the apparent cornucopia was a nightmare in disguise, a vast misuse of natural resources; and the consumerist pluralism was less a happy outcome than a flattening of character.[117]

It remained to Herbert Aptheker, the best-known and most politically influential of communist historians since W. E. B. DuBois (and indeed, himself the designated editor of the DuBois Papers) to pronounce a definitive view from the Old Left. Asked to write a second review for *Studies*, Aptheker the seasoned politico was uncharacteristically judicious. If Williams's sweep of all U.S. history did not fully succeed, the partial failure "does not dim the reviewer's admiration for the boldness of the effort, the brilliance of its insights, the humanism of its commitment, and the transparent honesty with which the case is offered."[118] Aptheker criticized

Williams's American-centeredness, his often narrow focus on the machinations and mentality of the ruling classes, his indifference to the contributions of Abolitionists, and his converse unwillingness to consider the dangers of fascism. Behind these particulars lay a sense that in failing with black history, the Civil War, Reconstruction, and all their historical implications, Williams had missed a very large trope in national experience. This was the other side of Williams's single-minded concentration upon expansionism.[119]

The Pan-African scholar and culture critic C. L. R. James, reading *Contours of American History* in the final years of his long and varied life, analyzed the problems raised by Aptheker more simply. Urged by a youngish devotee to read Williams, he pored over the pages, and putting the book down asked only: "Where is DuBois?"[120] Had James known that Williams began his political life in the civil rights movement, his puzzlement might have been greater. Somehow, the impulses which helped to set Williams's ideas in motion and prompted him to become a historian had gotten left behind. Perhaps he felt, as his British counterpart E. P. Thompson was wont to say about the limits of his own work, that there was a larger historical/intellectual conversation going on and no one scholar could expect to encompass it all in his own writing.[121] But this would be something of an evasion. In moving toward a synthesis (as his contemporaries moving into social history rarely attempted), he could create a sense of unity only from above, drawing from below those who, like labor leader Samuel Gompers or Populist leader Jerry Simpson, had been admitted to the club. Williams lacked the capacity or the energy to go any further with an alternative line of thought.

Decades later, when Williams devotees and former students reflected on the meaning and significance of *The Contours of American History*, they came to very different conclusions. Thomas McCormick was still impressed by the text's holistic "integration of domestic and foreign affairs," its providing "radical ways to think about whole epochs . . . and fascinating new notions about corporate liberalism" thoroughly overturning the familiar "liberal notion of cycles of history." Black historian Manning Marable found the treatment at its weakest points utterly lacking in social dynamics, an "old-fashioned, elitist history from the top down," ignoring "the dynamic, creative role of social protests by African Americans, working people, women and other oppressed groups . . ."[122]

These differences were instructive, for in a slightly earlier or later age when Williams's plain radicalism or his clumsy grappling with social history would have been far more defeating, *Contours* might have passed quietly as an eccentric work with some interesting insights. In the half dozen years after its publication, however, it was the open sesame to the younger radical historians, graduate students, and undergraduate students who wanted to take a large and long view of the national experience. As interesting and valuable (also better documented and more smoothly written) as synthetic accounts by other radical historians might be—and there were still relatively few of the species—none had the sweep of social formations and personalities in the historical process, and none had the intensity of identifying the specific role of ideas. By a large but not illogical leap, Williams's readership proved themselves as the core group who could explain the historical origins of the gigantic U.S. war upon the tiny jungle nation of Vietnam.

5

By no accident, the developing perspectives of the 1960s social movements seemed to coincide, for a time, with Williams's own. The Old Left, which the *Studies on the Left* editors avowed that they had outgrown, had hidden its socialist ideas inside a liberal casing and identified the enemy as the Far Right, when in reality a bipartisan corporate liberalism had long guided the State. The same Old Left had romanticized the top-heavy labor movement, and in true bureaucratic spirit urged youngsters to attach themselves to centralized institutions. Research and active discussion, according to the *Studies* editors, could make known alternative truths. Hence the journal bristled with the vision of the "citizen-scholar" that Williams more than anyone else had laid out for them. James Weinstein, soon to become the journal's leading political spokesman, pointed to Williams's understanding of the decision-making capacity of ordinary people as an inspiration for the New Left's commitment to "participatory democracy," even as he called for greater clarity and outright socialist organization.[123]

The political and tactical originality of this position was striking for the times and for the development of the American Left, precisely because the political dinosaurs of earlier eras—the fading Communist Party and the nearly defunct Socialist Party—had shared for decades a basic commitment to liberalism and the enlarged federal government. While various leftists continued to quarrel over foreign-policy questions decades old, they nearly all saw the levers of power and mass influence as lying within the Democratic Party and the AFL-CIO.

The peace movement, dominated by pacifists, had injected something new during the 1950s, leading demonstrations against nuclear testing as well as providing tactical models and volunteers to a determinedly nonviolent civil rights movement. Along with the aura of Martin Luther King, Jr., then drifting leftward (or acknowledging socialistic positions he had held privately for years), the passionate protests against the arms race and against the ceaseless maneuvering of Russians and Americans to control the rest of the world went far to define what "radical" meant. Williams's mentor and friend William Hesseltine was a sponsor of the pacifist *Liberation* magazine, and although disclaiming his own capacity to become a pacifist, Williams quietly sympathized with these most American of left-wingers.

But Williams, *Studies*, and the pacifists alike suffered major disadvantages in defining the changing radical turf. Scions of the Old Left still held charge of many institutional mechanisms as well as access to major media. Liberal Socialist Irving Howe, a talented scholar and cultural critic with rising influence among liberals, for instance joined sociologist Louis Coser in denouncing militant opposition to U.S. adventures abroad as "New Styles in Fellow-Traveling."[124] Tom Hayden, a *Studies* editor who sat in on editorial meetings of Howe and Coser's *Dissent* magazine, later reported laconically that Howe repeatedly asked him "how he could be an editor of a journal that was part of the Soviet world."[125] *Studies On the Left* might inspire campus intellectuals, but Howe's protégé Michael Harrington wrote *The Other America*, reputedly inspiring Lyndon Johnson's War on Poverty and winning for himself a special status as moral spokesman of a socialist politics determinedly loyal to those cold-war liberals despising Williams. Compared to the kind of celebrity so obvious in the pages of the *New York Times* and in the high-profile liberal organizations' banquet circuit, the New Left and Williams could only be suspect outsiders.

Busy with his teaching and local appearances, Williams barely bothered himself with such matters until the Cuban Revolution's sharp leftward turn in 1960-61. C. Wright Mills issued in his *Listen Yankee!* (1960) the most stirring and popular manifesto of anti-interventionism since at least the middle 1930s. Williams's own short volume, *The United States, Cuba and Castro: An Essay on the Dynamics of Revolution and the Dissolution of Empire* (1962), seemed in ways an echo of Mills's far more successful work. Williams's publishers, Monthly Review Press, lacked the outlets and cash for a major promotion even on a most topical theme. Besides, Williams was not entirely at his best writing current or international history, where the impish or unexpected side of his work was least effective.

Still, *The United States, Cuba and Castro*, written in the aftermath of the failed Bay of Pigs invasion, cried out against the long legacy of U.S. bullying in the hemisphere. In offering a critique of the several current popular treatments, it appealed most uniquely to the enlightened conservative tradition of voluntary restraint. "Had American policy in action between 1859 and 1959 actually been successful according to its own standards," Williams argued,

> then there would have been no Castro and no CIA invasion. The current argument about whether or not the United States should intervene in Cuba and other Latin American countries is ridiculously

irrelevant. It has been intervening ever since the 1780s and is still doing so today. The real issue concerns whether or not any kind of intervention is capable of effecting the traditional and existing American objectives.[126]

The error or deception of the current literature, especially Theodore Draper's *Castro's Revolutions: Myths and Realities* (1962) was, indeed, its studied indifference to the weight of history. Draper's determined compartmentalization of post-1959 events troubled Williams most. An affront to larger vision of "interrelatedness," it was also the hinge of the liberal-interventionist argument that any Latin American revolution which refused to accept the U.S. economic-political model (and State Department guidance of its functioning) had been "betrayed." An argument that forever displaced the facts of American wrongdoing into a disposable past, it neatly avoided the difficulty of U.S. business interests' resistance (with State Department and CIA support) to popular calls for expropriating the expropriators of national wealth. Williams insisted that the issue was inevitably more complicated.[127]

Patiently, and familiarly to many of his regular readers, Williams traced U.S. rule from the 1890s onward, stressing the ways in which American leaders had raised and then dashed the expectations of Latin middle classes. In passing, he revealed how deceptively American "non-recognition" had been used to block Cuba's ability to gain acceptance by any major power. That kind of tactic, to "intimidate a society through the belly," had been scarcely recognized as "intervention" unless Marines were sent in to protect American investments. Adolph Berle himself described the consequences of U.S. hegemony as "great luxury for a relatively small group in Havana and a small rise above the starvation level for the masses."[128] Yet nothing had changed significantly until 1959. Efforts by Draper and others to paint Cuba as a semi-prosperous nation on the basis of a relatively high (for Latin America) per capita income entirely passed over the actual division of wealth, as well as the overwhelming control of the Cuban economy by American interests.

Seen differently, *The United States, Cuba and Castro* suggested in one case study that when New Deal–style liberalism collided with Third World nationalism, the world had come to the brink of nuclear catastrophe. In that light, Williams was surprisingly sympathetic to Castro's predecessor, Fulgenci Batista, for seeking to establish a corporatist balance of interests against overwhelming U.S. hegemony. At a time when liberals and Castro supporters alike portrayed Batista as a monster, Williams went out of his way to praise the dictator's 1940 Constitution and suggest that Fidel Castro had sought to "honor" its radical possibilities. Castro the declared communist was therefore also, to Williams, the Cuban patriot that many radical nationalists of the

Caribbean and Latin America took him to be, a left-wing *caudillo* in a long line of conservative or politically ambiguous *caudillos*.

Williams envisioned, in a conclusion that must have flabbergasted real-life Cuban revolutionaries, Herbert Hoover ("the last great conservative to honor the bedrock principle of self-determination") having appreciated the notion that crusades to shape other peoples in the U.S. image violated fundamental American ideals. He sincerely, but not very realistically, hoped that America could withdraw gracefully from Cuba, as England had from its colony, India. Williams had made the right argument for the wrong audience, or the wrong argument for the right audience. The readers of Monthly Review Books wanted something very different about the hopeful new beginnings in Latin America, and the book reached hardly anyone else. Williams came off as well-meaning but definitely eccentric, offering the first of a number of volumes to strike off center. Within the academic world, *The United States, Cuba and Castro* was scarcely reviewed at all.

If Williams stirred little radical or mainstream interest, he ran squarely up against the steamroller of cold-war liberalism. Theodore Draper, a former Communist functionary with a reputation for hard-nosed Stalinism and for hardball tactics against dissenters, had changed political camps but maintained his style of invective.[129] Draper's essay, "The Strange Case of Professor Williams," was an attack on Williams's scholarly integrity disguised as a complaint against factual errors and mistaken conclusions. In the main, Draper debated particulars, showing himself a true master of the selective quotation. Here and there, his complaints found their mark. Williams had carelessly referred to a book that Castro did not write; his treatment of Cuban history was occasionally erroneous, stemming from his attempt to wrestle with the past as Draper himself had not. Most of all, Draper pointed to a familiar ambiguity in Williams's writing: he wished to insist upon the possibility that in spite of all the crimes committed by administrations in the past, the U.S. might still have made peace with the Cuban revolution, giving Castro the opportunity to backstep toward constitutional democracy.[130] It was not a realistic expectation, but Williams obviously hoped against realism that a crisis of conscience might prevail.

In pursuing a somewhat tortured logic, Williams had indeed mangled his argument, but not in the ways that Draper suggested. Draper's choice of the *New Leader* for attacks on the Cuban Revolution, a sort of mirror-opposite of the communist *Political Affairs* in its hard-line impulses and its enthusiasm for superpower hegemony, tended to confirm this expectation. Remembered especially for its ideological assault upon the reform Arbenz government in Guatemala and its enthusiasm for a U.S.-guided 1954 coup, the *New Leader* had its own unmistakeable agenda for the Americas. "Liberal democracy," very much like "People's Democracy" in the Soviet lexicon, meant nonresistance to the large neighbor's wishes. In a small-scale special operation directed against Williams and the post–cold war radicalism that he seemed to represent, the *New Leader* sent out extra copies of the Draper issue far and wide. Noting with the original publication of the Draper piece that "too little space is being devoted these days to serious dialogues," the *New Leader* editors predictably refused to publish Williams's response. The "dialogue" was only one-sided after all.[131]

On the other side of the political fence, Williams had also begun to experience serious difficulties with the New Left. The non-historians at *Studies On the Left* had always been somewhat restive. "Our readership," the managing editor complained in 1960, "is getting a bit irritated by the Williams-crowd American history, diplomacy and foreign policy surplus of articles in *Studies*."[132] The shift of the journal from Madison to New York in 1963 coincided with a modestly growing radical movement. True to the history of American social movements and notwithstanding the campus base of most current enthusiasts, the "Movement" was more activist than intellectual. Inevitably, the need for "relevance" grew steadily and Williams's influence in the more narrow political sense sank, more or less as he had gloomily anticipated.[133]

Williams mourned in advance the larger consequences of these shifts in political taste. While *Tragedy of American Diplomacy* and *Contours of American History* carried his intellectual reputation to higher and higher levels, he would soon be trapped between the New Left and the Old Liberalism. The Vietnam War, which proved the validity of his insights more than did any other development, almost seemed to preclude any other possibilities. These two forces, in Williams's eyes, had altogether too much in common. Neither constituency had any appeal to or even clear perception of intelligent conservatism; neither could anticipate a Middle-American crisis of conscience over Empire or win people over to a different politics.

6

Things were not all that good at home. By 1960, fractures had begun to develop in his second marriage. As happy as Williams could be at times, he could also feel at loose ends over a series of problems with child-raising. These tensions, and Corrinne's suggestions that she would want to return to school at the first realistic opportunity, precipitated conflicts that would stretch out for nearly a decade. Determined to be head of the household, he could brook no open opposition, but the conflict inevitably reappeared in one guise or another. By 1964, his adopted son had been sent to a private school in LaCrosse to deal with various emotional problems. A daughter appeared to be plagued with something similar. Both children seemed so troubled that Williams considered shipping them off to Oregon grandparents. "God," he wrote his friends,

> What an endurance test this is. I think of those nuts who used to fly airplanes around and around and around over some city for days on end, and decide that I am in a similar situation . . . this has been a three weeks to cap six years.[134]

The problems had only begun. Once the memorable part of the new era had arrived, his daughter recalled, the fighter for a socialist worldview in the previous dark age simply did not know what to do with unloosed energies beyond his ken.[135]

5

TROUBLE, FOREIGN AND DOMESTIC

WILLIAMS THE DEEPLY AMERICAN RADICAL could not have met the late 1960s without a considerable degree of stress. Not so different from Irving Howe, a socialist at the center of the New York Intellectuals and at nearly the opposite end of the cold war debate, Williams had weathered the 1950s with verve and a large degree of satisfaction. Not much could be done politically, but that dismal fact had reinforced the scholarly vocation. The universities had been in some places quite accommodating, the younger dissenting intellectuals hopeful if not numerous, and the civil rights movement offered promises of better things ahead for American society at large. If the early 1960s revealed the discomforting prospect of a bohemian undercurrent rising above ground and threatening to capture the attention of the college crowd, the steady growth of student idealism in general still augured well for senior radical savants.

For many of those who came of age at this time, Williams had captured exactly the logic that they intuitively grasped but could not fully comprehend. Orators against the Vietnam War on campus and in the community, it is fair to say, crammed the *Tragedy of American Diplomacy* before mounting the stage and calling for the nation to consult its sleeping conscience. In their free time, the same student leaders often turned to *Contours of American History*, along with Herbert Marcuse's *One Dimensional Man* and a small handful of other vital books. Williams's stature notably rose as that of the cold-war liberals fell; Vietnam proved him right, and showed them by contrast to be hypocritical and self-serving or (at a generous estimate) simply dead wrong. The University of Wisconsin at Madison was only one spot on a large national map of rising antiwar and generally radical political activity. But it played a special role in providing Williams a supportive milieu and an intellectual sounding board.

In Madison and far more elsewhere, however, the young radicals took from Williams only what they wanted or what they understood. Even as they underlined key passages of his books, they rendered him into a monument and sought to move beyond the particular prescriptions for change which they viewed as either quirky or outdated. As the too-well remembered "Summer of Love" days of cheap dope and free love (or loose sex) unfolded, Williams was confounded. This was not at all what he had in mind.

Suddenly, the generation barely coming of age during the last major phase of radicalism in the later 1940s felt old, indeed. Their presumed constituencies continued to listen to them in the classroom (when the universities were not on strike), but as if from increasingly far away; the drumbeat of the times sounded action and more action. The more adept or adaptable ones rode the tide, but often felt in danger of being swept away.

Nothing in this development *should* have surprised Socialist intellectuals. The American Left and radical reform movements had never been especially cerebral, a reality that had often caused theoreticians to wring their hands and wish that they had been born (or stayed) in Europe. At their best, generations of radicals published newspapers, staged lecture tours, organized unions, and generally agitated against the status quo and for "the good time coming" (as a nineteenth-century "movement" song put it). Even college students, extremely active for a few years during the 1930s, spent most of their political time on the picket line; if they had serious intellectual aspirations, they wanted badly to write novels, not analytical studies. A handful of intellectuals had by that time good-sized followings; nearly all of them were novelists or review mavens in the *Nation* and *New Republic*. Few professors of those days could afford to risk being activists themselves, but not many had ever aspired to roles beyond teaching the young and testifying at public hearings on social issues.

Thirty years later, amid the largest college generation by far, the majority of professors had probably not changed so greatly in the role they saw for themselves. But many of the academically situated 1940s political veterans, who had gone on to support civil rights movements, now increasingly found routes to bolder action. National personalities like Howard Zinn and Staughton Lynd mirrored the lesser-known hundreds active on the lecture platform and, where permitted, in the television studios as the movement against the war spread. Many of them roughly the age of Williams or Howe had long hoped for still more, the fulfillment of their life's work in a solid, popular radical movement which heeded their intellectual contribution. These experienced the keen disappointment of having waited, planned, and prepared themselves for a big personal letdown. Even the 1950s had been personally better, certainly happier for those who had had good jobs and eager protégés.

Williams had his own sources of frustration. Dissidents of considerably less standing than himself became overnight celebrities, often borrowing his ideas wholesale. At antiwar marches and rallies, orators intoned unmistakeably similar ideas, hailing a children's crusade which older people joined sheepishly, feeling always somewhat out of place. The ordinary middle-class and working-class Americans that Williams had hoped to convert were sometimes on hand, but rarely in numbers. Increasingly skeptical toward the brutal and seemingly senseless war, a large part of the nation remained unable to break with gung-ho patriotic traditions, the bread-and-butter logic of defense-related employment, and the feeling that irresponsible young people had no right to challenge the morals and the politics of the older generations.

Unsettled by such events and dragged down by intensifying back pain and deepening personal problems, Williams sometimes acted the part of the disappointed parent who, feeling betrayed by apparently uncontrollable teenagers, rages into the night. But even that sentiment would be hard to separate from his gut feeling that some vitally important moment was passing and that the one splendid chance for social transformation was being lost. Like so many other writers, but always with his own distinct mark of originality, he tried repeatedly to work out in print what he could not resolve in his own life.

He also continued to go his own way, managing often enough to make the best of a bad situation. He rose to the occasion when increasingly large numbers of students came to believe that knowledge *could* facilitate structural change in society—so long as they kept their quest to the classroom. He also reached out politically, even as he expressed his resentment at the direction of campus and New Left politics generally. In contrast to some other sharp critics of contemporary social movements including Howe and a host of erstwhile liberals or former socialists, Williams never sided with faculty conservatives who urged a crackdown on student demonstrators.

Nor did he follow them in cursing the antiwar movement more fulsomely than the Vietnam War itself. As in so many other instances, Williams continued his own way alone, paying the costs in his own fashion.

I

Until at least the middle 1960s, tensions between Williams and his youthful admirers were held in check by a variety of common sentiments and common foes. The political scene intermittently simmered toward a boil, but the classroom remained the focus for the great majority of sympathetic students. A professor extraordinarily hard at work packing the lecture halls, guiding seminars, and directing graduate students, Williams attracted attention and gained support.

He had many local sources of satisfaction and encouragement. As Fred Harvey Harrington moved further into administration, he saw Williams less, and the rest of the older generation of Beardians including a beloved Merle Curti gradually faded from the central avenues of intellectual life. But Williams had two intimate colleagues who, together, helped him realize his aspiration for a larger view of the world, and who with him set the pace for the extraordinarily rich classroom experience shared by thousands of undergraduates. In a way, he had found his own successor to the Beardianism of the 1940s-50s, this one not American-centered or heavily Protestant but cosmopolitan and disproportionately Jewish.

The older of the two colleagues was George Mosse. Active in the liberal wing of the local Democratic Party, Mosse was not a Socialist much less a Marxist, but prided himself on his continual dialogue with the faculty and student Left. Warning against the seductive power of ideologies, Mosse analyzed Marxism as one avant-garde trend among many, several of the key ones set in motion by a Hegelianism that he described carefully and sympathetically in his packed lecture courses. Personally more approachable than Williams, Mosse charmed even those pained by his long-standing ties with certain cold-war intellectuals.

The second figure was Harvey Goldberg, hired away from Ohio State in 1963 at Williams's initiative. If the ever worldly and amiably cynical Mosse taught European ideas, Goldberg taught European (and other international) social movements with a markedly different emphasis. The plump and gentle Mosse impressed students with his range, his genial and provocative ironies, playing especially upon the middle-class backgrounds and radical visions of Jewish undergraduates. Goldberg, by now terribly thin, cigarette chain-smoking and coughing, orated with torrents of narrative detail, wild hand-waving, and generally spellbinding sincerity. In a sense, much of the best of Mosse was reborn in his many books, and those of dozens of graduate students. Goldberg, who wrote little, put everything into his presence, and fairly swept the campus in the first year of his appearance there. As if that were not enough aura, he went out with students for coffee and drinks, frequently in public and always seemingly "on." After a few years, he employed half the teaching assistants allotted for all the European historians, and enrolled ten percent of all history majors of the Europeanists in one or another of his courses. He also marshalled his graduate students (forty-nine took PhDs with him over the decades) to write a veritable collective history of the French Left, touching on many other subjects.[1]

Office mates for several years, Goldberg and Williams also spent countless hours in less formal conversation. Delivering the first Goldberg Memorial Lecture after his close friend's death, Williams recalled the two throwing their arms around each other after characteristically long days of lecturing and meeting students. Williams had a family, of course, and a circle of other friends from the faculty and elsewhere. Goldberg shunned most faculty events, spent time with students, and had many lovers (some of them bailed out, after minor legal violations, by Mosse or Williams). Emotionally, Williams was Goldberg's sustaining intimate. And so the straight and gay man had a kind of "marriage," not unlike that of Williams and his wartime Jewish roommate at Annapolis. They could be gruff with each other, but the degree of love they felt can hardly be overestimated. Their relationship can surely be appreciated better from today's more sympathetic perspective on the hidden roles of gays in America's intellectual and cultural worlds.[2]

Williams, Goldberg, and Mosse at any rate made up a magic trio, in tandem unexcelled anywhere for the young cerebral leftist or attentive activist. Compared to the earlier triad of Williams, Mosse, and Gerth, it was less introspective and more directed to dynamic social developments. It might be said that hundreds or perhaps thousands of students lived the political excitement of the later 1960s a few years in advance, a more fulfilling experience in some ways than the real thing. Over-enrolled lectures and seminars, wildly enthusiastic undergraduates, and deeply committed (and usually radical) teaching assistants created an atmosphere of perpetual excitement. Many professors and not a few students remembered these as their happiest, least conflicted days, after the glum fifties had passed and before the confrontations ensued.[3]

A changing spirit gradually infused the scene. The students most enthusiastically devoted to the trio of Williams, Goldberg, and Mosse also responded to early stirrings of political movements. Madisonians' trips to Cuba had inevitably stirred conservative legislators' wrath, but actually involved few students and no professors. The Congress of Racial Equality (CORE) campus group, like the Friends of SNCC, at first engaged mainly in support work for events elsewhere. Some of the most eager radicals indeed soon left town for the South, in order to be part of the real action. In 1963 the CORE chapter launched a campaign against the local Sears and Roebuck, which refused to hire local African Americans in sales positions. Hundreds of students and community members joined picket lines, and some were arrested. But so clear were the moral issues and so marked the links between community and campus liberals that the university seemed to be resuming its legendary moral leadership familiar to the 1930s or 1910s.

Williams, too, welcomed this activity, albeit ambivalently. He believed strongly in the division between the classroom and society, and seemed to anticipate that with the continued rise of activism he could easily become an increasingly distant figure, more icon than palpable presence. He complained privately that young radicals seemed too eager for political shortcuts. He probably sensed already that he would not be in on the action or even urge it forward dramatically as Harvey Goldberg did in public orations to demonstrators and in countless private chats with students.

Other changes left him still more uneasy. Increasingly restive undergraduates, not yet very many but a considerable portion of students attracted to Williams and Goldberg, adopted habits and personal mannerisms somewhere between the Beat Generation and the later counterculture or New Left. Like Williams they often loved jazz, but Count Basie and Duke Ellington interested them far less than the more avant-garde varieties of free jazz and musicians like John Coltrane. They were likely to find Williams's great vocal favorite, Frank Sinatra, downright repellent.

These young radicals also dressed down with cultivated scruffiness, sometimes experimented with marijuana, and generally placed themselves outside the cultural mainstream that Williams regarded as politically mistaken but morally decent. They experienced major elements of the Sexual Revolution and even (more selectively) an early Women's Liberation. The tough-minded young women were not his type, in any sense. They raised troubling questions about male authority in political and intellectual life. Above all, by distancing themselves from their families they deeply offended Williams's socially conservative sensibilities.

Williams made no public issue of his disdain. Indeed, the avant-gardists who had direct contact only with his teaching assistants could simply admire the 1940s version of nonconformity (his red vest or tie, and rumors about his jazz drumming) as part of the fascinating character they loved to hear lecturing. Graduate students were at this point likely still more conventional socially if not politically, pipe-smoking family men en route to respectable jobs.

He surprised many devotees and close readers, then, with the undercurrents in his next book, bearing the whopping title *The Great Evasion: An*

Essay on the Contemporary Relevance of Karl Marx and the Wisdom of Admitting the Heretic into the Dialogue of America's Future. Published in 1963 by his friend Ivan Dee at Quadrangle Books of Chicago, it was in no small part his response to the young radicals' anticipations of a New Left. He had nurtured the idea of a "Marx Book" for several years, but the outline had actually emerged through his participation in a seminar during 1962-63 directed jointly by himself and George Mosse. According to Mosse, the writing coincided with Williams's rediscovery of religion through the reading of a few British Christian Socialist texts on loan from Mosse. It was for Mosse, who listened carefully as Williams developed his ideas aloud, a "very American" book in the sense of a moral quest or pilgrim's progress toward the horizon of Marxism but settling for a decidedly non-Marxist oasis.[4] For himself, Williams characteristically saw the manuscript in Spinozan terms. As he wrote Merle Curti shortly after its publication, *The Great Evasion* gave him true satisfaction because it had integrated "all parts of the story" in modern society by tracing central ideas about capitalism back to Marx.[5] Or so he believed.

In another sense, Williams had been anxious to do something on politics and theory rather than history, both because of his long-standing interest in Marx and his weariness with the usual professional demands for more and better monographs. He often expressed the feeling that as far as foreign relations in particular went, he had already trained his students to do better, to work on documentary sources more intensively and extensively, than he chose to do anymore.[6]

Serious students of Marxian exegeses could immediately recognize that Williams was espousing something closer to a Socialist Americanism than an American understanding of socialism—let alone Marxism. Like a later generation of texts but without their cumbersome language or psychoanalytic theoretical underpinning, the *Great Evasion* contained a very particular "reading" of Marx. It recalled Edward Bellamy's utopian novel, *Looking Backward*, the best-selling American Socialist work of all time and the third-best-selling book of the nineteenth-century United States. Both Bellamy and Williams were pained by social disorder and believed that citizens of all classes, properly educated to their real interests, could move towards a cooperative order. Bellamy, writing at the end of the nineteenth century, never suspected the dark potential of the behemonth State. He also found a better medium to express ideals than Williams's attempt at sophisticated social criticism.[7]

Williams began with the remarkable premise that "America's great evasion lies in its manipulation of Nature to avoid a confrontation with the human condition and with the challenge of building a true community." The ecological suggestion here, which Williams scarcely pursued, would alone have made this volume farsighted for 1963. But he also struggled with a unique interpretation of why Marxism had historically seemed unnecessary but become increasingly vital for the Americans to confront and accommodate. Unfortunately, as critics noted, his method of placing moral pleas and materialistic analyses side by side puzzled more than satisfied.

Williams spent about half the book detailing the means and byways through which Americans had evaded Marx's telling criticisms. These evasions rested upon the fertile but familiar idea that the "frontier is a cast of mind as well as a stretch of open territory," an "escape hatch" that eventually stretched around the world and now threatened to reach the infinity of outer space. Expansive America conquered everything in its path, but could not create community, and—as the young Marx had predicted about the upward climb of industrialization—produced estrangement and alienation among its citizens. With their own version of collective amnesia, Americans had ignored serious criticisms of capitalism, making "Marx into Lenin" and "Lenin into Stalin," and thus "Marx into the Soviet Union." They did not or would not see that Marx had "challenged capitalism's ability to honor the West's historic and declared values and to achieve its avowed objectives."[8]

Williams had said much of this earlier, if not in quite the same terms. The unique methodological hinge of *The Great Evasion* could be traced to that indirect reference to "feudal socialism" that Williams mentioned in passing in the acknowledgments section of *Contours*. Here, he wanted to explore the possibilities more theoretically. Williams's leap from Marx's concept to the mental world of the Founding Fathers was a big one, based upon a few phrases in *The Communist Manifesto*. He insisted once more that Jefferson and Madison, among others, could be fit perfectly into the Marxist model because mercantilism, as Marx and Engels had noted polemically, "appears as a higher form" of precapitalist self-organization. Growing out of a particular view of Christianity, it contrasted with the dog-eat-dog realities of modern industrial society. In Williams's words and not Marx or Engels', mercantilism thus

> acknowledged its avowed commitment to the ideal of the whole man based on an aristocratic model, and recognized its political, social and intellectual achievements as well as its success in organizing and carrying through the crucial first steps in developing a capitalist political economy at the national level.[9]

The quasi-feudalism that Marxism's own Founding Fathers offered as an immanent critique of capitalism, Williams cited almost reverentially as the best of the American promise. Rather like Staughton Lynd's *The Intellectual Origins of American Radicalism*, published a half dozen years later to a wide readership, Williams proceeded to insist that Marx's recognition of moral values (and their erosion by invading capitalism) was mirrored in the best of American thought. But Lynd cited the Abolitionists and Thoreau, traditional heroes of radicals; Williams had instead looked to John Quincy Adams.[10] Williams also suggested that Marx had seriously underestimated the *continuing* importance of mercantilist criticism, a most critical point of Williams's heterodox Marxism. And yet with its limitations, Marxism alone was capable of "bringing our capitalistic ego into a confrontation with our capitalist reality."[11] Somehow, the ego as reality principle in Freud's system had slipped into the ego of street parlance, as in "egotistic." The back cover sported a quotation from the *Library Journal* comparing Williams to Erich Fromm as a "non-doctrinaire student of Marx."[12]

In this queer theoretical setting, more Frommian than Marxist or Freudian, Williams bore down on familiar themes. The "bourgeois Socialists," Abolitionists, and Populists thus spoke for freedom but failed to grasp the increasingly divisive influence of the marketplace. Again in street or perhaps pulpit parlance, Williams declared that by looking at the marketplace, "the rich as well as the poor white can verify [that it] does not transform the ego into the soul."[13] All classes alike were trapped, he insisted, by sharing key assumptions of expansionism consciously or unconsciously. The "Corporate Socialism" of the New Deal, widely and mistakenly believed to be the highest degree of idealism reached by the national polity, likewise presented no serious alternative. Williams inevitably preferred the caution, and the social criticism, of Herbert Hoover.

These would be odd formulations for any other writer, but Williams needed them to repose the question of alienation, then popular among the readers of Fromm's *The Sane Society* and the "Young Marx" of the *Economic and Philosophical Manuscripts of 1844*, newly translated into English only a few years earlier. Others made much of the "lost" feeling widely prevalent (but especially keen among the young) under contemporary capitalism. Williams's own Marx became the "paradoxical prophet of affluence and of the irrelevance of affluence once it is attained," anticipating the possibility of a realized community in a fully technological, i.e., cybernetic society. Carefully calibrating the implications of industrial production and human needs, Williams insisted that "the issue is not whether to decentralize the economy and the politics of the country, but rather how to do so" through an inevitable but also "exhilarating" new constitutional movement. *That* America could truly aid the poor countries of the world, and even project "the rational (as opposed to political) exploration of space."[14]

Easily the oddest sections of the book identified—but never admitted as much—the problems in his own campus and family with the presumed ravages of alienation and consumerism. Under the heading of "Increasing

Misery and Increasing Proletarianization," he bemoaned the fate of mechanized labor, the loss of familiar jobs, the spread of psychological ailments among African Americans, women, and youth. But he chose campus sexual promiscuity as "the most dramatic sign of a sad and desperate search for a human relationship," the devaluation of sex as a commodity. Changing partners in bed now substituted for changing the society, he observed, and obviated hopes for the honest relationship of two adults within a real community. He could appreciate the young hot-rodder (like his adopted son) for using the mechanical means at hand to revive an almost handicraft creativity. But he castigated the struggle for women's emancipation in a male world, on male terms of equal access or competition for jobs and services. To Williams, this last was clearly an unendurable extension of community disintegration. Judgments like these, common enough among intellectuals during the 1950s, could not have been more ill suited for the era ahead. Within a few years, when so much had changed, Williams's sexual and gender observations could only be taken as eccentric or idiosyncratic, part of a larger problem in the volume.[15]

Williams had evidently drawn deeply, over a long relationship and correspondence, upon Warren Susman's work seeking to interpret the personality type that predominates in mass society.[16] In turn, Susman and others had culled ideas from neo-Freudians like Karen Horney, Fromm, and the anthroplogical followers of "Culture and Personality" studies analyzing behaviors in all societies as variants of distinct "factors." The perceived problem for these clinicians and writers was not "interpsychic," the individual mind wrestling with the innate drives described by Freud, but rather interpersonal, in conflicts which could be socially understood and hopefully resolved. But unlike Susman (who published little in his lifetime), Williams had no sophisticated critique of consumerism except as a form of alienation. And unlike *Contours of American History*, *The Great Evasion* did not surround its social-psychological assumptions with historical interpretations but instead exposed them in their fragile state.

Williams was also almost certainly drawing upon a Frankfurt School theorist's very particular observations on family authority, a side of the Frankfurt theorists conveniently neglected by radical devotees but later vividly recalled by intellectual historian Christopher Lasch. During the late 1940s, Max Horkheimer had attributed the rise of fascism to the decline of the patriarchal family. In an earlier era, boys internalized authority and grew up properly. The self-control of the individual, the ability to take pleasure in constructive activity all depended upon the mixture of fear and authority that the father provided. The undermining of that authority in the twentieth century had produced a growing insecurity for the whole family, encouraging the retrograde impulse of "unsatisfied, spiritless," and fearful women.[17]

Merging a critique of consumerist materialism with a hand-wringing complaint at the loss of paternal authority was so commonplace in intellectual circles during the 1950s that one might almost call it the thread connecting critical theory to cold-war liberalism. But it had slipped down several notches by the time *The Great Evasion* was published and was doomed to slip down many more before the 1960s had ended.[18] As the political lines on race seemed to coincide with generational tastes in music, so did attitudes on the war in Vietnam; those on the other side from Williams in age and culture had no reason to bemoan the crisis in family authority and growing reasons (with the rise of feminism) to celebrate the attack on Father from all sides. In one more way, Williams had written a book badly out of time. It might be contrasted, finally, with another reading straight out of the Frankfurt School: Herbert Marcuse's *Eros and Civilization* (1955) which anticipated and shaped young people's changing attitudes toward intimate subjects which interested them at least as much as political events.

The critics were in any case far from kind to the *Great Evasion*, and no major historical journal even bothered to review it. Many commentators already unfriendly toward Williams leaped at the chance to nail him. Among the most mean-spirited, Robert Heilbroner in the *New York Review of Books* found the *Great Evasion* "vulgar, self-serving, imprecise and shallow."[19] Political Scientist Floyd A. Cave called the book itself a "great evasion" for misunderstanding Marx's scientific socialism and for evading the doctrines of class warfare and the dictatorship of the proletariat.[20] Even in the columns of the *Nation*, Williams's long-reliable ally, labor historian Milton Cantor, described the volume as "disappointing," marked by idiosyncratic formulas and "careless generalizations."[21]

Eugene Genovese, the leading scholarly light of *Studies on the Left*'s New York–based operation, was considerably more impressed, but for reasons that would finally do Williams little good. He saw in Williams mainly an antidote to permissive individualism at large and to the emerging New Left in particular. Despite its plain ignorance of Marxism, the *Great Evasion* was to Genovese "both instructive and urgent" because Williams had "masterfully [exposed] capitalism as a process of dehumanization." Williams's desire for an organic community might just as easily have been a vision of a Catholic feudalist, a patriachal slaveholder, a utopian socialist, or even an Italian Fascist; it was, as other critics had said about *Contours*, more Hegelian idealism than real Marxist thought. But Williams had grasped the failure of the modern welfare state, and above all its encouragement to false emancipation of women through their participation in the marketplace.

Most tantalizing for Genovese, Williams had denounced those "quasi-beatnik anarchists" (in Genovese's words) of the New Left. He had restated the "spirit of Puritanism—of discipline, civil responsibility self . . . a respect for order" and genuine family values that Americans could appreciate. Contrary to the young radicals, Williams did not "expect [America] to jump into revolutionary transformations of any kind." Genovese obviously hoped, with Williams, that Americans could "reclaim their soul" in ways distant from the present young and rebellous generation, i.e., with a firm sense of admiration for their patriarchal-minded elders.[22]

George Mosse would later reflect that when he asked students,

> why on earth they were not reading *The Great Evasion* instead of Herbert Marcuse's books, they replied that Williams did not give them the kind of theory into which they so much wanted to fit the American situation. They had this hunger for theory, and the only theory that answered their needs was European. Williams's democratic vistas should have appealed mightily, but the radical students were in love with the philosophy of history of Marx, and with a sort of Kantian moral imperative that meant to be politically active while harmonizing means and ends.[23]

Mosse did not quite go to the heart of the problem, but he had detected the source of a significant misalliance. As an intellectual progenitor of the New Left, Williams resisted not only the student radicals but the drift of scholarship as well.

If the 1950s and early 1960s mainstream theorists of alienation such as David Riesman stressed the importance of norms and roles, seeking above all psychic adjustment and the restoration of social stability, the students and radical scholars of the later 1960s and after placed their main emphasis on creative destabilization and the dynamic elements in American history and society that seemed to disprove both the permanence and the desirability of consensus. Warren Susman, writing in 1979, would propose that as the late 1940s Age of Anxiety had given way to an Age of Identity (delineated in the writings of psychoanalyst Erik Erickson), the successor mood had yielded, in turn, to an Age of Liberation.[24] In a way, Herbert Marcuse had provided the middle term between the last two psychological "ages," and Williams had indeed used Marcuse's *One Dimensional Man* extensively in *The Great Evasion*. But far from doing so in ways that Marcuse (who looked favorably on student radicals and women's liberation) would have imagined either likely or desirable, Williams transported Marcuse's ideas back into the theoretical framework of the 1950s.

If students now wanted "theory" much as Williams fifteen years earlier in Madison had wanted it, they would get a great deal more, from Mosse, Goldberg, and others. Still, the accumulation of theoretical hints did not meet the scale of the problem they perceived, perhaps because no solutions existed. *The Great Evasion*, in any case, was left swiftly behind, a kind of marker to unsuccessful transitions. Most ironically, Genovese and Williams's later defender Christopher Lasch both would ride the antifeminist backlash of the 1980s-90s by renewing theories of family disintegration that Williams had found so absorbing.[25] By this time, socialism was no longer seen as an antidote but an impossibility. The envisioned organic society had become, for this day's ideologues, something closer to the market liberalism with individual solutions that Williams had shunned all his adult life.

2

Campus disruption came relatively slowly to Madison, in part because the Left could operate so freely already and in part because the forbidding Wisconsin winter limited demonstrations to early fall and spring. The explosion of the free speech movement in Berkeley during 1964-65 took everyone by surprise, thoroughly unnerving cold-war socialists (or former socialists) like sociologist Seymour Martin Lipset, who imagined omnipresent communist infiltration and urged a tough-minded response. At a distance, Williams and Mosse surely didn't like campus uprisings much more than the Lipsets did, but the generally relaxed atmosphere of Madison and its wise administrators both minimized the periods of unrest and kept the ardor of students for their classes high. The preliminary stages of the Vietnam protest movement, moreover, gave Williams an early sense of the ways in which his intellectual contributions had shaped the emerging radical thought. As a political (rather than intellectual) hero of the day, he now enjoyed his last moments of high visibility.

By March 1965, a month after Lyndon B. Johnson ordered intensive bombing of North Vietnam, the first Peace March on Washington occurred, sponsored by the Students for a Democratic Society. With twenty-five thousand on hand (more than twice what organizers had expected), it was the largest such demonstration in U.S. history, however small by standards soon to come. For the first time, a New Left was projected onto the nation's consciousness. SDS president Paul Potter, the rally's chief speaker, went beyond war and peace issues as such to say that "we must name the system" which produced brutal war-making.

A decade or two earlier, leftists would have concluded that Potter simply meant capitalism but had been too cautious to say so openly. The SDS leader hinted, however, at something far closer to Williams's concept of a *Weltanschauung* that categorically and irrationally rejected Third World revolutionary aspirations. SDS's next president and most popular orator, Carl Oglesby, was yet closer to Williams's way of thinking. An advocate of "decentralized socialism" and somewhat of a Christian Socialist, Oglesby agonized visibly on platforms about the betrayal of national ideals.

America, he often averred, had broken his "liberal heart." Only a kind of spiritual rebirth, he seemed to suggest, could salvage America from the sins of avarice plainly apparent in its international policies.[26]

Williams's articulation of "corporate liberalism," a phrase introduced by Martin J. Sklar, offered young radicals a major insight into how Lyndon Johnson could combine a Great Society at home with a senseless war in Southeast Asia and how an apparently left-of-center Democratic Party could be an integral part of bipartisan corporate control of politics. Sklar was himself seeking to distinguish various forms of corporatism, some of them considerably more consensual and, he believed, more benign.[27] Study groups on "Corporate Liberalism" became a fixture for several years on the Madison campus. Caught up in protesting the war, few young radicals elsewhere perceived the historic complications, and still fewer could likely have correctly identified the sources of the insight.

Later in the spring of 1965, teach-ins swept college campuses and found professors at the center of antiwar attention for perhaps the last time. Hundreds of students in Madison listened as speaker after speaker recounted the causes of the war and proposed peaceful solutions. Williams told the crowd which had waited until after midnight to hear him speak that they had the "makings of a community" forced to "assemble as citizens" because the government was violating America's "best traditions" and "threatening grave harm to [its] highest moral ideals and aspirations." The duty of those assembled was to try "to bring [the] government back into a dialogue with its own citizens . . . to transform America into a more humane and creative community."

Williams saw two alternatives to the present disastrous policy. One was to "embark upon a sober and informed imperialism designed to establish and maintain an American Empire of optimum size, efficiency and benevolence." The other and better solution was "to honor our moral commitment to the principle of self-determination . . . . We can clearly learn a good deal from others if we will only give them a chance to teach us; if we can only give ourselves the chance to learn."[28] Notably, he did not denounce the commander-in-chief of current U.S. policies. In private, he expressed admiration for Lyndon Johnson's domestic program of inclusiveness, especially the Civil Rights Act of 1964. He hoped almost desperately—and contrary to his own system of thought—that the New Deal liberal Johnson, outsider from Texas, would extricate the U.S. from Vietnam and go on to prove that an adopted *noblesse oblige* could point the way toward a better future.

In public, Williams could still seem close to the young radicals. At the annual banquet of the weekly *National Guardian*, in New York City, twelve hundred attendees watched pacifist David Dellinger and community organizer Tom Hayden, along with Eugene Genovese, Carl Oglesby, civil rights leader Fannie Lou Hamer, lawyer William Kunstler, and Williams together on the dais, the last four as speakers. Complaining at the exhausted visions of the Old Left and insisting upon the necessity of going beyond antiwar activism, Williams urged the new generation forward toward a decentralist vision of socialism, rebuilding in practice "an inspiring and exciting and practical alternative for a different and better America."[29]

But mostly, Williams seemed prepared to withdraw from the centers of action himself. In New York during the same fall of 1965, a handful of prominent academics formed the Socialist Scholars Conference, dedicated to holding large, annual meetings for intellectual and political exchange. Williams was notable for his absence among a circle of rising intellectuals who owed a great deal to him.[30] Neither did he participate in the Madison Teach-in of 1966. Already the local political scene had soured for him, and he was not sorry to be on leave in Oregon for the 1966-67 academic year.

In Madison as across the nation, liberals gave up on Johnson, and ever larger groups of students determined to express themselves against the war at any cost. In the spring of 1967, activists warned against the use of campus facilities by the Dow Chemical Company, notorious for its production of napalm, jellied gasoline dropped by airplane and used notoriously to terrorize Vietnamese civilians. A small group of Madison intellectuals and graphic artisans, disproportionately history students, set up an engaging campus "underground" newspaper, *Connections*, whose journalists enormously admired Williams but also ridiculed college administrators and urged mass action against both the war and the university's role in it.[31]

University officials now found themselves in a quandary which Williams largely shared. From Fred Harvey Harrington down, many and perhaps most of them personally opposed the war but felt compelled to obey the wishes of the regents. The contradictions sharpened further as a crisis emerged. Scholarship into the university's "power structure" by graduate students and others offered convincing proofs of how thoroughly the university had become enmeshed, over the years, in research destined for use in unconscionable anticivilian activities. Specific sections of the university also had records of long-standing cooperation with intelligence agencies guilty of widespread human rights abuses.[32] Those who opposed the war found it harder and harder to accept without question the university dissimulation of rights and wrongs, even as the university administrators proudly defended their own record of protecting antiwar freedom of speech against demands of conservative state legislators for a campus crackdown. Each side had important points to make, but could not hear the other.

Williams returned to Madison in this tense atmosphere for the school year 1967-68. Once again the Dow Corporation promised job-placement interviews, foolishly (or brazenly) coinciding with a declared "Vietnam

Week" nationwide, October 17-18. Antiwar demonstrators in many cities sought to halt the escalation of the war, which included a half million GIs stationed in Vietnam, with hundreds of resulting U.S. casualties and thousands of Vietnamese victims every week. Madison rallies appealed for nonviolent action against Dow. The peaceful sit-in of the building where the interviews were to be held might easily have ended in a draw, with Dow cancelling interviews or quietly moving the location. Instead, city officials unwisely called in by the university's chief of security ordered local police to clear the area by any means necessary. Given the esprit of uniformed student-haters unleashed to be bullies, a police riot was predictable. Swinging their clubs wildly, breaking glass doors, and dragging bloodied students out, they meanwhile fired tear gas and mace at the assembling crowd of incredulous and increasingly enraged bystanders. As the melee continued, the campus exploded.

A student strike quickly became inevitable. That night, after a stormy session in the Memorial Union auditorium, the attending faculty meekly voted to support the administration's decisions rather than join the strike. Students stood outside singing "Solidarity Forever" and watching disappointedly, sometimes whispering, "Shame, shame" as the faculty members filed out. Harvey Goldberg later addressed the crowd of embittered students in strident tones, offering no tactical advice but reminding them of their responsibilities to history. Williams was noticeably absent.[33]

Instead, he had been corralled by a young *New York Times* reporter, Nan Robertson, and over more than a few drinks he spilled out his anxiety. While student leaders appealed for idealism and set themselves to educate intensively within the dormitories (as Williams himself had long urged them to do), he described the era's undergraduates as the "most selfish people I know," determined to create a society which "an orangutan wouldn't want to live in."[34] The next day, as energy continued to build, a half dozen graduate students passed out bananas at the door of his diplomatic history lecture class, as if they were leafletting in the fashion of the day. Williams mounted the stage slowly, looked out at the banana-laden students, and smiled sheepishly. Rumors of his drinking spree had been passed around with copies of the *Times* article, and students accepted with compassion their beloved mentor's obvious moment of weakness. He went on that day to give a characteristic denunciation of U.S. foreign policies. Although he observed the week-long strike at close range, Williams kept a low profile while his friend Harvey Goldberg sparkled.[35]

The strike soon passed, the winter freeze set in, and students returned to the libraries until spring—a veritable fixed pattern in Madison's campus political life. Some professors melodramatically spoke of being "terrorized" by student activists. Aging refugees among them with memories of fascist

Europe knew better what terror meant and did not mean. Many committed faculty found these years a time of constant troubles but also of idealism, high cerebral energy, and above all, little apathy.

Williams continued to make personal gestures towards those student radicals who sought intellectual and political alternatives closer to his own heart. When a "free university" atmosphere encouraged the proliferation of study groups, especially active in times of campus strikes but often lasting for entire semesters, Williams readily arranged reading credit for a circle of choice graduate students analyzing liberalism. He also devoted entire days to a serious critique of a community organizing program set out by a new off-campus group, the Wisconsin Alliance.[36]

But for the most part, Williams did not have the heart for an active response. He could not reconcile himself to the politics of student demonstrators or to the response of the administrators, but he was disturbed even more by the cultural atmosphere emerging around campus. Madison rapidly became a center for counterculture or "youth culture," a Midwest-style, small-scale Haight-Ashbury with the full complement of marijuana, LSD, poster-and-incense stores, and even transgressive gay bravado. Bohemian in his own mind and intimate with gay intellectuals, but happiest when he could talk and drink with faculty and neighborhood friends, Williams felt more and more alienated.

Moreover and more personally, the rise of youth culture literally hit too close to home. He had developed problems, almost from the beginning, with his own sense of authority in the family. He wanted or demanded the kind of respectful attention that he imagined he might have given his own father. Like so many other parents in the 1960s, he found rebellion in the domestic setting impossible to accept. According to his ex-wife Corrinne, he typically sought to subject his (and her) children to absurd Annapolis rituals such as shining their shoes and holding them up for inspection when he came home. His Frankfurt School readings bolstered him theoretically in the belief that he deserved a respectful order.

Naturally, these kinds of demands elicited the very reverse of what he had hoped. The small and large rebellions of his stepchildren and children as they reached their teen years in turn hardened a view he had already developed, that somehow the harmful breakdown of authority was due more to the selfishness of the rebels themselves than to the failure of established institutions and leaders. Drugs, to take an obvious case in point, seemed as repellant and destructive to him as alcohol appeared benign or at least controllable in his own increasingly hard-drinking personal life. He simply could not acknowledge any link between his own alcohol consumption or his addiction to cigars and the larger addictive patterns in society.

A double irony pervaded these confused and sometimes strident generational conflicts. In the first place, a belief in decentralization that Williams viewed as the *sine qua non* of a democratic socialist society had continued to grow apace in the New Left from 1965 to 1968. Madison, partly because of his presence, was one of the intuitive centers of this kind of perspective. Despite the heavy influence elsewhere by the Leninist-style centralism of Trotskyists and Maoists, the vast majority of New Leftists and "movement" activists here continued to believe deeply in the potential power of the "community" (however it was defined) to meet individual and collective needs.

Unfortunately, the war and the particular forms that rebellious culture assumed inevitably continued to polarize opposing sensibilities. The inclination of the radical youth "community" to define itself as a counterculture against the dominant moral order (especially against the guardians of order) inflamed Williams. He believed that the mass of ordinary Americans *could* be won over, and no doubt he also resented the generational lines of division. Speaking in largely working-class Madison East High School once or twice gave him the kind of audience he wanted far more than the middle-class campus did. Without doubt, he had mastered the art of opening the minds of instinctively patriotic youngsters to the possibility of a patriotic anti-imperialism. But such opportunities remained rare. The New Left emphasis on the more impoverished, the lower layers of the working class, and the ghetto minorities left Williams cold, probably because he saw marginal classes as unable to lift themselves out of their misery.

In a second irony more obvious outside Madison, Williams's writing grew steadily more popular among political circles with which he found little or no spiritual common ground. The "anti-imperialist" wing of the New Left, concentrated in the coastal universities from Columbia and Harvard to Berkeley and San Francisco State, tended toward versions of Leninism, but schooled themselves in *The Tragedy of American Diplomacy.* Institutions like New York's "Alternative University" (the very idea of free-floating classes teaching "revolution" could only dismay Williams) considered I. F. Stone and Williams their patron saints, for these two had opened wide the book of American sins abroad. If liberals and conservatives increasingly viewed Williams as an "America-hater", the self-defined anti-imperialist activists, never a large section of the Left but increasingly present, manifested adulation precisely because they sought to overthrow what they usually referred to as "Amerika" or even "Amerikkka." It seems hard to imagine that the same readers could have comprehended *Contours of American History*—but hardly impossible in those strange days, either.[37]

For these contradictory reasons among others, Williams's familiar successes continued. His undergraduate course was larger than ever. He had not changed his political-minded critique of the past, nor his critique of the war in Vietnam. He maintained his graduate seminar at a high level, commenting privately that he had had enough of this work for a lifetime. He complained that even the graduate students had become rabid activists (indeed, in large numbers around the history department they set themselves to organizing a Teaching Assistants Association whose leaders would eventually guide the state federation of labor). Meanwhile, his private generosity included a helping hand to *Radical America*, a new graduate student radical history journal on campus and successor to *Studies On the Left* but distinctly drawn to the history of radicalism and labor rather than the history of elites. He successfully lobbied the Rabinowitz Foundation to offer a small grant making continued publication of the journal possible.[38]

One route out of the frustrations that seemed to surround him was an academic career move. He received in 1966 an offer from the University of Rochester, which had a strong history department with important Madison connections (notably his graduate school friend Loren Baritz, but also Herbert Gutman, a former teaching assistant to Howard Beale and a promising labor historian) and two new professors of note, Eugene D. Genovese and Christopher Lasch. Williams was drawn to and uncertain about Rochester for almost the same reasons. He would have plenty of intellectual stimulation but would also be swamped by another crew of ambitious young men (and a few women), determined to get him to lead seminars, read dissertation chapters, and write endless recommendations. He admired Genovese not least because the expensively dressed, cigar-smoking, self-defined gentleman on the Left shared many if by no means all of his values. He may also have suspected that Genovese's important works on slavery, *The Political Economy of Slavery* (1965) and later *The World the Slave-Holders Made* (1969) were, notwithstanding Genovese's greater Marxist theoretical acuity, in large ways shadow versions of *The Contours of American History*.[39]

Both scholars felt a repugnance at feminism and the activist campus New Left, with sentiments that grew steadily stronger. But Genovese, a rising master of the academic power play, also made Williams nervous. Williams had taken real pride in his various roles in the University of Wisconsin History Department, from training students to editing the department newsletter. But like a man who has raised a family, divorced, and had no wish to start over with a new wife, Williams did not intend to begin graduate training again. Nor did he want to take the time and emotional effort to become involved in Machiavellian professional maneuvers that he suspected Genovese probably had in mind, all the more because he guessed that he would be used as a symbolic chess piece for unspecified ends.[40]

Williams visited Rochester twice with Corrinne, and postponed until the last minute a final decision. He sought to blame his reluctance on her wanting to commute to Buffalo for courses toward a social work degree, thus fragmenting their family life. By staying in Madison, he concluded, he would do the best thing for them all. But he confessed to having other motives as well. The University of Wisconsin came through with a better salary offer, including some paid leave. He and Harvey Goldberg had worked long and hard in the department to win a special kind of freedom for both of History's stars (thereafter Goldberg regularly commuted to Paris for alternate semesters, as Mosse would similarly alternate with appointments abroad, years later). Williams thought he would stay.[41]

Williams also had a backup plan. He had wanted to return to Oregon's climate and its beautiful coast almost from the day he left. Now he could do so for an entire year. He thought that it would be good for the troubled marriage, which he insisted he hoped to save for everyone's sake including the children's. But it was also an unmistakable control move. He meant to take his teenagers and near-teenagers out of the rampant youth culture environment into the small and insular town life of Oregon. The implications for Corrinne were still more one-sided. She would not be able to continue coursework en route to a career. Although Williams rationalized that Corinne could now be near her own extended family, she simply did not want to leave Madison. He made the decision for everyone.

Renting a home in Newport, Oregon, for the school year 1966-67, the Williamses quarreled often. They also socialized, danced, and drank heavily with two other couples: all three were later divorced. On the positive side, Williams and Corrinne enjoyed the natural beauty of the scene and revisited, together, something of what they had experienced in their courting. But basic conflicts could not be avoided for long. As Williams angled for a job somewhere in the state, Corrinne felt trapped and looked forward to returning to Madison and going to school.

Williams owed the University of Wisconsin a year in any case. The return to Madison was fraught with emotional tremors on all sides. Daunted no longer, Corrinne applied and was accepted into the social work section of the sociology department at the University, and she completed her first semester more than satisfactorily.[42] Williams, on the other hand, told himself and his friends that he wanted to set down roots in small-town Oregon while he still had productive years, sparing himself both Wisconsin winters and the university-urban setting. Further problems with his back, which demanded he virtually give up active sports, also prompted him to think about his retirement still almost twenty years away. These perfectly logical reasons, however, also had the sound of a man frantic to control the elements of his marriage and, in other ways, tired to the bone.[43]

Williams measured his withdrawal from the New Left with a sort of anti-manifesto published, significantly, in *Liberation* magazine. There, the "Movement" (at least beyond civil rights) had arguably begun, recorded in the words of participants. *Liberation* had subsequently become more and more a magazine of direct (albeit nonviolent) action, raising the extreme ire of anti-Communist Socialists loyal to the Democratic Party and ambivalent about Vietnam. But for Williams, it undoubtedly displayed a more promising side. *Liberation* had been resolutely anti-imperialist without succumbing to Leninism, an ideology very suddenly gaining popularity within the New Left. It was also never anti-intellectual.

Thus Williams delivered, in early 1969, the damning complaint that the movement seemed incapable of forming around itself a social bloc capable of compelling structural change in capitalist America. Worse, in Williams's eyes, it had in many cases invited political repression through pseudo-militance and wild rhetoric. It showed little ability to discern conflicts among dominant groups of society (he would later say that any effective Left had to figure out how to split the ruling factions), and it had no sense of what kind of order should emerge from the chaos. Its utopian counterculture offered ordinary people ("the straights," and he counted himself among them) nothing but put-offs and put-downs. Williams unfailingly referred to this "do-your-own-thing" behavior as particularly destructive, mirroring marketplace individualism. Demonstrations, more and more followed by bloodlettings, could not convince in the way that quiet door-to-door or dormitory-to-dormitory dialogue could do. Unless and until the New Left found a way to reach the majority of the population with a vision of a better society, unless it learned how to use the campus for the testing of ideas, and unless it abandoned its sheer arrogance toward others, all the energy expended in protest would bring no significant, structural change.[44]

The young radicals needed more than anything else a positive vision of "what it means to be an American," and how Americans could make "their lives . . . richer and more purposeful." This demanded not only a better attitude (another age would say, less of an attitude) but also a blueprint of some kind: "how will socialism be any better than a capitalism without the Vietnam War, and with a continuing (and improving) pattern of permissive welfarism."[45] In short, he demanded more than Marx or Lenin, Trotsky, Mao, Castro, or the existing New Left had to offer.

Williams raised serious questions about the frantic pace of demonstrations against the war and the absence of any other apparent strategy. He pinpointed quite accurately the failure of New Left intellectuals to put forward some kind of long-range perspective. But in truth, such strategy (or nonstrategy) from the Left had evolved during the wild escalation of the war against the Vietnamese, and in a virtual vacuum for his kind of thinking.

The campus might well be considered, as Williams insisted, so precious a "center of serious intellectual activity" as to be sacrosanct from potentially destructive protest.[46] But such an attitude—if the many hawkish adminis- trators away from Madison could be forgiven their own sordid intentions of keeping the campus a cold-war intellectual reserve—did not neatly resolve the problems of university complicity. All the free speech of professors and students together could not blunt the harm done. As Harvey Goldberg had said, you don't call it free speech when an island of truth is surrounded by an ocean of lies. Nor was it self-evident that student activists taking their visions of peace into working-class (or middle-class) communities would have any particular success reaching people.

Those who determinedly heeded Williams's advice shaved off their beards or put on dresses and went door to door in Madison. They usually had the doors slammed in their faces.[47] No doubt they and many more like them should have persisted. But as the death toll mounted in Vietnam, antiwar activity remained centered in the one place where students could not only avoid being ignored but actually effect a sense of national crisis. Various liberal politicians including future candidate George McGovern offered peace proposals while vigorously condemning student actions. Hubert Humphrey, whose career-long behavior rendered his peace propos- als entirely suspect, staged a dramatic appeal late in his 1968 presidential campaign to be given his opportunity to halt the American mayhem in Vietnam. But meanwhile the military machine moved onward, troubled more by drugged and rebellious GIs than by conflicts within Congress. Demonstrations at least brought the nightmare back home in small doses.

There was also a larger issue which Williams left unresolved. The intel- lectual guidance behind a new blueprint for socialism belonged properly not to undergraduates nor even to graduate students but to the mature intellectuals whom they most admired, including Williams himself. His appeals for a new constitutional convention attracted few listeners. Discussions revived along somewhat similar lines in many intellectual cir- cles during 1968-70, including those of former *Studies On the Left* editors, by this time placed highly in the history profession. Various groups strug- gled for a perspective, a statement on where a socialist movement should be going. None succeeded in doing more than launching new journals.

Unable to reach beyond its limits on the campuses and in the ghettos, the social movements exploded or collapsed. They had considerable help in both regards from the largest national intelligence and local police "Red Squad" campaign in American history. As Williams might have recognized from his personal experience, episodes of violence very frequently left the telltale print of outside provocation. FBI, Cointelpro, and police groups offered weapons and explosives—or as in Madison at the time of the Army

Math Research Building bombing in 1970, apparently watched quietly as the plot was hatched by politically naive youngsters, shrewdly calculating that it would discredit the radical community.[48]

The severe repression of the Black Power movement, including the police assassination of Chicago Black Panther leaders, the wild factionalism of the Students for a Democratic Society, and the disintegration of the larger student movement had many causes but one result: they left almost nothing behind. As Williams would have predicted, the counterculture survived for the most part only in commodified forms, style rather than substance of rebellion. The underground press dragged on despite a continuing and highly illegal goverment campaign of harassment, but largely succumbed by 1973. The Women's Liberation Movement loomed steadily larger and the Gay Liberation Movement took shape as a social force. But Williams evidently looked askance at such phenomena (he never actually commented on the Gay Movement) as a further individualization of "freedom" at expense of community values.

Besides, the appeal of moving a consumer society off the mark of individual material pursuits had rarely reached beyond the middle class and other milieux who perceived a *need* for America to change gears. Outside those groups, relatively small numbers ever felt anything like the Depression-era sense that American capitalism had failed in some deep and fundamental way. Most other whites at any rate wanted to protect what they had gained (or might gain) from the real or imagined threats of communists, student protesters, enraged racial minorities, and liberated women. The suburban home and second car beckoned, not to the materialistic wife as Williams imagined but to the whole family. As Kevin Phillips later observed, these were the real "silent majority" of voters increasingly strong in the Southwest and West, often scarred by Vietnam but in no large way disillusioned with what capitalism could bring them.[49] Williams himself grasped, quite brilliantly, why liberalism had no more appeal for them. But neither he nor anyone else offered a serious plan to get them to move leftward from liberalism rather than moving rightward.

3

By the time he left Madison in June 1968, Williams had almost put the finishing touches on his next volume and final monograph. He had ruminated on the project since the *Great Evasion*, convinced that conservative and radical scholars of Populism alike had failed to give credit to the sophistication and unique insights of Populists as reflected in their own press. His letters to friends had for several years described with excitement his criticism of the polar positions taken by Richard Hofstadter and Norman Pollack.

Hofstadter, who coincidentally died in 1968 of a heart attack at age 52, had of course portrayed the Populists as irrational and often anti-Semitic agrarian losers who simply could not adjust to the realities of the market economy. Pollack, a victim of academic politics at Harvard, quoted many Populist newspapers to demonstrate a semi-socialist idealism and a solid economic consciousness hard at work.

Williams, as he eagerly wrote his friends during the middle 1960s, concluded after looking at many newspapers and the personal archives of key agrarian leaders that these estimates were equally off base. Unresolved questions in *The Great Evasion* prompted further inquiries and an extremely odd defense of the farmer. Far from irrational, backward, and untutored, farm folk were keenly aware of the changing shape of the world as well as the domestic economy. Far from renouncing competition and conquest for a cooperative or socialistic perspective, they actually previewed the idea of overseas colonies.

Confirming this perception played several other parts in Williams's long-term projects. If he had spent his time in the middle 1950s working out U.S. foreign relations since the 1890s (and especially since 1917), he had remained committed to an earlier notion of the "frontier" thesis as an American outlook developed before Frederick Jackson Turner's explication of it in 1890. *Contours* had of course been the major theoretical outgrowth of Williams's wider view. Expansionism, indeed, had been a *leitmotif* since well before the nation's Founding Fathers. But something of Williams's own sensibilities, along with the work of a student on a master's thesis under Williams at Oregon, sent him searching for evidence he had long intuited to be present.

The Roots of the Modern American Empire: A Study of the Growth and Shaping of Social Consciousness in a Marketplace Society, published by Random House in 1969, was also without question a response to critics' complaints that he could not (or at least did not) "do footnotes," i.e., serious archival work. The dense documentation proved, really for the last time in his career, his eye for the archival detail when he made up his mind to find it. The book also offered yet another flash point in his relationship with Corrinne when he sought to transform her career ambitions into wifely research assistance. He reveled in his findings in the National Archives when they took a family trip to Washington, D.C. By all accounts she found the work intolerably boring. More likely, she saw no good reason to do *his* work when she had waited so long to begin her own.

Modifying some earlier views, Williams now sought to prove that during the three decades following the Civil War, farmers (i.e., the majority of Americans) rather than financiers and industrialists were in the forefront of the campaign for foreign markets and overseas expansion. Extensive economic summaries of agricultural exports, along with plentiful quotations from the agricultural press and farm state politicians, provided ballast for his argument. In a logic less theoretical or sweeping than *Contours* but just as hard to follow, he drew out the steps leading to his conclusions. His argument hinged on the growing surplus of grains, animals, and other farm goods, and the crisis posed for the farmer.

Decades of troubles had dogged agricultural businessmen, frustrating their efforts to succeed by more intensive and extensive production. Higher capital costs, more expensive transportation to market, and the increased difficulty of obtaining inexpensive farm locations put agriculture in an intermittent squeeze despite the farmers' best efforts. Government action, moreover, had never been on their side. Tariff laws intended to boost national manufacturing by keeping out low-priced foreign goods had penalized them without compensation. Likewise, federally funded internal improvements had been devoted largely to railroads, benefitting elite shareholders. As European nations sought to restrict American agricultural products, farmers concluded that a shift of markets from Europe to Latin America and Asia offered the best and perhaps the only way out. Empire held, in short, their deserved slice of the pie.[50]

If not perhaps convincing readers that various pro-imperialist political leaders of the time actually represented farmers, *Roots* had made a strong case that the ruling groups of the nineteenth century had shrewdly turned an impending social crisis into its opposite. They responded to the agrarian demands creatively and boldly. Farmers and workers supported Empire because they had accepted the large program of materialism offered them. Indeed, farmers at the least had demonstrated their acuity by insisting upon such a solution! Put differently, a culture driven by expansionism would produce imperial ambitions, whoever made the decisions.[51]

Williams was on his strongest ground when he tackled symbolic or emotional issues, such as the struggle over currency issues that had long puzzled observers. He could show that the debate between "goldbugs" (those who sought to maintain gold as the exclusive basis of currency) and "silverbugs" (those who wished to move the treasury to a parity of silver and gold) really rested upon the best means of facilitating expansion. As in the study of so many other great or obscure figures of American democratic history, contemporaries and scholars debating various sides of the issue had failed to keep their collective eye on the ball. William Jennings Bryan in particular, long seen as a forlorn moral leader of rural mores, might be better seen as the spokesman for a relatively conservative Democratic outlook which hoped to bring prosperity without armed activity abroad. But he, like his constituents, had his own plan for advancing America's world interests. William McKinley, long condemned for his consolidation of industrialists' political power in the Republican Party, might be better seen as a competent manager of the emerging world economic relations. Williams thus agreed with mainstream or conservative historians' historical accounts of McKinley's 1896 victory over Bryan as a successful appeal to the self-interest of urban dwellers, businessmen, and working people alike. He confirmed this conclusion in a characteristically Wisconsin way: Robert LaFollette had been a loyal follower of McKinley, bolting the party only with the later mismanagement of Empire.[52]

All this led Williams to an extremely strange conclusion in *Roots*, one as deeply personal as political or historical. He warned that the "schizophrenic discipline of the historian is a harrowing way to stay sane," the effort to tell the absolute truth despite recognizing the egotistic weight of the scholar's own opinions.[53] The aphorism of Max Horkheimer (which Williams must have read in graduate school) that "Again and again, ideas have cast off their swaddling clothes and struck out against the social systems that bore them," he evidently grasped as a saving grace. The imperialist consensus had determined the American past, as he believed he had demonstrated so clearly. But he hoped, if perhaps he did not quite believe, that the future remained open.

Americans should not want to create a different society still ruled by the dominant logic, he insisted. His grandmother long ago warned him to beware of what he wished for, because he might get it. The counterculture idea of "doing one's own thing"—once more that phrase and notion that he loved to hate—seemed to Williams a travesty because it reproduced the irresponsible market way of thinking. Americans desperately needed real models of decentralized, autonomous but interrconnected communities, and the political movements to create the necessary support systems.

Williams urgently asked, in closing, "whether or not there is time to accept short-run defeat rather than win a minor battle by becoming more like the enemy."[54] This was not a rhetorical question. He seemed to be suggesting that the New Left and all the associated movements (especially, perhaps, Women's Liberation) would be better off defeated, so that a more worthy challenge to the system could take shape. That was not so different from (if far less harsh and vituperative than) the curses that Irving Howe hurled at the New Left from the pages of the *New York Times Magazine*, suggesting that liberal college adminstrators joining pro-war conservatives in ordering police sweeps against antiwar students and other disruptive demonstrators could bring a sane and sensible liberalism back to light.[55] Williams remained unwilling to go this far or he was simply vague on the implications of his proposals. Unlike Howe, he viewed the American Empire as an unambiguously ominous force and had no reservations about the positive value of GIs getting out of Vietnam. But he, too, felt the passion of the moment turning against the ordered process of structural reform.

Subsequent scholarship on Populism and agrarian movements of the late nineteenth century confirmed what many critics of *Roots* had immediately suspected. Williams's eagerness to generalize from what he took to be his Iowa legacy, his consequently one-sided focus on a conservative or business-oriented Populism, could not be sustained as an accurate view of Populism as a whole. Meanwhile, the various odd implications of the book from premise to conclusion placed him at odds with his most likely sympathetic, i.e., radical reviewers. This probably was an advantage within the mainstream and would have been more so in any time but the height of the Vietnam War. But it left Williams's latest work, if not the larger body of his *oeuvre*, at odds with those who had loved him best.

Judging from reviews alone, it ranks as Williams's third most important book, after *Tragedy* and *Contours*. Indeed, a few of his closest friends such as Lloyd Gardner consider it his most original and important volume. Yet *Roots's* lengthy introduction and a broad overview of his conclusions might have been easily excerpted into a separate essay with more thematic clarity, in the manner of *Tragedy*. The unnecessary difficulty of the text pointed to other internal problems.

The sheer volume of the research certainly impressed reviewers, even if they usually could not agree with Williams's analysis. Patient readers delved into the bulk of the book, either to note how well-anchored the arguments were or to point out contradictions and omissions. Even the most severe critics took Williams's effort seriously. As the nation agonized about its imperial overreach and familiar cold-war liberals sought desperately to separate apparent errors from the generally proper course of post-1945 strategy, Williams offered at least a well-documented fresh view.

The *New York Times*'s Christopher Lehmann-Haupt, in the book's banner review, found it "certainly among the profoundest and most important books of the year," considering *Roots* to be a contribution "beyond mere concern, beyond protest, beyond tears, beyond politics, and beyond hope that what is troubling this country these days can be cured by minor surgery." Unfortunately, *Roots* had concluded with "an almost idiotic faith that by understanding history, we can reverse its course." Other reviewers showed more ambivalence. Writing in the *New York Times Book Review*, Amherst College historian John William Ward complained that the volume was "tedious, dull and repetitious," with little consideration of other hegemonic factors than market forces. Still, Williams had pointed in a direction which alone could save historians from irrelevance, an "admirable" stance of both courage and insight.[56]

A handful of the academic reviews revealed a resentment, even an envy of Williams's acquired status, mixed with a sometimes thoughtful series of criticism of his methods. The distinguished liberal historian Carl Degler, widely known for his condescension toward Old or New Left scholars complained that Williams was too narrowly economic and ignored sentimental, psychologial, and political factors.[57] Minnesota historian Gretchen Kreuter struck hardest from a methodological standpoint, questioning whether Williams was imposing a thesis upon his research and in the process dismissing twenty years of scholarship on farm protest and reform movements, especially by sympathetic scholars of Populism. David Pletcher found that Williams's sources spoke less for farmers than for rural congressmen, farm journals, processing industries, and the Midwestern press, while ignoring the significance of the millions of dollars of investments abroad by corporations in railroads, sugar plantations, and refineries.[58]

Other American reviewers divided along political lines more predictable than the ambivalences of *Roots* should have allowed. His reputation preceded and suffused the reading of his book. Among economic historians, for instance, J. R. T. Hughes deeply resented Williams's suggestion that the desire for economic growth was "sinister" and business itself a "grand conspiracy against the people"—quite a remarkable misreading of his work.[59] Liberal opinion magazines, relying upon former Marxists accustomed to defending the general outline of cold-war policies, used Williams to refine their own approach in light of the Vietnam debacle. In *Dissent*, which until 1970 supported the U.S. presence in Vietnam while opposing the particular course of the war, Henry Pachter approved Williams's special innovation of calling attention to the rural roots of the imperialist impulse. In that way, the fault could be generalized to a culture at large rather than attributed to a certain stage of capitalism, as New Left writers often asserted.

Partisan Review, favorite magazine of the New York Intellectuals in their aesthete and anticommunist mode, had surely rejected an earlier Williams outright. Grown temporarily shaky about the familiar justifications of military overreach, it devoted a roundtable over two issues to a remarkable discussion of *Roots*. Socialist intellectual Michael Harrington framed his response to *Roots* in terms of his own current political imperatives. A Catholic moralist by background, he might well have found a common ground with Williams on other issues. But he was personally close to Arthur Schlesinger, Jr., (who praised him, in turn, as one of the very few intelligent commentators on the Left) and characteristically muted his own criticism of the Vietnam War in order to maintain his influence among the upper bureaucratic reaches of the extremely hawkish AFL-CIO. Harrington could not abide Williams's description of a consistent American imperial tradition. Simply to acknowledge its existence, Harrington insisted, negated the possibility of significant change, much less a Socialist transformation. Williams thus lent ammunition to the "fifth column guerillas of the Third World" living in the United States, presumably those who celebrated the victories of

Vietnam's National Liberation Front or disdained the electoral process—just the New Leftists that Williams despised.

Harrington saluted Williams's *Contours* (as he had never done previously) for a dialectical complexity absent in *Roots*, and observed that farmers had actually shown more hostility to commercialism, more interest in the possibilities of socialism (this was surely a stretch on Harrington's part) than in the potential benefits of imperialism. But Harrington's main complaint had an unmistakeably personal tone: Williams was a "Leninist," code word among democratic socialists and liberals for a communist sympathizer who willfully excluded himself from respectable debate. Williams's longtime self-identity as a Guild Socialist or decentralist was once again drowned out by his impermissible view of cold-war history.[60]

Decades later, Williams still smarted from the sheer unfairness of Harrington's comments. He had even written Harrington personal notes and received no response.[61] The nearest successor to Norman Thomas, a sort of lesser-prestige "Mr. Socialism" in popular books and on the lecture trail, Harrington might have drawn Williams in to a pact against the confrontationism of the campus New Left and toward a different politics. But Harrington had his roots in the Democratic Party and New York Intellectual circles; to these, Williams remained an unrespected outsider. Perhaps he was seen most hatefully as mentor to younger Jewish radicals who had turned against liberalism and toward some suspect populist spirit west of the Hudson.[62]

Howard Zinn, the historian and civil-rights and peace movement veteran, might well have been another scholar at the leftward fringes of academic life to draw Williams into a different intellectual orbit. Unexpectedly invited to add his perspectives to this discussion, Zinn complained that Williams was actually losing his radical edge and becoming too much like other professional historians. Assembling a "barricade of citations against the assaults of fellow professionals" and posing academically interesting questions (such as which classes had originated imperialism), he had failed to ask what the radical readers wanted to know. *Why* had change taken place, *what* changes should take place, and *how* could such changes be brought about? Placed as few other contemporary scholars to exert a wide political influence, Williams had failed to seize the time.[63] Zinn, whose own radicalization as a pilot during the Second World War had prompted him to become a civil rights activist while teaching in the South, could not manage the scholarly detachment Williams sought and did not want to make the effort.[64]

If Harrington considered Williams a dangerous figure and Zinn considered him not dangerous enough, the inevitable *Partisan Review* choice for Williams critic, Arthur Schlesinger, Jr., sought to outmaneuver his *bête noire. Roots*, he argued, was no proper Marxist text at all (a claim which Williams never made) "except in an épater-l'académie sense," the same canard that Schlesinger, Jr., had hurled against the New Left historians. Marx himself had believed that imperialism and colonialism were necessary if often atrocious stages in world development; furthermore, Williams had miscast the eighteenth-century legacy. What the Founding Fathers meant by Empire ("secure national sovereignty") was wholly different from the twentieth-century connotation ("territorial expansion"). Williams had overstated his case and manipulated evidence to suit his thesis. The empire, if it could be called one, had been created for reasons of state, not economics. The Open Door, Schlesinger, Jr., reiterated, was merely a benevolent free-market system for equal trade.[65] As usual, Schlesinger, Jr., exercized a remarkable capacity for denial in place of dialogue.

Williams had ready answers for his critics. If one wanted to build a social movement, it was "crucial to know a great deal more than we do about the *Weltanschauung* of the majority." Only then could a dialogue begin to change it. He dismissed Schlesinger's "hyperbole and gingerbread," noting that Otto Bauer, Rudolf Hilferding, and Rosa Luxemberg, and not Lenin, were the major Marxist theorists of imperialism. The notion that key American imperialists of a kind of "warrior class" identified with the state rather than the economy made sense only if such men had rejected the belief that marketplace expansion was necessary to sustain the economy. On the other hand, Williams accepted the criticism that he had ignored subsistence farmers, migrant farm laborers, tenant farmers, sharecroppers, and the huge black rural population of the South generally. These, he added in a telling admission, had simply not been central to his work.[66]

Foreign reviewers, no doubt reflecting the appearance of several of his books in translations and the general growth of his international reputation, saw the issues of American town and country more clearly. Edmund Ions observed that going all the way back to Schlesinger, Sr., "historians East of the Appalachians—even East of the Hudson Valley" had fashioned the traditional perspectives on the nation. Williams spoke for the other America, and thereby for a larger truth. The *Times Literary Supplement* complained at his emphasis on imperialism, but congratulated Williams for supplying a healthy corrective to traditional views of the American "agrarian myth." Noted foreign correspondent David Schonbrun was effusive: *Roots* had challenged the "cherished and firmly held self-image" of Americans as "descendents of freedom-loving people who have cast off the yoke of Empire and set themselves to build a model of demoracy for all the world to envy and emulate." Who else but Williams had ever been willing to characterize U.S. foreign policy as "interventionist, imperialist, or anything but freedom-seeking?" Many had, of course, although usually without being heard. But Williams the prestigious scholar had found a *sui generis* mode of puncturing national self-delusion.

For non-historians in the United States who could wade through the tough academic prose, Williams was likewise very much the phenomenon that he took himself to be. In the liberal Catholic *Commonweal*, Richard H. Miller proposed *Roots* for the 1969 Pulitzer Prize. While the "practicioners of establishment self-deception . . . led by a lesser luminary of the Pulitzer emiriti, Oscar Handlin . . . continue to denounce . . . revisionism et opera omnia," raining their polemics on Williams, he had "helped train more important diplomatic historians than the rest of the profession combined."

One of the shrewdest reviews of all, by fellow historian Richard Leopold, spotted in between the lines of the text "a revealing self-appraisal of the author's previous writings," as if Williams were courageously seeking to come to grips with the limits of *Contours* and the rise of social history. Whatever his weaknesses, he had also fashioned a "laudable attempt to make history relevant" to a traumatized age.[67] Williams, never quite predictable, had done it again. But *Roots* could not achieve the political force of his earlier texts both because he had arrived at uncomfortable views for radicals and because the fruits of his narrowed purpose had to be judged on their analytic merits alone. The Williams of *Roots* was neither the bold anti-cold warrior of *Tragedy* nor master of the synthetic overview.

Williams had taken up, consciously or otherwise, that sector of Populism most clearly expansionist-minded. He had ignored the militant antiracist action of southern Populists which threatened for a moment to tip over the post–Civil War reestablishment of the caste system, and he also ignored the vast intimidation and illegal procedures required to prevent a multi-racial victory. Williams made no sense of the sometimes ardent Populist support of anticapitalist workers' movements and mass demonstrations of the unemployed, the interest of many thousands of Populists in utopian socialism and their later membership in the Socialist Party. Nor did he connect Populism, looking further backward, with Radical Reconstructionism and its remarkable moment of shared black and white political history of the South.

More important by far, as Lawrence Goodwyn argued so carefully in *The Democratic Promise: The Populist Movement in America* (1976), the vast enterprise of agrarian cooperatives, especially in the South, pointed in another, very different direction. The Farmers Alliance, embodying an "ethos" in Goodwyn's term, sought to integrate elements of capitalism and what can be called socialism into a "belief in the power of man as a cooperative being," potential agency of a "cooperative commonwealth." To do so, the Populists knew they needed to overcome the thickening web of finance capitalism which took control of them through the railroads and the wholesalers. To be sure they faced overwhelming odds, they lost everything in 1896, and many of their adherents embraced the emerging system that they had so abhorred.[68] The party of business successfully "created in the larger society the cultural values" dominating the twentieth century.[69] The centralization of farming steadily eroded remaining pockets of autonomy. The very idea of popular control over the banking system, however poorly expressed by agrarian radicals, now fell to the ground forever.

Williams came close to admitting the *possibility* of this interpretation in acknowledging his failure to treat the lower-class element of Populism. Goodwyn reflected enough of the marketplace reality of the farmers' cooperationist vision to offer a conceptual bridge. But if the evidence laid out by Goodwyn should have persuaded him, Williams offered no significant reinterpretation of the subject in his later, mostly passing remarks about nineteenth-century agrarian movements.

For Williams to have accepted a fundamentally different view would have been to contextualize his particular organic vision of Midwestern America within a larger rural frame, limiting its universal significance. But his system of thought was buried as deeply in him as the rectitude of massive cold-war militarization and unchecked presidential prerogative was in the mentality of Arthur Schlesinger, Jr. Not only childhood recollections and subsequent projections, but a large portion of Williams's energies since 1953 had gone into demonstrating the validity of Turner's thesis before Turner, i.e., how much expansionism had been a popular doctrine.[70] He could not encompass an opposite view, even a partial one.

On the markedly positive side, as Williams's friends and devotees argued, *Roots* was important less as a book about agrarian politics than as a book about American life at large. Richard Van Alstyne insisted in the *Nation*, with pardonable exaggeration, that Williams's "intellectual tour de force" hit traditional interpretations of American domestic history with almost the same force as his earlier work had hit foreign-policy history. Michael Meeropol, who had come to Madison hoping to study with Williams and subsequently sought to draw him into local neighborhood organizing projects, concluded similarly in the pages of *Radical America* that Williams remained the "great myth-destroyer" clearing away the "mechanistic Marxist cobwebs." Thereby, he had fostered a "creative Marxism" far larger than himself. A well-circulated special issue of the same journal, *Radical Historiography*, which sold widely at the 1970 American Historical Association convention, accorded Williams the honor of having laid foundation stones for the ediface of a reinterpreted national history.[71]

In that specific sense, *Roots* was the logical successor to the *Great Evasion*, *Contours*, and *Tragedy*. Those close and distant who believed that they observed his work falling off in pertinence to contemporary politics and historical scholarship and found themselves reading each volume with less interest after *Contours*, missed an elusive but all-important point. Very much like a novelist who creates works that cover various fields but always refers back to the deeply personal experience of youth, Williams continued to work out the place of Atlantic, Iowa, within the Empire at large, and to pose the moral dilemmas of American success. Karl Marx's theories and "Sockless Jerry" Simpson's personal version of Adam Smith alike offered grist for Williams's particular mill. He simply could not have written *Roots* any other way than the particular way he wrote it.

4

Roots also completed a major *modus operandi* and even a way of life for Williams. He would never work on another full-scale monograph, devoting the remainder of his intellectual energies to moneymaking textbook projects (however little money they actually made), synthetic essays, and autobiographical ventures. Only rarely did he acknowledge any regrets over unfinished projects or ones never begun; often he confided to friends, inaccurately as it turned out, that he had written his last book.

But now personal troubles became more and more overwhelming. Williams had enjoyed enormously the early years of his own three biological children, set off in a sense from problems with the older ones. He wrote close friends repeatedly relating, in passing, his special delight with his girls. But troubles were never far away. Almost predictably, one of his grown children, moving into her own apartment in Madison, was arrested hiding a substantial "stash" of marijuana: the most transgressive nonviolent behavior imaginable. Williams, like so many other parents in the 1960s, continued to resist the implications. He could not help feeling that he had provided luxuries and security that he had never enjoyed, but that he received in return no gratitude and precious little acknowledgment.

He naturally blamed Corrinne and Madison for the growing problems that he experienced with his children and hers. Close observers might have detected that while he had bragged of changing diapers, he took little role in the considerable household duties, such as cleaning, and he could hardly boil water let alone cook. He considered the gender roles of parents as fixed and satisfying. No doubt, in his own mind, he had achieved after great effort what had been denied his mother's family after his father's death.

In 1964, as Corrinne Williams tells the story, she tuned in state radio station WHA while doing the family ironing. On a show of daily readings, the narrator offered chapters of Betty Friedan's *The Feminine Mystique*.[72] Corrinne's consciousness, like that of millions of other American women, had already begun awakening. By the middle 1960s, middle-class Madison's faculty-heavy and politically progressive West Side fairly buzzed with doctrines foreshadowing the Women's Liberation Movement. Several of Williams's social circle, wives of faculty friends, took part in local chapters of the International League for Peace and Freedom or Women Strike for Peace where such doctrines quickly took root.

Williams met this ideological invasion with a sense of intellectual scandal and personal outrage. He needed someone or something to blame, a superstructural theory to explain his own growing discomfort. Feminism, as he wrote often privately and a few times publicly, was not a true theory of emancipation but only a theory of individualism. It had no spirit of community, and indeed it aimed at breaking up that most fundamental community, the family itself. He had *always* made the large decisions on family funds, and preferred (as he had with Jeannie) to view his withdrawal from emotional closeness as the result of mutual differences rather than a power play with nearly all the power on his side.

Corrinne, who had announced early in the marriage her determination to return to graduate school when her youngest child was enrolled in first grade, now made clear that she intended to follow through. Williams viewed this move as a further effort to undermine his family status. An extremely revealing passage in a later book intellectualized the quarrel by trivializing its origin. Note the almost bizarre shift of subject from the 1890s to the present and back again:

> [President Grover] Cleveland's almost obsessive concern with the silver question serves to illustrate a more general aspect of interpreting the raw facts of history. Even at the individual and highly personal level, major confrontations often become displaced—symbolized—by secondary aspects of the crisis. Two people who are living together and who have come to understand their potentially destructive differences often argue about their fundamental incompatabilities (a matter of value systems), for example, in the language of who earns the most money and how it is spent. That also happens on the social level, between two or more groups of people, and just such a debate was well advanced in 1892 in the United States.[73]

No more transparent passage had ever been written, at least by Williams. He was right about displacement but dead wrong about what was being displaced.

Drinking more steadily, throwing himself into secret sexual liasons, he seemed to lose the personal control that he valued so highly in himself and others. It was, above all, time for a fresh start. But no midlife renewal is ever really free from the ghosts of the past.

6

At Home in Oregon

WILLIAM APPLEMAN WILLIAMS SPENT MORE than a third of his adult life, twenty years, in the relative seclusion of the Oregon coast, living in the manner he planned well in advance of his retirement. As he later wrote in the outline of a never-to-be-published autobiography, he wanted to give himself the "chance to get beyond History into dealing with alternatives for a better America."[1] His reputation grew and his scholarly influence spread. With the publication of several more popular and well-received books (and despite several others that could qualify on neither count) he became an admired senior figure. New generations of historians seeking fresh insights into the large picture of American development found, at any rate, no equal to his work.

Yet it was intermittently a bitter time rather than the well-earned rest and reinvigoration he had anticipated. He imagined himself happy in the small town of mostly working-class people, and he was certainly so at times. He could hardly avoid the national dialogue that he, more than any other scholar, had helped to generate along historical lines. When he sought to intervene directly in questions of foreign policy and its domestic consequences, however, he found himself more and more at the margins, both geographically and politically.

Williams's best books continued to carry considerable weight, but he somehow never received the high academic status virtually automatic to others who had refigured major paradigms. He reached the wide-circulation periodical press only briefly, in a series of *New York Review of Books* essays, while confronted with continual attacks from various critics and afforded scant opportunity to respond. He also rightly suspected that new careers in academic and public life had been based on the mining of his ideas, often without the proper acknowledgment. Finally, he felt hemmed in by the self-defined secondary status and intellectual mediocrity of Oregon State. He acknowledged what he had suspected for a long time, that he had depended upon the excitement of intellectual exchange and intimate friendships of Madison more than he had realized.

More than all this, he suffered from the growning awareness that the hopes of changing U.S. foreign policy and U.S. life in general had almost certainly been lost for a generation or more. Liberals at or near the apex of the Democratic Party establishment had learned almost nothing, despite the presence of a few intelligent diplomatic figures like Cyrus Vance. After the Vietnam episode passed, the party center tipped steadily back toward military-industrial economics and the centrist effort to outbid Republicans as swaggering cold warriors. Intelligent conservatives, if they existed at all at the upper levels of government—a few surely advised Nixon's China policy—folded ignominiously before the New Right of Jesse Helms and Ronald Reagan. Through recession and better times alike, many millions of Americans appeared to thrive psychologically in a fool's paradise of knee-jerk nationalism with no need for the likes of a conscience like William A. Williams.

Increasingly pained at the irrelevance of the Left in this dreary slide, Williams drew his own predictably idiosyncratic conclusions. The great historian seemed at times very wise, at others almost misanthropic and convinced that the "new social movements" such as feminism only contributed to the national dilemma by diminishing resistance to ever advancing individualism. His continued troubles with publishers reinforced his sense of frustration and isolation as a prophet in the wilderness of intellectual fads and political regression.

Seen from a longer view, he still had much to contribute. Nothing could have offered a clearer picture of government conducted behind closed doors than did Watergate. The widespread disillusionment with government, the energy shortage, the slow perpetuation and sudden flare-up of the cold war when the Russians clearly wanted peace, the accelerating environmental degradation and other such developments could not have surprised veteran Williams readers. The "overextended society," as the 1970s came to be called popularly, had the unmistakable look of a characteristically American self-made national tragedy. Such vindications, however, consoled him little when his mood was dark.

Williams was nevertheless personally resilient. Publishing important books at the center of acrimonious debates during the final years of the Vietnam War, he remained an intellectual inspiration to antiwar intellectuals and cold-war revisionists. Despite growing physical ailments, he lectured widely in the U.S. and on occasion abroad. On the platform and in the seminar room, if not in the *New York Times*, *Harper's*, or the *Atlantic*, he reached audiences willing and eager to listen.

I

Williams started his return to Oregon on a high note. *The Roots of the Modern American Empire* was published almost precisely as he reached campus, and he seemed to be cruising along toward ever greater heights. Critic (and literary agent) Clifford Solway, writing in the *Saturday Review* in 1970, hailed Williams as the nation's "leading radical historian." Occupier of a "special, soulful niche of Great Teacher" and an author of vital works, Williams had brilliantly articulated the widespread but mostly inarticulate desire to "find a moral substitute for the market place in American society." He had made himself the grand narrator of a society which failed to realize its original aims but might still turn "in on itself, responsive to its own needs . . . harmonizing its conflicting interests, redeeming citizens from alienation, giving them a handhold on their own destiny."[2] Eugene D. Genovese, in an interview, described Williams simply as "the best historian that the Left has produced in this country."[3]

In 1970, the *New York Review of Books* had solicited from him a series of lengthy essays on various topics, producing the largest immediate circulation his writings had ever achieved. The *Review*, then at its peak readership of perhaps 200,000 and at its peak political prestige as an intellectuals' journal opposed to the Vietnam War, had unique highbrow cachet as a kind of American *Times Literary Supplement*. In the *New York Review's* pages, Williams seemed to hold court. Much as his later friend and correspondent Gore Vidal would do there decades later, he wrote as quirkily as he chose on a given topic, challenging Americans to think about their mixed legacies. To some of his old friends, it was the oddest Williams yet. But by flaunting orthodoxy on all sides, Williams successfully disarmed in advance the stock conservative complaints while compelling many sympathetic readers to rethink their assumptions—and once more inflamed liberals who, despite their shaken confidence and the generational downward drift, still dominated U.S. political history. All in all, it was his most public performance and (along with his late-life classic, *Empire As a Way of Life*) his most eloquent text in the typically Williamsesque mixture of horse sense and moral pleading.

Williams insightfully imagined a mercantile America run by Alexander Hamilton–type conservatives choosing a smaller land empire and thereby leaving large numbers of Indians (along with the environment) to a better fate. He further imagined the North letting the South go to its own destiny, presuming with more than uncertain judgment that slavery would have to fall. He imagined Herbert Hoover rather than Woodrow Wilson setting the tone for post-1930 politics and diplomatic engagement, with open candor about the proper and practical limits of international influence. He imagined that the paternalism of Wilson and Roosevelt once done could nevertheless be undone, and that Dwight Eisenhower had begun the process by exposing what Roosevelt had hidden, the economic agenda that the military had been ordered to carry out in alliance with giant corporations.

Williams's views of many subjects, particularly Wilson and Hoover, would be familiar to his readers, if reworked here in terms of current books. He had no difficulty explaining Wilson's commitment to "an organic, conservative, corporate America in which all constituent elements would be integrated under the leadership of a benevolent elite."[4] Doing so cut neatly through the standard liberal interpretation of the old-fashioned individualist Wilson poised against the corporate giants which, of course, he aided enormously. Likewise assessing Wilson's preparations to invade Mexico ("the first Cubans, the first Russians, even the first Vietnamese," Williams called the Mexicans), the essayist plucked an appropriate gem of true American imperial psychology in Wilson's phrase that "*when properly directed*, there is no people not fitted for self-development."[5]

Williams had only a bit of trouble with Hoover, convincing himself if not many readers that the much-maligned president was "done in by his faith in the dream of a cooperative American community, and by his ruthless intellectual analysis of what would happen if the dream was not honored."[6] The crusader against paternalism looked to Williams like a philosopher, holding off various versions of state capitalism and state socialism. Williams could barely conceive that Hoover's faith in the redeeming power of business might have vitiated his other admirable qualities or prepared the way for other kinds of business-centered presidencies.

In his most creative stroke, Williams took up military questions as a radical or merely sensible military man might. The Second World War looked different when the historian considered that Eisenhower and

Marshall had been eager to assault the Germans in 1942, so as to assist the Russians actually doing the vast bulk of the fighting. Ike boldly resisted the temptation to look at war as a vast engineering project, an idea fostered by those convinced they could win easy victory through more and more intense bombing strikes against German industrial (i.e., urban) centers. Eisenhower knew better, and with the same wisdom refused Churchill's plan to "end World War II by forming a skirmish line for World War III in Berlin" and confronting the Russians.[7] Ike's wisdom recalled John Quincy Adams saying "no" to the annexation of Texas, and even to George Washington declining a chance at kingship. He looked bigger and bigger in Williams's eyes, morally much larger than the golf-playing former general could to those who recalled that the arms race had never slowed under his regime nor had the CIA or FBI hesitated in their heavily funded pursuits.

Against the benign image of Eisenhower, Douglas MacArthur offered a study in personal arrogance. But Williams managed to see him sympathetically as warrior trained for no other purpose than the acquistion and expression of authority. More to the point, MacArthur had seized only the opportunities for overreach that the civilian authorities had eagerly handed him. The ominous "military industrial complex" of Eisenhower's phrase was for Williams actually "but one facet of the industrial-political conglomerate that has dominated the political economy throughout the twentieth century." In function if not personality, MacArthur was a creature of their making.[8]

A proud military veteran responding to the Vietnam-era revulsion at violence, Williams likewise suggested that the exposure of the U.S. massacre of Vietnamese civilians at My Lai and other American war crimes should prompt not the scapegoating of the military (which, as usual, carried out civilian orders) but an investigation of where the abuses originated. He thought that military officers, imbued with the concept of Duty, might take the course of public resignation when orders conflicted with constitutional responsibilities—if only they were honored for that brave act as they had been honored for battlefield heroics. Arguing against a national exercise in public trials he proposed eloquently:

> It would be tragic to externalize all moral energy in a righteous trial of what we all now know is wrong. It is not really to the point to say simply that if all of us are guilty, then no one is guilty. The trouble is that when all of us are guilty we much prefer to shovel it all off on a few so that we can go on with business as usual. It is time we recognized the potential health in honest guilt, acknowledged our mistakes, and healed ourselves through political action to create an America that will no longer be hated and feared. That is, incidentally, the only

sure way to solve the problems of the military. And, also, the problem of law and order.[9]

This reasoning had its limits, mostly those of class and race within the armed forces. Rather than an orgy of blame, the chief danger was that America would brush aside the war crimes issue entirely. (Indeed, Oliver North first emerged here as a public figure, sponsored by William F. Buckley and denying that any massacres had taken place.) Vietnam Veterans Against the War offered more stark and better testimony about the nature of the war, returning their medals and marching on the White House with broken bodies, than Williams with his references to Duty and constitutional authority could possibly provide. Active officers knew that terrible orders had been given or implied, and many of them carried that consciousness into later civilian and military life. But the effective acts of conscience or passive resistance took place with the rarest exceptions only at the lowest military levels.

That said, Williams made his points with an authority that no one else in public life could match in this respect. For the last time, he was the war veteran who glimpsed the big picture from within the field of battle and lived to develop the immanent critique of the civilization that had pro-grammed conquest without admitting the cost in blood. Other future historians had certainly gone to war and returned both sadder and wiser, but none had brought back this kind of eloquence.[10]

Williams waxed eloquent on Lyndon Johnson and John F. Kennedy because he had found a remarkable foil for his favorite villains. While Johnson was never much respected by Eastern liberals and was regarded by 1968 as a lower form of life (perhaps only a bit higher than Nixon), Williams did not approve of "the computers . . . overheating under the load of all those Brownie Points coming in from the Ivy League" calibrated for comparing Johnson unfavorably to Kennedy.[11] A vintage Williams passage, in form as much as content, followed:

> If the Liberal Establishment were prepared to lead us plebs into the Golden Age, it would have neither the time nor the need to bela-bor Lyndon and his merely human torments. Having won the battle at the crossroads with their shiny new crossbows, the prodigies would be fingering the Grail.
>
> Alas.
>
> Rather, thank God. (Remember the Bay of Pigs, the Green Berets, the Missile Madness, and the noble call to Define Ourselves in Terms of the State.)[12]

Johnson, he insisted, had been sucked into abandoning the best vision of any president in the century. He had been duped or self-duped into believ-ing that enough economic growth would solve any problem—if only he could explain water power to the Vietnamese, he honestly believed that they would halt their rebellion—and he had simply continued down the primrose path of New and Fair Deal liberalism. He had been miseducated in diplomacy by Kennedy advisors in particular. One final time Williams recalled Herbert Hoover's public objection of 1950 to the famous Truman global overreach. Eisenhower was, at his best, closer in spirit to the Iowa-born engineer than to the former Missouri haberdasher that he succeeded. But Kennedy revived Truman-style international "activism." He initiated the new arms buildup and computerized the counterrevolutionary appara-tus at the Pentagon. He opened the door to Asian war in Laos, nearly provoked a military confrontation with the Russians in Berlin, sprung the Bay of Pigs (Williams was convinced that in this matter, anyway, Nixon was worse: he would have followed up with the Marines), and learned nothing from all this except that he *really* wanted to win:

> He gave serious consideration to any proposal that seemed likely to blot out the defeat. There was open talk of another invasion, and he persistently discussed the assassination of Castro.
> Irony of ironies.
> Terror of terrors.[13]

Khrushchev had been expansive enough to grasp, at the crucial moment of the Cuban Missile Crisis, that Kennedy could not psychologically make the first gesture pulling back from the nuclear brink. And Kennedy learned something from near-catastrophe. But he did not not learn enough, cer-tainly not the lesson that "a social movement can unzip a nuclear empire."[14] Thus Vietnam.

Even here, on an issue where millions of words had been spilled by 1970, Williams had something original to say. Johnson had (in Williams's famil-iar terms) failed to honor his own commitments and thereby failed the nation. He actually went to Congress in 1965 with the war issue, as Roosevelt, Truman, and Kennedy would surely not have done. He grossly misrepresented the Gulf of Tonkin incident there, as Williams did not note. But the North Vietnamese handed him a rationale by launching ground attacks in February 1965. Aroused, Johnson set out to finish an awful job. Only much later did he begin to understand the full measure of the harm he had done. The Kennedys, minus two assassinations, might have somehow given a credulous public the illusion in Southeast Asia of "another classic American victory." Johnson, in his blunders, had prompted Americans "to the visceral confrontation with ourselves that offers us a chance to break out of our traditional outlook."[15] It was an enormous potential contribution, if only Americans could take their opportunity.

But the great chance for change had been squandered in the sixties, twice over. The racial egalitarianism that white southerner LBJ proposed at home would, in itself, have been a magnificent democratic leap forward decades earlier; by 1964, and notwithstanding the Civil Rights Act, it was simply inadequate to the social problems at hand. When Johnson went down, Nixon came up a colorless figure who might possibly have made himself an American Disraeli but instead became (under the tutelage of Henry Kissinger) just another would-be successor to Woodrow Wilson. Williams still hoped Nixon would reconsider his course and become a statesman and even an intellectual, although he had few illusions on that score. Williams obviously did not foresee Watergate ahead, although he would have been the last one surprised at presidential debacle rooted in the unconstitutional imperatives of the security state.

Reprinted by the *Review*'s own press the next year as *Some Presidents*, the essays had little further distribution (as the publishers anticipated when they informed Williams they could offer only a small advance for the book). Nor was it much reviewed, a process which might have found critics unraveling the fascinating contradictions within Williams's narrative. One could imagine friendly commentators showing that Williams had tried more than ever before to speak for himself, not the foreign-policy expert or professor so much as the military man, the non-Easterner, the citizen.[16] The book seemed to fall anomalously from sight, probably because anyone interested in it had already read the contents serially in the *New York Review*. Its impact had been, for Williams personally, important nevertheless. As the U.S. involvement in the Vietnam War reached a climax and wound down, he seemed to have gained stature continuously, and by now, not quite fifty years old, to be at the top of his game. He was properly prepared for the stiffest challenges he would receive from cold-war traditionalists.

2

Behind the accolades and general wide appreciation for Williams with all his warts, a geological shift had taken place in the teaching and writing of U.S. history. The Vietnam War and the rise of social movements dampened the aging cold warriors' spirits as bright youngsters researched dissertations on "radical" subjects and looked to favorite historians to oppose once orthodox views in the public arena. On the merits of the arguments as much as the political shift of the profession, the antiwarriors won much historiographical ground, but not without facing well-placed challenges. For the last time, Williams seemed to be in the middle of the controversy, even when personally on the sidelines.

Defections from the erstwhile scholarly mainstream counted heavily at the end of the 1960s. As a handful of neoconservatives and traditionalists rushed into print condemning the rise of "New Left" history generally (and in particular the early volumes produced by scholars of women's history), other notables showed remarkable signs of rethinking their positions. Richard Hofstadter's *The Progressive Historians* (1968) suggested that historians needed to ask new questions about "the complex texture of apathy and irrationality that holds a society together." Thinking aloud about the radical historians, some of them his final graduate students, Hofstadter observed that scholarship *should* restore "our slave insurrections, our mobbed abolitionists and lynched Wobblies, our sporadic, furious militant Homesteads, Pullmans, and Patersons; our race lynchings and ghetto riots."[17]

Hofstadter more than answered the sputtering critics such as Oscar Handlin, who had insisted that the radicals were forcing a political agenda upon scholarship. Admitting that developments themselves had changed the agenda, conservative David Potter lamented that historical studies became irrelevant in the "intellectual riptide" which occasionally swept through society at large. Scholars who had once forced their own agendas upon the profession during the not-so-distant 1950s found themselves demoralized, bitter, and often uncomprehending. Others like David Donald, in 1940s youth a radical sympathizer and in early middle age a doughty conservative, began to see the history that they wrote with new eyes. Radical fanatics had become heroic fighters for black rights. New scholarship in their fields, rather than enraging them, prompted admiration and rethinking.[18]

This flexibility remained more rare on issues closer to the present such as the cold war. Rather than altering their views, hardliners found themselves displaced in prestige, and replaced at lower levels of academic privilege by younger men and women with strikingly different assumptions. The "realist" Norman Graebner, one of Williams early admirers, discovered in distributing a questionnaire to several hundred colleagues about the "success" of U.S. foreign policy in the nineteenth and twentieth centuries that the old questions could not be posed in the same way. A great number of teachers had come to the conclusion that "success" in attaining standard U.S. national objectives might well be moral disaster for the world. When the work of younger scholars began overturning some of the most basic assumptions of the cold war (such as Stalin's supposed aggressiveness on Greece, which in actuality was an acquiescence to Western interests), and when even George Kennan's *Memoirs* showed an anguished diplomatic veteran seeking to grapple with the nation's obsessions and errors, traditional positions simply could not retain their familiar credibility.[19]

U.S. escalation of the bombings and the war generally played a central role in turning minds, but before Vietnam's effects had been fully realized, Williams had one more round of spirited debate with his major critics. Arthur M. Schlesinger, Jr., early on signalled the beginning of an intensified controversy with a letter to the *New York Review of Books* in 1966, declaring it was time to "blow the whistle before the current outburst of revisionism regarding the origins of the cold war goes much further."[20] Within a year, the debate had attracted the attention of the *New York Times*.[21] A month later, Schlesinger, Jr., fired a major broadside in *Foreign Affairs*, the voice of the Council of Foreign Relations. Although historiographical revisionism had occurred after every major war, he noted, "past exercises in revisionism have failed to stick." This time, however, the challenge appeared to have a dangerous staying power. The United States no doubt made some mistakes, and the failure of communication on both sides had been harmful, but Marxist ideology and Stalin's paranoia made certain that even the "most rational of American policies could hardly have averted the cold war."[22]

Williams countered wryly in the *Nation* that Schlesinger, Jr., lacked the professional training to make psychiatric judgments. Besides and more importantly, no major U.S. policymaker between 1943 and 1948 had dealt with Stalin as a paranoid. Cold-war psychologizing could have found plenty of unbalanced minds at the top of both superpower governments, as subsequent studies of the James Forrestal (one of Schlesinger's early favorites), John Foster Dulles, J. Edgar Hoover, and arguably also Truman in his public tantrums suggested. In any event, Russian leaders need not have been paranoid to be upset by the way the U.S. flaunted its atomic bombs. Besides all this, Schlesinger, Jr., ignored the real historic origins of an ideologically driven anticommunism: not the 1947 of Stalin's misdeeds but 1917, when the Russian Revolution struggled for life.

Historian Christopher Lasch, who admired Williams while assailing New Left historians as a group, followed the Schlesinger, Jr.–Williams exchange with an extremely odd essay in the *New York Times Magazine*. It was good, he suggested, that revisionists could continue their work "(inconsequential as it may eventually be) without fear of being whistled to a stop by a referee." Historians should take such arguments more seriously in any case, not only to expose the "inadequacies" in orthodox positions but also the "ambiguities" in the revisionist cause. This lefthanded defense of Williams and the revisionists was weak enough. Lasch added that due to Williams, young radicals now foolishly considered it "axiomatic" that U.S. foreign policy had been counterrevolutionary and that no fundamental change was possible short of domestic revolution.[23] Even most of Williams's critics would consider this a bizarre caricature, closer indeed to Lasch's own position that the Empire could not be halted short of socialism.

The distinguished European intellectual historian and sometime peace candidate, H. Stuart Hughes, also weighed in to defend the intelligence services and anticommunist public opinion from what he took to be Williams's slights. Offering in *Commentary* magazine some personal testimony from the time he had served with the Office of Strategic Services during the world war and later with the State Department's Division of Research for Europe, he insisted that the revisionists simply lacked the "feel and taste" for the complexities of the 1940s. Although they had properly rehabilitated "those of us who originally opposed the cold-war mentality," they wrongly believed that the U.S. leaders could or should have seen the world in terms of spheres of influence, with Russia's unique history and its needs given special consideration. They also improperly saw anticommunism as "evil or misguided," when on a case-by-case basis "hostility to communism made sense in certain contexts and was blind and self-defeating in others."[24] Hughes could not account, however, for the out-of-control quality of the state security apparatus, or for the failure of presumably moralistic insiders to speak out early and often against the clear violations of international law and morality—to say nothing of the corrupting influences that secret funding exerted within American academic life.[25] While offering what seemed to be a balanced and personal perspective, Hughes actually anticipated a revulsion at anti-imperialism fully realized in the neo-conservative tilt of *Commentary* editors and contributors during the 1970s-80s.

Meanwhile, Williams emerged an admired figure in steadily wider academic circles. A poll of members conducted by the Organization of American Historians in 1971 showed that the *Tragedy of American Diplomacy* was one of the most influential books of any kind on college campuses. By this time, revisionist interpretations had begun to find their way into college textbooks, and even many traditional scholars had shifted ground to some degree on the cold war.[26] Gar Alperovitz, Gabriel Kolko, Lloyd Gardner, Diane Shaver Clemens, D. F. Fleming, Thomas G. Paterson, and non-campus intellectuals Carl Oglesby and David Horowitz were only a few of the heavily read revisionists caught up in scholarship, popularization, and controversy around views often heavily influenced by Williams. A *Wall Street Journal* reporter called him the "dean of leftwing diplomatic historians."[27]

Williams must have found the Congressional summons for 1971 on the origins of the cold war psychologically fulfilling. Only a decade ago, he had been hauled in front of HUAC. Now, he joined experienced cold warriors like Schlesinger, Jr., and Adam Ulam, fellow revisionist Richard Barnet, and the dean of revisionism, D. F. Fleming, in the spotlight. Schlesinger, Jr., restated his familiar perspective, insisting that the Truman administration had conducted no "crusading policy" until the Korean War and that the U.S. had never overreacted until 1953, when John Foster Dulles came to power at State—conveniently forgetting NSC-68 and the largest peacetime military buildup in American history. From that point on, Schlesinger, Jr., now saw what he had missed before, a runaway conflict with nationalism gradually undoing the assumptions of a bipolar world. Cold-war institutions were viewed ever more skeptically, now that the "old Stalinist Russia had gone," and that was "immensely to the good." No world power should continue to insist "that it has exclusive possession of the truth . . . [and] that it looks forward to the day when its absolute truth obliterates competing truths in the rest of the planet."[28] It would be difficult indeed to find a more forceful vindication of post-1953 relativism. If only Schlesinger had been expansive enough to admit the Kennedy administration's large burden of guilt in its dealings with the Third World as well as its escalating arms race with Russia, he and Williams might have found valuable common ground for the decades remaining to them.

Williams seemed for his part determined to be as cooperative as possible, almost as if to build upon Schlesinger, Jr.'s tacit admission of earlier errors of judgment. Because the U.S. had insisted upon a "world marketplace on capitalist terms" and wrongly analogized the Soviet Union with Nazi Germany, it had projected unrealistic expectations, including the long-term dominance of the Third World. He proposed that "Professor Schlesinger is absolutely correct . . . that the government generally engaged in a kind of massive overkill in its selling" of cold-war views to the public—but added politely that the exaggeration had come "much earlier than Professor Schlesinger allowed." The U.S. had thereby become locked into policies that misallocated resources, disregarded anticolonial and postcolonial nationalism, and harmed America. Stepping "outside my defined role as a historian," he concluded with a citizen's appeal:

> I am very pleased by what this subcommittee is doing. I think you have a great opportunity. I would like to see it be the beginning of Congress reasserting its role in the active ongoing dialog about foreign policy. I would like to see it as the House of Representatives, close to people every two years, broadening and deepening the debate about foreign policy. And I would like to see and like to hope, finally, that out of these hearings would come a decision and a will by the House of Representatives to take the lead in reallocating our resources and reordering our priorities.[29]

There the discussion practically ended, with a series of reiterations. Schlesinger, Jr., rebutted that capitalism played no "kind of significant role" in American postwar policy, and that the U.S. had simply been compelled to act; Williams responded that patience and understanding had never been tried, especially not by the "terribly impatient, hurryup" Truman who wanted everything settled in America's favor at the outset.[30] The two decades-long antagonists had obviously not reached agreement. But the fact that he and Schlesinger, Jr., found each other on the same platform and at an equal level of public acceptance was a great step forward. Within the profession, meanwhile, there was no doubt where the sympathies of the younger intellectuals lay.

Other scholarly assessments of the revisionist controversy dragged on mainly among specialists in the academic journals. Daniel M. Smith, for instance, hoped that revisionism would initiate a "scholarly dialectical process" that would ultimately yield "a more intellectually satisfying historical synthesis." If current revisionism had emerged in reaction to the "alleged failures of an affluent middle-class society, disillusioned by cold-war rhetoric, and appalled by the dangers of thermonuclear destruction," Smith complained, then the "moralism" of the New Left that prompted its members to embrace foreign revolutions tended "merely to substitute one kind of interventionism and American concept of mission for another."[31]

Charles S. Maier was more typical of intellectuals defending their familiar turf from scholars who seemed to represent the troublesome student activists. Revisionists had showed themselves "interested in certain specific modes of explanation and no others," with a value system and vocabulary that made meaningful dialogue impossible. Just as guilty as traditional cold-war historians of producing tautologies, they offered propositions that could not be proven or disproven. Others who styled themselves "realists" lamented similarly that New Left interpretations perceived "only evil in U.S. motives rather than merely setting forth the facts and explaining them."[32] This line of argument had the strangely reminiscent sound of the 1950s, when cold-war defenders had cursed criticism of America as based in "ideology," defending their own views as disinterested logic.

Lloyd Gardner, Hans Morgenthau, and Schlesinger, Jr., made what might be regarded as one final effort at dialogue or scholarly detente between cold warriors and their critics, setting forth respectively the revisionist, realist, and liberal perspectives in a roundtable. The discussion foundered when Schlesinger, Jr., could accept no element of the "spheres of influence" position. Had the West equivocated, Stalin would have "used Eastern Europe as a springboard for further leaps to the West," a view Gardner easily rebutted by pointing to specific instances of calculated and restrained Russian actions.[33] Seemingly, the differences of historical interpretation had proved irreconcilable.

For a brief moment in time, the various players nevertheless shared an opposition to the current Southeast Asian conflict. The logic of escalation had led to massive U.S. bombings (including unprecedented use of chemical warfare, with the volatile herbicide Agent Orange dumped on millions of biologically rich acres of rainforest), "free fire zones," and the "secret" invasion of Cambodia. Jolted by the opening of a technological nightmare and the popular response in protests across the U.S. and Europe, Schlesinger, Jr., joined Morgenthau as a prominent if cautious critic of the war. But Schlesinger, Jr., and most of his old-time colleagues in the leadership of Americans for Democratic Action (ADA) found the implications hard to swallow. During a heated White House meeting of 1967, when Schlesinger called for the replacement of the State Department team around Dean Rusk, Vice-President Hubert Humphrey (himself absolutely convinced that the Vietnam War was an extension of a Chinese Communist plot) reportedly shot back, "Arthur, these are your guys. You were in the White House when they took over. Don't blame them on us." Schlesinger, Jr., went silent.[34] Liberalism was in disarray, and would remain so for a long time, arguably because it could not handle the contradictions of its own conflicted history.

Later, the traditionalists' mood turned vindictive. After the high point of military conflict and the antiwar protest had passed, counterrevisionism entered full swing, both conservatives and liberal hardliners determined to shrug off the significance of recent events. Oscar Handlin, for instance, blustered in the conservative press at the publishing houses, attacking the media and fellow historians for "flaccid acceptance" of the "shoddy work" of the revisionists. Although the claim that the U.S. had the principal blame for the cold war was "inherently absurd," the revisionists had somehow "persuaded a considerable segment of liberal opinion" by supplying "a pseudo-historical basis for the wishful thinking of present-day isolationists."[35]

In the now swiftly rightward-drifting *Commentary*, veteran ideologue Walter Laqueur went for the jugular. Cold-war revisionism smelled to him like the German revisionism of World War I that had produced the myths upon which Hitler had been able to capitalize. The possibility that these myths reflected a revanchist, military-minded conservative nationalism far closer to Laqueur's own sentiments about America's war on Vietnam— which had supposedly been sabotaged from within—did not seem to occur to Laqueur at all. The Germans themselves had no revisionist views of the cold war, Laqueur insisted—overlooking the very considerable New Left influence in German scholarship—because Germany had experienced communism at close range and Germans were "more likely to trust their own recollections than the work of historians from . . . Madison, Wisconsin." The American New Left writings contained "a good deal of inanity, misjudgment and even hysteria" like that of the anticommunists they condemned (Laqueur obviously did not include himself). One could respect William Appleman Williams "as a writer on American history . . . but once he ventures outside his field, as in *The Tragedy of American Diplomacy*, the result is often embarrassing, if not laughable."[36] Just what did Laqueur think Williams's field of history was?

The indomitable Schlesinger, Jr., meanwhile moved his assault against the revisionists into the *Wall Street Journal*. He recalled, with only a trace of irony, "those brave days when America was manning the battlements of freedom against the wicked communist hordes." He now admitted that the Soviet Union had some "clear and legitimate concerns" and had been "acting more on defensive grounds and on local considerations" while the U.S. replied with "universalist principles." Nevertheless, the Soviet scheme for expansion had been heroically met with the Marshall Plan and NATO. Reiterating his familiar positions, Schlesinger, Jr., also previewed the coming attraction of a new book that would be "a quiet but devastating indictment of revisionist scholarship," showing the revisionists' "unscrupulous manipulation of documents."[37]

The book that Schlesinger, Jr., glowingly (or perhaps gloatingly) described was *The New Left and the Origins of the Cold War*. The scholar behind it, Robert James Maddox, not only began as a Williams student but owed his career to Williams's personal intervention. One of his graduate school classmates remembers him as a thoroughly cynical young man with a great sense of humor. After Maddox twice failed his comprehensive examinations, Williams got him into the doctoral program at Rutgers (through Warren Susman) without penalty or delay. Maddox later got a job at Pennsylvania State University and wrote a volume on William J. Borah with a distinctly Williamsesque revisionist flavor.[38]

Souring on his own views and seeing a unique literary opportunity at hand, Maddox carried an antirevisionist manifesto to Princeton University Press, which successfully solicited the endorsements of Schlesinger, Jr., Handlin, Kennan, and the noted Vietnam hawk, Eugene Rostow, for the contents of the book.[39] *The New Left and the Origins of the Cold War* examined accounts by seven revisionist writers (Williams, Alperovitz, Gardner, Fleming, Horowitz, Kolko, and Clemens) as they treated the four-month period of diplomatic history in early and mid-1945. Maddox believed that he struck gold finding discrepancies between the original documents and how the seven writers used or interpreted them.

Right-wing reviewers and embittered liberals were initially delirious. Writing in the *National Review*, Jack Chatfield declared that Maddox had literally "done in" Williams, showing up *Tragedy* "for what it really was: a novel rather than a work of history." Claire Z. Carey in the *Intercollegiate Review* congratulated Maddox for uncovering an "academic Watergate" (an unconsciously hilarious criticism coming from part of erstwhile Nixon enthusiasts, but also from defenders of presidential prerogative at large) which had jeopardized "the effort of honest and genuine historians." The *New York Times Book Review* assigned the review to the undistinguished Francis Lowenheim, who expectedly concluded that New Left histories

were "filled with systematic omissions, unwarranted insinuations, misstate-
ments of fact, gross misconstruction and misrepresentation, and quotations
wrenched out of context." Williams in particular, Lowenheim claimed,
"unable to locate evidence to support this or that of his basic premises, has
engaged in an unscholarly manipulation of the evidence," by splicing documents together.[40]

The *New York Times* uncharacteristically permitted seven "culprits" to
respond in the same issue. Each of them refuted a specific charge or two.
Horowitz and Kolko complained that Lowenheim was a lazy reviewer for
not checking the accuracy of Maddox's charges. Williams responded
methodologically, defending the use of "seriatum quotations to document,
illustrate, and communicate to the reader the substance and texture of the
Weltanschauung of the protagonists." Even if Stalin's precise words referred
to the Italian situation, Williams explained, they accurately reflected
Stalin's sentiments (corroborated by other evidence) about German reparations. A literal reading of documents certainly had its place in historical
scholarship, "but that place is at the beginning—by no means at the end—
of historical understanding."[41]

A wave of pro-Williams sympathetic commentary followed. Writing in
Commonweal, Richard H. Miller accused Maddox of having "committed a
verbal mugging on behalf of the cold-war liberals," using the "technique of
obscuring the message by slandering the messengers." Those "who gave us
McCarthyism years before the Wisconsin demagogue," by which Miller
obviously meant Truman, Schlesinger, Jr., and company, had resorted once
again to slander. After all, Miller concluded with pardonable exaggeration,
"Schlesinger's *Vital Center* and the professional anti-communists in the
American Committee for Cultural Freedom . . . [had done] more than the
FBI to stifle intellectual freedom on the nation's campuses."[42]

From the *New York Review of Books*, Ronald Steel likewise found
Maddox's book "highly disagreeable," marked by "personal vindictiveness"
and "nastiness." The author had suggested through innuendo, but could not
prove, that the revisionists' arguments were actually false. Maddox had also
proposed an amazing degree of "collusion and conspiracy" among a disparate
group of historians who often disagreed sharply among themselves. Certainly
the revisionists had "sometimes been inaccurate in their use of source material and unduly eager to jump at predetermined conclusions," but this was also
true of orthodox, liberal, and reactionary historians alike. Naturally historians
interpreted "the same evidence differently, depending on their own time,
place, and view of the world," but this did "not prove distortion." Nor was
Maddox in the least immune from wrenching quotations out of context.[43]

Mainstream historians delivered the real *coup de grâce* to Maddox and to
his defenders' influence in promoting the book. From the *American*

Quarterly to the *Journal of American History* to the *American Historical Review* and the smaller venues, Williams was defended against what the distinguished foreign-policy historian Norman A. Graebner called the "spirit of vindictiveness." Robert D. Schulzinger found Maddox's work "irrelevant, nasty [and] boring." He recalled that following World War I, an entire generation of scholars, following von Ranke's dictum to tell history "as it actually happened," had "exhumed letters and treaties from every European depository" to explain the causes of the world war. Only later did historians realize that "merely rummaging in the archives until the last mis-filed memorandum had been found" did not necessarily lead them any closer to "the Truth." Maddox likewise seemed "incapable of believing that documents [could] reveal anything about any subject other than the one under consideration in a particular memorandum." Graebner concurred, insisting that distinguished historical work embodied a framework "often based on contemplation and not easily documented, which creates the meaning that transcends the immediate sources themselves."[44]

The most middle-of-the-road or diplomatic history establishment assessment, by Warren F. Kimball in the *American Historical Review*, admitted that while Williams's use of *ad seriatum* quotations sometimes troubled historians including Williams's own students, he certainly had the scholarly prerogative to employ "stream of consciousness arguments" and an "intuitive ordering of the facts."[45] On this understanding, the worst charges against Williams collapsed. An enraged Handlin responded by charging "the ultimate betrayal of the discipline" in which "truth and untruth become matters of choice; and fact yielded to intuition." Hard put to defend himself, Maddox answered weakly a decade later that orthodox historians had obviously felt too much guilt and frustration over Vietnam to confront the abandonment of critical analysis for "ideological preferences."[46] These kinds of arguments steadily lost force save among neoconservatives, often the former colleagues of Schlesinger, Jr., and Hofstadter from the intellectual circuits of the 1950s, now housed in private institutes and seen in magazines like Irving Kristol's *The Public Interest*. And for the time being, they had other fish to fry.

Williams himself offered a parting shot in "Confessions of an Intransigent Revisionist," a paper given at the American Historical Association in 1973 and published in *Socialist Review* (its then leading editor, James Weinstein, was a friend from Madison and *Studies On the Left*). He admitted to honest occasional errors in taking notes from documents, in condensing them into summaries and those into narratives, as well as to being a poor proofreader of his own books. But he avowed his fundamental identity as a revisionist, "one who sees basic facts in a different way and as interconnected in new relationships." Just as he did not believe that his errors subverted the values of his work, he insisted that his critics "have yet to respond to the fundamental issues that I have raised."[47]

He could easily have been rephrasing Jean-Paul Sartre, who answered critics by proposing that they had not begun to comprehend his contradictions. But he intended something more. Challenged to explicate his worldview, he confessed to being a "Gestaltian who does not think that Freud or Jung or Adler wiped the slate clear of Dilthey or James—or even Marx."[48] In other words, if he believed that empirical examination remained the essential work of the scholar, he also had his own distinct framework for looking at things. He frankly sought the particular documents and the precise intellectual perspectives that allowed him to interpret the big picture in his own way. Seeking to "explore and reveal all the internal relationships that give meaning to a group of positivistic facts" had sometimes produced logical gaps or redundancies in his narratives, raising hackles for instance when he explained one era by a piece of evidence from another. But he was doing "my best to encapsulate the history that I then explore."[49] If he were proven wrong on this or that point, if scholars disagreed, he still saw things where other people did not. For sympathetic readers, this *mea culpa* would be sufficient. He did not seriously expect to convert the inveterately hostile.

By the middle 1970s, at any rate, no one appeared eager to challenge him or his methods any more. For that matter, the whole revisionist controversy seemed to wind down. Perhaps both sides had simply wearied of writing polemically, or perhaps the Watergate fiasco, the end of the Vietnam War, and the collapse of the 1960s social movements had left so little behind that the edge of expectations had dulled all around. Williams meanwhile plunged himself into private life.

3

Williams's return to Oregon was almost as rocky and uncertain as its famous coastline. A friendly and insightful colleague later recalled the "man with the compact frame, with oversize hands, a generous smile, and the smell of cigar smoke" meeting with Oregon State's history chair in November 1966. It seemed unlikely that an acclaimed genius at mid-career peak would choose an agricultural school. But new friends vigorously lobbied departmental colleagues on Williams's behalf. As the college's bureaucratic procedures suddenly slowed to a full stop, Williams looked elsewhere in the region without effect. Administrators at Portland State made clear that they wanted nothing from a man bearing Marxist credentials, and at his former home base of Eugene, University of Oregon historians seemed astonished that he could even consider OSU—not that they had anything else to offer. One of the nation's most influential scholars had seemingly run out of luck in the Northwest.

Then OSU moved ahead. The liberal arts dean, gazing at Williams's credentials—he had carefully listed his involvements, including his early campaigning against the Vietnam War—wondered aloud if the candidate were "safe." Madison Chancellor Robin A. Fleming reassured the dean on that score.[50] A lone hostile letter of reference among the laudatory ones described him as "abrasive," "dogmatic," and "stubborn." The History Department's initiative now almost fell through again, but not quite. The acting chair reassured the dean that Williams would not be an "uncooperative" faculty member, and OSU made him an offer.[51]

His old friends and Madison admirers were deeply disappointed by his decision. Merle Curti grudgingly supplied a "damnable letter" which facilitated the departure of "a man I admire as much as anyone I know," and the further prospect that "Wisconsin would suffer an irreparable loss by his departure."[52] Madison's graduate student Americanists regarded Williams's disappearance as the end of an unforgettable era, in no small part because it climaxed the retirement and disappearance of the once-dominant Progressives as a group. Williams's relocation did not mean the end of the Wisconsin School as a body of thought, for it was renewed in virtually ceaseless diaspora of individuals and generations. But it no longer had a center.

Williams's decision meant for him, a family head and a proud man, both a sharp reduction in salary to less than $20,000, and starting over without tenure for at least a year. He dickered, first on salary and then on moving expenses. He made it clear to OSU officials that he could not be expected to be present more than three days (it later became two days) per week. And he soon let his prospective colleagues know that he wanted no early morning courses. Those concerns answered, he eagerly made the leap, both because he had resolved to live at the ocean and because he hoped that his marriage might be patched up. Newport was indeed as spectacular as he remembered. A few blocks from the Corvallis campus, a cousin on his mother's side worked in the downtown candy store. In short, he felt he had come home.

But for a number of related reasons it was not, at least for some years, an especially happy homecoming. Above all, the move away from Madison not only failed to heal the damaged marriage but made matters worse. Williams saw his plan to halt his wife's career stopped cold when Corrinne announced that she was determined to return to school. She could manage by commuting for several days each week, she insisted; he took this as an outright attack upon the family and attempted to forbid it. She moved out, accepting his custody of the children and expecting them to return to her eventually (as they all did but one).

In an outline for a never-to-be-written autobiographical volume, he referred to "marriage in the midst of social traumas," and the "frustration of trying to be a historian writing books from 10 p.m. to 2 a.m." Only once, in a personal reference to his first marriage decades after its ending, did he acknowledge that he might have been partly at fault for his repeated and now enveloping problems. He considered himself a martyred single father. He drank much more heavily, swore he would cut down or cut out—and then returned to pattern.

In a still less mellow vein, Williams addressed a handful of students in the Home Economics Auditorium in 1973, decrying the women's movement for misconstruing the task of liberation as freeing the individual rather than women joining men to break away from "the miserable and dehumanizing system which defines freedom as the opportunity to do battle with each other, man against man, man against woman, adults against children."[53] Sometimes in letters he also railed against the new and exciting field of women's history, even as he sought increasingly as a scholar to grasp the importance of women's various roles in U.S. history.[54] He must have been relating larger social developments to his own life, consciously or unconsciously, with its two failed marriages. Far too much like the stuffier senior members of the profession whose elitism he had long disdained, he took personal offense at the idea of a women's experience as somehow distinct from or even opposed to that of men.

Despite his determination to be positive about the regional tilt to life in the Northwest, it was hard to deny a certain intellectual-political sense of absence. What attracted him to Oregon, the joy of daily life rather than cerebral competition, had a definite down side as well. If he had complained that in Madison he often felt "trapped half-way between the 1920s and 1940s, reliving all the strange individualism and the brittle leftwingism of that period," he might now in Corvallis and Newport have felt he had slipped in somewhere between the blue collar 1950s and the earth-toned 1970s, with very little conscious political sensibility to speak of.[55] He also felt intellectually unchallenged and at times just plain lonely.

His new geographical locus also seemed to finalize his tendency, evident since the mid-1960s, to withdraw from things national. In 1969, for instance, a dozen radical historians including Eugene Genovese, James Weinstein, and Warren Susman, nearly all of them heavily under Williams's influence, gathered privately in Chicago to discuss the formation of a new Socialist Party or intellectual nucleus for one; Williams chose not to be on hand. The next year, some of this group formed the journal *Socialist Revolution*, a successor to *Studies On the Left*, published not so far from him in San Francisco, with many of the familiar *Studies* editors and a perspective seemingly quite close to his.[56]

The new journal occasionally published him and drew considerable inspiration from his intellectual framework; indeed, it might be regarded as potentially forming a third "Williams School." But he drew no closer. Nor did he make any effort to hook up with the post-New Left New American Movement founded in 1970 and aligned with *Socialist Revolution*, and the subsequent merger of NAM with the Democratic Socialist Organizing Committee to form Democratic Socialists of America, the largest non-Communist Left entity in the U.S. for some time. At an editorial meeting of *Socialist Revolution*, or at the founding convention of NAM in Davenport, Iowa, welcomed by the progressive mayor, he would surely have been accorded a central spot, his views considered an inspiration to begin again with Socialist education. Feminism aside, he would have found wide agreement with his vision of a decentralized socialism and appeal to a Socialist Americanism. Yet he opted out, perhaps correctly judging the sharp limitations in advance or perhaps simply leaving all of it behind.

He instead adapted himself and his aspirations, not without losses, to his Oregon life. He made friends and lovers, and especially when his health was good, he relished out-of-door activities like hiking in woods and along the shoreline. He rarely complained about being far from the national scene. But the longer he was away from Madison, the sweeter that camaraderie seemed to have been and the more he treasured visits from old friends stopping by to drink and swap stories with him. The University of Wisconsin, as he unintentionally revealed in interviews of the time, had joined Iowa and the Navy as sources of his own political and intellectual vigor, steadily idealized the further he grew away from them.[57]

He made one last, major change in his life during the early 1970s. In late 1973, he married Wendy Margaret Tomlin, a returned student fifteen years his junior who had emigrated from the UK to the United States via Canada and who met him on the OSU campus. At last he had made what he considered, according to frequent and effusive descriptions in his letters, a soul match. A peacenik or anti-imperialist of nonconformist family background with anthropological training and a keen sense for the dangerous expansiveness of American life, she understood his political worldview perfectly. She helped him raise the children still at home; and, in time, she returned to work. This time, a wife's career seemed to him a reasonable choice, and he began to feel more comfortable with the growing independence of American women.

The family moved up the coast from Newport to Waldport, a still smaller town of about 1,500, where Williams bought a very modest house near the water. There he nursed his spinal ailments and mulled fusion surgery, choosing instead the path of "reasonable control with exercise, some good sex, and once in a while an extra drink or two."[58] A few years later, with all the children gone, he did the carpentry for an expansion and took considerable pride in his work. From a captain's chair just outside the house, he could survey the cliffs and the water below, somewhat sheltered from the steady winds and from the drizzle which fell intermittently. As a skilled and occasionally prizewinning amateur photographer, he relished the opportunity to snap cormorants sunning themselves, or capture the shading of the light in different weather or seasons. Above all, he loved to catch fish and to eat them fresh. Development arrived slowly to the roadside in Waldport, so gradually displacing a feeling of insularity that the changes seemed, as so often elsewhere, almost welcome at first. The coming strip malls and the significantly heavier volume of traffic (much of it former Californians seeking a new retirement haven) with its accompanying noise and pollution were still years away.

The coast and Corvallis now suited him better and better. He genuinely loved spending time with locals, from truckdrivers to fishermen to lumberjacks to small business people to students and like-minded academic colleagues. A bit like the legendary idealists Gene Debs and Wendell Phillips, he was known to empty his wallet occasionally to a destitute old-timer on the streets of Waldport. He wrote self-effacingly to his in–laws about his professional life, claiming that it was "satisfying to have superior students and create books which were translated into six languages." But "compared with finding the way to create sound and happy and even passionate relationships with other human beings," writing seemed only "a kind of finger exercise."[59]

This sentiment fit well with his happiest sense of life among colleagues in the OSU History Department. A fellow historian wrote, apparently without exaggeration, that Williams had "reached out right and left with words, gestures and manuscript assistance." After four years the chair could say that "no one in his experience, so well qualified to play the role of prima donna, resisted the temptation so completely." A small circle of colleagues drew close, shooting pool with him, sharing a drink (or several) during his days in Corvallis and occasionally visiting in Waldport. Of all these, a young labor historian with a Connecticut working-class (and military) background and a growing interest in environmental history earned Williams's greatest affection. William Robbins, in turn, became Williams's first in-house historian, peppering him with biographical questions and laying the groundwork for the most personal sections of a *Festschrift* published in 1986. To Robbins's wife, Karla, he became a rare male confidant, and to their children he was "Uncle Bill," a frequent playmate and sometimes correspondent.[60] He had become part of another family.

Williams also became something of a public personality. He wrote sharp political letters to the statewide and local press, took part with congressmen and other politicians in public hearings, appeared in a wide variety of other venues from church-sponsored lecture events and demonstrations against U.S. imperial adventures to an occasional tribute dinner for himself (such as a 1981 event at the Corvallis Country Club). He was seen much as he wished to be, an adopted Oregonian with a national and even international reputation. Even if the business community ignored him and the OSU administration remained indifferent to the true value of their noted faculty member, other elites were not entirely blind. Liberal Republican senator Mark Hatfield, with a reputation for mild anti-imperialism or at least international caution, avidly shared Williams's enthusiasm for Herbert Hoover and proudly announced that he regarded this adopted Oregon historian as the finest practitioner in his chosen field.[61]

Williams meanwhile made good on his promise to devote his main energies to undergraduates. Although few of his students were aware of his full stature, they quickly got an idea of his commitment to learning. Especially in the early years, he found many eager to take all he had to give. He set himself to "design a course that would engage students with the teacher and yet enable [them] to experience the excitement and relevance of history by beginning to act as their own historians involved in an on-going dialogue with other citizen-historians." To that end, he devised elaborate experiments in pedagogy to interest students into doing serious reading, dividing them up in groups to consider documents and to make up their own minds about what historical interpretation meant. He also "learned once again how difficult it is to prepare and deliver one good lecture a week."[62]

Williams also reaffirmed his belief that students digging into original sources and arriving at their own conclusions remained their own best teachers. Especially at a school like OSU, however, "they were not disciplined or engaged enough" to do it rigorously "unless it was required and unless I was involved."[63] Over the years, such demands proved more and more tiring, especially in the foreign-policy course that he sometimes felt he had done to death. He was also saddened when Greyhound cancelled its bus service on many less-traveled routes, including Corvallis to Waldport (the camera team for PBS's McNeil-Lehrer Report just happened to catch Williams on the last ride), forcing him to make a wearying and, after dark, a potentially dangerous drive. But even when his energy level and his interest in school waned, he still had his moments. One day walking across campus, he stopped to watch an undergraduates' pickup softball game and a couple of his students yelled "Come on, Prof, have a hit!" He knocked a series of long balls and then gave them a demonstration of old-fashioned, windmill-windup fast-pitching, to his own immense satisfaction.[64] He had, perhaps, delivered a blow against the self-perception of advancing old age.

The administration's lack of commitment to excellence, however, particularly frustrated Williams. The state had never "mustered the sustained will to act on its peculiar kind of incipient radical ethos," taxing resource production in timber or water power to pay for education as some Midwestern states had.[65] Oregon State got the worst of a bad deal. He believed the school should either fight for more stature and funding within the state system or else simply merge with the University of Oregon. The administrators reciprocated his criticism by refusing to defend him against occasional public attacks on "the radical professor." For all this, he had no patience. "In typed and scribbled messages," a colleague recalled, Williams "bombarded the administration from top to bottom," sometimes on behalf of himself but mostly on behalf of a better learning environment at large. He occasionally suggested that certain administrators deserved a good old-fashioned ritual humiliation of having a scholar's hood torn from their heads and ground into the mud.[66]

4

His frustrations in Oregon were minor, in the larger sense of his career, compared to the consequences of his writing. He had always felt, as most authors do, that he lacked a certain creative control over marketing and had probably been too gullible in dealings with publishers. Increasingly, however, he considered himself cursed with bad luck and perhaps swindled to boot by the arrangements he had made. Asked by his agent in 1978 to "go public in the marketplace," he responded that he could not "take it very seriously because my books are not earning anything at all any longer," nor did he expect they ever would again.[67]

For years, he exchanged anxious and occasionally exasperated letters with his literary agent and with publishing house editors. He cajoled and threatened, even filed legal briefs to get what he considered his due. But his new book projects seemed stymied while royalties on his old books were steadily diminished by changes in scholarly fashion and by corporate takeovers. He swore repeatedly never to write another book. Although he did attempt half a dozen projects and completed several, he almost certainly earned more through the sale of his mother's modest property than he had from all his books together.[68]

It was an old story. Going back to the middle 1960s, he consistently failed to get the kind of publishers' attention and healthy advances that one might have expected for the author of *Tragedy* and *Contours* as well as an earlier successful classroom text. Nor did he get any lucrative fees for journalism and commentary. *Tragedy* continued to return several thousands of dollars each year in paperback sales, but by no means large sums. *The Roots of the Modern American Empire* garnered a thirty-five hundred dollar advance from Random House, with an additional five hundred dollars for publication of the Vintage edition.[69] But it faded after a strong beginning, never to reach the status that he had anticipated for it.

To a degree, Williams resisted suggestions to frame his work in the ways sympathetic editors thought the most propitious. Even a radical editor like Knopf's Angus Cameron expressed frustration when Williams refused the timely notion of carrying the vision of community into a popular history book devised with that purpose squarely in mind. Perhaps the *Great Evasion* had been his one "concept" book and he had no more patience for a nontraditional narrative style.[70]

But there was always another element, quite despite the apparent success of Williams's writings in the *New York Review* and the *Nation*. The response of the influential Theodore Solotaroff, liberal but firmly nonradical editor of the *New American Review*, might be taken as characteristic. Without quite saying so, Solotaroff politely rejected Williams's work as simply unsuited—as it certainly was to the New York Intellectuals' literary and political tastes alike.[71] They might be under severe attack from the younger generation, but they and their heirs still held the majority of the prestige literary cards. Neither the *New York Times*, *Harper's*, the *Atlantic* nor other high-profile magazines like the *New Yorker* or *Saturday Review* ever invited the extraordinarily talented historian and essayist to contribute. The efforts of his agent to land his essays in such magazines were hopeless.

At any rate, Williams had a bad publishing decade after 1970, partly but not mainly of his own making. According to his hardworking agent Gerald McCauley, Williams was perennially "overcommitted to publishers in what he wanted to write." Flattered by the attention and drawn to even comparatively modest financial offers, he then felt tortured by the response of editors to what he was actually trying to do. He signed contracts overhastily for several trade books including a survey text of U.S. history and another overview of foreign policy, in addition to revisions of both the *Shaping of American Diplomacy* and *Tragedy*. It was an unrealistic and, for a normally slow writer (in his own opinion), a simply unmanageable pace. As the seventies wore on and he found himself increasingly wracked with spinal pain and facing unexpected bills, he pressed publishers to pay the full advance, scheduled on delivery, while he still worked on the manuscript. In this, too, he had little success.[72]

The sudden transformation of the publishing industry, from a low-profit-margin but high-prestige field of capital to a rapidly changing corporate shuffle of ownerships and staffs, badly undermined his confidence in editors and book production generally. Sinking college history enrollments steadily eroded the commercial market that Williams had rightly expected his reputation and accomplishments entitled him to reach. The Franklin Watts company, for instance, took over his books that had been originally published by Quadrangle, on the sale of that latter company to the *New York Times*. After delays in payments and other frustrations, Williams demanded to buy back his contracts. In turn, a Watts editor wrote him peevishly that *History as a Way of Learning*, the collection of his older essays that Franklin Watts published in 1972, was mainly considered a stimulant to get him to write a popular book; they thought of *Way of Learning* itself as a born loser. He was not wrong to conclude that the book had been written off rather than promoted seriously.[73]

This was not only a personal disappointment but an editorial and political injustice. From the highly personal preface to the eclectic contents taken from virtually every phase of Williams's life and interests, *Way of Learning* should have attracted attention due to Williams's stature alone. Even the thinnest collections of essays by adversaries such as Handlin and Schlesinger, Jr., had been promoted heavily and given ample attention in the commercial press.[74]

By this time, an increasingly frantic Williams implored his agent and publishers about his needs for cash due to family medical bills and his children's education. He complained about the unwillingness of foundations to underwrite radical explorations, and joked about going on welfare when he was faced with a loss in salary if he accepted a Fulbright to Australia in 1976. He contracted a local bank loan in order to take a semester off to finish a volume and thanked the banker personally in his acknowledgments.

Soon, even the once-regular returns from *Tragedy* and *Contours* melted away in the corporate shuffle. What small royalties he received had passed through three or four hands en route, leading Williams into continual uncertainty and the ironic reflection that he was "becoming dim-witted" with the strain of figuring out the cash flow. To make matters worse, younger scholars had by now produced highly readable texts and collections of readings on foreign policy with a strong revisionist bent, adaptable for classroom use. Indeed, several of Williams's own students turned out their own foreign-policy overviews. These texts inevitably made *Tragedy* less useful.

More than once, Williams had in hand what he mistakenly took (from the responses of his former colleagues or friendly locals) to be a "mind-blowing" set of chapters. The publishers rarely thought so, and his work interested them less and less as the sixties grew further away.[75] Perhaps the worst experience for Williams involved trying to write a mainstream textbook. He signed a contract for thirty-two thousand dollars and promptly collided with editors fixed in their ideas about how to reach a rapidly diminishing market. Williams wanted to experiment with the text, including a radically different design with many illustrations, from photos to

Beatles sheet music. He also wanted to use documents alongside text in different and (for the publishers) unexpected ways. He aspired to produce a unique text prompting "more creative . . . more oral, more ecological, more playful . . . more responsible, and more equitable" responses of young readers to events around them. He was, perhaps, a generation ahead of time with a CD-ROM vision of how history might be taught beyond the limits of traditional texts.[76]

But the manuscript that he produced in 1975 did not satisfy the editors at all; one of them pronounced flatly that it would not "play in Peoria." He parted with the ostensible publishers, Wiley and Sons, in what he considered a spirit of mutual resignation, ultimately returning two-thirds of the advance. He complained that his out-of-pocket expenses during the protracted revising process did not figure into the financial settlement. He had been treated like a bush leaguer rather than the world-class historian that scholars and many popular readers believed him to be.

Americans in a Changing World: A History of the United States in the Twentieth Century, finally published by Harpers in 1976, was certainly an odd volume, and a measure of Williams's difficulty meeting the changing times. At its best, the text had the feel of lectures to undergraduates, probing for ways to clarify large ideas without patronizing the reader. He insisted, for instance, that the text be considered an argument rather than absolute truth, and Williams ended each chapter with references to books with opposing arguments. At worst, the main historical figures chosen in the chapters seemed to appear almost from nowhere and then again disappear, as a friendly critic observed, unexpectedly bearing and then deserting the large historical tendencies that they represented.

Williams also weighed down the book with judgments that otherwise sympathetic readers found doubtful or downright repugnant, such as a condemnation of late-nineteenth-century women's "false choice" for either marketplace equality or satisfying family life. Privately, Williams was increasingly fascinated and impressed by the contribution of women's history to scholarship. But he lacked the sensibility to make the emerging research and insights his own.[77] On the other hand, he appeared eager to congratulate contemporary corporate leaders such as George Perkins of the House of Morgan for being "honestly paternalistic," keenly aware of the need for reforms to preserve the system. He seemed to ask a greater sagacity of reformers than he demanded of genteel thinkers or politicians.

From the viewpoint of younger historians slated to assign or not assign the text to undergraduate classes, the book was also plainly short on social history. Historical conceptualizations had changed drastically since Williams had himself first taught surveys during the 1950s, and since his own cutting-edge work had changed the diplomatic-scholarly map. A large new literature had meanwhile appeared on black history, women's, and working-class history, with important contributions to Asian American, American Indian, Chicano, and other minority history fields as well.

It was not so much that he lacked the requisite sympathies. He expressed admiration for leaders of various downtrodden groups, especially the Socialist idol Eugene Debs. But the detail in the newer social history simply overwhelmed him. As he mulled with various former students the question of American labor, for instance, he returned repeatedly to the absence of imagination on the part of labor leaders, their inability to envision any other possible system of social organization.[78] The emerging labor historians would hardly have disagreed with this estimate. But they sought imaginative possibilities where Williams did not look, in the lives and day-to-day culture of ordinary people. This was simply not to Williams's taste. Feeling provoked, he lashed out in private at the scholars who somehow thought the people at the bottom of society were morally superior, or would operate the system more effectively than the people currently on top.[79]

He had wanted to make a very different point, that a consensual belief in expansionism drew even dissident groups, with few exceptions, into that strategic posture. Class and race conflict had never overridden this fundamental fact in his reading of U.S. history, and he would be hard put to accept the idea that any other sort of difference (the contemporary assault on male privilege, for instance) short of a community vision of socialism or at least of international restraint could change matters fundamentally. He confused the issue by teasing friends and especially younger historians with jibes against social history that he knew would get under their skin. But in truth, he could not transcend the limits of his fundamental perspective, including his fascination for elites and a certain reverence for "enlightened conservatives." He was plainly out of fashion, but also badly limited in his understanding.

To be fair, Williams was in this last respect among abundant and prestigious company even at this late date of historical revisionism at large. A host of traditional liberal historians in mid-career or a bit older continued to turn out fresh editions of survey textbooks devoted to political history from the top down, with a staggeringly familiar cast of heroes and a far less interesting or original treatment than Williams's. For them, the shock of the sixties and the emergence of social history had not changed anything interpretively, even as they made minor adjustments to include more material here and there on women, minorities and sports history. These books had their fixed constituencies among the older historians, with the further advantage of the standard textbook format and a large sales force. Williams's challenge to cold-war assumptions effectively barred his book from the classrooms of traditionalists, while the younger radicals who might have assigned it were not yet sufficiently numerous and besides, had other objections or reservations.

Americans in a Changing World can also be read in an entirely different way. It was a book written consciously or unconsciously about himself, his personal sources of influence, and his ostensibly private tastes. The novels, films, music, and sports he described from the 1930s onward were clearly part of his own experience, the older fiction he lovingly described mainly the books that he had learned to cherish. He finally had something good to say about Franklin Delano Roosevelt who, having established an intimate rapport with the American people, died "deeply mourned." But something fundamental in Williams's world had obviously ended with the loss of faith in Herbert Hoover's vision of dynamic equilibrium. As Warren Susman once observed, the outbreak of the Depression marked the end of Turner's thesis as an explanatory device: the meaning of the frontier, at least in its original form, had been exhausted, and nothing else equally clear followed. Williams was clearly out of his depth in domestic history at large after that point.[80]

Americans in a Changing World had its moments in the post-Hoover society only when the text seemed to speak directly from Williams's personal experiences. He wrote feelingly about the Second World War, the terrible sense of battle, and its effects upon the survivors. He analyzed the GI Bill's effects as greatly assisting a large generation but also prompting in most of them both a desperate quest for middle-class status and the abandonment of any political lessons they had learned in the war. He predictably seared Truman, but not without crediting even this prime agent of the Imperial Presidency with serious desires to enact needed domestic reforms.

American history had no apparent happy ending in sight. For almost the last time, Williams showed a certain respect for Dwight Eisenhower and how Ike had tried to ease the cold war. But more recent events, from at least the middle 1960s on, looked terribly disappointing. By no accident, these were historical moments when the actors might conceivably have taken heed from Williams's writings. As the possibility of U.S. hegemony disappeared, administrative leadership had been utterly unable to respond to the challenge; Kissinger and Nixon disguised their blundering through bluster. Williams could still not believe that a "Class B movie actor" and rising candidate for the Republican nomination during the 1970s would prove to be the culmination of all the turmoil. In Congress, the rising political influence of neoconservative academics like Daniel Patrick Moynihan, whose "new" ideas were both wrongheaded and mean-spirited, showed that the same mental bankruptcy prevailed among supposed moderates. The dream of a democratic citizenship receded ever further from reality. Sounding like an aging but radical World War II veteran remembering a strip show seen in youth, he concluded that America by the mid-1970s just "continued to bump and grind around the dead center: a once revolutionary society unable to break free of the status quo."[81]

He had apparently intended to say something more grand, but could not quite find the words. Nothing quite so characterized the better moments of *Americans in a Changing World* as much as his motto-like insistence that

> As you begin history, you will develop a feel for the ironies related to a sense of what might have happened at those moments known as turning points at which nobody turned, those instants when as a society, as well as in our individual lives, we came to a fork on the road and choose to go down the path that seemed safe and secure.[82]

Unfortunately, American history now seemed littered with almost nothing but such disappointments. Even as an exercise in mordant observations, his literary efforts got lost in the effort to render his polemical, almost novelistic approach into a textbook narrative.

The in-house reviewers of the manuscript who described the text as off-center for a course book had thus not been all wrong. His effort to "make sense out of the American experience" and to "give the student some meaningful essence of where he is today," had not succeeded despite what Williams regarded as the crucial test of the classroom setting. His self-belief of being keenly prepared, "the same sense of being ready to work that I had when I did the readings-and-documents text in foreign relations," had ingloriously let him down. Or the publishing world had let him down by not encouraging and promoting a format in which he thought he could exploit his best talents and create a text which somehow spoke directly from the writer's soul to the student's mind.[83]

For the Bicentennial, Williams produced *America Confronts a Revolutionary World, 1776-1976* (William Morrow, 1976) in which he argued that the nation had been counterrevolutionary from its inception. Fearing the "Future" and unable to examine the "Past" fearlessly, American leaders had with few exceptions sought to freeze the national experience into a mythical "Present" (all three concepts capitalized), continually denying the right of self-determination to other peoples. Although most of the book reiterated familiar themes, e.g., how Empire had negated community, at the end Williams proposed a return to the days of the Articles of Confederation so as to break down the continental U.S. into units over which citizens would have effective political and economic control. Williams's own chosen region, including Washington, Oregon, Idaho, Montana and perhaps part of Canada, might, he thought, assume the Indian name, "Neahkahnie."

Williams had imagined himself writing a lucid, conceptual, "what if" book-length essay dealing with his favorite subject: the Open Door. It turned on the crucial moments—the Constitutional Convention, the Civil

War, the Spanish American War, two world wars, and the Asian conflicts—when U.S. leaders might have said "no" to Empire, and prepared American society for a decisively widened democratic practice.[84] All too aware of the rightward current drift of the nation, and alienated from the post-McGovern drift of liberalism both to the Left (toward feminism) and to the Right (toward a renewed acceptance of military Keynesianism and cold-war diplomacy), Williams made a valiant effort to cut through traditional lines of division. Not only did he appeal repeatedly to conscience conservatism, upholding as models J. Q. Adams and Henry Adams along with Herbert Hoover and Dwight Eisenhower; he directed his invective almost exclusively at the traditional heroes of the liberals. If only the Founding Fathers had chosen the ideal not of Empire but of the Republic, or if their successors had heeded the danger signs of its subversion by liberal mechanisms, he repeatedly suggested, America would be a different place.

Williams took exceptional risks by expanding his critique of Lincoln and Franklin Roosevelt. Cold toward the Abolitionists for decades, he now nearly suggested that slavery would have been better left alone, or at least its life would not have been significantly longer without a Civil War. Lincoln, who indeed exceeded his constitutional powers more than once, came to be seen as a railroad lawyer who desperately *needed* Southern rebellion in order to justify and extend the imperial presidency. Never had Beard's view of the Civil War as the "Second American Revolution" been recreated quite so starkly, nor had a prominent radical historian made so little of slave and free black activity before, during, and shortly after the war. Once again, as in *Contours* but with a generation of further research available, he seemed to have missed entirely W. E. B. DuBois's point about the possibilities of Black Reconstruction. Not since the relatively conservative historiography of the 1950s, when former Marxist David Donald held Lincoln up to scorn, had so distinguished a scholar confronted the favorite American president of the nineteenth century.

Williams had once again chosen to be outrageous. A wiser rhetorical strategy for his antebellum nineteenth-century treatment, such as attacking the ever familiar sentimentalization of Andrew Jackson the slaver and Indian-killer by Arthur Schlesinger, Jr., and the traditional liberal historians, apparently did not occur to him despite his increasing stress upon the plight of the "First Americans." He needed to make Lincoln the empire-builder as he much as he needed to hammer once more at Woodrow Wilson.

Tackling Truman was elementary, especially as the Wisconsin School of Williamsesque scholars made the case against the cold-war leader in ever increasing detail. Savaging Franklin Roosevelt meant risking the wrath that fell upon Beard and continued to fall upon Harry Elmer Barnes. Williams carefully pointed out that Roosevelt's long-term policies had encouraged Germany and Japan against Russia and then failed to articulate the consequences to the American public. Unwilling to undertake fundamental reform at home, Roosevelt had actually opened the door to the frightening atomic arms race that followed. By contrast to Truman, Roosevelt still looked pretty good; by contrast to Hoover, he looked terrible. Behind these particulars lay Williams's familiar credo: "the act of imposing one people's morality upon another people is an imperial denial of self-determination. Once begin . . . and there is no end of Empire except war and more war."

If the *Philadelphia Inquirer* hailed it as an important and fresh look at U.S. history, *America Confronts* had few other unequivocal enthusiasts. One of these, Robert M. Senkewicz, in the Jesuit magazine *America*, hailed the "well-written and eminently readable volume," which made "the basic premises of a very sophisticated argument available to a wider public" than just the younger historians who had been enormously influenced by Williams's creative inventions.[85] Michael Zuckerman, writing in the *Nation*, was by contrast plainly disappointed. Unlike the "White House-broken" Arthur Schlesinger, Jr., Williams had "affected the tenor of public affairs where the Presidential chroniclers and court jesters have not." He was "probably the most influential—and perhaps the only influential—American historian of our day." But if his present narrative was "often convincing, occasionally outrageous, and always engaging and alive, his judgments . . . fresh and provocative," much of the book was "certainly problematic if not preposterous."[86] Thomas G. Kennedy likewise believed that many scholars would agree with Williams's description of the "ill effects of the sense of national uniqueness and destiny or the penchant for crusades," but not his oversimplifications or "assumptions of a calculated rationality and consistency on the part of policy-makers."[87]

Other reviewers were less than kind. Yale diplomatic historian Gaddis Smith attacked the book on the front page of the *New York Times Book Review*. Subtitled "the United States as Villain," Smith's essay (which also covered a recent volume by Gabriel Kolko) made Williams into a mere "pamphleteer." Smith's view was hardly surprising; he would continue to attack Williams's positions well after the latter's death, as an obstacle to the triumph of the neorealist scholarship that Smith represented. The assignment of Smith to the book demonstrated that the somewhat favorable tilt of noted liberals toward Williams in the Vietnam years was swiftly coming to an end. The *Times* had returned to a center from which Williams was an unwanted heretic or perhaps the relic of a recent dissenting past.[88] The reaction of the *New York Review of Books* was similar, where the most charitable thing Edmund S. Morgan could say was that *America Confronts* seemed "eccentric."[89]

Roscoe Drummond in the *Christian Science Monitor* saw the book only as an intended "total antidote against any reverence or warmth of the nation's Bicentennial." Williams had "set out to prove that just about everything the United States could do wrong, it has done wrong year after year for the first two centuries—deliberately, eagerly, grievously wrong." Noting that "the kindest and most complimentary works in the book go to Marx, Mao and Castro," Drummond expected that the book would "please the communists and may win some allies and recruits." He warned, "We had better know what they are up to."[90]

Professionally, Williams's stature nevertheless continued to ascend, even as the dialogue among differing scholars that he had always hoped to see now disappeared from any foreseeable future. The American Historical Association devoted a second session to his works at its annual meeting in 1973. Antirevisionists attacked Williams personally for perpetrating a "historical fantasy," while David Horowitz, the author of the popular anti-imperialist volume *Free World Colossus*, lashed out at other panelists and the audience. Obviously, the panel had made no progress in facilitating discussion across political lines.[91]

The Organization of American Historians offered its own version of a collective critique of Williams in 1978. William Leuchtenberg, widely regarded as a dean of liberal historians and who served shortly as OAH President, presided over a panel of Christopher Lasch and N. Gordon Levin, Jr., with Williams himself and peace scholar Martin Sherwin serving as commentators. Lasch stressed the importance of Williams's contributions to U.S. history at large—and also why Williams's roots in Progressive history prevented him from moving beyond the limits of his own remarkable views. Although Levin had himself earlier followed revisionist leads in studies of World War I diplomacy, he now typed Williams a "radical isolationist" who inexplicably refused to acknowledge the heroic "strategic and moral roles" played by the U.S. in assisting world democracy. Martin Sherwin deftly noted that Williams had moved scholars from peripheral questions about public postures to unstated assumptions of U.S. policies. Right or wrong on details, he had aimed bravely at explaining Americans' various contradictory and conflicting assumptions and urging them to accept change as progress, not capitulation.[92]

In the most prestigious presentation of the panel, a definite irony prevailed. Lasch praised Williams's "distinguished work" and insisted that no other historian had "taught so many outstanding students or imbued them with such a passion for critical scholarship," effectively defining the questions asked by diplomatic historians. He had made clear that "American liberalism cannot be understood as an anti–business creed" and liberalism had been shaped in part by corporations, and that Progressivism and the New Deal had stabilized society rather than "revolutionized" it.

But Lasch also had in mind a very different purpose. Williams the "lonely radical" of the 1950s-60s had inspired so much ridicule that many young scholars (including, Lasch freely admitted, himself) had ignored his work. After the "brief rise of radicalism to academic respectability and even fashionability," many of his erstwhile opponents had become supporters. Now, his work could be "acknowledged not as a formative influence on a nonexistent school of New Left historians but as an inescapable influence on American historians in general."[93] Useful radicalism had been absorbed, transcended, or extinguished, as proved by Williams's own case.

This was certainly an odd formulation, all the more so in the doldrums of the 1970s, and it had far more to do with the conflicts Lasch felt within academic and public life than with Williams's work. If, indeed, the New Left scholars of foreign policy, women's labor, and minority history had originated with Williams more than with anyone else, and if they taught his ideas with a fury when entering the classroom (as well as launching local public history forums), it would be strange indeed to imagine these ideas vanishing into thin air. A better case could be made, as Jon Wiener did a decade later, for declaring that their influence had been stamped upon virtually every corner of the profession and had shifted it leftward in a variety of important ways. If many of Williams's former critics had come to agree with him, it was hardly their amiability or his growing respectability but surely the Vietnam War that broke their faith in cold-war liberalism's narrative of the American saga and found them accepting many criticisms set forth by Williams and the New Left.[94]

Lasch could accept Williams's view of Empire as an extremely useful reformulation of Progressive history. But Lasch focused his hostility upon Charles Beard and Beard's demand that American capitalism solve its own problems without expansionism. An inner-focused capitalism could only bring fascism, Lasch insisted; rather than criticizing Franklin Roosevelt, Williams should have congratulated Roosevelt for aiming outward and setting the pace for administrations to follow. So long as capitalism survived, Lasch seemed to be suggesting, expansionism was at least an outlet for its aggressive energies. Any attack upon expansionism which was not an attack upon private property could only assist in creating a regionalist democracy in place of the imperial state, and end up encouraging "the very escapism it condemns."[95]

Thus Lasch had reversed the logic that Williams urgently sought to extend beyond the barriers separating the Left and Right, ruling out in advance the vision of a medium-range strategic alliance of students, minorities, workers, citizens at large, and small business united against the expansionist-minded Establishment. In levelling his attack on Beard, Lasch also seemed to rule out any final vindication of the Beardian circles where Williams's worldview took shape. Believing himself also an heir to Frankfurt School themes and insights, Lasch (as he would detail in a few years) had actually assimilated Williams into his own sense of a moral tradition armed against consumer society and feminism alike. Williams thus became, most oddly, a prime source or at least a scholarly reinforcement for Lasch's *The Culture of Narcissism* (1978) on which President Jimmy Carter was said to have based his disastrous speech lamenting the American "malaise." [96]

At any rate and for apparently contradictory reasons, Williams continued to pick up admirers within the scholarly mainstream. In 1976, he was nominated for but narrowly lost the presidency of the OAH to noted slavery and Civil War scholar, fellow Hesseltine student Kenneth Stampp. Responding to disaffection of younger members, OAH officials grudgingly permitted a sweeping rules change. Rather than the officers of the organization only, the entire membership now voted. In 1980 Williams swept easily into office. Williams was not the first radical historian to be named president of a major historical association. Merle Curti had served in the depths of the McCarthy era and unabashed Marxist Eugene Genovese occupied the OAH presidency in 1977. But unlike these others, Williams clearly represented a new constituency, the antiwar generation of the 1960s. As unlikely as Williams was to represent their main scholarly interests—by this time, women's, labor, and minority histories—he readily offered them the chance to legitimate their growing claims upon the profession. [97]

His election could be properly seen as a happy climax to his decades of work with colleagues in Madison and his participation in the far-ranging controversies among historians. According to his student Edward Crapol, Williams had always felt "the ambivalence that all self-defined mavericks and outsiders have about a community that shuns them and considers them and their work beyond the pale." He had rarely showed up at conventions unless on committee work, and often expressed disdain for the hierarchical, individualist attitudes that belied the ideal intellectual community of peers. And yet naturally enough, as the generational shift brought more and more of his admirers into the mainstream, he was flattered and honored. [98] It was also, if he cared to think of his election in this way, his personal vindication over the cold-war zealots who had so often sought to belittle him. He had long since developed definite ideas about what scholars could do to remedy their collective failings. This was his opportunity to make a difference in the way historians practiced history among themselves and in public.

Vindication in Defeat

WILLIAMS'S FINAL DECADE COULD NOT very well have been a happy one, given the triumph of a demonstrably unenlightened conservatism in Washington, the rapid acceleration of military spending, the unembarrassed plundering of natural resources, and a mean-spirited celebration of wealth that seemed to bring out all the worst in the American character. While these events unfolded, Williams's health slipped downward. He occasionally mulled over projects that he thought he might have tackled under different conditions, if he were younger and unmarried. He thought he could have written a biography of antiwar senator J. William Fulbright, the "Rhodes Scholar from Arkansas [who] was the best we had to offer, but . . . failed."[1]; this exercise would have returned him to several interests of his graduate student years, including biography and a Raymond Robins–like statesman who looked beyond the cold war. By now, however, Williams had accepted narrower limits. His projects and plans remained closer to home.

Williams began to project himself somewhat beyond the passions of the times, taking the long view of the nation and, increasingly, of his own life as well. He found new interests, scholarly and pedagogical, as he approached retirement. He also re-learned how to play, devoting himself to building model airplanes as in childhood—including replicas of Charles Lindbergh, Jr.'s *Spirit of St Louis*, which had flown over his family's home. In tune with all this, he struggled to reap the benefit of accumulated wisdom. If he could not hope to turn back the incoming toxic tide of politics, he could tell those listening how they could get a better sense of the world before their eyes, and how they might act upon the hopes of coming generations.

Here Williams found the strength for his remaining work. As a former student wrote in an obituary, Williams had the talent and, even more, the will to dialogue with ordinary people about the nation's dilemmas.[2] If he appeared at times to throw his hands up at the sight of a "weary and nostalgic Empire," he still had mental resources aplenty to prompt fresh views of liberalism, conservatism, and radicalism. As Warren Susman remarked about the Williams of graduate school days, he seemed ever ready to "discover America" in ways that others did not. And in this crucial respect his vision grew keener at the end of this life. Even while attacks by unrepentent cold warriors continued in high-brow venues generally closed to the dissenter, he refused to be dragged to their polemical level, taking the high road instead. And there he could be found, to the last day.

I

Williams rounded out his public life in two distinct ways during the early 1980s. Controversial scholar one last time, he briefly placed himself near the center of intellectual challenges to the rising imperial arrogance of the age. President of the Organization of American Historians, he worked at the center of a profession which had moved beyond his generation's mindset but desperately needed its administrative support.

Williams had long since ceased writing monographs by the time of his OAH presidency, having made his mind up to work on projects more intimate to his memories and to his unfulfilled aspirations. If his scholarly reputation continued to grow, it was due to past accomplishments and to one more volume, his last: *Empire as a Way of Life*. Urged by his agent to meet the requests of publishers for a cogent overview, he delivered to Oxford University Press in 1979 an extraordinary book-length essay.

By the time it reached publication, the 1980 election season had begun and the *Nation* decided to publish a longish section of a chapter with responses. Lawrence Goodwyn, the leading historian of Populism, and foreign affairs critics Richard Falk and Norman Birnbaum starred among the commentators. Copies of that issue, as planned, were made available to delegates and attendees of the Democratic party convention. "Devoting this special convention issue to Williams's manifesto," the *Nation*'s editor commented, was intended not to undercut President (and candidate) Jimmy Carter but to show "the limitations of the sameness" among the various presidential hopefuls on the central issue of Empire. This examination would highlight the necessity of coming to terms with the "vital work of internal reconstruction" as well as a better international policy. From the standpoint of America's outstanding left-liberal weekly, no one put the issues better than the Oregon anti-imperialist. From the standpoint of a Williams who had first made his name in the *Nation* nearly thirty years earlier, it marked a satisfying return.[3]

Carrying the Williamsesque subtitle of *An Essay on the Causes and Character of America's Present Predicament Along with a Few Thoughts About an Alternative*, the book was Williams's most cogent and artistically complete. Published shortly before his sixtieth birthday, it was also, very self-consciously, his last major salvo. Here, Williams examined every major action in U.S. history, from the nation's origins in Elizabethan England to the present, as premised on unlimited expansion and imperial dominion over internal and external foes. American politics and ideals and the American way of life itself had been premised on endless abundance, making expansionism almost literally an "opiate of the American people." By the 1970s, the world seemed to be closing in, and Americans needed urgently to reassess their traditional values and assumptions. While most of his arguments were familiar to Williams readers, he revealed a fresh grasp of current studies in the cultural dynamics of imperialism. He subtitled his second chapter in a way unimaginable to the Williams of the 1950s: "The Myth of Empty Continents Dotted Here and There with the Mud Huts, the Lean-tos, and the Tepees of Unruly Children Playing at Culture."

Williams also responded to critics, and added some subtle methodological touches to his earlier formulations. He now saw the drive toward a worldwide Open Door as shaped not only by economics but also by a mix of politics, culture, and even sheer diplomatic energy. In response to critics who had challenged not so much his focus on economics as his basic interpretations, Williams once again stubbornly declared himself an "intransigent revisionist." As far as he was concerned, Henry Kissinger had summed up an entire school of official diplomatic thought with the observation "I don't see why we need to stand by and permit a country to go communist due to the irresponsibility of its own people," rationalizing the U.S.-choreographed overthrow of the elected Chilean government in 1973. But Williams's book was no narrow indictment of State Department officialdom. The collective psychology that demanded intervention somewhere or anywhere to stroke the national ego, and the apparent voter willingness to incur a matching federal debt from past military-industrial waste, were scarcely better than Kissinger's personal cynicism.

Perhaps more effectively than ever before, Williams told the familiar story as Greek tragedy and self-evasion. Each chapter ended with a detailed chronology of intervention from the first days of the American Republic, but the narrative disputed any Manichean interpretation of the virtually uninterrupted warfare. White Americans accepted the Empire because, for a long time, it had worked for them—whatever the price to others. "Marx would very probably have shrugged his shoulders (and ideology) and said only that socialism is *unimaginable*, let alone pragmatically possible, until capitalist Empire has run its course," Williams reflected laconically.[4] The crusading expansiveness of the Spanish American War (against the colonial Spaniards, and then against the presumably liberated Cubans and Filipinos) had established a fresh precedent of extra-continental warfare, creating a demon which no subsequent administration could readily exorcize.

Williams gave new exactitude to the self-image of Americans as benevolent rulers of the planet and of themselves, offering various definitions of Empire's key terms and noting how the images blurred with each other and with reality. Bullies looking at their image in the mirror imagined they saw Greek gods staring out at them. The vision of the imperial chase thus became larger and more satisfying than any possible reality, occluding hopes for a wiser "philosophy that viewed . . . restraints as part of a community of reciprocal benefits and obligations."[5]

The State filled the gap between imperial grasp and desiccated democracy. World War II, seen afresh, offered the chance for American leaders either to admit to Empire and pay the cost, or to give up their imperial designs. Letting the Red Army and other exhausted allies pay the cost in human terms while asserting U.S. leadership of world democracy, Roosevelt sowed dragons' teeth for the postwar world. Having lost only four hundred thousand to Russia's twenty million, the United States emerged unquestionably the strongest nation on earth. But faced with the challenge of a postwar world slipping out of the U.S. grasp, leaders fell back upon NSC-68, written *before* the outbreak of the Korean War to rationalize a massive military buildup against potentially revolutionary changes everywhere.

Imperial optimists of the 1990s would insist that Williams had badly misjudged the future balance of power when he labeled the cold-war era "the Empire at Bay." The cold war had tested the U.S. ability to outspend and outlast its opponents across a planetary graveyard of threatened, war-torn or starveling populations (not to speak of devastated flora and fauna). But Williams would not likely have been put off and certainly not satisfied by this victory-through-exhaustion. He admired most the peaceful pioneers who had been able to challenge their own assumptions and had taken the measure of alternatives to Empire: former advocates of Empire, like W. E. B. DuBois, Eugene Debs, Robert M. LaFollette, or Congresswoman Helen Gahahan Douglas (defeated by young Richard Nixon in a 1950 campaign notable for its red-baiting smears). Extrication would not be cost-free. In getting out of the Empire and paying the price long overdue, "some of us will die. But how one dies is terribly important. It speaks to the truth of how we have lived."[6]

Not surprisingly, the last page of his last book brought Williams back squarely to the Atlantic, Iowa, of his childhood where "we did miss much of the so-called American Way of Life" in materialistic terms but believed in the ideal nevertheless. Becoming a part of the imperial ethos which "informs one with the assumption that the goodies should be here and now—and forever," young Billy had stolen an expensive knife from the best hardware store in town. His grandmother discovered the knife and told him that he had not earned it and had to take it back. He resisted, insisting that he couldn't return it now. Around her response and the following action, he framed his last parable:

> She said: You *will* do that. *Now.*
>
> Oh, my: the power of the declarative sentence.
>
> And so I walked back along those long and lonely blocks to the store. And in through the door, and up, face to face, with the member of that small community who owned the store.
>
> And I said: I stole this knife and I am sorry and I am bringing it back.
>
> And he said: Thank you. The knife is not very important, but you coming down here and saying that to me is very important.
>
> Remembering all that, I know why I do not want the Empire. There are better ways to live and there are better ways to die.[7]

Did the incident really happen this way, if it happened at all? Perhaps the "facts" do not, as usual with these things, matter so much. The vividness of real or mythical small-town Atlantic of the 1930s to Williams's wide view of American and international life allows the reader a parting glimpse of the patriot appealing to the public as eloquently as he can. It was also a last testament, from a man who still had no apparent inkling of the cancer that would strike him down in a few years.

If *Empire As a Way of Life* was a remarkable book and a courageous personal statement, it brought Williams's enemies out of the woodwork and into the columns of the *New Republic*, among other places. But for Williams admirers from the U.S. to Europe and Latin America to Israel and Asia, he had reaffirmed his stand like a Biblical prophet of old. "Might

Makes Wrong," proclaimed the Oxford University Press advertising campaign, inveighing against the "binge" of consumptionism, expansionism, and militarism.[8]

It was tragically a message out of time, an effort that an admiring German historian called a "farewell song . . . just at the close of that short period of postwar history during which the political mood of mainstream America could permit critical reflections on premises, judgments and results."[9] Some Americans were indeed ready to hear. But the Carter reelection campaign, running scared, drifted steadily rightward as Carter himself had done during his final two years in office. Already the vision of a reduced cold-war budget and the modest social alternatives that George McGovern had endorsed were long gone from the Democratic party centers of influence. Worse still, the future belonged to Reaganism, an immoderate Republicanism which allowed no guilt or self-doubt whatsoever. As the same admirer of Williams wrote, the "rhetoric of national revival" was now full-tilt, with revisionist criticism reduced to "one more bit of postmodern pluralism easy to ignore in the halls of power."[10]

Critics tended to be deferential toward Williams's new status, even when they were sharply critical of his arguments. Historian Lawrence S. Kaplan complained that the book distorted materials to fit a pattern, but he nevertheless admired its "folksy ways, pungent expressions," its "well-turned phrases" and the author's imagination, revealing Williams to be a "deeply caring person who wants to purge the nation of its original sin." Diplomatic historian Robert H. Ferrell likewise admired Williams's "intense humanity" and could "share his apocalyptic feeling for the present-day confusions . . . compounded with ignorance and pat phrases out of the distant past." He had indeed made himself a modern-day Beard. Intellectual historian Rush Welter charged Williams with "imputing consistency of purpose to actions that were at best confused responses to a variety of circumstances," further burdening the argument with "allegation, insinuation and indignation." Yet he admitted that Williams's "theology is probably true" and his argument "highly persuasive" on at least some level.[11]

Conservatives predictably waxed wroth. A. J. Beitzinger considered the book "an embarrassment to read," the manifestation of a "'rap session' leader" spouting the puerile language of a "righteously indignant Marxist populist." Joseph M. Siracusa, borrowing a phrase from Oscar Handlin, wondered if Williams had prepared yet another "elaborate hoax," with a concept of community resembling "the ancient Greek city-state with Williams himself as philosopher-king, surrounded by a chorus of former graduate students."[12] This was normal fare for Williams.

Those journals which might be called cold-war social democratic or neo-liberal offered the most vicious attacks outside New Right circles. The attack upon *Empire* in the *New Republic* easily exceeded the usual dosage of that magazine's political venom. For reviewer John Lukacs, Williams had in the twenty years since that "artless book," the *Tragedy of American Diplomacy*, "learned nothing and forgotten everything. Truth has further decayed, and lying has become worse." Williams was no "American idealist," as his devotees claimed, but a "vulgarian and a pedant." Henry Pachter, a familiar figure around *Dissent* magazine (and once an admirer of Williams's *Roots of the Modern American Empire*) writing in the *New Leader*, hit a similar low note of intellectual abuse.[13] Not much else could be expected of erstwhile moderates never especially regretful of U.S. misdeeds and now furiously backpedaling from the 1960s—although Williams claimed to have received an apology from the *New Republic*'s review editor for the sheer crudeness of the attack.[14]

With *Empire as a Way of Life*, at any rate, Williams had offered his last and his most cogent overview of American history and its meaning, to the nation and to the world. He could be satisfied that those who sought to understand his message *sans* the troubling complexity of earlier works would find it here.

2

A sympathetic writer in the *Manchester Guardian* observed that the influence of the "deeply American figure" had found "readier and wider acceptance among non-Americans than among his own countrymen."[15] This view, perhaps a bit exaggerated, had the same perceptive insight as Gerda Lerner's *bon mot* that each reader took away from Williams what he or she had come to search for, rather than the author's whole *oeuvre* and driving purpose. Williams's work reached different cultures at different times, touched academic and activist, and its effect varied at least as much with the political situation and academic interests as with the particular text adopted. Altogether, it was a deep international penetration for a dedicated Americanist, with no end in sight.

The Williams influence had been felt earliest, and perhaps the most profoundly in terms of the internal scholarship of another nation, by the Germans. There, the older generation of historians had been guilty of compliance with Hitler's actions or at least with atavistic German nationalism. By the later 1950s or early 1960s an interpretive vacuum became obvious. The Marxism of East German intellectuals, rigid in its familiar delineation of ruling-class manipulators and oppressed masses, could not fill the gap. Younger scholars, some of whom had studied in the U.S. and even in Madison, drew upon Williams for a fresh perspective on Empire. Others looked to Williams through the lenses of his devoted friend George Mosse, who had personally rewritten the cultural history of modern Europe.

Hans-Ulrich Wehler, who trained in part with German scholars in the U.S., might be considered the most prominent of the new generation. No more a Marxist than Williams (but perhaps also no less influenced by Marx's ideas), Wehler sketched out in *Bismarck und der Imperialismus* (1969) and in *Das Deutsche Kaisserreich 1871-1918* (1973) a view of Bismarck's rise to power and the consequences for the new German nation. Like Williams, whose influence he readily acknowledged, Wehler saw divided ruling groups and domestic conflicts unified and resolved through expansionism and the German version of the Open Door. The Bismarckian clique, like Williams's Progressive-era rulers, could be admired for the intelligence of their overview, their acuity in planning reforms and social welfare to preserve the system—even when their successes led to national disaster. Particularly noteworthy, from a different standpoint in Williams's work (and the complimentary influence of Hans Rosenberg, a German exile historian who remained in the U.S.), was Wehler's attempt to see the workings of the system in its entirety.[16]

Wehler and a handful of other German scholars also had a more direct lineage to Williams's view of imperialism and foreign policy. Werner Link's *Die Amerikanische Stabilisierungspolitik in Deutschland 1921-32* (1970) owed a reading of several manuscript chapters (in English) to Williams and although heavily archival, also owed its overview of American leaders' intentions to Williams's insights. Ekkehart Krippendorf's *Die Amerikanische Strategie: Entscheidungsprozess und Instrumentarium der Amerikanische aussenpolitik* (1970) acknowledged Williams only indirectly, but clearly followed the line taken by the diplomatic revisionists. Wehler's more general anthology, *Imperialismus* (1970), refined terms and offered analyses somewhere beyond Marxism, but intimately close to Williams's interpretations.[17]

British radical historians, like the Germans, had internal divisions which shaped Williams's significance for them. The older group had graduated from the Communist Party with a passion for lower-class social history and a firm grasp of historical materialism. Their luminaries, including Christopher Hill, E. P. Thompson, V. G. Kiernan, and Eric Hobsbawm, were often taken as models for New Left scholars in the U.S. A younger group, by contrast, had evolved through the political New Left via Louis Althusser and the journal *New Left Review*, defining itself less through social history than in terms of ideologies and the capitalist system as seen from above. Despite Williams's early stay in Britain and his attachment to Guild Socialism, he had surprisingly little contact with the first circle. But Kiernan, an encyclopedic scholar, penned *America: The Newer Imperialism* (1978) within an unmistakable Williams framework. Seeking to comprehend the nature of economic control and political overlordship without the formality of a Colonial Office, he popularized American perspectives thirty years in the making.[18]

The *New Left Review* circle, which naturally tended to place Empire alongside class as a central historical category, cast Williams in terms that New Left Marxists the world over would recognize. On the one hand, Williams had deftly grasped the changing contours of Empire and its powers to lull the masses. On the other hand, Williams seemed in European Marxist terms a naif, the all too typical American Socialist who viewed the world in his own parochial terms.[19] Not surprisingly, when *Review* editor Perry Anderson selected a dozen intellectuals as his chosen subjects of a book-length essay on Western Marxism, Williams did not make the list (neither, it is fair to say, did E. P. Thompson, W. E. B. DuBois, or indeed any other historian). If British scholars of U.S. history leaned more and more heavily upon Williams to explain how the successor to their own nation's Empire had both built and destroyed, the more prestigeous Marxist intellectuals took too little account of him as an important international writer and theorist.[20]

Something of the same might be said for academic life in Holland, Sweden, France, and most other European countries in terms of Williams's early usefulness and the ultimate difficulty of incorporating his work. If during the Vietnam years Williams helped explain the American Empire, he stood too far outside Marxist and other currents to fit the study of the societies at hand. Italy marked an exception, because here American Studies was influenced early and heavily by American antiwar and New Left cultural perspectives. *Contours of American History* was translated and published in 1968 by Laterza, a liberal publishing house long associated with the works of Benedetto Croce. As *Storia degli Stati Uniti*, it replaced the translation of the familiar and conservative Morison and Commager textbook for a handful of mostly youngish professors. *Contours*, whose cadence defied translation, proved daunting to average young Italians who had little or no background in U.S. history. The book also proved difficult to assimilate in its own terms, as an auto-critique of American civilization. But for teachers and graduate students who had plunged themselves into American culture, it opened eyes and made for especially exciting dialogues over the logic of imperialism and the meaning and direction of ongoing Italian "Americanization."

During the 1970s and after, Williams's Italian impact took more unexpected turns. His influence on a budding school of Italian "corporate" theorists had hardly consolidated before it was subjected to a sharp criticism by Americanists inspired instead by the social history of Herbert Gutman's and David Montgomery's labor-based scholarship. The subsequent rise of post-revisionist diplomatic history in the mainstream of

American studies—and the rightward drift of Italian society itself—tended to push Williams to the side, but never entirely. For former New Leftists now greying at the temples but reaching their stride in writing and teaching, Williams remained with a few others the lasting guide to the immanent critique which they sought, in their own ways, to apply to Italian as well as American history and life.[21]

Since the 1960s, Williams's works had also reached Japan and the People's Republic of China. For Asian scholars, the U.S. Open Door to the Pacific in the nineteenth and twentieth centuries was naturally of enormous interest. To the Japanese, Williams offered not only a somewhat mitigating look at Japanese expansionism, but also a parallel or contrasting view (as in the German case) of how Empire becomes a mechanism to quell internal contradictions. The Marxist traditions in Japanese scholarship, and the handful of graduate students who actually studied in Madison, made the academic New Left especially receptive of his work. As Williams devotee Yui Daizaburo put it, "studies of American diplomatic history have inevitably been influenced by the dominance of ideas that underlay specific policies," a perspective wide open to a leftish or Williamsesque interpretation. Shimizu Tomohisa's *Amerika teiloku* (The American Empire), written very much under Williams's influence, likewise defined Empire as a "system of capitalistic control and domination," a system as old as the American republic. Expansionism is for Shimizu and other Japanese scholars influenced by Williams the consistent and inevitable theme of U.S. history—in part because it helped explain Japanese history *sans* illusions as well.[22]

Yet other Asian studies in a variety of areas of U.S. diplomatic history, shaped in part by the interest in ethnicity, increasingly adopted topics of the immigration question and its relation with the logic of race and Empire. Beyond all this, Williams has a continuing appeal for those scholars across the world drawn to what the Germans called *Staatswissenschaft*, the ways in which the State mechanism operated through the political economy and social-cultural life of the nation. To the Chinese, opening at last to a wide world of scholarship, Williams was recently "discovered" for the first time.

In China and elsewhere, a growing debate about the history and meaning of the Open Door was bound to prompt discussion over the value of Williams's (and more generally, the revisionist) approach. Regardless of the direction taken by particular societies, and regardless of the scholars' political credentials, the work he had done would prove heuristic into the foreseeable future. Almost certainly, for at least some of the scholars from Europe to Africa and Asia to the Pacific archipelago, it would be inspiring as well.[23]

3

Williams entered his year as President of the Organization of American Historians on strong ground, with a real mandate from vigorous sectors of the membership. He had, at the time of his election, great hopes for the coming generations of scholars, and he made real progress along certain lines. His expectations were undercut, however, by an underlying pessimism and by the inevitable organizational inertia.

Writing an open memo to department colleagues in 1976 based on a version of the program intended for the OAH presidency, Williams concerned himself mainly with the consequences of academic specialization. Historians more and more tended to address each other (and graduate students) rather than undergraduates and the public. "As a historian and a citizen, " he reflected,

> I see a strong probability, if we do not rapidly and drastically change our ways, that the next generation will be masters of particulars that have little or no bearing on the general state of mankind—East or West, or North or South.[24]

Looking ahead to his presidency of the OAH, he envisioned addressing this problem with exhortation and personal example, meanwhile revolutionizing the inner life of the organization. In his official statement for election, he argued that "the immediate health, creativity and welfare of our profession is dependent upon the imaginative regeneration of the undergraduate history major in close alliance with young political theorists, political economists, teachers of literature and young scientists." Revitalization demanded the capacity to pose the question "What If," so as to ask Americans to consider breaking free of their collective past.[25] On the practical side, he planned to raise three quarters of a million dollars for an organization that (unlike its sister American Historical Association) had never possessed a capital fund. In doing so, he would also raise up those categories of scholars, like women and minorities, who had the least resources and the least opportunity to benefit from the traditional grants.

He had a most pleasing base of initial operations. At the behest of his student Ed Crapol, the College of William and Mary (whose *Quarterly* had published him during the dark 1950s) invited him to be the James Pinckney Harris Chair in the Spring semester of 1980. One of precious few honors accorded Williams, it was also a joy, according to his private letters, for the aging and insular radical to meet new people, to explore the vicinity of Williamsburg, Virginia, and to play fierce rounds of bridge with Wendy as his partner against friendly adversaries Ed and Jeanne Crapol.[26] Here, he spent the first months of his term as OAH president and hatched his plans for its transformation.

A few months earlier, he had written to a National Endowment for the Humanities officer pleading assistance to help resolve a "major problem involving the intellectual health of our society and culture" and the situation of historians in particular. Unable to find work as professors, large numbers of talented youngsters and especially women and minorities were in the process of drifting away, depriving the profession of its future resources. Meanwhile, the government had set about to destroy large numbers of important documents, effectively narrowing the historical record. Against these associated threats, he sought the basis for a capital fund and major grants for two programs: an oral history of citizen "experiences and responses" to the atomic bomb, Korea and Vietnam; and "a documentary foundation for a history of the culture coming to terms with a drastically new reality."

In effect, Williams wanted a historians' version of the New Deal's Works Progress Administration, an idea often discussed informally in those days as a solution to the employment crisis but rarely addressed formally.[27] He put the same proposition to Senator Mark Hatfield, pleading for the documentation of the atomic bomb's implications on ordinary American lives and suggesting that if the federal government began the funding, state historical societies and legislators would feel compelled to add enough to get the job done.[28]

"If we can save Lockheed and Chrysler, we can save history! Or am I naive?" Williams probed and asked his favorite politician, recalling the recent taxpayer bailout of corporations.[29] He was indeed naive, for most leaders of a society lurching toward Reaganism proved eager to literally bury the radioactive past in favor of the pleasant movie-style myths of happily government-free yesterdays.

By the time he had returned to Corvallis, just about everything seemed to go wrong with his plans. A small flood of memos aimed at the OSU administration placed claims upon stamps, long-distance phone use, travel and half-time salary. He received less than he had hoped (the OAH actually provided most of the traveling expenses), but he managed. More galling by far to him was the indifferent response of fellow historians, either to assist him in obtaining a National Endowment for the Humanities matching grant or corporate funding. By the spring of 1981 he wrote bitterly that he had "attempted over the better part of two years to engage the members of the OAH, various agencies of the government, and sundry corporations and foundations, in various programs and projects to re-energize historians to revitalize the place of History in our culture."[30] He had invested a great deal of time, thought, mundane labor, and even money of his own that he could not easily spare.

Williams concluded in a low moment that the organization was nothing more than a "white middle class gentlemen's club that is long on rhetoric about the importance of history but unwilling to act on the rhetoric." If historians would not "put their money or their backs to work in support of their rhetoric," they could guarantee that "neither the government, the corporations, or the public takes us seriously." As far as Williams could see, historians did not take themselves seriously enough to care.[31]

He had exaggerated the indifference, or taken the widespread uncertainty toward his plans as blanket refusal. He announced to the OAH governing council early on that he would approach corporate heads directly and through fellow scholarly volunteers. Such volunteers proved indeed few, but Williams's own approach to a regional giant, the lumber corporation Weyerhauser, produced no model for others to follow. Plans for contacting some one hundred and fifty other major corporations evaporated. He seized the only available alternative source for funds, the members themselves, writing personal letters to one hundred well-off members asking them each to equal his own five-thousand-dollar contribution. The total he raised by this method did not come to five thousand dollars altogether. He had expected that scholars with the two-income family that he had never been fortunate enough to experience (and had at some points admittedly resisted) would see their savings as excess. Not even his old-time Madison mentors agreed.

The failure to raise a capital fund and to create a historians' WPA was only, as it turned out, a small part of his legacy. Isolated among his own generational cohort of historians, Williams in office ironically found his readiest allies among women's history enthusiasts and above all the OAH president-elect, distinguished women's historian Gerda Lerner. Herself a veteran of political wars—widow of a prominent Hollywood blacklistee—and an adept organizational activist, Lerner made plans to push harder for some of the key programs that Williams wanted but by the less direct method of asking prestigious historians to devote their lecture fees. In the end, his initiative had been most valuable as a call from an unusual activist president for worthy goals achievable down the road.

In one other extremely important respect, he succeeded quickly and admirably. He established two ad hoc committees on the issue of government control of information: one to grasp the implications of the Freedom of Information Act on record preservation and release, the other to target the State Department's policies towards foreign relations documents. Now at last, historians would act in a collective, public manner to anticipate and to prevent the destruction of records—something which the Reagan administration clearly intended.

The first committee, headed by distinguished civil libertarians William Preston (a Madison PhD from the early 1950s and the nephew of famed ACLU founder Roger Baldwin) and Blanche Cook, had an immediate impact on publicizing the FBI plan to destroy its massive field office and headquarters files. A personal deposition in *AFSC v. Webster* noted Williams's own discoveries that the Wilson administration had misused its authority to seek the destruction of Senator William Borah; and that the State Department during the 1930s had begun determinedly "redlining" (destroying) revealing documents. Based on these discoveries, he condemned the "self-interested destruction of documents [as] a subversive act in the truest meaning of that much abused term."[32] Historians also joined as plaintiffs, filing an eloquent amicus brief. Drafted partly by Williams, the Brief challenged on behalf of the OAH the notion "that government documents have no other purpose than to serve the needs of the agency creating them." Nor, it went on,

> does the OAH believe that the law gives no recourse to private parties to challenge the destruction of documents that constitute this country's historical past. Such acts of self-inflicted amnesia cannot have been intended by a people that have revered the documents of their heritage and erected a magnificent archival system for their preservation and appraisal .... Should the government motion prevail, Washington will indeed have discovered a new way of fouling its own nest .... Historians and their many doctoral candidates working in 20th century history could no longer describe unique aspects of dissent, the civil rights movement, radicalism, and antiwar and student protests, and other activities that the FBI deemed worthy of investigation. This vision of an historical future in an environment without a documented past is surely not one that can escape challenge and rejection.[33]

The historians had not merely made a scholarly intervention or plea. Their action marked a complete rejection of the cold-war patronage in which certain prominent historians had argued for executive privilege free from public scrutiny or had cooperated quietly with CIA subterfuge operations conducted beyond the reach of reasonable documentation. The case was won on freedom of information grounds, even if future violations could hardly be precluded. An East European writer with a similarly bitter taste of state authority described "the struggle of man against power [as] the struggle of memory against forgetting," and that was surely the framework for Williams's most successful OAH committee.[34]

At the State Department, where the in-house Historical Office grew increasingly protective of secrets, the other OAH committee (and a sister committee from the Society of Historians of American Foreign Relations) failed to prevent the parallel drift toward secrecy. Indeed, a new classification system stopped publication of State's own Foreign Relations Series and it further classified documents that had been earlier available. More than a decade later and with a Democrat in the White House, many records dat-

ing from the 1950s still awaited declassification. As a new Russian government allowed *its* files to be examined and scholars rushed to look for the
evidence of charges made decades earlier, many Americans (and not only
historians) continued to wonder when similar U.S. archives would be open.
Only then could the real story of covert U.S. policies from Europe and
Africa to Asia, the Philippines, Central and South America, and the
Caribbean regions, and the participation of Americans in those programs,
be opened for discussion and debate.

The two committees, in their three years of life, could hardly manage to
lay open the books of highly guarded state secrets. They nevertheless
accomplished much and boldly attempted more: they testified at congressional hearings against legislative amendments and executive guidelines
limiting openness, worked to see that the FBI met criteria of the court on
record preservation, opposed budget cuts intended to limit the National
Archives' ability to respond to requests, convened OAH panels on issues of
access, and supported the idea of a politically independent National
Archives.[35]

Williams and committee members also anticipated, in important ways,
the dangerous burst of illegal behavior late in the cold war and the gaps in
the curtain of secrecy which prompted the Iran-Contra hearings. Stunned
by the crude manipulations of fact by Reagan's State Department team
(most notably Jeane Kirkpatrick and Elliott Abrams) toward Latin
American events, senior liberal historians probably came closer than at any
previous time to endorsing Williams's sentiments. Tragically, neither they
nor other scholars and investigators could prevent Congress from limiting
its probes and the media from loosening their pressure on the President at
a time when the evidence became too damning and too revealing of the
Democrats' all-too-willing participation in deceptive procedures. With a
little more political courage or the simple abandonment of cold-war traditions, the efforts of the freedom of information activists might possibly
have prepared the way to shatter the administration's authority and bring an
early end to the era of unprecedented waste and plunder.[36]

In the emerging context of Reagan-style neoconservativism, Williams
lacked the patience to look ahead to possible vindications, and to consolidate or simply enjoy the real victories he had won. His manner, more than
his properly ambitious programs, alienated him unnecessarily. Historians,
he now complained bitterly, were "cub scouts without a den mother." The
same attitude had made him, a decade earlier, eager for the insularity of
Oregon. If he blamed himself on occasion for helping to create a specialized professoriate less accessible to the public, he blamed others far more
severely. He seemed to rage at the gentlemanly sensibility that he had once
considered the *sine qua non* of educated citizenry in professional life, mean-

while expecting yesterday's rebels to haul out their wallets. Once again, the fact that so many younger historians held him in enormously high esteem scarcely altered his view favorably, as if he considered their failings more egregious because they should have known better. A different Williams would surely have pursued and cultivated them as a political base from which to build the needed support for his programs after he had left office.

The conflict of sensibilities had long since turned explosive when Williams addressed the largest of the handful of emerging radical and public history groups, the Mid-Atlantic Radical Historians Organization (and sponsor of the *Radical History Review*) in New York City in 1978. Inebriated and upset by rude challenges from the floor, he went on for nearly an hour, mortifying a mostly adulatory audience. Some years after the confrontationist campus New Left had disappeared, he plainly still felt uncomfortable with this generation of radicals—even when they pointedly shared his concerns for the classroom. He probably felt uneasy with this new breed of *Eastern* intellectuals. He could not have understood that more than a few in the New York audience remembered their own Madison days as the best of their lives.

He also felt plainly uncomfortable, he often wrote in letters, at being a highly lauded figure. The OAH spotlight sometimes seemed to make him especially queasy. Faced with the prospect of major audiences listening to him as president-elect, and with his back problems making travel uncomfortable, he turned to the cocktail glass for relief. His introductory remarks—normally a glowing tribute to the predecessor in office—were only two sentences long. His presidential address the next year was, however, an intellectual triumph of typical Williamsesque vintage.[37] After the OAH experience, at any rate, he had reached a point from which retreat to Waldport and his public or private life as an Oregon citizen was paramount and nearly absolute.

4

Since his return, Williams had been vitally concerned with the Oregon scene. Here he found some degree of real satisfaction. By the 1980s, with his triumphs and disappointments well behind him, the elderly Williams poured his energies into matters that the young Williams would have recognized as a contribution to public life.

One strain passed through the sciences and their relation to Liberal Arts at OSU. Williams had never entirely left behind his fascination with science and technology, and could often be found in the university library at Madison or Corvallis looking at technical journals. Very late in life, he became deeply interested in the construction of a new bridge near his home, photographing it in process and exhibiting the photos on an easel at a Waldport store. At OSU, he repeatedly emphasized the importance of finding ways to draw scientists into a dialogue, a small but important contribution to that discussion necessary "if we are to survive and create a humane new world." He asked scientists to consider anew the ends as well as means, and liberal arts scholars to make themselves aware of the scientific developments which did so much to reshape the world.

Williams argued, in venues as distant as the *Nation* and the shortlived but highly esteemed quarterly journal, *democracy*, that such regionalism held the promise of a democratic and radical future. He premised his 1981 call in the *Nation* for "Backyard Autonomy" on the seemingly unlikely appeal, by the president of the Mormon Church, for elimination of the MX missile system. The inability of radicals to grasp the importance of such religious and regional resistance pointed to their inability to "imagine a *different* America," their lack of staying power in the "rudimentary work of people-to-people politics," and their reluctance to commit themselves "to changing conditions in the places in which we live." They needed to look at democracy afresh, to drop an all-or-nothing perspective and instead set themselves to "fragmenting centralized power" via a variety of means. Radicals, Williams concluded, must "develop a different conception and practice of America and then persuade our neighbors that we are honoring the true spirit of America. That we together are the bearers of the torch. That *We* rather than *They* decide our common future."[38]

This was a bit vague, but he claimed (during an exchange of views in the Letters Column of the *Nation*) to have received many letters and phone calls urging him on. As one of the letter-writers noted, Williams aimed in fact at piecemeal disarmament in the frame set forth across the Atlantic by END (European Nuclear Disarmament) led by Englishman and fellow historian E. P. Thompson. A particularly brilliant pamphleteer, Thompson had recently penned *Protest and Survive*, a bestseller in the U.K., and become a major international peace spokesman through ceaseless public engagements. Williams lacked the European setting in which even radical intellectuals could become public heroes, and above all he lacked the personality for this kind of political work.[39]

He felt more at home, anyway, linking present-day perspectives with historical experience. Thus writing in *democracy*, he insisted that after the Civil War and during a situation of severe national flux, Americans *could* have developed a different view of the world including an acceptance of a regionalized socialism. "But in the end," he concluded sadly, "we crab-scuttled away from the challenge." No one sounded the alarm (he had forgotten, again, to treat aspects of Populism at variance with his own interpretation). The Marxist acceptance of the population megalopolis and over-centralized industries only reflected the subsequent muddle of radical thought. The "friendly and erotic fascism" of technocratic fantasy as well as capitalist reality had repeatedly swept aside the quieter dreams of subsequent regionalism, most notably the decentralist spirit of the early Tennessee Valley Authority (TVA) project, leaving behind fewer and fewer real community resources. If "twentieth century radicals followed Marx in becoming victims of his fascinating combination of capitalist assumptions and socialist utopianism," they needed at long last to unburden themselves of these illusions.

He also echoed the somber tone of late-life considerations so vividly expressed in *Empire as a Way of Life*. We "twentieth century radicals are aging. Realistically we are old. Candidly we are dying." In the time remaining, space had to be won to create time for this generation's children to "refine our thoughts" and set them right. "If we fail," above all in halting the drift toward nuclear war, "we destroy time." To halt the drift, radicals needed to look at community and at religion, "another word for community." Rather than saving the world, American radicals should turn to saving their own communities, the space around them. They needed to create something like the Federalist Papers, through discussions with a lot of nonacademics. Was it a utopian conception? Yes, if "the purpose of a radical utopia is to create a tension in our souls." To evoke a widespread feeling that the nation was not doing well enough demanded the effort by intellectuals to imagine something better, something which "defines us as people who offer our fellow citizens a meaningful choice about how we can define and live our lives."[40] If *The Great Evasion* had been Williams's version of *Looking Backward*, he urged radicals and intelligent conservatives to dream again, and better than he had done.

These were bold strokes and thoughtful ones, in tune with the early moment of mass disillusionment and radical hope, Washington protest parades, and Latin American radical insurgencies during Reagan's first two years in office. The political turnaround, with Truman-style heavy military expenditures boosting economic growth, ensured the former actor's popularity; the successful conspiracy to finance the Contras secretly meanwhile buried hopes for a peaceful adjustment to hemispheric inequalities. Localism seemed either like the last gasp of a dated 1960s counterculture vision, or an expression of the narrowness of the emerging NIMBY (Not In My Back Yard) movements. Even the journal *democracy*, off to an intellectually promising beginning, folded after a few years. For that matter, so did Eugene D. Genovese's own journal, *Marxist Perspectives*, which had also invited contributors from Left and Right seeking dialogue but which foundered on its editor's rocky personal temperament.

Williams had meanwhile already taken his own advice and turned to the state and regional scene. From 1981 to 1986, he wrote semi-weekly (sometimes weekly or monthly) columns for the *Capitol Journal* and the *Statesman Journal*, working hard to attain a regional sensibility. The West, he often emphasized, was a different place, with a relatively small population controlled or directed from the East (and more recently, the South). The West had a "different attitude, a different psychology, a different hierarchy of values," some involving escapism but others set in the aspiration for a human scale of life and politics. Westerners learned to say "No" to becoming a mere natural raw material center for the rest of the nation, a "surplus of land and resources" that others could exploit at will. But if they did not learn to say no to central government and to find their own way forward, "the West is dead. And so is America."[41]

Williams specialized as a regional columnist in developing extended examples such as water policy. He exposed how such a purportedly water-conscious political leader as Washington's Senator Henry "Scoop" Jackson (an undaunted Democratic hawk on Vietnam, best known in the Northwest and the nation's capitol as the "Senator from Boeing") actually supported the vast wastage of resources while claiming to protect regional supplies from incursions by Californians. Jackson was barely more than a vulgar lobbyist for military spending, despite a vigorous campaign of foreign-policy hard-liners for his nomination in 1972. But the ordinary adopted Oregonian who "built a retirement home with two full bathrooms, including water-jet toothbrushes, a hot tub, a sauna, a jacuzzi, an automatic dishwasher, a five-cycle washing machine and a sprinkling system" for the lawn and flowers represented a popular constituency which shared large parts of Jackson's worldview.[42] Unfortunately, although Williams neglected to say so, this retiree was a member of the fastest growing population on Williams's own coastal territory, which during the 1980s began to blossom with strip malls and garish housing complexes.

Williams's rapier thrusts at Truman and Kennedy also probably earned him more hostility than admiration. Oregonians did not like any more than other Americans to admit that, as Williams put it, in the struggle to conquer the planet, "success is failure," and the "truth about power is defined by its limits."[43] Likewise, if peace demonstrations in Europe inspired him (and especially Wendy, who shared moments of enthusiasm for her fellow Britons), his appeals to join the anti-nuke crusade almost certainly struck home to the peacenik constituencies of Oregon Public Radio more than to the "ordinary folks" of the pool halls and fishing docks.[44]

Perhaps, however, Williams had earned the satisfaction of writing about himself and his interests, saying whatever he chose for whoever would listen. One week he might address the foolish funding of college athletics, complaining that organized sports wasted precious university funds, encouraged vicarious pleasure-taking, and discouraged real play. He had early on discovered, he recalled, that even the scholarship given him to attend Kemper for basketball would have been better awarded to more worthy but less athletic kids. Another week he might ruminate on history as art, his views of the Middle East (where he believed that Israelis badly needed to rethink their occupation policies if they hoped for future accord), or anything else that struck his attention.[45]

His public talks increasingly had a similar let-it-all-hang-out tone, heavily flavored with personal experiences. For instance, he addressed journalism students recalling (perhaps from high school days) that he had nearly joined the Fifth Estate fraternity of newspapermen himself. He had learned in the subsequent decades that the mass audience was "assumed to be largely uninterested . . . in serious and sustained information and analysis about their natural and human environment." Information was therefore presented them at random, while a tiny minority was treated "as honorary members of the information and opinion elite."

He had found, especially in regard to Vietnam and Central America (even after Watergate and Contragate) that the *New York Times* for instance rarely encouraged a "fundamental debate about the nature, necessary limits, or consequences of Empire, and similarly with nuclear weapons, poverty, racism, sexism, unemployment or education." For that reason, the journalism of the elite "misleads the elite" by defining "what is fit to take seriously." Falsely defined by their exercise of power, Henry Kissinger and even Ronald Reagan were made somehow to look like intellectuals, while intelligent ordinary citizens were treated as dummies and responded by tuning out. If "history is thoughtful reflection upon critically evaluated human experience," and so little of it was available in intelligent form, "I hope but I also weep."[46]

He urged, as in his newspaper columns, that the Constitution be used to attack the oppressive national state through diminishing its power of taxation. He urged the state legislature be used to return authority to the citizen, and take it away from the corporation. He likewise urged regional public enterprises "not so much [because] small is good, as that small is human" even if sometimes less efficient. He saw no other way out of the morass of distant authority and citizen apathy.[47]

In that melancholy tone, he repeatedly treated what he often described as the crisis of American democracy, seeing the nation's "Weary and Nostalgic Culture" as the heart of the problem. The non-perception of a crisis during the massively destructive 1980s was the most certain evidence that the crisis had reached epic proportions. Reagan's promise to start the world over with "morning in America" was at once crazed and unworkable "short of having the Lord on hold on the Hot Line." The Reagan plan to free corporate or individual philanthropy to care for the poor until the economy gave them all jobs reminded Williams of the capitalist John D. Rockefeller giving away dimes on the streetcorner.

Anguished by the sheer banality of it all, Williams reached his eloquent apex as Cassandra:

> There is no community and no commonwealth in contemporary America. Instead there is a Superpower within which there is not even a dream of the common welfare. As for shared values, there are two: first, get it while you can; second, anybody who gets in the way is a Communist. On four days a week the Superpower asserts its meaningless military power by subverting the Constitution. It uses the other three days to offer various excuses about why it can neither help improve the quality of life of its citizens nor allow them to change the society.
>
> America is indeed weary. Only a handful of its citizens seek seriously to create a community and a commonwealth. There are no strikes, as there were within memory (say the 1930s) to define and sustain the essence of being an artisan or a yeoman.
>
> The heroes of the moment, not just today but for long years past, are people who lie. Most of our leaders admit that they lie, and nobody gives a damn. It is taken as a given. So? Granted his serious competition in those sweepstakes, Colonel Oliver North captured the affection of the American public with his candid remark to a Congressman: "I lied to you in good faith."
>
> Yes, America is weary when it takes that as honest. It is a dreary and scary epitaph for the idea, or the ideal, of community and commonwealth.

Somehow—and now Williams could no longer quite imagine how—America had to move beyond its now-ancient vision of itself as the City on the Hill ready to instruct or bulldoze everyone who saw things differently. As Williams turned repeatedly to the historic wars waged upon Vietnam, Mexico, and the Philippines, the message came back again and again. Once "the dream and the magic of Arcadia, of Walden Pond, no longer had a basis in reality," America would logically be compelled to join the human race like everyone else. But its leaders refused. For that reason, they had to try to style history in their own image, preserving half-truths as to render "a once vibrant people frightened of human beings who are trying to realize the ideal of community and commonwealth."[48]

It would have been impossible for Williams to miss not only an echo of the "low intensity" brushfire wars ongoing, but also the ill effects of current unconstitutional conduct by highly-placed former Naval officers on the *élan* of the U.S. military. He took great pride in Oregonians' demonstrations against U.S. interventionism here and there. But he evinced still more interest in the uproar around Oliver North and the Contragate scandal. He corresponded with career Navy men who readily agreed with Williams's view of the demoralization brought by civilian misleadership. And from Williams's testimony, so did the rising star and future Joint Chiefs commander Colin Powell.

Williams therefore enthused when his Naval Academy alma mater invited him back to lecture the midshipmen. He gave his audience a dramatic picture of Alfred Mahan's importance both in devising a global-imperial overview and elaborating the *noblesse oblige* mission "to be honorable and generous." Every midshipman, he recalled, was assigned the "Pocket Bible," a handbook stressing that the oath of service was taken neither to persons nor offices but to the Constitution. Williams read that as the "crucial right and responsibility" to "challenge an order that violates his oath to the Constitution and his tradition," a promise demanding "courage beyond combat." Colonel North and those other fellow Annapolis graduates John Poindexter, Robert McFarland, and James Webb could have said "no" to illegal orders. Instead they lied or pretended not to remember. (Williams claimed that many in North's class returned their rings in disgust.)[49]

The enduring naval connection also excited Williams's last (and mostly unrecorded) scholarly passion: for the sea and everything connected with it. From the middle 1970s, he had urged Oregon State to take up its potential for an original and outstanding program in which, by no accident, he could play a central role. Maritime Studies never achieved the solidity that Williams hoped for, but it drew upon some outstanding younger scholars, such as Michael Sprinker—an English teacher and a personal bridge between Williams and Edward Said.[50] Bringing scientists into the program as equal partners also fulfilled a long-term ambition of Williams, who continued to scan a variety of scientific journals, recalling his undergraduate training and discussions with some of his closest Madison academic friends.

Classroom discussions inspired his own research and rumination in a number of related areas. He sought more information on the Chinese explorer Cheng Ho, who had halted his historic journeys of fleets to Africa before da Gama rather than draw China into a sea empire (fulfilling Williams's notion of saying "no"—certainly a strange interpretation, as friends noted, of a land dynasty).[51] He urged the study of pirates as a proto-community which sought in the Renaissance era and afterward to create its own rules, and prompted widespread fear in the existing empires.[52] And he set out to learn more about a very particular wreck famous on the Oregon shore, the grounding of a British ship in October 1913. Its captain was Captain Owen Williams from Wales, a not-so-far-fetched possible relative to the family. The more Williams probed, the more he was hooked. He recounted, in an exceptionally lively tone, the results in the *American Neptune*, a noted maritime journal.

"Walking along the fist-sized basalt rocks and looking out to sea," he recalled his view of the wreck's sight exactly sixty years afterward:

> One could see the curtain of water vapor rolling upward from the water. One felt that awe of forces beyond control. . . . Today it remains hazardous despite electronic navigational aids . . .
>
> Several reasons had prompted me to come north from my home on the beach just north of Waldport to seek an understanding of what it was like at that place at that time. Like everyone else who has seen the photographs taken by Charles Wood (and others), I had been initially baffled and intrigued. But I was drawn into it further because I had sailed the sea aboard a wishbone-staysail-rigged ketch, and had later navigated the Caribbean and much of the Pacific as the executive officer of a ship that could be as tricky and as difficult to handle under some conditions as the *Glenesslin*.
>
> Those experiences evoked in me a sense of awe and mystery about the sea—not the sea as romantic myth or metaphor, just the sea as a very necessary and demanding friend. And so, when I much later became a historian, I thought of the sea . . .
>
> Facts are not simply discrete entities proceeding on their individual way. Facts are interacting parts of a whole. Hence I have always thought of the historian as one who tries to discover and explain those interrelationships. There are many guides: from Spinoza to Henry Adams, from Adam Smith to Karl Marx; but also oceanography and geology—disciplines that deal with particulars as part of a whole.[53]

Here, Williams expressed almost a whole life's interests together. He condemned the corporate planners who described the sea as the "next frontier," not only because of the brute treatment given to other frontiers but because the sea had obviously been *the* frontier that had led to the industrial revolution. Sailing was integral to human development, probably beginning before writing. It expressed for Williams the development of a community, in the complexity of shipbuilding and of navigation. The three-masted bark (like the *Glenesslin*) he could see as at once an imperial instrument and a "poem to man's creativity." It was finally, from a military angle, the "first inter-continental missile" aimed by one part of the world at another far away.[54]

He sought to explain the wreck in detail and with great empathy for the victims. The crews of such ships had been reduced, since the emergence of steamships, to a skeleton of often inexperienced and nutritionally deprived men little able to handle themselves or even to see properly at night. As water rushed over the deck, the sailor faced many sudden jerks which could easily throw him overboard. Standard histories of the incident had from the first blamed the captain, suggesting the influence of alcohol. Williams drew out of himself the memories of aching tiredness and the inevitable reliance upon mates who often did not entirely know their job. Tragedy could have struck quite without any notable blundering human assistance, in Williams's estimation. Now, as he looked at rubble from a highway construction project covering the "bones of the *Glenesslin*," he mused:

> The sea will have its way. Slowly, but certainly, the sea will free *Glenesslin*. And perhaps someday we will recover the essence of *Glenesslin*: that awareness of common purpose; that knowing that being a sail master rather than a master does not demean a person; and that commitment to behaving like a captain even if one is an apprentice seaman.
>
> Once we did all those things in the name of Empire. Perhaps now we can do it to create a different and more human kind of community.[55]

The subject had touched his inner being; Williams was not likely in any scholarly effort to become more eloquent and intimate. It was also an observation of a man who at sixty seemed to have seen as much of life as he wanted.

In the same spirit, he turned to a past that he had never previously written about, perhaps as a way to tie up loose ends. During the later 1970s he had refused a five thousand dollar offer made on the basis of an outline about his life's story. A few years later, he used some of the research materials for a family memoir, "A Good Life and a Good Death: A Memoir of An Independent Lady," ostensibly to leave a record of his mother's life as a kind of gift to his children. He sent an outline to a press or two, but without any serious hope of publication. The result was a family self-justification, often charming in its details and revealing of a way of life he had left far behind. It was also, transparently, about the making of William Appleman Williams.

The eighty-page essay undoubtedly captured the positive side of prosperous Iowa commercial and small-town society, and offered particularly incisive glimpses of the family's two strong-minded women. It spoke honestly to the trials of Mildrede Williams, interpreting with extraordinary empathy her stresses and her decisions. The Iowa and the family scenes he depicted were mainly Williams's imagined human-scale society struggling through a difficult but in some ways hopeful period, chiseled in outline against the darker, militarized and bureaucratic future of the post–World War II era. This vignette might have been better projected fictionally onto Iowa's genuinely isolationist districts (as Atlantic was not) or to the Farmer-Labor and Progressive Party voting counties of Minnesota or Wisconsin.

But he portrayed what he chose to see about the only home town and the only family that he could call his own.[56]

During his final years, he set out on a very different project, a fictional treatment of his own Civil Rights days. A lifelong reader of novels, he had for decades been convinced that he could turn out a novel with an effective story line and well-developed characters. Once he claimed to have written a novel before any of his historical works, and burned it. However that might be, he resolved now to bring 1945-46 back to life, recalling fictionally "the effort to make the victory against The Axis in World War II into a better and more equitable culture and society . . . and the frustration of that effort through prejudice, violence and indifference."[57]

His current friends had difficulty telling him how far he was from the stylistic mark. His dialogue—nearly always the most difficult element for the amateur fiction writer to master—never lost its artificiality. His characters all seemed underdeveloped except the protagonist "Cat," i.e., Williams himself. At that, he could hardly imagine the human frailties required to fill out his narrative realistically. Not that Cat lacked human desires or vices, especially sex (with his wife) and liquor. But he and his mates—to say nothing of the African American locals courageously throwing their weight against armed racism—were too good, too narrow. Encouraged by his new friend Gore Vidal, who had spent days with Williams in Corvallis and struck up a correspondence afterward, he nevertheless pressed ahead. He was crestfallen although hardly surprised at various publishers' indifference.

5

Williams's status as a scholarly giant and historiographical influence had risen to an apex, ironically, a decade after his authorial success seemed to hit bottom. Part of this was generational. The younger historians shaped by the Vietnam War experience were now moving into senior positions, and the Schlesinger, Jr., generation of liberal cold warriors looked toward retirement. The New Deal had obviously ceased to be at the center of the twentieth-century experience, and even the Second World War grew further and further away. Yet a good number of older historians, mostly those beyond the range of the East Coast notables, had also seen their views of U.S. foreign relations significantly changed. Even when they rejected Williams's political suggestions and declined to credit him with influencing them, they nonetheless appropriated portions of his analyses of foreign policy and imperial overreach. Williams had, in short, by this time gained a kind of almost unimpeachable integrity within a history profession prone to personal rifts and intellectual vendettas.

From another and more practical standpoint, Williams certainly did not provide the particular cutting edge that social historians sought in treating women, labor, and minorities. But at the classroom level, it was his perspective (often retailed and refurbished through books by Walter LaFeber and Lloyd Gardner, among a growing multitude of others) that informed lectures not only on foreign policy but also, increasingly, on various other aspects of the eighteenth- and nineteenth-century experience. Seeking a fresh synthesis of U.S. history not yet nearly in sight, scholars and teachers began to incorporate the themes of Empire and imperial consensus along with African American history, Indian people's history, and women's history.

Outside the profession, the thin slice of the public which read popular history books might not even have noticed the trend, so much did Civil War history and the flattering mode of "insider" histories like Arthur Schlesinger, Jr., on the Kennedys and David McCullough on Harry Truman continue to dominate limited shelf space. Yet Williams's classics, especially *The Tragedy of American Diplomacy*, remained in the hearts of now-experienced teachers and at hand on the scholar's shelf, trustworthy conceptual guides to the movement of large trends.

After the Maddox flap had almost passed from memory, historical meetings on foreign policy no longer elicited what John Lewis Gaddis described as "torrents of impassioned prose . . . provoking calls for the suppression of unpopular points of view, or threats of lawsuits."[58] As Lloyd Gardner put it at the 1983 meeting of the Organization of American Historians, neither side felt capable any more of convincing the other. Many scholars opted out of the conflict entirely, citing "irreconcilable differences."[59] Middle-of-the-roaders sought an elusive compromise.

Harvard Europeanist Stanley Hoffman thus observed characteristically that in their assessment of Soviet diplomatic behavior, the revisionists were probably closer to the truth, whereas in their assessment of American diplomatic behavior the traditionalists were more accurate. The Soviets had acted defensively as nationalists; no monolithic worldwide Communist conspiracy had existed. But the revisionists had failed to take into account the inconsistencies within U.S. policies.[60]

A new school, labelled "post-revisionist," quickly emerged. Many historians considered it tepid, but it offered a roundabout vindication of liberal-skeptical positions and mainly for that reason succeeded cold-war liberalism at the prestigious ramparts of influence. Hence, for example, the "post-revisionists" conceded that the U.S. was an Empire, that it did bear a heavy responsibility for the cold war, and that economic factors did heavily influence American policies. Yet, while the Soviet Union reacted defensively and cautiously, Stalin's Russia represented one of the most repressive regimes in world history. If mistakes were inevitably made on both sides, the U.S.—constrained by bureaucratic considerations and the force of public opinion—never followed a clear or consistent policy. The leading exponent of post-revisionism was none other than John Lewis Gaddis.[61]

The great weakness of this position was its too-evident attempt at adjustment *sans* synthesis. Traditionalist Warren F. Kimball called Gaddis's position "orthodoxy plus archives." Bruce R. Kuniholm added that the questioning of fundamental assumptions "is what revisionism was all about," and without which nothing had been seriously revised.[62] Noted left-liberal Barton J. Bernstein admiringly observed that unlike many anti-revisionists, Gaddis was "never angry or polemical, never sharp-tongued or snide . . . [but] polite, modest and even disarming."[63] Yet he fundamentally missed "the subtle formulation of Williams's conception of the 'Open Door' ideology" of which the economic component was only a part. Gaddis treated the concerns of American policy-makers with economic expansion, self-determination, and collective security as independent variables, "not as integrated parts of an ideology" in Williams's understanding.[64] Williams himself, who mostly stayed largely out of the debate, was also unimpressed with the recent nuances.[65]

In a notable address to diplomatic historians in December 1992, Gaddis revealed the extent to which and ways in which post-revisionism could be used to reinforce the interpretations of traditional orthodox historians. He began by praising *The Tragedy of America Diplomacy* as "one of the most influential books ever written about the history of United States foreign relations." But he fretted that Williams's views, shared by many scholars, now risked becoming a new orthodoxy, presumably the last thing Williams would have wanted. Presenting his own perspective as if it represented a new twist, Gaddis reiterated Schlesinger's familiar argument that the United States during the early cold war was dealing not "with a normal, everyday, run-of-the-mill, statesmanlike head of government" but rather with "a psychologically disturbed but fully functional and highly intelligent dictator." Throughout the twentieth century the U.S. had played a central role in resisting authoritarianism, whether that of Lenin, Stalin, Hitler, Mao, Ho Chi Minh or Fidel Castro. The "American Tragedy," reread as the distance between its aspirations and accomplishments, therefore faded in comparison with the tragedies of other great powers.[66] As Bruce Cumings quipped memorably in response,

> Bill Williams gets flogged whether he is a pro-Communist, a revisionist, a reductionist, an American Exceptionalist, the author of the new orthodoxy in diplomatic history, or, by implication, a dishonest historian who ignored the millions who died at the hands of world-historical monsters. And we still wait, through two decades of writing,

for John Lewis Gaddis to take one of his arguments seriously and try to refute it.[67]

Not only had Gaddis come to honor Williams in order to bury him. In linking Ho and Castro to Hitler and Stalin (conveniently ignoring the bundle of authoritarian governments that the U.S. had propped up with cash and intelligence or direct military assistance), Gaddis seemed to be justifying the Vietnam War, as well as past and future interventions into Latin America. No wonder Gaddis felt dismayed that so many historians still subscribed to Williams's views. Indeed, at the time of Williams's death and after, many conservative and liberal historians—often those who still smarted from perceived personal slights during the Vietnam campus protests or who resented the career advances of New Left and feminist historians and scholars of minority cultures—treated the fall of communism as a long-awaited vindication of America's cold-war policies and of themselves personally as well. Or, from more detached perspective, they saw the opportunity to take a slap at Williams for his decades-old support of foreign revolutions and revolutionaries.[68]

Williams would not have found it difficult to formulate responses to their arguments. Obviously, as he had long suggested, if the U.S. had accommodated and cooperated with revolutionary movements at an earlier date, many of the helpful changes at the end of the cold war would have come more peacefully without bringing the world to the brink of nuclear war and devastating large parts of the civilian population and planet itself with militarization and environmental poisoning. We could have learned something humanly invaluable from the societies that our government and its clients proceeded to destabilize and overthrow.

His critics almost invariably overlooked the enormous tragedy endured by American society precisely because of its counterrevolutionary posture. "If everyone elsewhere *does* deny us the chance to realize ourselves by changing them," Williams wrote half-ironically in the preface to *History as a Way of Learning*, "we nevertheless have a magnificent fall-back position: we can finally confront the question of what we are going to make of America."[69] That dialogue had now been postponed so long since the unresolved social dilemmas of the 1960s had burst into crises, it seemed almost beyond recollection. Political leaders of both parties, as Williams might have observed, had abandoned anything like a vision of a better or more democratic society. They offered nothing more meaningful than the universal panaceas of growth and economic expansion; all else was calculated spin control.

And of course, it remained to be seen how well the capitalist world would survive the legacies of the cold war, especially when capitalism had nothing more to absorb. As frequent mainstream commentators noted gloomily, the early post-Communist prediction of democracy as world destiny was swiftly and rudely shaken by events in Afghanistan, Somalia, Haiti, the former Soviet Union, and the former Yugoslavia, to name only a very few locations. As the rainforests toppled, the cities of the world grew more ugly and crime-scored and the ozone layer thinned, happy endings were indeed scarce. George Frost Kennan, the last surviving formulator of Containment, observed that the cold war, with its enormous costs, really had no victors at all.[70]

Williams's theses remained at the center of other debates over U.S. history as well. An aging Schlesinger, Jr., clearly disturbed by the concerns of younger generations of scholars and nervously looking over his shoulder for his old foe's shadow, compulsively lashed out again and again. Schlesinger's effort to rewrite his own synthesis so thoroughly revolved around Williams and the New Left that his late scholarly effort can be regarded as a sort of mirror-image or *doppelgänger* to Williams's texts, its author possessed by the notion of expunging the dissident voices and reestablishing the canon unchanged at its essence.[71]

The Open Door theorists were not open-minded like himself, Schlesinger, Jr., insisted in *The Cycles of American History* (1986), and they felt compelled to commit "historical malpractice," to "distort evidence in order to bolster their thesis." The Open Door argument was "evidently not falsifiable. Because it explains everything, it explains very little. It is not a testable historical hypothesis at all. It is a theological dogma." Schlesinger, Jr., unwilling to respond to the variety of criticisms rained down on him by younger historians for especially dark moments of his own political past and for his sometimes doubtful scholarly ethics, wrapped up the collective critic into Williams and found it "difficult to understand why any thesis so intellectually parochial, so thinly documented, and so poorly argued . . . should cast a spell on a generation of American historians."[72]

Much of the rest of *The Cycles of American History* was cast in light of Reaganism, which Schlesinger, Jr., thoroughly disliked but adamantly refused to see in any way as emblematic of American society and politics. Where Williams perceived the wastefulness and self-destructive shortsightedness of the 1980s as all too typical of a way of life, Schlesinger Jr., cheerfully insisted that, at worst, the excesses of the period merely encouraged the swing of the pendulum back from the Right, preparing another phase centerward or slightly beyond.[73] No permanent harm had been done. Williams privately described this pendulum theory as the "birth control method of history," pointing instead to the 1980s as one disaster after another in a compounding and culmination of past conservative and liberal mistakes. The predecessor of Reagan as military budget-buster, world policeman, and domestic political smear artist had not after all been

Eisenhower or Hoover but Harry Truman.

Schlesinger, Jr., also implicitly assailed Williams's views on larger trends. If Williams's *The Great Evasion* described a society which could not face up to its limits, Schlesinger, Jr., insisted that Marx had precisely failed to anticipate the power of the democratic citizenship which outstripped class theories of structural inequality by encouraging social responsibility (and, he might have added, by outreaching all possible limits). If many of Williams's works had insisted that imperial policy corrupted what was best in America, Schlesinger, Jr., simply wished that policy out of existence. Certainly, he admitted, conflicts existed between policies of human rights and national interest, but after all, "a nation's supreme interest is self-preservation." Conquest of the Third World by force had in any case always been exaggerated, since at least some portion of natives in each conquered society had collaborated with the colonialists and used imperialism for their own purposes. The American Empire, as anything like an oppressive force, had scarcely ever existed at all and certainly not in recent decades. Vietnam was a judgment error. Lyndon Johnson's other misadventures of Gunboat Diplomacy and the CIA-backed coups following the 1954 overthrow of the Guatemalan government— including those Latin American activities of the early 1960s in which Schlesinger, Jr., himself had a hand—dropped from sight. Because public opinion no longer tolerated such CIA moves, they had, Schlesinger, Jr., suggested, finally been abandoned.[74] What policies did Schlesinger imagine the Reagan administration practiced in Central America?

Williams and his favorite social critics had, for many generations, deplored the centralization of power as a loss of democratic possibility. For Schlesinger, Jr., however, national "leadership is really what makes the world go round . . . . Numerical majorities are no substitute" for leaderly action, and democratic decentralization of the type Williams favored was obviously undesirable as well. Centralization of power had grown not from overweening ambition, Schlesinger, Jr., insisted, but from the complexity of society and the "psychology of mass democracy." Kennedy had obviously been a model leader, Nixon a bad leader, Reagan evidently a dreadful leader. But the excesses of presidential power, even Watergate and Contragate, cast no doubt for Schlesinger, Jr., on the underlying mechanisms themselves. Presidents needed to be strongmen at home and abroad.[75]

The oddest touch in *Cycles of American History*, and the one most clearly related to his struggle with Williams, was Schlesinger, Jr.'s confidence that Kennedy's guiding influence had "touched and formed a generation of young men and women in the 1960s . . . moved by his aspirations and shaped by his ideals." But those must surely have been the anti-Vietnam protestors and erstwhile civil rights activists who fell under Williams's influence and whose university protests Schlesinger, Jr., had cursed in the

New York Times and elsewhere. "Their day is still to come," he promised.[76] But would he welcome it then?

Schlesinger, Jr., devoted his next volume to a blistering polemic against the epicenter of this very generation's influence on the universities, seen in the rise of multiculturalism. *The Disuniting of America* made no mention of William Appleman Williams (nor of Empire, nor imperialism) in the text. But it might be said to have moved toward a triumphal defense of Schlesinger's views of thirty years earlier, just as Williams had sought in his last few books to move beyond the limits of his own older work toward an egalitarian, tragic, and multiracial view of the American saga.[77]

Because Williams did not live to comment on this book, the dialogue (or rather, the exchange of criticisms) between the two historians ended here— or at least one side of it did, because Schlesinger, Jr., has continued to defend himself against a ghost, filing charges against those younger historians seen as proxies of Williams. Observers expected another large dose in his memoirs. Would the exchange finally end with the demise of Schlesinger, Jr.? Presumably not, because just as he had long since assumed the archetype of the Cold War Democrat, Williams had been the archetypal anti-imperial democrat, big "D" against little "d" in an intellectual set piece of the half century after World War II. Others would continue these positions, with or without the names of the original debaters.

In a field ostensibly far from foreign affairs, Williams's side meanwhile received a vindication and extension that neither he nor Schlesinger, Jr., had probably ever imagined. A decade or so after the last U.S. withdrawal from Vietnam, a fresh generation of scholars in Western history, confronted with a virtual absence of acceptable interpretations, found in Williams a guide to a new and drastically revised view of national experience. Yale professor John Mack Faragher, the award-winning biographer of Daniel Boone, notes that in graduate school during the Vietnam days he was struck in reading *Contours* by Williams's view of continental expansion as a substitution of Manifest Destiny for the earlier vision of the Christian Commonwealth. *Roots of the Modern American Empire* made the connection between continental and overseas expansion explicit. The problem of expansion and its implications for community, as described and analyzed by Williams, neatly became, in Faragher's considered view, the catchspring for some of the most influential and radical scholarship of the emerging scholarly generation.[78]

Williams certainly did not set the course for this field, as he did in diplomacy. But his provocation came at just the right moment to prompt young scholars in the direction that already called them, and to give them what their own predecessors in Western history could not: a view at once personally sympathetic and realistically (even harshly) critical of the consequences. Without placing any particular stress upon the fate of Mexican Americans, Indians, or of the land—at least until his last books—Wiliams had also made it possible for the next generation of scholars to pursue the inner logic and the various meanings of expansionism from the viewpoint of victor and victim.

Williams's own intellectual lineage can be interrogated one last time in this regard. His classmate David W. Noble has suggested that Williams's true importance on this matter can be understood best through re-examining the problems for U.S. history which Frederick Jackson Turner earlier articulated: if the frontier were the key to American specialness and success, what would happen when the frontier closed? Warren Susman, Williams's intimate friend, saw the continual scholarly reevaluation of Turner as the clearest symptom of changing attitudes about American life, and how these attitudes tended nevertheless to return to the same, almost obsessive questions of expansion.[79] Williams discerned in Turner less the master scholar than the essayist looking for a grand metaphor; perhaps Williams understood this best because it so matched his own temperament. Williams offered the freshest insights of any historian for generations on that continuing controversy about the frontier.

How, Noble asks provocatively, can we explain the enormous impact of a youngish scholar like Patricia Limerick, whose *Legacy of Conquest* (1987) may be said to have precipitated more than any other work the change in the way the history of the American West is taught? Limerick's innovation was, foremost, in periodization: the history of the West does not begin in the eighteenth century and end in 1890, but must instead be seen as a continuous history of contest and conquest. The study of contestation, in Limerick's work, becomes a reconceptualizing of that history as a continuing saga where a seemingly fragmented and discontinuous past gains coherence at last.[80]

Limerick does not invoke Williams directly and has no need to do so. Williams shaped the background against which subsequent scholarship's patterns now move. The next generation also demonstrated, in passing, many of the smaller points that Williams struggled to make against an unwilling profession. For instance, Richard White has pinpointed Woodrow Wilson as the first massive betrayer of evolving conservation policy toward the West, stripping millions of acres of proposed national parkland for exploitation.[81] The fighting idealist of Arthur Link and Arthur Schlesinger, Jr., is extraordinarily difficult to find in this Wilson, precursor of Reagan and Bush's woodlands sell-off policies.

Noble elaborates what Faragher affirms: that by drawing domestic conclusions from diplomatic history, and by perceiving the limits of earlier progressive history, Williams cut the famous nexus of 1890 (or thereabout) which bedeviled Beard with conflicting contemporary impulses of democracy and Empire. Already in *American-Russian Relations* and *Tragedy*, Williams assumed the kind of community of interests or *Weltanchauung* which unified America. *Empire as a Way of Life*, most fittingly, drove home the lesson again and finally. He thereby placed a capstone on his lifetime of work by reminding readers of the consequence of market choices: the wages of conquest which deprive the conquered and conqueror alike of the possibility for a higher purpose.

6

The future impact of Williams's works can hardly be foreseen. Much depended, of course, upon the shape of scholarship, even more perhaps on the shape of politics. One scholarly direction obvious long before the end of the cold war predicted, however, a large body of work reflecting the current sense of political stasis. Several of the older revisionists, notably Thomas McCormick and to some extent Walter LaFeber and Gabriel Kolko, as well as a few younger neorealists such as Michael J. Hogan, adroitly moved revisionism in the direction of corporatism. Merging the influence of Williams into a larger pool of resources including recent European and Latin American studies, they moved beyond the study of business corporations to make room for corporate-minded labor and the increasingly vital role of the State.

Closely examined, corporatist functional groups had worked in voluntary but often intimate association to shape national policies. Basic to their shared belief has been the concept of "productivism," the determination to increase the size of the overall pie in order both to avoid a redistribution of wealth and to forestall revolutionary threats. Corporatist theories have been applied particularly to the U.S. foreign policies of the Progressive era (sometimes defined as 1913-33) and the early cold-war period, 1945-53.[82] Martin J. Sklar, for some years a very Williamsesque editorial writer of the Socialist weekly *In These Times*, applied his own corporatist perspective to a close study of turn-of-the-century America and, in his collected essays, to a somewhat larger time frame.[83]

The political implications are yet more difficult to see. Hugh De Santis perceptively analyzes this corporatism as a hybrid of Beardian Progressivism and Marxism, resurrecting from the top of society the dichotomy of the Establishment versus the people.[84] A methodologically similar tendency from seemingly opposite sources has a surprising consequence: the addition of "world systems" theory to corporatism, embracing the entire Western world. This view, largely inspired by Immanuel Wallerstein's work, is in some ways a sharp departure from Americo-centric approaches, because New

York and Washington become only two of the rotating centers of the "informal Empire" on a wide-wide scale. Even before the end of the Second World War, American foreign policy, although still largely shaped by domestic needs, had been increasingly influenced by "an international marketplace and a culture created by a new technology," as Walter LaFeber puts it. In truth, "later twentieth century capitalism . . . has little respect for national borders," perhaps the most significant implication of all.[85]

If the national framework increasingly falls away—even with Washington firmly at the strategic center of the New World Order—does Williams's immanent critique of Empire lose its meaning or value? Only in the sense, one could argue, that the modes established by Americans tend to become a world norm. Business and political elites from impoverished African nations to rising Asian "Tigers," and from Latin America to the former Soviet Union, look to the U.S. for behavioral norms. From business suits to the proliferation of golf courses, the respective middle classes likewise copy the American style of consumption. No matter that nationalism rises sharply and competition adds to the already dangerous effects of world trade arrangements on the living standards of ordinary people. The world's winners, jettisoning concerns for growing class disparities or ecological degradation, adopt neoliberal strategies of rapid development and capital accumulation. Neoliberalism, already the kernal of corporate intellectual reflection in Woodrow Wilson's day, becomes a grim, final ideology of liberalism, worthy successor to the rampant individualism of the eighteenth and nineteenth-century American "great barbecue" frontier-style. This time more than ever, the planet is on the spit, revolving just above the flame.

This is the future Williams perceived from another angle, the apparent collapse of Socialist hopes, in one of his last pieces of sustained correspondence. Responding in the summer of 1989 to the question of whether he still considered himself a Marxist, he had "no apologies and no denying of the problems inherent." Marx had viewed nature as a resource to be exploited at will, and Williams readily admitted that as a young man he had shared that view. By now, he had learned better. Ecological crisis more and more frighteningly raised the right question: what is the purpose of economic growth?

Capitalism had its own answer, as Williams had detailed at great length. But efforts to create socialism had, at least at points, been on another track. Contrary to popular belief, Williams insisted, Lenin had urged a sort of de-centralization in the New Economic Policy period just before his death. If centralization had won out in Stalin's version of Elizabethan mercantilism ("with that kind of romantic personalized violence institutionalized in the Gulag"), it was a distorted mirror reflection of capitalism's world project.[86] Centralization, Williams continued, had served Stalin's purpose for primitive accumulation just as Queen Elizabeth had sent Sir Francis Drake off to piracy against the Spanish and Portuguese expropriation of the New World. The newly rebellious colonies of Europe, after the Second World War, attempted a similar strategy, adopting centralized mercantilism as the only way to become modern. All this had been finally swept away in the world market and the recuperation of capitalism's hegemony, without acknowledgment that the underlying premises of socialism had barely been glimpsed. The humane purpose of economic planning, to satisfy human and now more obviously, planetary needs, had been lost in the shuffle and needed to be found again.[87]

Williams's characteristic contribution to this future discussion remained what it had always been, his ability to see far beyond the ideologies and assorted claims of the moment to the operation of the system over centuries' time. No doubt his frequently repeated revelation that Marxism had shown "the interplay of ideas and reality" and "made my work as useful as it is," reflected both the Marxist-influenced content and the unique quality of his achievement.[88]

Then again, it would be as mistake to forget the underlying moral element of his life's effort. A keen-eyed British observer, writing in 1987, noted that Williams's importance had often been attributed to the Vietnam War's effect on Americans and to the rise of the New Left. Yet many of his closest and most sympathetic readers were not particularly radical, nor even Americans. His widespread and continuing influence might just as well be traced to "his own remarkable qualities," above all

> his striking intellectual integrity, manifested not so much in his treatment of historical evidence (which has sometimes raised scholarly eyebrows) as in his unswerving allegiance to the logic of his own thoughts and values.[89]

This, almost certainly, was the way that Williams would have chosen to be remembered. A self-made intellectual in many ways, he had risen out of his insular Iowa background, his Navy experiences, and his civil rights activities into a dialogue with professors and fellow graduate students which allowed him to shape his narrative according to conclusions he had reached very much independently. Whatever the limitations of his two great works, the *Tragedy of American Diplomacy* and *Contours of American History*, the ideas in them had the unmistakable marks of originality. He lived out the rest of his life, less as a scholar and more as a public citizen, likewise according to his own credo.

Had he failed, and does the rebel—the intellectual and political loner who bucks the system—ever really succeed? The socialistic-minded science fiction writer Philip K. Dick, who rose from similar obscurity to a mass 1960s-70s following and a late-life spiritual commitment, observed in his penultimate work that one fundamental postulate survives through the ages: "the empire has never ended." Empire, the very codification of derangement, imposed its madness upon everyone through the violence which is endemic to the phenomenon. The ancient destruction of community, according to Dick, left its victims "idiots" (a word drawn from the Greek for "private"), unable in their aloneness to make sense of what their eyes told them.[90]

The LSD-dropping Dick from the postmodernist hometown of Berkeley, a college ROTC-resister to boot, was as far from Williams's personal mentality as one could imagine. And yet the two, both astonishingly keen observers of Empire and its various manifestations, had moved through very different paths of the 1950s toward similar ends. Indeed, as Dick became a late-life Gnostic before his death in 1974, Williams reconciled himself to the Episcopalian Church (Wendy, for her part, was a Unitarian) in Waldport. Perhaps he sought solace, and with spreading cancer he had every reason to do so. But Christianity heavy with symbolism also signified his mental return to the premodern era where, in *Contours of American History*, he had placed the origins of the modern historical imagination. There, whatever the enormity of society's flaws, a sense of community had persisted, perhaps as remnant of a distant age.

Williams sometimes remarked comically that he remained determined to stay alive if only to give Arthur Schlesinger, Jr., more restless nights. But the real point was of course to move ahead, to develop an overview which worked by explaining or helping to explain events and ideas. Williams frequently said, especially in later years, that to do so made arguments with the likes of Schlesinger, Jr., irrelevant, because their constant pursuit of ideologies showed that they simply had no idea of how the system actually worked. Perhaps they did not wish to know. A valid explanatory framework, at any rate, would serve a hundred times better than debating those who wished to lay Williams low.

And so he passed, in March of 1990, after repeated surgery, never finished but still struggling for understanding and expression.

An intimate friend speaking at the memorial service imagined William Appleman Williams at the service himself, saying,

Well, this is all getting a bit much, a little dreary. After all, I haven't really gone, I just got bored and terribly tired, and finally found the time to be constructively lazy. If you want to find me, don't look in the lecture halls or the library. Come to the top of Cape Perpetua and watch the sun set, and the moon rise to claim the sky and dance its path across the water. Look at the beach at Seal Rock, or south near Waldport or Yachats. I'll be there with you poking around the tidepools, and sizing up the surf fishing, and taking photographs of the cormorants and the sea anemones. Take my hand and climb the dunes at Florence; taste the salt wind and watch the gathering of a winter storm—and wonder at the hard beauty and the eerie power of the ocean and the interconnectedness of it all.[91]

This neatly-done picture offers us Williams at his happiest, near the end of a remarkable life often connected with the ocean and more often with solitude. It tells us little about the content of his ruminations, if he had any, as he walked, looked, fished, and photographed the spectacular scene. Perhaps Oregon, the last frontier of the small businessman and reputedly also of the farmer more interested in leisure than profits, was Bill Williams's natural last frontier as well. When he reached it, he stayed until crossing over to an Unknown that his self-styled Christian Socialism had never delineated.

But he could satisfy himself, if he needed the consolation, that of all his remarkably creative work, his own most marvelous creation had been himself. Neither U.S. history, nor the writing of any kind of history from the world's dominant power, would see his like soon again.

NOTES

INTRODUCTION

1 Quoted by Howard Schonberger, "In Memoriam: William Appleman Williams, 1921–1990," *Radical Historians Newletter*, May, 1990.

2 Bruce Cumings, "Global Realm with No Limit, Global Realm with No Name" *Radical History Review*, 57 (Fall, 1993), 55.

3 William Appleman Williams, "Thoughts on the Fun and Purpose of Being an American Historian," *Organization of American Historians Newslette*, February, 1985.

4 Interview with Merle Curti by Edward Rice-Maximin, May, 1993.

5 Edward Said, *Culture and Imperialism* (New York, 1993), 64–65.

6 Amy Kaplan, "'Left Alone in America': the Absence of Empire in the Study of American Culture," introduction to *Cultures of American Imperialism*, ed. Amy Kaplan and Donald E. Pease (Durham, 1993), 14.

7 Sylvia Wynter, "The Counterdoctrine of Jamesian Poiesis," in *C.L.R. James's Caribbean*, edited by Paget Henry and Paul Buhle (Durham, 1992), 66–67.

8 Amy Kaplan, "'Left Alone with America,'" 13–14.

9 Amy Kaplan, "'Left Alone with America,'" 14.

10 George F. Kennan, "The Failure of Our Success," *New York Times*, Mar. 14, 1994.

11 A public opinion poll reported in the *New York Times* that seventy-five percent of Americans agreed when asked the question "Don't you think Americans over-consume?"; most of the same people insisted that overconsumption was one of the best things about being American. Wade Greene, "Overconspicuous Consumption," *New York Times*, Aug. 28, 1994.

CHAPTER 1

1 This insightful suggestion was made by W. A. Williams's daughter, Kyenne Williams, in an interview with Paul Buhle, June 10, 1993, and confirmed by Jeannie Williams in an interview with Paul Buhle, Oct. 20, 1993. In writing the memoir, Williams had the advantage of detailed correspondence and other records that his grandmother had saved. We are not so fortunate. He disposed of the raw material when he finished the memoir, a decision that may have been a matter of convenience as he cleaned out his grandparents' effects. But as Kyenne Williams suggests, it may well speak also to his determination to have the final word.

2 "A Good Life and a Good Death: A Memoir of an Independent Lady," n.d., William Appleman Williams Papers, Oregon State University; and "Ninety Days Inside the Empire," by "Billy Apple," an unarchived manuscript very kindly made available to us by Karla Robbins. See Chapter 7, on Williams's attempts at straightforward autobiography.

3 Only the use of the word "visceral" probably exceeded "honored" in Williams's published and unpublished prose. He sought to convey a physical sensibility, a more than cerebral way of seeing and engaging the world, but without neglecting those traditions which made life and sensibility possible.

4 "'New Left' Historian Williams, Iowa native, dies of cancer at 68," *Des Moines Register*, n.d., clipping in Williams Papers.

5 Interview with Lloyd Gardner by Edward Rice-Maximin, June 10, 1994; interview with William Robbins by Paul Buhle, Oct. 12, 1993.

6 For his father's side of the family, see the *Compendium of History and Biography of Cass County, Iowa* (Chicago, 1906), 557–58. Williams's great aunt Katie Williams, his paternal grandfather's twin, was a schoolteacher "and a student in an advanced course at the State Normal School, Cedar Falls." Thanks to Neil Basen for supplying this reference. Williams, "A Good Life and a Good Death," II, 6 (manuscript not paged consecutively).

7 Williams, "A Good Life and a Good Death," II, 10.

8 William J. Peterson, *Iowa: The Rivers of Her Valleys* (Iowa City, 1941), 280–91.

9 Alan Bogue, *From Prairie to Corn Belt: Farming on the Illinois and Iowa Prairies in the Nineteenth Century* (Chicago, 1963), Ch. 6-9.

10 Williams, *Roots of the Modern American Empire: A Study of the Growth and Shaping of Social Consciousness in Marketplace Society* (New York, 1969), xxi.

11 Bogue, *From Prairie to Corn Belt,* 205.

12 "A Good Life and a Good Death," II, 11.

13 We wish to thank Neil Basen for supplying this information.

14 *Iowa: A Guide to the Hawkeye State, Compiled and Written by the Federal Writers Project of the Works Progress Administration for the State of Iowa* (New York, 1940), 495–96.

15 Williams, "MacCormick Reports on Russia: A Study of News and Opinion on Russia in the Chicago Tribune from 1917–1921," unpublished master's thesis, University of Wisconsin-Madison, 1948, 159–62. William J. Peterson, *Iowa,* 291.

16 Bogue, *From Prairie to Corn Belt,* 184–86.

17 "A Good Life and a Good Death," II, 18–19.

18 "A Good Life and a Good Death," I, 3-II,1.

19 "A Good Life and a Good Death," II, 17.

20 Williams, *Americans in a Changing World: A History of the United States in the Twentieth Century* (New York: 1977), 179.

21 Outline for "A Historian Reflects Upon his Memories," Williams Papers.

22 Telephone interview with Corrinne Williams by Paul Buhle, July 10, 1994.

23 "A Historian Reflects Upon his Memories."

24 "A Good Life and a Good Death," V, 22.

25 See, e.g., Colin Wilson, *New Pathways in Psychology: Maslow and the Post-Freudian Revolution* (New York: 1972), Ch. 3-4.

26 Williams, *Roots,* xxii.

27 Williams, *Americans in a Changing World,* 267.

28 "A Good Life and a Good Death," VI, 1-2.

29 Lloyd Gardner to William Robbins, Mar. 19, 1985, lent to the writers by William Robbins.

30 Certificate from Secondary School, in, William W. Jeffries Memorial Archives, Naval Academy, Annapolis.

31 See his comments in Williams, *Americans in a Changing World,* 198.

32 Williams, *Americans in a Changing World,* 184–85.

33 Williams, *Americans in a Changing World,* 64–65.

34 "A Good Life and a Good Death," VIII, 12.

35 Interview with Jeannie Williams.

36 "A Good Life and a Good Death," VIII, 21.

37 See Paul Buhle's biography of James: *C. L. R James, the Artist as Revolutionary* (London, 1988), Ch. 5.

38 Grade transcript, 1941, Kemper Military School, in Naval Academy Archives.

39 Interview with Williams by Michael Wallace, in Henry Abelove et.al., eds., *Visions of History* (New York, 1983), 126.

40 Interview with Jeannie Williams; "A Good Life and a Good Death," VIII, 13.

41 Williams, "Notes on the Death of a Ship and the End of a World: The Grounding of the British Bark *Glenesslin* at Mount Neahkahnie on 1 October 1913," *American Neptune,* 41 (1981), 131.

42 Transcripts, 1944, United States Naval Academy, William W. Jeffries Memorial Archives.

43 Telephone interview with former classmate John Piro, Nov. 17, 1993; "William Appleman Williams," *Lucky Bag* (Annapolis yearbook). n.p., 1944.

44 "William A. Williams, '45," "The Flame of Faith," *The Trident Magazine* (Spring, 1944), 12, 38–41. Copies of the magazine were kindly made available by the Nimitz Library of the U.S. Naval Academy.

45 "William A. Williams '45," "Today is Russia," *The Trident Magazine* (Winter, 1944), 12–13, 39–44. While this essay reveals a characteristic naïveté of the time about the leadership of Stalin and the success of the Five Year Plans, it has a keen interpretation of the Soviet appeals for Western alliance against the Nazis and the indifference of the future Allies. (Williams carefully also excluded the U.S. and American leadership from any complaints).

46 Williams interview, *Visions of History*, 126; "William A. Williams," *Lucky Bag*, 1944.

47 Fred Harvey Harrington, interview with Edward Rice-Maximin, June 12, 1992. See also Williams interview, *Visions of History*, 126–27; Henry W. Berger, "The Revisionist Historian and His Community," introduction to Berger, ed., *A William Appleman Williams Reader* (Chicago, 1992), 13–14; William Robbins, "William Appleman Williams: 'Doing History is Best of All. No Regrets,'" in Lloyd Gardner, ed., *Redefining the Past: Essays in Diplomatic History in Honor of William Appleman Williams* (Corvallis, Oregon, 1986), 4–5. Berger has the text of Williams's speech on his return to Annapolis in 1987. See Chapter 7 for an analysis of it.

48 Williams, *Americans in a Changing World*, 322.

49 Williams, *Lucky Bag*, 1944.

50 "Dear Jim," July 22/23, 1989, Williams Papers.

51 Williams, *Americans in a Changing World*, 332.

52 "Billy Apple," "Ninety Days Inside the Empire," 430.

53 Williams, *Americans in a Changing World*, 334.

54 Williams, "Notes on the Death of a Ship," 137.

55 Interview with Williams by David Shetzline, Williams Papers.

56 Interview with Williams by David Shetzline, Williams Papers.

57 Williams interview, *Visions of History*, 127.

58 "Ninety Days Inside the Empire," 66. It is interesting to note that the director of *The House I Live In* was to become a prominent Hollywood Blacklistee. The lyricist for Sinatra's tune, Abel Meeropol, later adopted the sons of "atom spy" victims Julius and Ethyl Rosenberg. One of the two sons, Michael, took classes with Williams and became one of his admiring interpreters.

59 Charlotte Gilmor, letter to Paul Buhle, Nov. 17, 1993.

60 *CORPUS CRISIS*, May 9, 1946. NAACP Papers, Group II, Box C 189, Branch File, Corpus Christi , Library of Congress. Typical headlines read "WILLIE FRANCIS FIGHTS FOR LIFE" and "NEGRO MOTHER HONORED FOR 1946."

61 Teresa Grace Herold to H. Boyd Hall, May 15, 1946; and Rt. Rev. Monsignor John F. Basso to H. Boyd Hall, May 15, 1946, NAACP Papers.
62 "Minimum Wage Bill Fighting Hard," and "Normal Contracts Needed," *CORPUS CRISIS*, May 9, 1946; "Local Chapter Sends Wire," and "Fight Inflation," ibid., May 17, 1946.
63 Williams, "My Life in Madison," in *History and the New Left: Madison, Wisconsin, 1950–1970*, edited by Paul Buhle (Philadelphia 1990), 266.
64 Interview with Williams by David Shetzline, Williams Papers.
65 Paul D. Meyer, "Book Review," *CORPUS CRISIS* May 17, 1946. Interestingly, Williams later claimed to have read W. E. B. Dubois's *Black Reconstruction* around this time. James S. Allen's book which stressed biracial action for justice, was seen at the time of its publication as a kind of antidote to *Black Reconstruction*, which portrayed Southern racism as a totalistic force.
66 Williams interview, *Visions of History*, 128. NAACP correspondence reveals a somewhat different story. See Boyd Hall to Walter White, May 19, 1946. Seeking guidance about how to act within a controversy-ridden situation, Hall was advised, via an internal memo to White, that the Corpus Christi chapter would do well simply to let the whole controversy pass. "Memorandum, To: Mr White, From: Miss Black. Re: Letter from H. Boyd Hall," May 27, 1945, NAACP Papers.
67 Williams interview, *Visions of History*, 134.
68 Williams interview, *Visions of History*, 128.
69 At first many veteran New Dealers resisted this divisive course, insisting that it aided the Right, but ADA spokesmen like Arthur Schlesinger, Jr., pressed ahead. See Steven M. Gillon, *Politics and Vision: The ADA and American Liberalism, 1947–1985* (New York, 1987), 21–32.
70 "Life Inside the Frontier," tentatively titled one-page outline for an autobiographical novel, Williams Papers.
71 Williams wrote to the national NAACP headquarters mentioning his Corpus Christi activity and noting he had "never received my official notification of membership or card" despite being "desirous of being active in all localities for many years to come." Williams to "The Executive Secretary, the NAACP" from Atlantic, Iowa, Aug. 13, 1946, NAACP Papers. Perhaps alerted to controversy, the organization simply "overlooked" his application, embittering Williams from another side.
72 In one of his published interviews, Williams insists that he had an earlier experience, teaching YMCA summer camp while at Kemper, learning the love of teaching. This cannot be confirmed, and Jeannie Williams insists that he imagined or at least greatly exaggerated this experience. No independent confirmation has been found.
73 "Billy Apple," "Ninety Days Inside the Empire," 437.
74 Outline, "Life Inside the Frontier."
75 Williams interview, *Visions of History*, 129; the insight into Williams's career belongs to Wendy Williams, in an interview given June 10, 1993.

Chapter 2

1 This anecdote was reported by Williams to Mitzi Goheen, and was relayed in a telephone conversation, June 12, 1993.

2 This cannot be independently confirmed, and Jeannie Williams casts doubt upon the memory.

3 Telephone interview with Mitzi Goheen by Paul Buhle.

4 Williams to William Robbins, n.d. [1985], made available by William Robbins.

5 Fred Harvey Harrington to William Robbins, Feb. 22, 1985, letter made available by William Robbins.

6 According to an interview with Merle Curti, Turner was intrigued by Simons's interpretations. Interview with Merle Curti by Paul Buhle, Nov. 17, 1993.

7 See, e.g., Bernard C. Borning, *The Political and Social Thought of Charles A. Beard* (Seattle, 1962), parts 2–3.

8 See John D. Hicks, *My Life With History: An Autobiography* (Lincoln, 1968), ch. 3. 9, 11; Warren Susman, in *History and the New Left*, 275–84; See also Howard K. Beale, ed., *Charles A. Beard: An Appraisal* (Lexington, 1954), discussed below in Chapter 3.

9 Fred Harvey Harrington, *God, Mammon and the Japanese: Dr. Horace N. Allen and Korean-American Relations, 1884–1905* (Madison, 1944); Harrington, *Fighting Politician: Major General N.P. Banks* (Philadelphia, 1948).

10 File Notes, William Hesseltine Collection, State Historical Society of Wisconsin.

11 Warren Susman, "The Smoking Room School of History," in *History and the New Left*, 44.

12 Williams to Walter LaFeber, Jan. 15, 1985, Williams Papers; and interviews with Fred Harvey Harrington.

13 Williams to Walter LaFeber, Jan. 15, 1985, Williams Papers; communication from David W. Noble to Paul Buhle, May 7, 1993.

14 Williams, "My Life in Madison," in *History and the New Left*, 267, n.1.

15 Williams to William Robbins.

16 Ibid.

17 Ibid. See also Evan Stark, "In Exile," in *History and the New Left*, 173–74.

18 Harrington to William Robbins.

19 See George Catephores, "The Imperious Austrian: Schumpeter as Bourgeois Marxist," *New Left Review* #205 (May-June, 1994), 3–15. We might expect Madison graduate students to have read an essay by Schumpeter, "The 'Communist Manifesto' in Sociology and Economics," in the *Journal of Political Economy*, 1949. Cited in Catephores, 8, n. 9. In an interview with David Shetzline, n.d. [1976], Williams suggested that he had read Schumpeter (without giving a specific volume) at the proper moment, in Madison of the 1940s. Williams Papers.

20 See Maurice Glasman, "The Great Deformation: Polyani, Poland and the Terrors of Planned Spontaneity," *New Left Review*, #205 (May-June 1994), 59–69.

21 Interview with Susman by Paul Buhle, September, 1982; these observations were confirmed by Curti in the interview noted above.

22 Harrington to William Robbins.

23 Not to romanticize this brief retrospect: during World War I, faculty members, by a large majority, demeaned themselves by signing a public document repudiating LaFollette's courageous stand. See Paul Buhle, introduction to *History and the New Left*, 10–17.

24 See a slightly later account of the *Cardinal* milieu in Richard Schickel, "A Journalist Among Historians," in *History and the New Left*, 85–100. Schickel joined the *Cardinal* staff in 1950, en route to life as a film reviewer and critic at *Time* and elsewhere.

25 Harrington to William Robbins.

26 "Marzani Case . . . the Editor's Mailbag," *Daily Cardinal*, Dec. 16, 1947; and "Filling Out the Picture of Campus Politics," *Daily Cardinal*, Sept. 23, 1949.

27 "University Society News—Marxists Convene," *Daily Cardinal*, Dec. 16, 1947; "Portrait of a Woman" (advertisement), *Daily Cardinal*, Dec. 12, 1947; "Golden Boy," *Daily Cardinal*, Dec 17, 1947.

28 "Thomas Blasts Foes in Madison Address," *Daily Cardinal*, Sept. 15, 1948; "Gerth Stresses German Needs," *Daily Cardinal*, Feb. 26, 1949; "Full House Hears Taylor," *Daily Cardinal*, Sept. 21, 1948.

29 Harrington to William Robbins.

30 An anonymous observer insists that Williams appeared at a civil rights meeting in Chicago around this time, attended by a wide range of the Left, including members of the Communist-oriented Civil Rights Congress. This memory cannot be verified.

31 See for example, "Badger Village Houses 78 New Families, Married Veterans continue to Occupy Apartments," *Daily Cardinal*, Sept. 23, 1948; Williams's own reflection on the GIs-turned-students of that day are in Williams interview by Michael Wallace, *Visions of History*, 129.

32 David W. Noble to Paul Buhle, May 7, 1993.

33 Williams, "McCormick Reports on Russia: A Study of News and Opinion on Russia in the *Chicago Tribune* from 1917–1921," MA Thesis, University of Wisconsin, 1948, 29, 75.

34 Williams, "McCormick Reports," ibid., 147–48, 199.

35 The fullest version of Robins's life is told in Neil V. Salzman, *Reform and Revolution: The Life and Times of Raymond Robins* (Kent, Ohio, 1991). Salzman interviewed Williams, used materials uncovered by him, and credited him with important archival discoveries.

36 Williams, "Raymond Robins and Russian American Relations," PhD Dissertation, University of Wisconsin, 1950, 126.

37 Quoted, from an unpublished manuscript, in L. P. Carpenter, *G.D.H. Cole, An Intellectual Biography* (Cambridge, 1973), 47.

38 Justus Doenecke letter to Paul Buhle, Sept. 19, 1993.

39 Charles S. Maier, "Marking Time: The Historiography of International Relations" in Michael Kammen, ed., *The Past Before Us: Contemporary Historical Writing in the United States* (Ithaca, 1980), 364–66; interview with Harrington by Edward Rice-Maximin, June 12, 1992.

40 See Ralph Miliband, *Parliamentary Socialism: A Study in the Politics of Labour* (New York, 1964), Ch. 9 for an overview of Labour's timidity, both on foreign policy and in regard to the possibilities of worker-controlled factories. Centralization of power dominated the few nationalizations of industry carried out.

41 Quoted and discussed in Peter Novick, *That Noble Dream: The "Objectivity Question" and the American Historical Profession* (Cambridge, U.K., 1988), 318.

42 See Michael Meeropol, "Cold War Revisionism," in *Encyclopedia of the American Left* (New York, 1990), 144–46.

43 Williams, *American-Russian Relations, 1781–1947* (New York, 1952).

44 Hugh Seton-Watson, *International Affairs* (London), 30 (October, 1954), 514–15.

45 Bradford Perkins, "A Matter of Interpretation," *New York Times Book Review*, Nov. 9, 1952, 20.

46 O. T. Barck, Jr., *American History Review*, 59 (January-March, 1953), 83–85; William A. Brandenburg, *Mississippi Valley Historical Review*, 40 (June, 1953), 169–70; Ruhl Bartlett, *Pacific Historical Review*, 22 (May, 1953), 422–23; Alfred A. Skerpan, *Indiana Magazine of History*, 49 (June, 1953), 225–28.

47 Harold C. Hinton, *Catholic Historical Review*, 39 (Fall, 1954); Paul A. Fitzgerald, *Catholic Historical Review*, 41 (Fall, 1956); and William A. Nolan, *American Catholic Sociological Review*, 14 (October, 1953), 198–99.

48 Richard Van Alstyne, *Far Eastern Quarterly*, 12 (May, 1953), 311–12; E. H. Carr, *American Slavic and East European Review*, 12 (1953), 392–94. Another, more predictably favorable review was by the American Socialist intellectual exiled to Paris, Samuel Bernstein, in *Science & Society*, 17 (Summer, 1953), 276–77.

49 Robert Friedman, "Crisis Laid to Anti-Soviet Policy by Oregon University Professor's Book," *Daily Worker*, Dec. 22, 1942.

50 Ernest B. Haas, *Journal of Political Economy*, 62 (June, 1954), 137–38.

51 Letter from David Noble.

52 Williams to William Robbins.

53 William Appleman Williams, "Brooks Adams and Expansion," *New England Quarterly*, XXV (June, 1952), 82–85.

54 Interview with Merle Curti by Paul Buhle, Nov. 20, 1993.

55 Interview with Thomas McCormick by Edward Rice-Maximin, June 11, 1992.

56 Telephone conversation with Charles Vevier, Jan. 7, 1994.

CHAPTER 3

1 Memo to William and Karla Robbins, Mar. 17,1985, Williams Papers.

2 Together with Raymond Robins's personal papers, these constituted a vital nugget of materials about those who strove to bridge the gaps between the U.S. and the early Soviet governments. While working on the recovered documents for his first book, Williams declined to make them available to cold war scholars, touching off Schlesinger, Jr.'s first recorded attack on Williams as "pro-Communist." Ironically, Schlesinger, Jr., would later bear the brunt of professional complaints that he had used Kennedy family sources available to no one else, and Williams as president of the OAH would lead the struggle against the destruction of State Department and FBI documents. See Arthur Schlesinger, Jr., to Boyd Shafer, July 1, 1954, American Historical Association Papers; Williams explained with frustration to Warren Susman that the Robins Papers had been uncollected in Florida for a quarter century and none of the pro-State Department scholars showed any interest until Williams's use of them. Williams to Warren Susman, n.d. [1960], letter made available by Bea Susman. See also Williams to Clifford Lord, June 4, 1955, State Historical Society of Wisconsin General Administrative Collection, and Lord to Williams, Aug. 20, 1952, General Administrative Collection. Special thanks to Scott McLemee for making the full set of documents related to Schlesinger, Jr.'s charges against Williams available to us.

3 Ron McCrea and Dave Wagner, "Harvey Goldberg," in *History and the New Left*, 244.

4 Interview with Peter Weiss, Nov. 20, 1993; and telephone conversation with Corrinne Williams, July 25, 1994. Therapist, musician, and former undergraduate student of Fred Harvey Harrington, Weiss was one of the closest social friends of the couple during the 1960s.

5 Williams, "Harvey Goldberg and the Virtue of History," Harvey Goldberg Memorial Lecture, Oct. 22, 1987, Williams Papers.

6 Quoted in McCrea and Wagner, "Harvey Goldberg," 244.

7 Memo to William and Karla Robbins [1985], Williams Papers; Interview with Jeannie Williams, Oct. 9, 1993. This episode is only briefly discussed in various interviews. See for example the Williams interview in *Visions of History* (New York, 1983), 132.

8 Telephone conversation with Corrinne Williams, July 11, 1994.

9 William A. Williams to Warren Susman, n.d. [1957], letter made available by Bea Susman.

10 Memo to William and Karla Robbins [1985], Williams Papers. Williams to Warren Susman, March, 1957, and undated [1957]. Letters made available by Bea Susman. In an explanation to Walter LaFeber, Williams added, "You know as well as I do: hell, I read so many damn Russian documents in the archives of the

American Embassy in Moscow that it would drive anybody out of their mind . . . we are so bloody good as imperialists that you get the other side's position in our documents as to make wandering-off to their archives a kind of exercise in funded vacations!!" Nov. 10, 1983, Williams Papers.

11 Jonathan M. Wiener, "Radical Historians and the Crisis in American History, 1959–1980," *Journal of American History*, 76 (September, 1989), 402; Peter Novick, *That Noble Dream: The "Objectivity Question" and the American Historical Profession* (Cambridge, 1988), 300. Novick quotes Arthur Schlesinger, Jr., as saying a few years later that the very words "capitalism" and "socialism" belonged "to the vocabulary of demagoguery, not . . . analysis." From "Epilogue: The One Against the Many," in *Paths of American Thought* (Boston, 1963), edited by Arthur Schlesinger, Jr., and Morton White, 536. The following owes much to Warren Susman, "The Historian's Task," a seminar paper written in 1952 for fellow Madison graduate students and published as "Appendix One" to *History and the New Left*, 275–84. Special thanks to William Preston for making this document available for publication.

12 Peter Novick says that historians' attacks on "moral relativism" were not systematic, but later offers evidence of Morison, Nevins, Schlesinger, Jr., and Handlin sharply attacking relativists and relativism. Novick, *That Noble Dream*, 286–87, 342–43. Susman was far closer to the mark in his comments, "The Historian's Task," 278.

13 Susman, "The Historian's Task," 281.

14 Quoted in Jesse Lemisch, *On Active Service in Peace and War: Politics and Ideology in the American Historical Profession* (Toronto, 1975), 69. In the *Harvard Guide to American History*, Morison with unconscious hilarity urged colleagues to offer their services chivalrously to such noted right-wing (and especially at that time, notably racist) ladies' organizations as the Daughters of the American Revolution and the Daughters of the Confederacy for patriotic festivals. Challenged on the racial politics of his own noted textbook, he suggested "some essential docility in their character" that made blacks a race ideally suited for slavery. Novick, *The Noble Dream*, 350, n.46.

15 Cited in Novick, *That Noble Dream*, 342; see also Lemisch, *On Active Service In Peace and War*, 70–71.

16 Lemisch, *On Active Service*, 74–78.

17 Sigmund Diamond, *Compromised Campus: The Collaboration of Universities with the Intelligence Community, 1945–1955* (New York, 1992), 151–66 and 139–45. According to Diamond, Buckley was a regular campus informant, and young Henry Kissinger, a particular protégé of Arthur Schlesinger, Jr., opened the mail of fellow graduate students and sent the contents to federal authorities.

18 Novick, *That Noble Dream*, 326.

19 Novick, *That Noble Dream*, 325–332.

20 Jon Wiener, "Radical Historians and the Crisis in American History, 1959–1980," *Journal of American History*, 76 (September, 1989), 411–12, n. 29. Wiener's sketch of the repressive atmosphere faced by future leading historians is also illuminating.

21 Interview with Fred Harvey Harrington, Nov. 19,1993, about his own experiences as a department head in 1957.

22 Novick, *That Noble Dream*, 308.

23 Quoted in Lemisch, *On Active Service*, 88–89.

24 Richard Wightman Fox, *Reinhold Niebuhr: A Biography* (San Francisco, 1985), 244–47, 272, 274–75. He also notes that Niebuhr's editorial, "The Evil of the Communist Idea," was published and widely broadcast a short time before the execution of Ethel and Julius Rosenberg. Niebuhr earnestly believed that they deserved execution, although he later recanted this conviction. Ibid., 254–55.

25 See Richard Reinitz, *Irony and Consciousness: American Historiography and Reinhold Niebuhr's Vision* (New York, 1980), 99.

26 Quoted in Lemisch, *On Active Service*, 53–54.

27 Quoted in Gary Dorrien, *The Neo-Conservative Mind: Politics, Culture and the War of Ideology* (Philadelphia, 1993), 362.

28 Susman, "The Historian's Task," 282.

29 Susman, "The Historian's Task," 282.

30 Michael Wreszin, "Arthur Schlesinger, Jr., Scholar-Activist in Cold War America: 1946–1956," *Salmagundi*, 63-64 (Spring-Summer, 1984), 255–285.

31 Arthur Schlesinger, Jr., "The Future of Socialism, III," *Partisan Review*, 14 (May-June, 1947), 229–241.

32 Schlesinger, Jr., "The Future of Socialism," 236–37.

33 Schlesinger, Jr., "The Future of Socialism," 241.

34 This tendency in Schlesinger's work was keenly identified by Elaine May, in her *Homeward Bound: American Families in the Cold War Era* (New York, 1988), 98.

35 A few years later, Niebuhr attacked Eisenhower as the "Chamberlain of our day," and "decent but soft." Still later, he developed the distinction between "authoritarian" allies and "totalitarian" enemies widely used by Jeane Kirkpatrick during the Reagan years. Fox, *Reinhold Niebuhr*, 265, 272, 274–75.

36 Susman, "The Historian's Task," 284.

37 See for instance, John Bellamy Foster, *The Theory of Monopoly Capitalism* (New York, 1986) and Paul Sweezy, "Interview," *Monthly Review*, 38 (April, 1987), for a basic sense of *MR* theory and history. We are grateful to Paul Sweezy and Harry Magdoff for letters of reminiscence about Williams.

38 Interview with Saul Landau by Paul Buhle, May, 1982. A part of the interview, but not this part, was excerpted into Landau, "From the Labor Youth League to the Cuban Revolution," in *History and the New Left*, 107–112. Landau and others were Left activists on the Madison campus of the 1950s.

39 Thanks to Alan Wald for pointing out Williams's status on the *American Socialist*, which merged into *Monthly Review* in 1960.

40 See David Goldway, "Science & Society," in *Encyclopedia of the American Left* (New York, 1990), edited by Mari Jo Buhle, Paul Buhle, and Dan Georgakas, 679–80; and Goldway, "Fifty Years of Science & Society," *Science & Society*, 50 (Fall, 1986). Williams also offered around the same time to contribute an essay on Big

Band jazz to *Mainstream*, a leftish cultural journal thought to represent former Communist intellectuals distancing themselves from the Party. Among the *American Socialist* pieces, his 1958 essay, "The Large Corporation and American Foreign Policy" was reprinted into his essay collection, *History as a Way of Learning* (New York, 1974). On the connection with *Mainstream*, we have benefitted from Alan Wald making available several of Williams's letters to Charles Humboldt, its editor, in 1959. See also Annette Rubinstein, "Mainstream," *Encyclopedia of the American Left*, 445–46.

41 See Margaret Morley, "Freda Kirchwey: Cold War Critic," in Lloyd Gardner, ed., *Redefining the Past: Essays in Diplomatic History in Honor of William Appleman Williams* (Corvallis, 1986), 157–68. Morley was one of Williams's final graduate students and his only female PhD; Interview with Margaret Morley, Nov. 15, 1993. The *Reporter* was known for its concocted revelations, such as an essay by a defecting Russian colonel on how the Russians had trained the North Korean Army. The colonel had been an invention of the CIA. See the American Social History Project, *Who Built America* (New York, 1992), 489. The *New Leader* was the leading publication of an intellectual milieu around the social-democratic wing of the garments trade whose foremost figures had established the CIA-funded international agencies of the AFL and later AFL-CIO. See Paul Buhle, "Lovestoneites," *Encyclopedia of the American Left*, 437; and Daniel Cantor and Julia Schor, *Tunnel Vision: Labor, the World Economy and Central America* (Boston, 1987), 34–48. See Chapter 4, on the Central American and Caribbean matters in which Williams dealt.

42 Williams, "Moscow Peace Drive: Victory for Containment?" *Nation*, 177 (July ll, 1953), 28–30.

43 Williams, "Irony of Containment: A Policy of Boomerangs," *Nation*, 182 (Apr. 5, 1956), 376–79.

44 Williams, "Babbit's New Fables: Economic Myths," *Nation*, 182 (Jan. 7, 1956), 3–6.

45 Williams, "Needed: Production for Peace," in "If We Want Peace: Barriers and Prospects," special issue of the *Nation*, 188 (Feb. 21,1959), 149–53.

46 William Appleman Williams, "The American Century: 1941–1957," *Nation*, 185 (Nov. 2, 1957), 297–301.

47 William Appleman Williams, "The 'Logic' of Imperialism," *Nation*, 185 (July 6, 1957), 14–15.

48 Williams, "The Tribune," 5.

49 Williams, "Cold War Perspectives: A Historical Fable," *Nation*, 180 (May 28, 1955), 458–61.

50 The term "public intellectuals" and the following description owes much to Russell Jacoby, *The Last Intellectuals* (New York, 1982), notwithstanding Jacoby's own narrow and eccentric views of which writers could be considered "public" or important (mostly authors for New York highbrow magazines) and which disregard not only widely-read public intellectuals such as Williams but film and television writers, popular critical poets and novelists, etc., as well as writers for the large sec-

tions of the leftish press, e.g., *Nation* and *Village Voice* to *Ramparts* and *Mother Jones* magazines.

51 Williams, preface to *Roots of the Modern American Empire,* xv–xvi.

52 Interview with Fred Harvey Harrington by Paul Buhle, Madison, Nov. 20, 1993. See also comments by William G. Robbins, "William Appleman Williams," in *Redefining the Past,* 9; William Marina, "William Appleman Williams," in *Dictionary of Literary Biography,* 17; *Twentieth Century American Historians,* ed. Clyde N. Wilson (Detroit, 1983), 17.

53 Preface to *Shaping of American Diplomacy I* (Cleveland, 1956), xiv. A. T. Volwiler, "Harrison, Blaine, and American Foreign Policy, 1889–1993," and Nelson M. Blake, "Cleveland's Venezuela Policy," in *Shaping of American Diplomacy,* 356–64 and 364–73, respectively.

54 Williams, *Shaping of American Diplomacy I,* xii–xiii.

55 Charles A. Madison, "Reviews," *Science & Society,* 21 (Fall, 1957), 372–73; Rufus G. Hall, Jr., *Southeastern Social Science Quarterly,* 37 (March, 1957), 380.

56 Paul A. Varg, *World Affairs Quarterly,* 28 (July, 1957), 1292–95. See also Alan Conway, *International Affairs,* 33 (April, 1957), 259.

57 James P. O'Brien, "Comment," *Radical America,* IV (August, 1970), 50.

58 William Appleman Williams, "Charles Austin Beard: The Intellectual as Tory-Radical," in *American Radicals: Some Problems and Personalities* (New York, 1957), 304, 305, 299.

59 Harvey Goldberg and Williams, "Introduction: Thoughts about American Radicalism," in *American Radicals,* 3, 4.

60 *American Radicals,* 8.

61 *American Radicals,* 12.

62 *American Radicals,* 6, 15.

63 Williams, preface to *Roots of the Modern American Empire,* xv–xvi.

64 This discussion is based on Williams, "Open Door Interpretation," in *Encyclopedia of American Foreign Policy, Vol.II, Studies of the Principal Movements and Ideas,* edited by Alexander DeConde (New York, 1978), 703–10; and "Confessions of an Intransigent Revisionist," in *A William Appleman Williams Reader: Selections from His Major Historical Writings,* edited by Henry W. Berger (Chicago, 1993), 342–44.

65 *The Accumulation of Capital—An Anti-Critique by Rosa Luxemburg/Imperialism and the Accumulation of Capital by Nikolai Bukharin* (New York, 1972), translated by Rudolf Wichmann. See especially Kenneth Tarbuck's Introduction which sets out the issues clearly. When Michael Harrington in 1971 accused Williams of being a "Leninist" because of his critique of imperialism, Williams could rightly point to the far greater importance of Luxemburg and Hobson on his views. See Chapter 6.

66 Williams to William Robbins, n.d. [1985], Williams Papers.

67 Williams to William Robbins.

68 Williams, "A Note on Charles Austin Beard's Search for a General Theory of Causation," *American Historical Review*, 62 (October, 1956), 59–80. This was the first of Williams's contributions accepted by the *AHR*.

69 William Appleman Williams, "Brooks Adams and American Expansion," *New England Quarterly*, 25 (June, 1952), 217–32; and "Communication: On the Restoration of Brooks Adams," *Science & Society*, 20 (Summer, 1956), 376–79. Williams also showed how the "frontier thesis" could still inspire a 1956 election in Oregon with all the heroes and villains of frontier imagery and the foreign policy of the classic frontiersman: "get more markets for raw materials and agricultural surpluses, and settle disputes by organizing a committee of vigilantes and arming oneself with more and bigger guns." See Williams, "Historical Romance of Senator [Richard] Neuberger's Election," *Oregon Historical Quarterly*, Vol. 56 (June, 1956), 101–5. See also his "Neuberger Ducked the Basic Issues," *Frontier*, 6 (October, 1955), 5–6.

70 William Appleman Williams, "The Frontier Thesis and American Foreign Policy," *Pacific Historical Review*, 24 (Nov., 1955), 379–95.

71 William Appleman Williams, review of Arthur S. Link, *Woodrow Wilson and the Progressive Era, 1910–1917* (New York, 1954), in *Science & Society*, 18 (1954), 348–51.

72 William Appleman Williams, "The Convenience of History," review of George F. Kennan, *Russia Leaves the War, Vol. I: Soviet-American Relations, 1917–1920* (Princeton, 1956), *Nation*, 183 (Sept. 15, 1956), 222–24. Williams took the opportunity here to reveal his inveterate hostility to "infantile leftism," affirming his sympathy for Lenin and Trotsky's reluctant signing of the Treaty of Brest-Litovsk "rather than go out in a blaze of romantic revolutionary pyro-technics."

73 Williams, "A note on American Foreign Policy in Europe in the Nineteen Twenties," *Science & Society*, 22 (1958); Williams, "The Loss of Debate," review of Herbert Hoover, *The Ordeal of Woodrow Wilson* (New York, 1958), *Nation*, 186 (May 17, 1958), 452–53. Williams found his favorite protagonists among those long ridiculed by the liberal historians, William Borah and the "Sons of the Jackass" from the West who (in Borah's words) considered "futile and unAmerican" any effort "to run the world by establishing an American system comparable to the British empire." Borah's vision of the U.S. supporting "movements of reform and colonial nationalism" could not be realized, but remained a monument to clear-headedness. See William Appleman Williams, "The Legend of Isolationism in the 1920s," *Science & Society*," 18 (Winter, 1954), 1–20, reprinted in *A William Appleman Williams Reader*, 75–88; and Williams, "Latin America: Laboratory of American Foreign Policy of the Nineteen Twenties," *Inter-American Economic Affairs*, 1 (Autumn, 1957), 3–4.

74 Williams, "The Legend of Isolationism," 129.

75 William Appleman Williams, "Schlesinger: Right Crisis—Wrong Order," review of *The Age of Roosevelt: The Crisis of the Old Order* (New York, 1956), *Nation*, 184 (Mar. 23, 1957), 257–60.

76 See Susman's important essay, "The 1930s," in *Culture As History* (New York, 1987). Little has been written about Susman's own scholarly legacy. The pamphlet-length collective tribute, *In Memory of Warren Susman, 1927–1985* (New Brunswick, 1985), unfortunately does not touch upon his intimate connection with Williams.

77 Novick, *That Noble Dream*, 450. A decade later, Schlesinger, Jr., admitted that "the fact that in some aspects the revisionist thesis [of Williams] parallels the official Soviet argument must not, of course prevent consideration of the case on its merits, nor raise questions about the motives of the writers, all of whom, as far as I know, are independent minded scholars," in "Origins of the Cold War," *Foreign Affairs* 46 (1967), 24. Novick rightly suggests that the phrase "as far as I know" left open the possibility that Williams and his colleagues might be Soviet agents after all.

78 Williams, memo to William and Karla Robbins, 1985, made available by William Robbins.

79 Bernard Malamud, *A New Life* (New York, 1961).

80 Williams to Warren and Bea Susman, Aug. 3, 1955.

81 Interviews with Jeannie Williams and Kyenne Williams.

82 Norman Thomas, "The New American Imperialism," *Socialist Call*, XXXVI (July-August, 1958), 8. Only a few years earlier, Thomas had joined Reinhold Niebuhr and others in denying that any such thing as American imperialism could exist in the present. See "Open Letter to USA Socialists," *Socialist Commentary*, IV (Mar., 1951), 70–72. For his part, Niebuhr continued generally to compare independence unfavorably to colonialism. See, e.g., Reinhold Niebuhr, "The Army in the New Nation," *Christianity & Crisis*, 35 (May 2, 1966), 84, in which he refers to Kwame Nkrumah's efforts as "ridiculous." Although Niebuhr supported Martin Luther King, Jr., he likewise directed torrents of abuse at Malcolm X and others who rejected continued Western (i.e., white) control of world politics and economy.

83 Interview with Harrington, Nov. 19, 1993.

84 Interview with Harrington, Nov. 19, 1993. In a letter to William Robbins, Feb. 22, 1985, Harrington confessed his own uneasiness at drawing Williams to Madison when he was not sure of his own advancement into the administration. "But we did persuade him," and gave him tenure by 1958. Letter given to the authors by Robbins.

CHAPTER 4

1 See for instance Arthur Hove, *The University of Wisconsin: A Pictorial History* (Madison, 1991). Fred Harvey Harrington, who assumed the reins in 1962, was quoted three years later as saying that in the last half dozen years there had been "more building in Madison than in the whole history of the campus," in ibid, 242.

2 See Paul Buhle, introduction to *History and the New Left*, 24–25; Saul Landau, "From Labor Youth League to the Cuban Revolution," in ibid., 107–112.

3 See Richard Schickel, "A Journalist Among Historians," 85–100; Warren Susman, "The Smoking Room School of History," 43–46; Herbert Gutman, "Learning about

History," 47–49; and William Preston, "WASP and Dissenter," 50–53, in *History and the New Left*. Preston would carry out Williams's program for an official Organization of American Historians committee to demand access to hidden government records; see Chapter 7.

4 See Jeffrey Kaplow, "Parenthesis: 1952–1956," in *History and the New Left*, 58–66. We wish to thank Larry Gara, a Madison graduate student of the early 1950s and later an activist for the War Resisters League, for offering his personal observations about pacifists' roles during this period. A small handful of Trotskyists had mainly an intellectual role, but figured interestingly in the later rise of social history. George Rawick, youth editor of a national Trotskyist tabloid while a graduate student at Madison, would become one of the most important scholars of slave history and a political disciple of C. L. R. James. See Rawick, "I Dissent," in *History and the New Left*, 54–57. Among the other radicals, Gabriel Kolko was a national leader of the small and scattered Student League for Industrial Democracy and in a decade or so, Williams's counterpart in the radical scholarship of diplomatic history.

5 Nina Serrano, "A Madison Bohemian," in *History and the New Left*, 67–84. Bertell Ollman, "From Liberal to Social Democrat to Marxist: My Political Itinerary Through Madison in the Late 1950s," in ibid., 101–6.

6 Interview with Saul Landau by Paul Buhle, Oct., 1980.

7 See Harvey J. Kaye, *The British Marxist Historians* (Oxford, 1984) and Harvey J. Kaye, *The Education of Desire: Marxists and the Writing of History* (New York, 1992). It is interesting, however, that the main journal that sought to coordinate such a New Left, the *American Socialist*, added Williams to its board of editorial advisors and that one of its major younger figures, David Herreshoff of Wayne State University, was a highly original scholar of American radicalism.

8 See Lee Baxandall, "New York Meets Oshkosh," *History and the New Left*, 127–33; and Appendix 2, by Lee Baxandall, Marshall Brickman and Danny Kalb, "The Boy Scouts in Cuba," *History and the New Left*, 285–90.

9 Telephone interview with Henry W. Berger, Nov. 20, 1993.

10 Karl Gutknecht, "Students Jam State Capitol for Joint HUAC Hearing," *Cardinal*, Feb. 22, 1961.

11 Sig Eisenscher, "Teaching to Think," *People's Daily World*, Apr. 20, 1990. A Wisconsin Communist, Eisenscher recalled the incidents decades later, shortly after Williams's death.

12 Jeff Greenfield, "Legislator Rebuffs HUAC Foes," *Daily Cardinal*, Mar. 2, 1961 see also Mailbox, "Anti-Anti-Huac," *Daily Cardinal*, Mar. 10, 1961.

13 "Peace Center Pickets Heckled at Meeting," *Daily Cardinal*, Mar. 11, 1961.

14 Letter from George Mosse to Paul Buhle, October, 1992.

15 Interview with Thomas McCormick by Edward Rice-Maximin, June 11, 1992; and comments by McCormick in Dina M. Copelman and Barbara Clark Smith, editors, "Excerpts from a Conference to Honor William Appleman Williams," *Radical History Review*, 50 (Spring, 1991), 44–45. Based on a memorial colloquium

and roundtable convened by the Institute for Policy Studies, June 10, 1990. Referred to hereafter as Copelman/Clark Smith.

16 Interview with McCormick by Edward Rice-Maximin, June 11, 1992.

17 Interview with McCormick, June 11, 1992. In McCormick's case, an Irish-American who already had no love for the British Empire and felt admiration for Herbert Hoover mistrusted the idea of socialism, but was in some ways a natural convert to Williams's views.

18 Taped version of oral presentations by Lloyd Gardner, Thomas McCormick, and Martin J. Sklar at Williams Memorial Conference, Institute for Policy Studies; tapes kindly made available by Dina Copelman.

19 Taped oral presentations by Lloyd Gardner, et al.

20 Fred Harvey Harrington interview by Edward Rice-Maximin, June 12, 1992; and McCormick in Copelman/Clark Smith, 46–47.

21 McCormick in Copelman/Clark Smith, 46–47.

22 Gardner in Copelman/Clark Smith, 45.

23 Interview with McCormick; Letter from J. Quinn Brisbane, June 30, 1993. Brisbane was an undergraduate in Williams's 1959 foreign policy course, later a southern "Freedom School" teacher, and still later the 1992 candidate for President on the Socialist Party ticket.

24 Margaret Morley made this point especially in an interview with Paul Buhle, Oct. 20, 1993, and in Copelman/Clark Smith, 48–49. Morley was one of Williams's very last graduate students, and one of his few women students; interview with Alan Bogue, Apr. 30, 1993; relevant correspondence in the Fred Harvey Harrington Papers, State Historical Society of Wisconsin archives, includes Williams to Harrington, Nov. 7, 1961, complaining of placement procedures; and Harrington to Williams, Nov. 9, 1961, chiding Williams gently for his overeagerness.

25 See for example Williams, "Memorandum on Diplomatic History Jobs: 13 November 1961," in Fred Harvey Harrington Papers, State Historical Society of Wisconsin.

26 He also wrote Susman that he had been denied a leave by the Research Committee which deemed the manuscript for *Contours of American History* insufficiently important. Williams to Susman, Nov. 1, 1960, letter made available by Bea Susman.

27 Williams to Susman, July 22, 1961, letter made available by Bea Susman.

28 Williams Memo to William and Karla Robbins, n.d. [1985], made available by William Robbins.

29 The most lucid overview of *Tragedy* remains James Livingston's obituary and tribute, "Farewell to Intellectual Godfather William Appleman Williams," *In These Times*, Mar. 28-Apr. 3, 1990. This account owes much to him.

30 For more detailed summaries of *Tragedy*, see Berger's introduction to *A William Appleman Williams Reader*, 19–22, 116, 133, 156; and William Marina, "William Appleman Williams," *Dictionary of Literary Biography, Vol. 17, Twentieth-Century*

American Historians (Detroit, 1983), edited by Clyde N. Wilson, 452–54; A telephone interview with William Marina by Paul Buhle, Nov. 10,1993, did much to amplify the published discussion.

31 Williams, *The Tragedy of American Diplomacy* (Cleveland, 1959), 2–3.

32 Williams *Tragedy*, 292–93. This passage was also quoted in Anders Stephanson's unpublished paper, "The United States," prepared for the Conference on the Cold War, in honor of William Appleman Williams, University of Wisconsin, Madison, October, 1992.

33 Marilyn Young, in taped version of William Appleman Williams Memorial Conference, Institute for Policy Studies.

34 Williams, *Tragedy*, 13.

35 Williams, *Tragedy*, 305, 308–9.

36 William Appleman Williams," in *Visions of History*, 132–33.

37 Foster Rhea Dulles, *American Historical Review*, 44 (July, 1959), 1022–23.

38 Armin Rappaport, *Pacific Historical Review*, 28 (August, 1959), 288–90. Rappaport's appointment at Berkeley had been held up in 1949 by general suspicions. See Peter Novick, *That Noble Dream*, 330.

39 Gordon M. Craig, *International Journal*, 14 (Autumn, 1959), 317–18.

40 Adolf A. Berle, Jr., "A Few Questions for the Diplomatic Pouch," *New York Times Book Review*, Feb. 15, 1969.

41 Berle, Jr., "A Few Questions."

42 Bernard C. Borning, *The Political and Social Thought of Charles A. Beard* (Seattle, 1962), 228–35.

43 Lloyd Gardner, speech to symposium on Williams at the Institute for Policy Studies, April, 1990.

44 Telephone conversation with Henry W. Berger, Nov. 20, 1993; Berger set up this meeting on the spur of the moment.

45 Williams to Susman, Nov., 1959 and Mar. 22, 1959.

46 William Appleman Williams, *Visions of History*, 133.

47 Ibid.

48 Williams to Susman, Nov. 1, 1990, letter made available by Bea Susman.

49 Telephone interview with George Mosse by Paul Buhle, June 20, 1993.

50 These methods, adopted extensively in Central America toward the end of the 1960s, produced an ecological nightmare. See for instance, Daniel Farber, *Environment Under Fire: Imperialism and the Ecological Crisis in Central America* (New York, 1993), which indicates that Salvadoran and Nicaraguan peasants had twenty to thirty times the pesticide levels in their blood as North Americans, with cancer and other premature death rates racing upward, large "dead" zones disrupting wildlife migration, and a growing pattern of U.S. toxic dumping in these lands, ruled by U.S. client governments.

51 Sigmund Diamond reports that a high-ranking CIA officer, later a special assistant to Yale President Kingman Brewster and the organizer of a special "company" team to overthrow the elected Arbenz government of Guatemala, apparently

arranged a meeting with Schlesinger, Jr., to prepare the White Paper on the Bay of Pigs operation. Schlesinger, Jr., afterward sent a memorandum to President Kennedy praising the "skill and care" of the disguise so as to make the invasion appear "a spontaneous Cuban effort," and to deceive the public at home and elsewhere into believing "that the alleged CIA personnel were errant idealists or soldiers of fortune working on their own." Schlesinger, Jr., reportedly went on, "When lies must be told, they should be told by subordinate officials" in order to protect higher-ups from damaging revelations of past deceits. U.N. Ambassador Stevenson, who had believed himself a trusted and longstanding friend of Schlesinger, Jr.'s, was stunned to learn that he also had been deceived, duped into swearing U.S. innocence at a U.N. session. Diamond, *Compromised Campus: The Collaboration of Universities with the Intelligence Community, 1945–1955* (New York, 1992), n. 39, 335–36.

52 William Appleman Williams," *Visions of History,* 133.

53 Telephone interview with Corrinne Williams, July 9, 1994.

54 Williams to Lloyd Gardner, n.d., letter made available by Gardner.

55 William Appleman Williams, *Visions of History,* 133.

56 HUAC's harassment no doubt further encouraged certain Wisconsin state legislators to make noises about investigating Williams themselves. They backed down after the university took his side. Harrington had rightly guessed that Williams could take care of himself, and if not, Harrington would no doubt have thrown his full weight behind his student.

57 Henry W. Berger, introduction to *A William Appleman Williams Reader,* 23; William G. Robbins, "William Appleman Williams: 'Doing History is Best of All. No Regrets,'" in Lloyd Gardner, ed., *Redefining the Past: Essays in Diplomatic History in Honor of Wiliam Appleman Williams* (Corvallis, 1986), 13–14.

58 Quoted in James Weinstein and David Eakins, introduction to *For a New America: Essays in History and Politics from* Studies On the Left, *1959–1967* (New York, 1970), 8–9.

59 Weinstein and Eakins, introduction to *For a New America,* 10–11.

60 Interview with Saul Landau by Paul Buhle, Oct., 1980.

61 Williams to Susman, July 22, 1961, letter made available by Bea Susman. In 1961, the Socialist Club, evidently on a lark, invited Khrushchev and Castro to speak on campus. They were promptly slapped down by the Student Council for improper procedure.

62 Williams to Susman, July 22, 1961; James Weinstein, "Studies On the Left," and Saul Landau, "From the Labor Youth League to the Cuban Revolution," in *History and the New Left,* 113–117 and 107–112. See also Martin J. Sklar, *The United States as a Developing Country: Studies in U.S. History in the Progressive Era and the 1920s* (New York, 1992), especially 46, fn. 7 and 152, fn. 3, in which Sklar acknowledges Williams's influence and describes his contribution.

63 Andrew Hacker, "The Rebelling Young Scholars," *Commentary* 30 (November, 1960), 404, 407.

64 Hacker, "Rebelling Scholars," 408, 412.

65 C. Vann Woodward, "Comment on Genovese," *Studies On the Left* 6 (November-December, 1966), 36.

66 Peter Novick, *That Noble Dream*, 332.

67 Reinitz, *Irony and Consciousness*, 162–68.

68 Richard Collins, "The Originality Trap: Richard Hofstadter on Populism," *Journal of American History*, 76 (June, 1989), 150–67.

69 The most extreme attacks on Populism, however, were made at the hands of cold war militants like Oscar Handlin who treated Bryan's famed Cross of Gold speech as an anti-Semitic outburst, or Edward Shils's *The Torment of Secrecy*, a shallow polemic against Populism, as the source of McCarthyism from a writer himself notably close to McCarthyism's defenders at the CIA-sponsored *Encounter* magazine, co-edited by Irving Kristol. This was exactly the kind of case that raised questions about intellectual integrity and not only on the Left: intellectuals both eager to whip up hysteria for a clash of titans and simultaneously determined to attribute its least loveable qualities to ordinary Americans.

70 Interview with Merle Curti, Nov. 20, 1993. Curti was particularly sharp about the influence of the Trillings on Hofstadter. A sophisticated argument by Peter Novick attributes the anti-Populist shift in historiography to an ethnic variation: the Jewish scholars in Eastern schools had European ancestors and relatives threatened by uncontrolled crowds of gentiles. But this insight is not sophisticated enough. During the 1950s, a notably left-wing tradition of Jewish thought, communist and noncommunist, was under fierce attack from Jewish mainstream institutions and officials. A new Jewish radical generation had come through the war or grown up shortly afterward and would fill out radical historians' ranks, including many supporters and some severe critics of Williams. See the essays in *History and the New Left*, and see Howard Zinn, *You Can't Be Neutral On a Moving Train: A Personal History of Our Times* (Boston, 1994), Part Two. We also wish to thank Alfred Young for his own account of a young Jewish radical historian in this period.

71 This draws directly on the memory of U.S. history courses taught at the University of Illinois from 1962 to 1966 but is consistent with many undergraduates' experiences. Alfred Young has also been very helpful.

72 In a 1983 essay, "American Historians and the Democratic Idea," Irving Kristol makes this point clear, even disparaging his unreflective fellow neoconservative Boorstin for misunderstanding the conservatism of Edmund Burke. See Kristol, *Reflections of a Neo-Conservative* (New York, 1983), 105.

73 The evidence for this thick pattern of friendship and collaboration is seen best in the Richard Hofstadter Papers, Special Collections, Columbia University. Here, for instance, Kristol, Lipset, and Riesman, among others, exchange ideas clearly previewing the corporate-funded neoconservatism that Kristol would personally champion. See e.g., Riesman's railing at C. Wright Mills and insisting as late as 1964 that "Big Business" could not possibly be the enemy of freedom because intelligent corporations allowed ample room for individuality. Riesman to Hofstadter,

Dec. 7, 1964. This account also owes a great deal to the interpretations by Reinitz, *Irony and Consciousness*; and to David W. Noble, "William Appleman Williams and the Crisis of Public History," in *Redefining the Past*, 45–62.

74 Robert M. Collins, "The Originality Trap," 166. The later Hofstadter should thus be contrasted with the later S. M. Lipset, Irving Kristol, or Daniel Boorstin. Interestingly, Williams was later a casual friend of the writer Harvey Swados, in turn brother-in-law of Hofstadter. Had the latter lived, it is more than possible that a dialogue between Williams and Hofstadter would have illuminated large territories.

75 William Appleman Williams, "The Age of Reforming History," *Nation*, 182 (June 30, 1956), 552–54.

76 See Alan Wald, *The New York Intellectuals* (New York, 1986), Part III, Ch. 9–11.

77 A most remarkable text in this regard from a non-historian influential on historians is Riesman, *Individualism Reconsidered and Other Essays* (Glencoe, 1954). The much admired author of *The Lonely Crowd* considered himself a pacifist and in that sense a dissident from the arms race, but his description of dissenters and radicals as alienated outsiders was anything but complimentary. More than anyone else except perhaps his associates Daniel Bell and Nathan Glazer, his mixture of psychological, anthropological, and sociological influences nearly reversed the emphasis of liberal writers from the New Deal and World War II years. See also Thomas L. Hartshorn, *The Distorted Image: Changing Conceptions of the American Character Since Turner* (Cleveland, 1968).

78 See Mari Jo Buhle and Paul Buhle, "The New Labor History at the Cultural Crossroads," *Journal of American History*, 75 (June, 1988), 137–41.

79 Walter P. Webb, *The Great Frontier* (Lincoln, 1952). See also Necah Stewart Furman, *Walter Prescott Webb: His Life and Impact* (Albuquerque, 1976), especially Ch. 10–12.

80 These phenomena were not entirely unrelated. Arthur Schlesinger, Jr., was easily the most unremitting liberal critic of the Hollywood Blacklistees, those writers, directors, actors, and technicians driven out of the movie business. See Dalton Trumbo's witty response to Schlesinger, Jr.'s *Look* magazine attacks on the Blacklistees, in Trumbo, *Additional Dialogue* (New York, 1971), 124.

81 Riesman, *Individualism Reconsidered*, 476–77.

82 Phone interview with Carl Marzani by Paul Buhle, Oct. 1, 1994. Marzani, a founder of the little Prometheus Books, noted that he had also offered to publish any of Williams's works which could not be published elsewhere.

83 See James Livingston, "Farewell."

84 Livingston, "Farewell."

85 Martin J. Sklar, "Dear Board Members," Nov. 19, 1960. Studies On the Left Papers, State Historical Society of Wisconsin.

86 Williams previewed this section of *Contours* with "The Age of Mercantilism: An Interpretation of the American Political Economy, 1763 to 1828," *William*

and Mary Quarterly, 15 (October, 1958), 419–37; and with "Samuel Adams: Calvinist, Mercantilist, Revolutionary," *Studies On the Left*, I (Winter, 1960), 47–57.

87 See Henry W. Berger's comments on *Contours* in his various introductions to *A William Appleman Williams Reader*, 24–26, 162, 221, 239.

88 Apart from the parallel impulse of British historian E. P. Thompson to recuperate William Morris through an expansive biography, a handful of Socialist writers sought to reinterpret the legacy of the Middle Ages. Among them, C. L. R. James's essay, "Dialectical Materialism and the Fate of Humanity," published obscurely in the later 1940s, reprinted by *Radical America* as a pamphlet in 1971 and finally in James, *Spheres of Existence: Selected Writings* (London, 1980), 70–105, is closest to Williams's intent.

89 Williams to Warren Susman, Mar. 10, 1958. Letter made available by Bea Susman.

90 William Appleman Williams, *Contours of American History* (Cleveland, 1961), 95–96.

91 See Paul Buhle, "Marxist Historiography, 1900–1940," *Radical America*, IV (December, 1970), 5–36; this argument is simplified and refined in Buhle's "Marxism and Its Critics," in Mary Kupiec Cayton, Elliott J. Gorn and Peter W. Williams, eds., *Encyclopedia of Social History* I (New York, 1993), 371–86.

92 Williams, *Contours*, 137.

93 Williams, *Contours*, 136–48.

94 A telling comparison on questions of Indian policy and slaves can be made between Schlesinger, Jr.'s Pulitzer Prize–winning *The Age of Jackson* (Boston, 1945), and a recent authoritative textbook, *Out of Many* (Engelwood Cliffs, 1994), by John Mack Faragher, Mari Jo Buhle, Daniel Czitrom, and Susan H. Armitage, especially 281–84.

95 Wilson's role in gutting parklands was little discussed by historians until a major reevaluation of Western history. Under Wilson, the Olympic Natural Monument lost half its land and the Rocky Mountain National Park was robbed of two-thirds of its original planned territory. Happily, Stephen Mather, an early Sierra Club member, created the National Park Service, lobbying for better care of national parks and using his own money to buy lands and pay staff. Without Mather's determination, Wilson's misrule would have been far more destructive. See Richard White, *"It's Your Misfortune and None of My Own": A New History of the American West* (Norman, 1991), 413–15. White's book was dedicated to Vernon Carstensen, collaborator of Merle Curti's in the multi-volume history of the University of Wisconsin and yet another favorite Madisonian scholar.

96 Williams had set out the outlines of "corporatism" in several of the essays he had written for the *Nation*, but even in *Contours*, never fully elaborated his conceptualization. Thomas McCormick, whose wife was typing the manuscript, says that Williams was "running out of steam" at this point in the book. Interview with McCormick by Edward Rice-Maximin, June 11, 1992.

97 The most important socialist theorists were William English Walling and Louis C. Fraina. See Walling, *Progressivism and After* (New York, 1914), the most cogent of his volumes, and Louis C. Fraina, *Revolutionary Socialism* (New York, 1918), for the two best primary sources; See also Paul Buhle, *A Dreamer's Paradise Lost: Louis C. Fraina/Lewis Corey, 1892–1953* (Atlantic Highlands, N.J., 1995) for a summary and discussion of the dialogue during the 1910s.

98 Anders Stephanson, "The United States," unpublished paper delivered at a Madison, Wisconsin, conference on the cold war, October, 1991. Thanks to Stephanson for lending us a copy of this address.

99 Ronald Radosh, "The Corporate Ideology of American Labor Leaders from Gompers to Hillman," *Studies On the left*, reprinted in *For a New America* (New York, 1970), 125–52.

100 James Weinstein, "Gompers and the New Liberalism, 1900–1909," *For a New America*, 101–14.

101 Martin J. Sklar, "Woodrow Wilson and the Political Economy of Modern United States Liberalism," *For a New America*, 46–100. This essay, the longest essay published in *Studies* and in *For a New America*, was a chapter from Sklar's MA thesis.

102 See Chapter 7.

103 Michael Meeropol and Gerald Markowitz, "Neighborhood Politics," in *History and the New Left*, 211.

104 See Casey M. Blake, *Beloved Community: The Cultural Criticism of Randolph Bourne, Van Wyck Brooks, Waldo Frank and Lewis Mumford* (Chapel Hill, 1990).

105 Williams, *Contours*, 472–73.

106 Williams, *Contours*, 491. As noted by Herbert Aptheker, "American Development and Ruling-Class Ideology," *Studies On the Left*, III (1962), 97.

107 *Selected Correspondence of Karl Marx and Frederick Engels*, (Moscow, 1955), 300. Thanks to Timothy Messer-Kruse for pointing out this passage. A section of the *Communist Manifesto* entitled "Reactionary Socialism—Feudal Socialism," indeed attributes to the anachronistic aristocrats a resistance which is "half lamentation, half lampoon," containing a "bitter, witty, and incisive criticism," striking the bourgeoisie "to the very heart's core." Karl Marx and Frederick Engels, *The Communist Manifesto* (New York, 1961), 49.

108 Ian Tyrrell, *The Absent Marx: Class Analysis and Liberal History in Twentieth-Century America* (Westport, 1986), 138–39. Unfortunately, Tyrrell's own understanding is severely limited by a certain prejudice but even more by an extremely vague notion of "New Left history" and a remarkable underuse of sources in which young historians sought to overcome Williams's weaknesses. See Chapters 5 and 6, and Jon Wiener's more reliable if brief account, "Radical Historians and the Crisis in American History, 1959–1980," *Journal of American History*, 76 (September, 1989), 399–434.

109 See for instance the "Introduction" by Lawrence Krader to *The Ethnological Notebooks of Karl Marx* (Assan, Netherlands, 1972), edited by Lawrence Krader.

110 William A. Williams to Lloyd Gardner, n.d. [1986].

111 Handlin, *Mississippi Valley Historical Review*, 68 (Mar., 1962), 743–45.

112 John Higham, "Communications," *Mississippi Valley Historical Review*, 49 (September, 1962), 407–08.

113 John Higham, "The Contours of William A. Williams," *Studies On the Left I* (Spring, 1960), 74–75.

114 John Higham, "Communications," 408.

115 John Braeman, *American Political Science Review*, 56 (December, 1963), 1005–06.

116 John C. Malin, *South Atlantic Quarterly*, 61 (Winter, 1962), 123–24. In an interview with Paul Buhle, Oct. 20, 1993, Alan Bogue described the conference in Kansas (in which Bogue first encountered Williams), hosted by a conservative foundation close to Malin, but featuring a Williams paper.

117 Letter from David Noble to Paul Buhle, May, 1992.

118 Aptheker, "American Development," 97.

119 Ibid. 97–105.

120 Conversation from c.1986 reported by Jim Murray to Paul Buhle, June 1994.

121 "E. P. Thompson," in MARHO, *Visions of History* (New York, 1983), 22. Fortunately for Thompson, the conversation was held at close range, with people he could see regularly.

122 Manning Marable, Thomas McCormick, and Lloyd Gardner, in Copelman/Clark Smith, 59–61.

123 James Weinstein, "The Need for a Socialist Party," *Studies On the Left*, VII (Jan.-Feb., 1967), reprinted in *For a New America* (New York, 1970), 338. See the parallel comments on Williams's importance in Eugene Genovese, "Legacy of Slavery and Roots of Black Nationalism," *Studies On the Left*, VI (Nov.-Dec., 1966), reprinted in *For a New America*, 419.

124 Maurice Isserman, *If I Had a Hammer: The Death of the Old Left and the Birth of the New Left* (New York, 1987), 109.

125 James Weinstein, "Studies On the Left," in *History and the New Left*, 117.

126 William Appleman Williams, *The United States, Castro and Cuba* (New York, 1962), 1.

127 Williams noted that Draper's anti-Castro thesis was quickly borrowed by cold war strategists and its perspectives adopted as the "central theme" of the State Department's White Paper of April, 1961. Many believed that the counter-strategy encouraged massive repression, not excluding ethnocide of troublesome indigenous peoples. Williams, *The United States, Castro and Cuba*, 70, 71.

128 Quoted in Williams, *The United States, Cuba, and Castro*, 15.

129 A communication from Alan Wald to Theodore Draper, July 9, 1987, made available to Paul Buhle, cites numerous interviews with former Communists recalling Draper as "the Commissar" of the literary left in the later 1930s, demanding loyal support of American intellectuals to Stalin's view on the Moscow Trials, attacking critics of those trials in the pages of the *New Masses* and slurring them as Nazi-like in their attack upon the Soviet Union. We are grateful to Wald for mak-

ing this document available. See Alan Wald, "Search for a Method: Recent Histories of American Communism," *Radical History Review*, 61 (Winter, 1995), n. 11.

130 Theodore Draper, "The Strange Case of Professor Williams," *New Leader*, 46 (Apr. 29, 1963), 13–19. Draper's earlier attacks on the Cuban Revolution had appeared in the British-based *Encounter*, for much of the 1950s a tainted outlet of CIA funds. The *New Leader* had its own Latin American story. Daniel James, a *New Leader* editor, had written in 1954 a cold war propaganda tract, *Red Design on the Americas*, and gone on a promotional tour for it. Responsible historians later confirmed the devastating U.S. role and the dissimulation involved in the press cover-up. See Walter LaFeber, *Inevitable Revolutions: The United States in Central America* (New York, 1983 edition), 113–27; and Van Gosse, *Where the Boys Are: Cuba, Cold War America and the Making of a New Left* (London, 1993), Ch. 2. Under restored U.S. hegemony and with American military training for officers, subsequent Guatemalan governments became notorious for human rights abuses in general and the premeditated slaughter of Indians in particular.

131 Williams's response finally appeared in *Studies On the Left* despite the private misgivings of some editors that Williams had missed the chance to meet Draper flatly and to quash his disingenuity. See William A. Williams, "Historiography and Revolution: The Case of Cuba, A Commentary on a Polemic by Theodore Draper," *Studies On the Left*, 3 (Summer, 1963), 78–102. See Williams's letters to Myron Kolatch, Executive Editor of the *New Leader*, May 6, 18, 1963, *Studies On the Left* Papers, State Historical Society of Wisconsin.

132 Eleanor Hakim to Martin Sklar, Oct. 4, 1960. *Studies On the Left* Papers, State Historical Society of Wisconsin.

133 See "Stanley" [Aronowitz] to Board Members, n.d. [1965], ibid. Aronowitz scribbled at the bottom of his letter, "either we move in these directions or I'm afraid the magazine will continue to decline in prestige and readership." See also Eleanor Hakim's retrospective essay "The Tragedy of Hans Gerth," in Buhle, ed., *History and the New Left*, 252–63, on the general decline of interest in theory after the early *Studies* days.

134 Williams to Lloyd Gardner and Warren Susman, Nov., 1964. Around the same time, he described family problems as "so damn enervating that I feel some times as though I would like just to go quietly to sleep[,] I am so weary." Williams to Gardner, n.d. These letters kindly loaned by Lloyd Gardner.

135 Interview with Kyenne Williams, June 9, 1993.

CHAPTER 5

1 One of the few written accounts of Goldberg, in Tom Bates, *Rads* (New York, 1992), is a travesty, treating him as a radical pied piper corrupting naive midwestern youth. For a partial antidote, see Ron McCrea and Dave Wagner, "Harvey Goldberg," in *History and the New Left*, 241–45.

2 Williams, Harvey Goldberg Lecture, Madison, 1989, Williams Papers. Goldberg destroyed his personal papers, but the Goldberg Center in Madison continues to keep his memory alive. We wish to acknowledge their sponsorship of a lecture by Paul Buhle on the late historian E. P. Thompson, in November 1993, during which research and interviews on Williams could be conducted.

3 See, e.g., Paul Breines, "The Mosse Milieu," and McCrea and Wagner, "Harvey Goldberg," *History and the New Left*, 246–51 and 241–45, respectively.

4 Letter from George Mosse to Paul Buhle, Sept. 20, 1993, stressed the signal importance of two volumes loaned to Williams in 1962, *The Church and the Working Classes* and *Through the Lord's Body*, both conveying a British "incarnational theoogy" with a heavy emphasis on a highly structured symbolic religious service. See also George Mosse, "New Left Intellectuals," in *History and the New Left*, 234.

5 Williams to Merle Curti, Oct. 5, 1964, Curti Papers, State Historical Society of Wisconsin.

6 Memo to William and Karla Robbins, n.d. [1985], Williams Papers.

7 For readings of Bellamy, see e.g., Daphne Patai, ed., *Looking Backward, 1988–1888: Essays on Edward Bellamy* (Amherst, 1988); Csaba Toth, "Utopianism as Americanism," *American Quarterly*, 45 (December, 1993), 649–58; and Franklin Rosemont, "Edward Bellamy," in *Surrealism and its Popular Accomplices* (San Francisco, 1982), edited by Franklin Rosemont, 6–16.

8 Williams, *The Great Evasion* (Chicago, 1963), 12, 20.

9 Williams, *Great Evasion*, 132.

10 Staughton Lynd, *Intellectual Origins of American Radicalism* (New York, 1968).

11 Williams, *Great Evasion*, 167.

12 Williams, *Great Evasion*, back cover.

13 Williams, *Great Evasion*, 142.

14 Williams, *Great Evasion*, 175–76.

15 Williams, *Great Evasion*, 111–13.

16 See Susman's "'Personality' and the Making of Twentieth-Century Culture," in Warren Susman, *Culture as History: The Transformation of American Society in the Twentieth Century* (New York, 1982), 271–86.

17 Max Horkheimer, "Authority and the Family," in *The Family: Its Function and Destiny* (New York, 1949), Ruth Nanda Anshen, ed., 367.

18 There was one vitally important exception: theories of Black poverty, attributed by Daniel Patrick Moynihan among many others to the African American matriarchy, gained new popularity among liberals and conservatives toward the end of the 1960s. Later, of course, Christopher Lasch would revive and restate the Horkheimer critique in a sustained polemic against feminism. See Chapter 6.

19 Robert Heilbroner, "Marx and the American Economy," *New York Review of Books*, 3 (Jan. 14, 1965), 21–22.

20 Floyd A. Cave, *American Political Science Review*, 60 (Jan., 1966), 127.

21 Milton Cantor, "Inheritors of the Faith, "*Nation*, 120 (Apr. 5, 1965), 366–68.

22 Eugene D. Genovese, "William Appleman Williams on Marx and America," *Studies on the Left*, 6 (Jan-Feb., 1966), 70–89. Among other sympathetic views of the book, perhaps the most insightful was written by a libertarian conservative: William Marina's "William Appleman Williams."

23 George Mosse, "New Left Intellectuals," 234.

24 Susman, "'Personality,'" 284–85.

25 See Christopher Lasch, *Haven in a Heartless World* (New York, 1977), Ch. 7.

26 Kirkpatrick Sale, *SDS* (New York, 1973), 188–89; Carl Oglesby, *Containment and Change* (New York, 1967).

27 Indeed, another Madison graduate student of the time, Ellis Hawley, would produce the most impressive theoretical analysis of consensual corporatism. At a panel of the Organization of American Historians in 1994, Hawley and Sklar shared the platform, arguing that contemporary corporatism as the governing system of the nation had evolved into something close to a merger of traditional Socialist and capitalist ideals. Hawley had always held beliefs close to what might be described as a traditional democratic-liberal pluralism; Sklar had evolved toward it, while continuing to insist upon the value of Williams's ideas. See his later essays *The United States as a Developing Country* (Cambridge, 1992), especially "The Corporate Reconstruction of American Capitalism: A Note on the Capitalism-Socialism Mix in U.S. and World Development," 209–18. See also Ellis Hawley, "The Discovery and Study of a 'Corporate Liberalism,'" *Business History Review*, 52 (Autumn, 1978), and Hawley, *The Great War and the Search for a Modern Order: A History of the American People and Their Institutions, 1917–1933* (New York, 1979), 91–105.

28 Williams, "Our Leaders are following the Wrong Rainbow," Apr. 1, 1965, reprinted in Louis Menashe and Ronald Radosh, editors, *Teach-Ins, USA: Reports, Opinions, Documents* (New York, 1967), 45–53.

29 "Williams on Policy for U.S. Radicals," *National Guardian*, Nov. 27, 1965. He claimed, in private correspondence, that the response in mail to him had been overwhelmingly positive.

30 The first Socialist Scholars Conference meeting was held in September 1965, with a steering committee which included Eugene Genovese, *Monthly Review*'s Paul Sweezy, and two *Studies on the Left* editors, James Weinstein and James O'Connor. See "1,000 Attend Socialist Scholars Meeting in New York," *National Guardian*, Sept. 18, 1965.

31 See Stuart Ewen, "The Intellectual New Left," in *History and the New Left*, 178–82.

32 Researchers pointed especially to the Land Tenure Center and to the School for Workers, apart from the various projects funded by military sources directly or indirectly.

33 An extremely misleading account has been offered of the day's events by *Rads*, evidently for the purpose of discrediting war protesters by crediting the club-swinging police as hardworking proletarians. Fire fighters, soon drawn to the side of the campus and community progressives by a mutual hostility toward the thuggish spe-

cial squad which was called out against demonstrators, were remarkably slow a few years later to answer a call to quell an accidentally exploded gas grenade in the basement of the police department. With major changes in city government instituted by the administration of a former peace demonstrator, Paul Soglin, a new, liberal élan and professionalization entered the police force and the hardliners were marginalized. See "Introduction" to *History and the New Left* for a more accurate version of the Dow events.

34 This article was reprinted in many places but see Nan Robertson, "Students Angry, but Frustrated," *Sunday Oregonian*, Nov. 26, 1967.

35 This recollection is a collective one, but depends primarily upon the memory of Paul Buhle, one of those who handed out the bananas in Williams's class. It may be worthwhile to add that this technique or theatrical stroke was entirely spontaneous on the part of several graduate students, none knowing the others would do the same. There was not a hint of resentment in it, nor did Williams take it as such.

36 Letter from Michael Meeropol, June 20, 1994.

37 We wish to thank Michael Hirsch, who attended the Alternative University in New York, for these recollections.

38 This recounts a conversation between Williams and Paul Buhle, the editor of *Radical America*, in November 1967, scarcely a month after the Dow Demonstration, in which Madison SDSers had played a prominent if by no means leadership role. *Radical America* went on, in later years, to emerge as a major voice of Socialist feminism and a Socialist version of gay liberation. Its leading editor of the 1970s, historian Linda Gordon, returned to Madison and became Vilas Professor. In some sense, then, the sceptre had almost literally been passed from hand to hand.

39 Our gratitude to Alfred Young for making this suggestion.

40 Williams to Lloyd Gardner, January, 1966, letter donated by Lloyd Gardner.

41 Williams to Gardner; and telephone interview with Corrinne Williams, July 11, 1994.

42 Interview with Phyllis Weiss by Paul Buhle, November 18, 1992.

43 Memo to William and Karla Robbins, 1985.

44 Williams, "An American Socialist Community?", *Liberation*, June, 1969, reprinted in William Appleman Williams, *History as a Way of Learning* (New York, 1972), 383–90.

45 Williams, *History as a Way*, 388.

46 Williams, *History as a Way*, 389.

47 The attempt to pass a ballot measure in Madison against the war in Vietnam brought just this hostility. See Michael Meeropol and Gerald Markowitz, "Neighborhood Politics," in *History and the New Left*, 214–15.

48 Tom Bates makes the very serious and unfounded suggestion, in *Reds*, that Harvey Goldberg in some way incited this traumatic event, resulting in the death of a researcher. Williams never thought so. And those who knew the youngsters personally, as Paul Buhle did Leo F. Burt in a discussion section for a U.S. History course, dismiss the charge out of hand.

49 Kevin Phillips, *The Emerging Republican Majority* (New York, 1969). Decades later, Phillips would offer real wisdom which sounded very much like echos of Williams's own views.

50 This account owes considerable to Michael Meeropol, "W. A. Williams's Historiography," *Radical America*, IV (Aug. 1970), 29–49.

51 This point is made best by James Livingston, "Farewell to Intellectual Godfather William Appleman Williams," *In These Times*, Mar. 28-Apr. 3, 1990.

52 Other devotees of LaFollette would answer plausibly that he had undergone a radicalization on questions of Empire. See for instance R. David Myers, "Robert M. La Follette," in Mari Jo Buhle, Paul Buhle and Harvey J. Kaye, eds., *The American Radical* (New York, 1994), 159–66.

53 Peter Novick has pointed out that Williams long believed the real truth and not just a relativistic truth could be told through a sufficiently determined personal effort. See *That Noble Dream*, 423.

54 Williams, *Roots of the Modern American Empire*, 452.

55 Irving Howe, "The New 'Confrontation Politics' is a Dangerous Game, "*New York Times Magazine*, Oct. 20, 1968, 27–29, 133–39; and "Political Terrorism: Hysteria on the Left," *New York Times Magazine*, Apr. 12, 1970, 25–27, 124–28. Alan Wald incisively describes this aspect of Howe's work and the drift of the New York Intellectuals toward neoconservativsm in Ch. 10–11 of his *The New York Intellectuals: The Rise and Decline of the Anti-Stalinist Left From the 1930s to the 1980s* (Chapel Hill, 1987).

56 Christopher Lehmann-Haupt, "Down on the Farm," *New York Times*, Nov. 24, 1969; John William Ward, "Does the Study of the Past Have a Future?" *New York Times Book Review*, Feb. 22, 1970, 10, 12, 14.

57 Carl Degler, *American Historical Review*, 75 (October, 1970), 172–74. Writing almost twenty years later on the influence of radical history on the profession, Degler warned against "celebratory" discussions, insisted that evidence and not opinion convinced true historians, and described only a small handful of radical scholars as worthy of mention; Williams was not among them, proving once more that old grudges die hard. He also freely admitted that he had advised against the publication of the essay by Jon Wiener describing the rise of the Williams-influenced trend. See Carl Degler, "What Crisis, Jon?" *Journal of American History*, 76 (Sept., 1989), 467–70.

58 Gretchen Kreuter, *Minnesota History*, 42 (Summer, 1971), 235–36; David M. Pletcher, *Journal of American History*, 57 (June, 1970), 172–74.

59 J. R. T. Hughes, *Business History Review*, 44 (Winter, 1970), 567–68. The more progressive Lewis E. Hill found *Roots* a "bold new approach to the interpretation of American economic development and growth," written with both creativity and courage.

60 Michael Harrington, "America, II," *Partisan Review*, 37 (1970), 498–505. Harrington himself later described his opposition to the New Left in terms strikingly like those used by Williams, while insisting upon supporting Hubert

Humphrey and while regretting the dramatic shift of his political mentors and long-term labor allies away from George McGovern into the Nixon camp. Breaking off from this political tendency, he went on to head the Democratic Socialists Organizing Committee (DSOC) and later Democratic Socialists of America (DSA), which vehemently opposed U.S. guidance and funding of the "dirty wars" in Central America and Africa. See Michael Harrington, *Fragments of the Century* (New York, 1973), 223–25, and Robert Gorman, "Michael Harrington," in *The American Radical*, 337–44.

61 Williams, Letters column, "Loose Lips," *In These Times*, Oct. 18-24, 1989.

62 Ironically, former Williams student Ronald Radosh had become by the 1990s a frequent contributor to *Partisan Review*, still run by the now elderly cold warrior William Phillips.

63 Howard Zinn, "America, II," 519–27.

64 Howard Zinn, *You Can't Be Neutral on a Moving Train: A Personal History of Our Times* (Boston, 1994), Ch. 1-2.

65 Arthur Schlesinger, Jr., "America II," 505–19.

66 Williams, "America II," *Partisan Review*, 38 (1971), 67–78. Schlesinger, Jr., and Harrington offered brief rejoinders, 78–83.

67 Richard Leopold, Reviews, *Pacific Historical Review*, 39 (August, 1970), 307–8.

68 Lawrence Goodwyn, *Democratic Promise: The Populist Movement in America* (New York, 1976), xi, xiii, xv. For a potpourri of various scholarly views on Populism, see William F. Holmes, ed., *American Populism* (Lexington, 1994). This edition does not excerpt from Williams's writing, and includes only a passage from Hofstadter among the 1950s "School" of anti-Populists. The rest of the essays take up Populism from various aspects, but none recycles the old charges of anti-Semitism and irrationalism. The discussion had simply moved onward.

69 Goodwin, *Democratic Promise*, 532.

70 Williams, *Roots*, xvii.

71 Richard W. Van Alstyne, "Beyond the Last Frontier," *Nation*, 210, Feb. 23, 1970, 214–15; Michael Meeropol, "William A. Williams's Historiography,"and James P. O'Brien,"Comment," in *Radical America*, 4 (Aug., 1970), 29–49 and 50–53. James O'Brien, et. al., "New Left Historians of the 1960s," *Radical America*, IV, (Nov.-Dec., 1970), 82–83.

72 Telephone interview with Corrinne Williams, July 11, 1994.

73 Williams, *Americans in a Changing World*, 3.

CHAPTER 6

1 Outline for "A Historian Reflects Upon His Memories," n.d., Williams Papers.

2 Clifford Solway, "Turning History Upside Down," *Saturday Review*, June 20, 1970, 62.

3 "Eugene Genovese: The Uncommon Marxist," *Intellectual Digest* (October, 1970), 79.

4 Williams, *Some Presidents: Wilson to Nixon* (New York, 1970), 26.

5 Williams, *Some Presidents*, 30, 31. Italics added.

6 Williams, *Some Presidents*, 39.

7 Williams, *Some Presidents*, 72.

8 Williams, *Some Presidents*, 77.

9 Williams, *Some Presidents*, 80–81.

10 Howard Zinn, a bombadier, came close but rarely wrote about his experiences in his historical studies. At a guess, most other World War II veterans-turned-historians remained Truman or Kennedy Democrats.

11 Williams, *Some Presidents*, 83.

12 Williams, *Some Presidents*, 84.

13 Williams, *Some Presidents*, 102.

14 Williams, *Some Presidents*, 103.

15 Williams, *Some Presidents*, 87.

16 Indeed, he urges the reader to "try to be a historian. Or if you (like me) prefer the idiom of Thucydides, try to be a citizen." Williams, *Some Presidents*, 84.

17 Richard Hofstadter, *The Progressive Historians: Turner, Beard, Parrington* (New York, 1968), 453. Quoted from Jonathan Wiener, "Radical Historians and the Crisis in American History," *Journal of American History*, 76 (September, 1989), 429.

18 Wiener, "Radical Historians," 430–31.

19 Peter Novick, *That Noble Dream* (Cambridge, 1988), 447–49.

20 Arthur M. Schlesinger, Jr., *New York Review of Books*, 7 (October 20, 1966), 37.

21 John Leo, "Some Scholars, Reassessing Cold War, Blame U.S.," *New York Times*, Sept. 24, 1967, 33.

22 Arthur M. Schlesinger, Jr., "Origins of the Cold War," *Foreign Affairs*, 46 (October, 1967), 22–52, especially 22–23 and 45–52. In grudging praise, Schlesinger, Jr., found Williams the "most subtle and ingenious" of the revisionists.

23 Christopher Lasch, "The Cold War Revisited and Re-Visioned," *New York Times Magazine*, Jan. 14, 1968, 26ff, especially 27, 51, 59.

24 H. Stuart Hughes, "The Second Year of the Cold War: A Memoir and an Anticipation," *Commentary*, 48 (August, 1969), 27–32. Hughes characteristically hardened his positions as well in the post–Vietnam War era, insisting only a few years later that one could never possibly trust a Stalin, who was "only a few degrees less loathsome than Hitler," in Hughes, "Cold War and Detente," *New York Review of Books*, 23 (Feb. 19, 1976), 3–6.

25 Martin Diamond devotes several illuminating chapters to the intelligence agencies' influence, secret and open, upon Harvard and Yale, and the quiet collaboration of such figures as Talcott Parsons in the process. See *Compromised Campus: The Collaboration of Universities with the Intelligence Community, 1945–1955* (New York, 1992).

26 Noted by a hostile critic in a heavily funded conservative magazine for undergraduates: Edward S. Shapiro, "Responsibility for the Cold War: A Bibliographical Review," *Intercollegiate Review*, 23 (Winter 1976-77), 113–20, especially 113–14.

27 A. Kent MacDougall, "Looking Back: Radical Historians Get Growing Following, Despite 'Myths' of Past," *Wall Street Journal*, Oct. 20, 1971.

28 *Hearings Before the Subcommittee on Europe of the Committee on Foreign Affairs, House of Representatives, Ninety Second Congress, First Session* (Washington, 1971), 9–10.

29 *Hearings Before Subcommittee*, 18–19. Williams added that Henry Wallace's experience was "classic." He was "disparaged as a mind and . . . labeled as a tool of the communists. He didn't happen to be guilty on either count," 18. Of course, Schlesinger, Jr., had been guilty of the labeling. Foreign relations (and Vietnam War) hardliner Adam Ulam disparaged Williams's views on the early cold war, warning against "this compulsive guilt feeling which we seem to have been experiencing in our national life," 22.

30 *Hearings Before Subcommittee*, 28, 44.

31 Daniel M. Smith, "The New Left and the Cold War," *Denver Quarterly*, 4 (Winter, 1970), 788; Charles S. Maier, "Revisionism and the Interpretation of Cold War Origins," *Perspectives in American History*, 4 (1970), 313–47, especially 338–39, 345–47.

32 Fred Warner Nal and Bruce D. Hamlet, "The Never-Never Land of International Relations," *International Studies Quarterly*, 13 (Sept, 1969), 281–305, especially 304–5. See also Willard L. Hogeboom, "The Cold War and Revisionist Historiography," *Social Studies*, 61 (December, 1970), 314–18.

33 Lloyd C. Gardner, Arthur M. Schlesinger, Jr., and Hans J. Morgenthau, *The Origins of the Cold War* (Waltham, Mass, 1970), 105–9, 115–16.

34 Quoted in Steve Gillon, *Politics and Vision: The ADA and American Liberalism, 1947–1985* (New York, 1987), 196. Ironically for Williams's personal sympathies, as Gillon notes, the ADA cold war hardliners around the AFL-CIO, like Gus Tyler, were more sympathetic to Johnson, while the "Dump Johnson" faction of the ADA, including Schlesinger Jr., hailed back to the Kennedy years. As usual, no branch of liberalism held much for Williams.

35 Oscar Handlin, "'Revision' Perverts 27-Year U.S. Policy," *Freedom At Issue*, 15 (Sept.-Oct., 1972), 2. This was a publication of the New Right.

36 Walter Laqueur, "Rewriting History," *Commentary*, 55 (March, 1974), 53–63.

37 Arthur M. Schlesinger, Jr., "Was the Cold War Really Necessary?" *Wall Street Journal*, Nov. 30, 1972. See also his effort to redefine terms and defend what the 1940s generation called "anti-Stalinism" in "Communication," *American Historical Review*, 78 (February, 1973), 190–91. This view was ironic or misleading in that Schlesinger, Jr., had in fact rarely used the phrase "Stalinists"—in those days largely a Trotskyist term to differentiate *real* Leninism from the current Russian variety—preferring to attack Russian "Communists" and their American counterparts.

38 Interview with David Shetzline, n.d. [1976], Williams Papers. Thomas McCormick interview, June 11, 1992.

39 A synopsis of the book was published in a conservative journal (and warmly prefaced by Oscar Handlin), as "Cold War Revisionism: Abusing History," *Freedom at Issue*, 15 (Sept.-Oct., 1972), 3–6, 16–19. See also Maddox's follow-up, "Revisionism and the Liberal Historians," *Freedom at Issue*, 19 (May-June, 1973), 19–21.

40 Jack Chatfield, "Refuting Gauguinism," *National Review*, 17 (August, 1973), 904–5; Clare Z. Cafey, "Uncovering an Academic Watergate," *Intercollegiate Review*, 9 (Winter, 1973-74), 51–53; Francis Lowenheim, "Who Started It? You Did! Who says So? We do! Who Are You?" *New York Times Book Review*, June 17, 1973, 6–7.

41 Lowenheim, "Who Started It?" 8, 10.

42 Richard H. Miller, "A Verbal Mugging," *Commonweal*, 98 (August 24, 1973), 457–58. Miller also reviewed Maddox's book for *Science & Society*, 38 (Spring, 1974), 90–91. Ronald Radosh, one of Williams's most devoted students and later a hostile critic, lambasted Maddox in "Hot War with the 'New Left,'" *Nation*, 217 (July 2, 1973), 55–58.

43 Ronald Steel, "The Good Old Days," *New York Review of Books*, 20 (June 14, 1973), 33–36, a review of several volumes.

44 Norman A. Graebner, *Pacific Historical Review*, 43 (February, 1974), 183–89; Robert D. Schulzinger, "Moderation in Pursuit of Truth is No Virtue; Extremism in Defense of Moderation is a Vice," *American Quarterly*, 27 (May, 1975), 222–36, a review of several books. See also Thomas A. Krueger, "New Left Revisionists and Their Critics," *Reviews in American History* (December, 1973), 463–70; Richard W. Leopold, *Journal of American History*, 643 (March, 1974), 1183–85.

45 Warren F. Kimball, "The Cold War Warmed Over," *American Historical Review*, 79 (October, 1974), 1119–36, especially 1128–34.

46 Oscar Handlin, *Truth in History* (Cambridge, 1979), 156–57; Robert Maddox, "The Rise and Fall of Cold War Revisionism," *Historian*, 66 (May, 1984), especially 421–24; and Maddox, "Diplomatic Blunders," *Society*, 23 (March, 1986), 9–10.

47 Williams, "Confessions of an Intransigent Revisionist," reprinted from *Socialist Review*, 1973, into *A William Appleman Williams Reader* (Chicago, 1993), 337–39.

48 Williams, "Confessions," 339.

49 Williams, "Confessions," 344.

50 R. W. Fleming to Carson, May 29, 1967, Williams Papers.

51 Don McIlvenna, "William Appleman Williams, the Historian and His Community, the Oregon Years," Williams Papers. Special thanks also to McIlvenna for making himself available for an on-campus interview. Among correspondence on the subject of Williams's departure from Madison, see, e.g., Williams to McCauley, Oct. 17, 1966, about Williams's love for the coast; and recommendations to George Carson from Gordon Wright, May 25, 1967; Merle Curti, May 26, 1967;

Warren Susman, May 26, 1967; and see Thomas McClintock to Dean Gordan Ghillie, Feb., 1967. Williams Papers.

52 Merle Curti to George Carson, June 24, 1967, Williams Papers.

53 OSU *Barometer*, Feb. 5, 1973, Williams Papers. Williams's talk was entitled, "Adam Smith and Female Persons: A Different Approach to Women's Liberation."

54 See his letter to "Dear Frank and All," dated June 19, 1985, Williams Papers, in which he complains that "truly emancipated women" should not care about special courses in women's history.

55 Williams to Merle Curti, June 1, 1967, Williams Papers.

56 Interestingly, so did Christopher Lasch, who had attacked the New Left, its scholarly elements often as much as its campus activism, but wanted to be part of a group of Socialist historians. See "History as Social Criticism: Conversations with Christopher Lasch," interviews by Casey Blake and Christopher Phelps, in *Journal of American History*, 80 (March, 1994), 1326. Among the younger radical historians at the Chicago meeting, held at the apartment of historian Jesse Lemisch and feminist-scientist Naomi Weisstein, were Mari Jo and Paul Buhle. *Socialist Revolution*'s editorial group included former *Studies* editors David Eakins, Saul Landau, James O'Connor, Martin J. Sklar, and James Weinstein (who emerged as the strongest figure, until his departure to found the newspaper *In These Times* in 1976). Among the younger editors were intellectual historian Eli Zaretsky and a graduate student, John Judis, who as a columnist for *In These Times* and later a contributing editor of the *New Republic* sometimes sought to bridge the gap between the ideas of Williams and those of opponents who sought to banish Williams's influence entirely.

57 Williams to Merle Curti, June 1, 1967, Williams Papers.

58 Williams to McCauley, Oct. 10, 1973, Williams Papers.

59 Williams to "Mother and Father Tomlin," Apr. 27, 1985.

60 See William G. Robbins, "William Appleman Williams: 'Doing History is Best of All. No Regrets,' " in *Redefining the Past* (1986), ed. Lloyd Gardner, 3–20.

61 Mark O. Hatfield, letter to Donald Wax, Chair of History, OSU, Mar. 19, 1986, Williams Papers. Hatfield recalls Williams's "profound" influence on Hatfield's views from the time of the historian's appearance on the OSU faculty. Williams allowed an essay on Hoover to be reprinted into a volume that Hatfield prepared.

62 "Seven Americas on the Way to the Future: An Exploration of American History," outline-prospectus for a textbook, n.d. [1975?], Williams Papers.

63 "Seven Americas."

64 Williams to McCauley, May 29, 1979, Williams Papers.

65 Williams to McCauley, Apr. 27, 1981, Williams Papers.

66 McIlvenna, "William Appleman Williams."

67 Williams to McCauley, Mar. 4, 1978, Williams Papers.

68 Conversation with Kyenne Williams, June 15, 1993.

69 John Simon to McCauley, Jan. 31, 1967, Williams Papers.

70 Angus Cameron to McCauley, Jan. 18, 1967, Williams Papers. Eventually, a major survey history text was produced with the "community" theme central to it: John Mack Faragher, Mari Jo Buhle, Daniel Czitrom, and Susan H. Armitage, *Out of Many: A History of the American People* (Englewood Cliffs, 1994).

71 Theodore Solotaroff to Jerry McCauley, Aug. 26, 1968, Williams Papers.

72 McCauley, draft of speech to Washington, D.C., IPS memorial symposium, Williams Papers.

73 Quoted by McCauley in speech, Williams Papers.

74 See William A. Williams, *History as a Way of Learning*, xiii, for bitter remarks about the *New York Times*–owned Quadrangle for dumping the book after promising earlier to publish it.

75 Patricia Irving to McCauley, Dec. 7, 1976, Williams Papers.

76 "Seven Americas."

77 Interview with Gerda Lerner by Paul Buhle, May 10, 1993.

78 Williams to Henry Berger, June 30, 1976. We are grateful to Berger for making this letter available to us.

79 Williams to William Robbins, n.d. [October, 1985], in the private collection of William Robbins.

80 Interview with Warren Susman, May, 1982.

81 *Americans in a Changing World*, 471.

82 *Americans in a Changing World*, 97.

83 Anonymous critique, prepared for Wiley & Sons., n.d., Williams Papers.

84 We owe the frame of "what if" to a conversation with Williams's sometime Oregon student and longtime close friend Mitzi Goheen, whom he acknowledged generously in the book's preface. Phone conversation, June, 1993. He became close to her parents, an Old Left Jewish academic couple who lived in Corvallis, and stayed in touch as she went on to foreign study and to teach anthropology at Amherst College.

85 Robert M. Senkewicz, *America*, 136 (Jan. 8, 1977), 57–58.

86 Michael Zuckerman, "Recasting American Historical Consciousness," *Nation*, 223 (Sept. 11, 1976), 214–16.

87 Thomas G. Kennedy, *American Historical Review*, 82 (June, 1977), 724.

88 Gaddis Smith, "The United States as Villain," *New York Times Book Review*, Oct. 10, 1976, 25.

89 Edmund S. Morgan, "The American Revolution: Who Were 'The People,'" *New York Review of Books*, 23 (Aug. 5, 1976), 29.

90 Clip of *Christian Science Monitor*, n.d., Williams Papers.

91 Notes from Noel Pugach phone conversation with Williams, Jan. 13, 1974, Williams Papers. In less than a decade, Williams's defender Horowitz—always given to caricature of complex arguments—had swung from far Left to far Right, arguing in *Soldier of Fortune* magazine and other conservative outlets for a bullying U.S. posture abroad. Even more remarkably, he played a starring role in a high-pro-

file Washington "Second Thoughts" conference of Reagan-leaning former New Leftists and others.

92 Special thanks go to Martin Sherwin for making available extensive correspondence and papers from this meeting.

93 Christopher Lasch, "William Appleman Williams on American History," *Marxist Perspectives*, 2 (Fall, 1978), 118.

94 Jon Wiener, "Radical Historians and the Crisis in American History, 1949–1980," *Journal of American History*, 76 (September, 1989), 399–434. The *Radical History Review* was by the later 1970s a main symbol of this activity, succeeding *Radical America* and *Studies On the Left*; but beneath and behind the literary production lay networks of former campus political activists who entered public history in many different venues, from documentary film to extra-academic conferences to historical exhibits and theater. In one thin sense, Lasch was correct: this activity more and more ceased to be called "New Left." But in the more meaningful sense of shared and continuous political commitments, it continues today among New Left veterans from the pages of the *Journal of American History, American Historical Review*, and the *Nation* to prestigious documentary film production companies, the Smithsonian Institution's museums, and the labor/social history exhibits, not to mention the libraries of notable scholarly volumes produced.

95 Lasch, "William Appleman Williams," 125–26.

96 Lasch's volume *The True and Only Heaven: Progress and Its Critics* (New York, 1991), a dense intellectual history, was finally (among a wide assortment of other things) an apotheosis of that cold-war master Reinhold Niebuhr.

97 Not until Eric Foner's election in 1993 did the sixties generation of historians take this symbolic position for themselves without an older generation intermediary. The 1994 annual meeting in Atlanta, featuring one major session devoted to re-examining U.S. foreign policy after the cold war (with Leonard Liggio and Marilyn Young, among others, presenting papers) and another devoted to the influence of the late E. P. Thompson, was in part an honoring of scholarly and personal influences from the older radical generation, now virtually all gone. A "Cold War Revisited" conference at the University of Wisconsin in 1992, dedicated to Williams, offered a smaller but more intense version of this apotheosis. A forthcoming volume of papers delivered at the conference discusses the Williams legacy extensively.

98 Edward Crapol, "William Appleman Williams: The Historian and His Community," Organization of American Historians meeting, 1991. Manuscript kindly supplied by Crapol.

CHAPTER 7

1 Williams to Jeff and June Safford, Jan. 12, 1976, Williams Papers.

2 Howard Schonburger, "William Appleman Williams," *Radical History Newsletter*, 62 (May, 1990), 8.

3 William Appleman Williams, "Empire as a Way of Life," *Nation*, 231 (Aug. 2–9, 1980), 104–119. Respondents included Robert Lekachman, Walter Dean Burnham, Philip Green, Thomas Ferguson, Joel Rodgers, Alan Wolfe, Clair Clark, Marcus G. Raskin, and Sidney Morgenbesser, 120–27; A later issue of the *Nation*, 231 (Nov. 1, 1980), included an exchange of letters over the Williams essay with Carl N. Degler, Martin Green, Lewis Perry, and Virginia Held adding their comments and Williams replying, 426, 443–45.

4 William Appleman Williams, *Empire as a Way of Life* (New York, 1962), 102.

5 Williams, *Empire*, 157. Italics removed from quotation.

6 Williams, *Empire*, 213.

7 Williams, *Empire*, 226.

8 Advertising copy, Williams Papers.

9 Frank Unger, "History as a Way of Learning: On the Death of American Historian William A. Williams," *Initial: Zeitschrift für Politik und Gesellschaft*, 7 (1990), translation in manuscript, Williams Papers.

10 Unger, "History as a Way."

11 Lawrence S. Kaplan, *Journal of American History*, 68 (June, 1981), 96–97; Robert H. Farrell, *South Atlantic Quarterly*, 80 (Summer, 1981), 361–62; Rush Welter, *Annals of the American Academy of Political and Social Science*, 455 (May, 1981), 202–3; See also *Choice* (April, 1981), 1158; and Roger R. Trask, *History: Reviews of Books*, 9 (Oct., 1980), 67.

12 A. J. Beitzinger, " 'Old' and 'New' History," *The Review of Politics*, 43 (Oct., 1981), 611–13; Joseph M. Siracusa, *Business History Review*, 86 (Oct., 1981), 906–7.

13 John Lukacs, *New Republic*, 183 (Oct. 11, 1980), 31–33; Henry Pachter, *New Leader*, 63 (Oct. 20, 1980), 724–25.

14 Williams's last major scholarly contribution, *America in Vietnam: A Documentary History* (Garden City, 1985), was co- edited by Williams with Thomas McCormick, Lloyd Gardner, and Walter LaFeber. An eminently useable collection of documents and introductory essays, the book gained quick adoptions in U.S. foreign policy and Vietnam War history courses. Williams's direct contributions, however, were limited to the period before 1945 and an essay that reiterated familiar themes. Daniel Hémery, Vietnam specialist at the Sorbonne and the only major reviewer, found Williams's essay "excellent" and the overall collection "first-rate." Daniel Hémery, *Pacific Affairs*, 59 (Winter, 1986-87), 724–25.

15 John A. Thompson, "Changing the Outline of American Historiography," *Guardian*, n.d. [March, 1990?], in Williams Papers.

16 Hans-Ulrich Wehler, *Das Deutsche Kaiserreich 1871–1918* (Göttingen, 1973). Special thanks to Volker Berghahn for making German-language sources available to us, and for a discussion of their relevance.

17 Werner Link, *Die amerikanische Stabiliserungspolitik in Deutschland 1921-32* (Düsseldorff, 1970). See also Wehler's translated essay, "Industrial growth and Early German Imperialism," in *Studies in the Theory of Imperialism* (London, 1972), edited by Roger Owen and Bob Sutcliffe, 71–92.

18 V. G. Kiernan, *America: The New Imperialism* (London, 1978). We owe thanks to Harvey J. Kaye, editor of several volumes of Kiernan's writing, for pointing to Williams's influence on him. See also Harvey J. Kaye, ed., *Imperialism and Its Contradictions: Writings of V. G. Kiernan (Volume III)* (New York, 1995).

19 Gareth Stedman Jones, "The Specificity of U.S. Imperialism," *New Left Review*, 60 (Mar.-Apr., 1970), 59–86. Jones suggested that although Williams "had tried to break away from conventional patriotic fantasies," he "remained imprisoned in a moralistic problematic," and yet "shows expansionism to have been a consistent theme running throughout American history," allowing others to "raise more adequately the problem of the specificity of American imperialism," 61, 62.

20 Perry Anderson, *In the Tracks of Historical Materialism* (London, 1983).

21 Many thanks for helpful letters on this subject from Bruno Cartosio and Nando Fasce among others; see also the survey essay on Williams by a Wisconsin PhD, Malcolm Sylvers, "Storia Nazionale e Imperialismo nella Riflessione di Uno Storico Americano 'Revisionista,'" *Qualestorica* 8 (June, 1980), 16–23. Sylvers treats at length yet another translation, of *History as a Way of Learning*, as *Le frontiere dell'impero americano. La cultura dell' "espansione" nella politica statunitense* (Bari, 1978).

22 Yui Daizaburo, "History of American Foreign Relations," in *International Studies in Japan: A Bibliographical Guide* ed. Sadao Asada (Tokyo, 1988), 93–103. Special thanks to Masahiro Hosoya for making this document available to us, and to Charles Neu for assisting us in locating Japanese scholars familiar with Williams's influence. Bruce Cumings added some crucial insights to this perspective in a letter to Paul Buhle, Jan. 7, 1994.

23 Michael H. Hunt, "New Insights But No New Vistas: Recent Work on Nineteenth Century American–East Asian Relations," in *New Frontiers in American-East Asian Relations* (New York, 1983), edited by Warren Cohen, 7–43, especially 24.

24 "To: All members of the History Department," May, 1976, Williams Papers.

25 "Organization of American Historians, Biographical Data for 1979 Nominees," Williams Papers.

26 Ed Crapol, "William Appleman Williams: The Historian and His Community," Organization of American Historians, 1991, manuscript supplied by Ed Crapol.

27 "Wm. A. Williams, President Elect," to Stephen Goodell, Program Office, National Endowment for the Humanities, Sept. 14, 1979. Document made available by William Preston.

28 "Bill Williams: President Elect," to Senator Hatfield, Sept. 14, 1979. Williams Papers.

29 Williams to Hatfield.

30 "From: Bill Williams, To: The Department," Apr. 16, 1981, Williams Papers; Williams to "Bill" [William Preston], Jan. 29, 1980, letter supplied by William Preston.

31 "From: Bill Williams, To: The Department," Apr. 16, 1981, Williams Papers.

32 Affadavit of William Appleman Williams, AFSC v. William H. Webster. Supplied by William Preston.

33 "Amicus Brief: Opposing the Government's Motion to Dissolve Judge Greene's Preliminary Injunction," supplied by attorney Marshall Perlin, at the suggestion of Michael Meeropol.

34 Milan Kundera, quoted by Sigmund Diamond in *Compromised Campus: The Collaboration of Universities with the Intelligence Community, 1945–1955* (New York, 1992), 285.

35 This information was helpfully summarized by William Preston.

36 See Arthur Schlesinger, Jr.'s hand-wringing account of CIA activities in *The Cycles of American History* (Boston, 1986), 60–61.

37 Published as William Appleman Williams, "Thoughts on Reading Henry Adams," *Journal of American History*, 68 (June, 1981), 7–15.

38 Williams, "Beyond Resistance: Backyard Autonomy," *Nation*, 232 (Sept.5, 1981), 161, 179–80.

39 See Monty Wiley letter and Williams's response in "Letters: Backyard Autonomy," *Nation*, Oct. 31, 1981, inside front cover; on Thompson, see for example, Paul Buhle, "E. P. Thompson," *TIKKUN*, 8 (Nov.-Dec., 1993), 82–84. The two historians admired each others' work enormously, but never met.

40 Williams, "Radicals and Regionalism," *Democracy*, 1 (Oct. 1981), 87–98. This journal was established and edited by the distinguished political scientist Sheldon Wolin. Under different historical circumstances, it might have become the ideal vehicle for Williams's effort to establish a dialogue transcending the usual political lines.

41 "Keeping a Hold on the West," *Statesman Journal*, undated clipping, Williams Papers.

42 "A Waste-Our-Water Lifestyle," *Statesman Journal*, Aug. 5, 1981. Fulfilling one of Williams's earlier historical themes of corporatism and labor leaders, Jackson's other major support came from the AFL-CIO chiefs who deserted George McGovern in favor of a Truman-like candidate with promises of heavy military spending and a vitriolic hatred for the peace constituencies.

43 "The U.S. and Uses of Power," *Statesman Journal*, Mar. 17, 1982.

44 "Why They March in Europe," *Capitol Journal* (Portland), May 19, 1982, and "Time to Rehumanize War," *Capitol Journal*, May 5, 1982.

45 "On Funding College Athletics," *Statesman Journal*, July 22, 1981; "Learning to Forget History," *Statesman Journal*, July 29, 1981.

46 "One Historian's Challenge to Journalists," unpublished address, n.d., Williams Papers.

47 "The Crisis of American Democracy," unpublished address, n.d., Williams Papers.

48 "America as a Weary and Nostalgic Culture," unpublished address, n.d., Williams Papers.

49 Printed for the first time as "The Annapolis Crowd," in *A William Appleman Williams Reader*, 385–92.

50 See *Edward Said: A Critical Reader* (Oxford, 1992), edited by Michael Sprinker.

51 Williams, "The Comparative Uses of Power: China on the African Rim and the United States on the Pacific Rim," unpublished address, Williams Papers.

52 We are grateful to Marcus Redicker for making available several letters from Williams to him on this subject.

53 Williams, "Notes on the Death of a Ship and the End of a World: The Grounding of the British Bark *Glenesslin* at Mount Meahkahnie on 1 October 1913," *The American Neptune*, 41 (1981), 123–24.

54 Williams, "Notes on the Death of a Ship," 127–28.

55 Williams, "Notes on the Death of a Ship," 138.

56 "A Good Life and A Good Death: A Memoir of an Independent Lady," with the inscription on the second page, "By Her Son William Appleman Williams for Her Grandchildren," Williams Papers.

57 Summary-outline prospectus, Williams Papers, titled "Life Inside the Frontier," later retitled in manuscript "Ninety Days inside the Empire," Williams Papers. Williams continued to work on this project until the year before his death.

58 John Lewis Gaddis, "The Emerging Post-Revisionist Synthesis on the Origins of the Cold War," *Diplomatic History*, 7 (Summer, 1983), 171, originally presented to the meeting of the Organization of American Historians, April, 1983.

59 See Peter Novick, *That Noble Dream*, 454–57.

60 Stanley Hoffman, "Revisionism Revisited," in *Reflections on the Cold War: A Quarter Century of American Foreign Policy* (Philadelphia, 1974), 3–6, especially 10–15, edited by Lynn H. Miller and Ronald W. Pruessen; for a different and unrecalcitrantly conservative overview see Joseph M. Siracusa, "The New Left, the Cold War, and American Diplomacy: The Case for Historiography as Intellectual History," *World Review*, 14 (March, 1975), 37–52.

61 John Lewis Gaddis, "The Emerging Post-Revisionist Synthesis," 171–72, 180–83. Gaddis first formulated his views in *The United States and the Origins of the Cold War, 1941–1947* (New York, 1972). For his comments on the revisionists, see 357–58. Among other leading "post-revisionist" works were George C. Herring, *Aid to Russia, 1941–1946*; Lynn E. Davis, *The Cold War Begins*; Daniel Yergin, *Shattered Peace*; and Bruce R. Kuniholm, *The Origins of the Cold War in the Near East*. For a good discussion of the post-revisionists, see Richard A. Melanson, *Writing History and Making Policy: The Cold War, Vietnam and Revisionism* (Lanham, Maryland, 1983), 97–119.

62 Warren F. Kimball and Bruce R. Kuniholm, replies to John Lewis Gaddis, in "The Emerging Post-Revisionist Synthesis," 198–99, 201.

63 Barton J. Bernstein, "Cold War Orthodoxy Restated," *Reviews in American History*, 1 (December, 1973), 453–62. Bernstein spoke too early or simply about a young Gaddis, as Bruce Cumings observed; the later Gaddis was none too polite.

64 Bernstein, "Cold War Orthodoxy Revisited," 454; See also Bruce Cumings, "'Revising Postrevisionism,' or The Poverty of Theory in Diplomatic History," *Diplomatic History,* 17 (Fall, 1993), 539–69, considered further below.

65 Williams, "Demystifying Cold War Orthodoxy," *Science & Society,* 39 (1975), 346–51.

66 John Lewis Gaddis, "The Tragedy of Cold War History," *Diplomatic History,* 17 (Winter, 1993), 1–16.

67 Cumings, "'Revising Postrevisionism,'" 555.

68 "[N]ow we can see the absurdity of the recently fashionable view that for two centuries the United States has been struggling to preserve a sclerotic Present and fight off the Future, as represented by a regenerative revolutionary world," said David Brion Davis in a 1989 presidential address to the Organization of American Historians, footnoting in the printed text *America Confronts a Revolutionary World.* A distinguished scholar of race and racism, Davis insisted that the "America Triumphant" cold war liberal or neoliberal (or conservative) view had not been vindicated, either. But in singling out Williams, he seemed to be making a personal point, related perhaps to Niebuhr's enduring influence upon him. David Brion Davis, "American Equality and Foreign Revolutions," *Journal of American History,* 76 (December, 1989), 729ff, especially 730–31. In a letter to the editor of the *New York Review,* Feb. 5, 1986, in the Williams Papers, Williams hailed David Brion Davis as "an exceptionally accomplished, thoughtful and insightful historian who reads documents with a fine sense of nuance and an unusual feel for relationships," a more generous judgment by far than Davis's of Williams.

69 Williams, *History as a Way of Learning* (New York, 1974), xvi.

70 George F. Kennan, "The G.O.P. Won the Cold War? Ridiculous!" *New York Times,* Oct. 28, 1992; Kennan's volume, *Around the Cragged Hill: A Personal and Political Philosophy* (New York, 1993) offered another installment of sobering reflections. In contrast to many observers, including Arthur Schlesinger, Jr., Kennan was distinctly pessimistic about the consequences of the cold war and modern culture at large.

71 We are grateful to David Krikun for suggesting that Williams and Schlesinger, Jr., mirrored each other for decades.

72 Arthur M. Schlesinger, Jr., *The Cycles of American History* (Boston, 1986), 137, 141.

73 Schlesinger, Jr., *Cycles of American History* 248–55.

74 Schlesinger, Jr., *Cycles of American History,* 161, 282, 311.

75 Schlesinger, Jr., *Cycles of American History,* 419, 285.

76 Schlesinger, Jr., *Cycles of American History,* 418.

77 Arthur Schlesinger, Jr., *The Disuniting of America: Reflections on a Multicultural Society* (New York, 1991). Consistent with the growth and development of scholarship in the multiple sources of American culture, an Organization of American Historians president skewered *The Disuniting of America* in his 1993 presidential address and in a subsequent sharp exchange with Schlesinger, Jr. In a none-too-subtly race-tinged commentary on non-European and specifically African traditions,

Schlesinger, Jr., had perceived only sources of "despotism, superstition, tribalism and fanaticism," as usual reserving for the Europeans all the good political traits inherited by Americans. Schlesinger, Jr.'s response to Lawrence Levine's shattering commentary was notably weak and self-contradictory; See Levine, "Clio, Canons and Culture," *Journal of American History*, 80 (December, 1993), 865–66; and the exchange of the two in "Letters to the Editor," *Journal of American History*, 81 (June, 1994), 367–68.

78 Letter of John Mack Faragher to Paul Buhle, Dec. 25, 1993. For his part, an elderly Schlesinger, Jr., no longer accused the critics of Western dispossession of Mexicans and Indians as potential subversives serving the interests of communism (as he had in *The Vital Center*), but he insisted that internal expansion was entirely exaggerated because the U.S. had never conquered Canada or all of Mexico! *Cycles of American History*, 149–52.

79 David W. Noble, "The American Wests: Refuge from European Power or Frontiers of European Expansion," in *The American West as Seen by Europeans and Americans*, ed. Rob Kroes (Amsterdam, 1989), 19–36. See also the discussion by Warren Susman, "The Frontier Thesis and the American Intellectual," in Susman, *Culture as History: The Transformation of American Society in the Twentieth Century* (New York, 1985).

80 Noble, "The American Wests," 31. For Limerick's own account see "Introduction" to *Legacy of Conquest: The Unbroken Past of the New American West* (New York, 1987), 17–32.

81 Richard White, *"It's Your Misfortune and None of My Own": A New History of the American West* (Norman, 1991), 411–12.

82 Walter LaFeber, "Liberty and Power: U.S. Diplomatic History, 1750–1945," in *The New American History* ed. Eric Foner (Philadelphia, 1990), 275–76; Michael J. Hogan, "Corporatism," in "Explaining the History of American Foreign Relations," *Journal of American History*, 77 (June, 1990), 153ff; Hugh De Santis, "The Imperialist Impulse and American Innocence, 1865–1900," in *American Foreign Relations* ed. Gerald K. Haines and J. Samuel Walker (Westport, 1981), 74.

83 Martin J. Sklar, *The Corporate Reconstruction of American Capitalism, 1890–1916* (Cambridge, 1988) and Martin J. Sklar, *The United States as a Developing Country: Studies in U.S. History in the Progressive Era and the 1920s* (Cambridge, 1992). Mark Leff has a perceptive commentary on the latter volume and Sklar's own political trajectory in a review of *The United States as a Developing Country* in *Journal of American History*, 80 (December, 1993), 1117–18.

84 Hugh DeSantis, "The Imperialist Impulse," 74.

85 Walter LaFeber, "Liberty and Power," 276–77; and Thomas J. McCormick, "World Systems," 125ff.

86 This remains an extremely unpopular view, but one heavily endorsed in a careful analysis of Lenin's last years by C. L. R. James. See "Lenin and the Problem," in C. L. R. James, *Nkrumah and the Ghana Revolution* (London, 1977), 189–213. This essay was originally published in a special "C. L. R. James Anthology" issue of

Radical America in 1970 edited by Paul Buhle and may well have influenced Williams's views.

87 Williams to "Jim" [no last name given], July 22/23, 1989. Williams Papers.

88 Williams to "Jim."

89 John A. Thompson, "Reviews," in *International History Review*, 14 (August, 1987), 513.

90 Philip K. Dick, *VALIS* (New York, 1981), 220, 221, 224.

91 Mitzi Goheen, untitled, Williams Papers.

BIBLIOGRAPHY

MANUSCRIPT COLLECTIONS CITED

American Historical Association Papers, Washington, D.C.
Columbia University
  Richard Hofstadter Papers
Library of Congress
  National Association for the Advancement of Colored People Papers
New York University, Tamiment Library
  Oral History of the American Left
Oregon State University, Kerr Library
  William Appleman Williams Papers
State Historical Society of Wisconsin
  Merle E. Curti Papers
  Fred Harvey Harrington Papers
  William Best Hesseltine Papers
  Radical America Papers
  Studies on the Left Papers
United States Naval Academy
  William Appleman Williams File

WORKS BY WILLIAM APPLEMAN WILLIAMS

Unpublished Manuscripts

"McCormick Reports on Russia: A Study of News and Opinion on Russia in the *Chicago Tribune* from 1917 to 1921," MA thesis, University of Wisconsin, 1948.
"Raymond Robins and Russian American Relations," PhD dissertation, University of Wisconsin, 1950.
"Ninety Days Inside the Empire," a novel.
"A Good Life and a Good Death: A Memoir of an Independent Lady, By Her Son . . . for Her Grandchildren," in William Appleman Williams Papers, Oregon State University.

Books and Edited Works

American-Russian Relations, 1781-1947, New York, Rinehart, 1952.
The Shaping of American Diplomacy, 1750-1955, two volumes, Chicago, Rand McNally, 1956. Revised 1972.
The Tragedy of American Diplomacy, Cleveland, World Publishing Company, 1959. Revised 1962, 1972. Twenty-Fifth Anniversary Edition, New York, Norton, 1988. Also published in Spanish and Japanese translations.
The Contours of American History, Cleveland, World Publishing Company, 1961. New Edition, New York, Norton, 1989. Also published in British edition and Italian translation.
The United States, Cuba, and Castro, New York, Monthly Review Press, 1962. Also published in Spanish translation.
The Great Evasion: An Essay on the Contemporary Relevance of Karl Marx and on the Wisdom of Admitting the Heretic into the Dialogue about America's Future, Chicago, Quadrangle Books, 1964.
The Roots of the Modern American Empire: A Study of the Growth and Shaping of Social Consciousness in a Marketplace Society, New York, Random House, 1969. Also published in British edition.
From Colony to Empire: Essays in the History of American Foreign Relations, New York, John Wiley and Sons, 1972. Also published in Italian translation.
Some Presidents: Wilson to Nixon, New York, New York Review of Books, 1972.
History as a Way of Learning, New York, New Viewpoints, 1974. Also published in Spanish translation.
America Confronts a Revolutionary World, 1776-1976, New York, Morrow, 1976.

Americans in a Changing World: A History of the United States in the Twentieth Century, New York, Harper and Row, 1978.

Empire as a Way of Life: An Essay on the Causes and Character of America's Present Predicament Along with a Few Thoughts about an Alternative, New York, Oxford University Press, 1980. Also published in British edition and Spanish, German, and Japanese translations.

America in Vietnam: A Documentary History, edited with notes and introductions with Walter F. Lafeber, Thomas J. McCormick, and Lloyd Gardner, Garden City, New York, Anchor Press/Doubleday, 1985.

A William Appleman Williams Reader: Selections from His Major Historical Writings, edited with an introduction and notes by Henry W. Berger, Chicago, Ivan Dee, 1992.

Selected Essays

"Today is Russia," *The Trident Magazine*, United States Naval Academy, (Winter 1944):12ff.

"The International Impact of National Economic Planning," University of Leeds, England, 1948.

"A Frontier Federalist and the War of 1812," *Pennsylvania Magazine of History and Biography*, 76 (January 1952):81-85.

"Brooks Adams and American Expansion," *New England Quarterly*, 25 (June 1952):217-232.

"A Second Look at Mr. X," *Monthly Review*, 4 (August 1952):123-128.

Review of Albert A. Woldman, *Lincoln and the Russians, Science & Society*, 17 (1953):363-364.

"Moscow Peace Drive: Victory for Containment?" *Nation*, 177 (11 July 1953):28-30.

"A Note on the Isolationism of Senator William E. Borah," *Pacific Historical Review*, 22(November 1953):391-392.

Review of Arthur S. Link, *Woodrow Wilson and the Progressive Era, 1910-1917, Science & Society*, 18(1954):348-351.

"Raymond Robins, Crusader—The Outdoor Mind," *The Nation*, 179 (30 October 1954):384-385.

"Collapse of the Grand Coalition," review of William H. McNeill, *America, Britain and Russia, Nation*, 179 (6 November 1954):408-409.

"The Legend of Isolationism in the 1920's," *Science & Society*, 18 (Winter 1954):1-20. Reprinted in Armin Rappaport, editor, *Essays in American Diplomacy*, New York, MacMillan, 1967, and in Henry W. Berger, editor, *A William Appleman Williams Reader*, Chicago, Ivan Dee, 1992.

Review of Michael Florinsky, *Russia: A History and an Interpretation, Science & Society*, 19 (1955):346-350.

"Cold War Perspectives—A Historical Fable," *Nation* 180 (28 May 1955): 458-461.

"The Historical Romance of Senator Neuberger's Election," *Oregon Historical Quarterly*, 56 (June 1955):101-105.

"The Frontier Thesis and American Foreign Policy," *Pacific Historical Review*, 24 (November 1955):379-395. Reprinted in Henry W. Berger, editor, *A William Appleman Williams Reader*, Chicago, Ivan Dee, 1992.

Review of Robert D. Warth, *The Allies and the Russian Revolution, Science & Society*, 20 (1956):84-86.

"Babbitt's New Fables," *Nation*, 182 (7 January 1956):3-6.

"Great Boomerang: The Irony of Containment," *Nation*, 182 (5 May 1956):376-379.

"On the Restoration of Brooks Adams," *Science & Society*, 20 (Summer 1956):247-253.

"Challenge to American Radicalism," *Frontier*, 7 (June 1956):3-6.

"The Age of Re-forming History," A review of Richard Hofstadter, *The Age of Reform*, *Nation*, 182 (30 June 1956):552-554.

"Reflections on the Historiography of American Entry into World War II," *Oregon Historical Quarterly*, 57 (September 1956):274-279.

"The Convenience of History," review of George F. Kennan, *Russia Leaves the War*, *Nation*, 183 (15 September 1956):222-224.

"A Note on Charles Austin Beard's Search for a General Theory of Causation," *American Historical Review*, 62 (October 1956):59-80.

"Introduction," with Harvey Goldberg, and "Charles Austin Beard: The Intellectual as Tory-Radical," in Harvey Goldberg, editor, *American Radicals: Some Problems and Personalities*, New York, Monthly Review Press, 1957. Essay on Beard reprinted in Henry W. Berger, editor, *A William Appleman Williams Reader*, Chicago, Ivan Dee, 1992.

"Taxing for Peace," *Nation*, 184 (19 January 1957):53.

"The Empire of Theodore Roosevelt," review of Foster Rhea Dulles, *The Imperial Years* and Howard K. Beale, *Theodore Roosevelt and the Rise of America to World Power, Nation*, 18(2 March 1957):191-192.

"Schlesinger: Right Crisis—Wrong Order," review of Arthur M. Schlesinger, Jr., *The Crisis of the Old Order, 1919-1933, Nation*, 18(23 March 1957):257-260.

"Go Left or Go Under," *Liberation*, (April 1957):14-17.

"The 'Logic' of Imperialism," review of Amaury de Riencourt, *The Coming Caesars, Nation*, 18(6 July 1957):14-15.

"The Nature of Peace," *Monthly Review*, 9 (July-August 1957):112-114.

"China and Japan: A Challenge and a Choice of the Nineteen Twenties," *Pacific Historical Review*, 26 (August 1957):259-279.

"Latin America: Laboratory of American Foreign Policy of the Nineteen Twenties," *Inter-American Economic Affairs*, 11 (Autumn 1957):3-30.

"The American Century, 1941-1957," *Nation*, 185 (2 November 1957): 297-301.

America and the Middle East: Open Door Imperialism or Enlightened Leadership? (pamphlet), New York, Rinehart, 1958.

Source Problems in World Civilization (pamphlet), New York, 1958.

"Loss of Debate," review of Herbert Hoover, *The Ordeal of Woodrow Wilson*, *Nation*, 18(17 May 1958):452-453.

"The Age of Mercantilism: An Interpretation of the American Political Economy, 1763-1828," *William and Mary Quarterly*, 15 (October 1958): 419-437. Reprinted in Armin Rappaport, editor, *Essays in American Diplomacy*, New York, MacMillan, 1967.

"A Note on American Foreign Policy in Europe in the 1920's," *Science & Society*, 22 (Winter 1958):1-20.

"Needed: Production for Peace," *Nation*, 188 (21 February 1959): 149-153.

"Take A New Look at Russia," *Foreign Policy Bulletin*, 38 (15 April 1959):118-119.

"Samuel Adams: Calvinist, Mercantilist, Revolutionary," *Studies on the Left*, 1 (Winter 1960):47-57.

"On the Origins of the Cold War: An Exchange," *Commentary*, 31 (February 1961):142-159.

"Protecting Overseas Investors," *Nation*, 193 (26 August 1961): 100-101.

"The Irony of the Bomb," *Centennial Review*, 5 (Fall 1961):373-384.

"Foreign Policy and the American Mind: An Alternate View," *Commentary*, 33 (February 1962):155-159.

"A Proposal to Put *American* Back into American Socialism," in "American Socialism and Thermonuclear War: A Symposium," *New Politics*, 1(Spring 1962):40-45.

"Fire in the Ashes of Scientific History" (review article), *William and Mary Quarterly*, 19 (April 1962):274-287.

"Cuba: The President and His Critics," *Nation*, 196 (16 March 1963):226, 236.

"Historiography and Revolution: The Case of Cuba," *Studies on the Left*, 3 (Summer 1963):78-102.

"American Intervention in Russia, 1917-1920," *Studies on the Left*,3 (Fall 1963):24-48; 4 (Winter 1964):39-57.

"The Acquitting Judge," review of Ernest R. May, *Imperial Democracy: The Emergence of America as a Great Power*, *Studies on the Left*, 3 (Winter 1963):94-99.

"Cuba: Issues and Alternatives," *Annals of the American Academy of Political and Social Sciences,* 351 (January 1964):72-80.

"The Vicious Circle of American Imperialism," *New Politics,* 4 (Fall 1965):48-55. Reprinted in K. T. Fann and Donald Hodges, editors, *Readings in U.S. Imperialism,* Boston, F. Porter Sargent, 1971.

"Last Chance for Democracy," review of John Bartlow Martin, *Overtaken by Events: The Dominican Crisis from the Fall of Trujillo to the Civil War, Nation,* 204 (January 29 1967):23-25.

Review of Tristam Coffin, *Senator Fulbright: Portrait of a Public Philosopher, Ramparts,* 5 (March 1967):57-59.

"A Natural History of the American Empire," *Canadian Dimension,* 4 (March-April 1967):12-17.

"The Cold War Revisionists," *Nation,* 205 (13 November 1967):492-495.

"The Rise of an American World Power Complex," in Neal D. Houghton, editor, *Struggle Against History: U.S. Foreign Policy in an Age of Revolution,* New York, Washington Square Press, 1968.

"The Large Corporation and American Foreign Policy," in David Horowitz, editor, *Corporations and the Cold War,* New York, Monthly Review Press, 1969.

"An American Socialist Community?" *Liberation,* 14 (June 1969):8-11.

"How Can the Left Be Relevant?" *Current,* 109 (August 1969):20-24.

"The Crown on Clio's Head," review of J. H. Plumb, *The Death of the Past, Nation,* 210 (9March 1970):279-280.

"What This Country Needs. . . ." Review of Gene Smith, *The Shattered Dream: Herbert Hoover and the Great Depression, New York Review of Books,* 15 (5 November 1970):7-11.

"Notes for a Dialogue with Messrs. Harrington, Schlesinger, and Zinn," *Partisan Review,* 38 (January 1971):67-78.

"Officers and Gentlemen," review of nine books on military history, *New York Review of Books,* 16 (6 May 1971):3-8.

"Wilson," review of five books on Woodrow Wilson, *New York Review of Books,* 17 (2 December 1971):3-6.

"Ol' Lyndon," review of Lyndon Baines Johnson, *The Vantage Point: Perspectives of the Presidency, 1963-1969, New York Review of Books,* 17 (16 December 1971):3-6.

"Excelsior!" Review of Rowland Evans, Jr., and Robert D. Novak, *Nixon in the White House* and John Osborne, *The First Two Years of the Nixon Watch, New York Review of Books,* 18 (24 February 1972):7-12.

"Confessions of an Intransigent Revisionist," *Socialist Review,* 17 (September-October 1973):89-98. Reprinted in Henry W. Berger, editor, *A William Appleman Williams Reader,* Chicago, Ivan Dee, 1992.

"A Historian's Perspective," *Prologue: The Journal of the National Archives,* 6 (Fall 1974):200-203.

"Demystifying Cold War Orthodoxy," review of George C. Herring, *Aid to Russia, 1941-1946* and Thomas G. Paterson, *Soviet-American Confrontation: Postwar Reconstruction and the Origins of the Cold War*, *Science and Society*, 39 (1975):346-351.

"Schurman's Logic of World Power," review of Franz Schurman, *The Logic of World Power*, *Bulletin of Concerned Asian Scholars*, 84 (October-December 1976):47-48.

"Raymond Robins," *Dictionary of American Biography*, Supplement 5, 1951-1955, New York, Charles Scribner's Sons, 1977.

"Social Protest in Three American Cities: Is Radicalism an Urban Phenomenon?" 48th Australian/New Zealand Association for the Advancement of Science (August 1977).

"Open Door Interpretation," in *Encyclopedia of American Foreign Policy: Studies of the Principal Movements and Ideas*, volume II, New York, Charles Scribner's Sons, 1978.

"Amerikas 'idealistischer' Imperialismus, 1900-1917," in Hans-Ulrich Wehler, editor, *Imperialismus*, Konigstein, Althenaum, 1979.

Review of David Burner, *Herbert Hoover, New Republic*, 180 (10 March 1979):35-36.

"You Aren't Lost Until You Don't Know Where You've Been," review of Frances FitzGerald, *History Schoolbooks in the Twentieth Century*, *Nation*, 229 (27 October 1979):405-407.

"An Interview with William Appleman Williams," by Mike Wallace, *Radical History Review*, 22 (Winter 1979-1980):65-91. Reprinted in Henry Abelove et al., editors, *Visions of History*, New York, Pantheon, 1984.

"Is the Idea and Reality of America Possible Without Empire?" *Nation*, 231 (2-9 August 1980):104-119, 120-127.

"America and Empire: An Exchange," *Nation*, 231 (1 November 1980): 426, 443-445.

"Notes on the Death of a Ship and the End of a World: The Grounding of the British Bark *Glenesslin* at Mount Neahkahnie on 1 October 1913," *The American Neptune*, 41 (1981):122-138.

"Thoughts on Rereading Henry Adams," *Journal of American History*, 68 (June 1981):7-15.

"The Whole World in Its Hands," review of Holly Sklar, editor, *Trilateralism: The Trilateral Commission and Elite Planning in World Management, Mother Jones*, 6 (June 1981):53-54.

"Regional Resistance: Backyard Autonomy," *Nation*, 233 (5 September 1981):161, 179-180.

"Radicals and Regionalism," *Democracy*, 1 (October 1981):87-98.

"History as Redemption: Henry Adams and the Education of America," *Nation*, 234 (6 March 1982):266-269.

"Procedure Becomes Substance," *Democracy*, 2 (April 1982):100-102.

"Missile Ban in Washington: 1921," *Nation*, 237 (26 November 1983):530-533.

"The City on a Hill on an Errand into the Wilderness," in Harrison Salisbury, editor, *Vietnam Reconsidered: Lessons from a War*, New York, Harper and Row, 1984.

"Thoughts on the Fun and Purpose of Being an American Historian," *Organization of American Historians Newsletter*, 13 (February 1985):2-3.

"William Appleman Williams: 'Doing History is Best of All. No Regrets,'" interview with William G. Robbins, in Lloyd C. Gardner, editor, *Redefining the Past: Essays in Diplomatic History in Honor of William Appleman Williams*, Corvallis, Oregon State University Press, 1986.

"Thoughts on the Comparative Uses of Power," George Bancroft Lecture, United States Naval Academy (September 1986), in Henry W. Berger, editor, *A William Appleman Williams Reader*, Chicago, Ivan Dee, 1992.

"The Annapolis Crowd" (August 1987), in Henry W. Berger, editor, *A William Appleman Williams Reader*, Chicago, Ivan Dee, 1992.

"My Life in Madison," in Paul Buhle, editor, *History and the New Left: Madison, Wisconsin, 1950-1970*, Philadelphia, Temple University Press, 1990.

SELECT SECONDARY STUDIES

Buhle, Paul, ed., *History and the New Left: Madison, Wisconsin, 1950-1970*, Philadelphia, Temple University Press, 1990.

Buhle, Paul, *Marxism in the United States: Remapping the History of the American Left, From 1870 to the Present Day*, London, Verso, 1987.

Buhle, Paul, "Marxism and Its Critics," in Mary Kupiec Cayton, Elliott J. Gorn, and Peter W. Williams, editors, *Encyclopedia of Social History*, volume I, New York, 1993.

Buhle, Paul and Edward Rice-Maximin, "War Without End: Why the U.S. Can't Stop," a review article considering Marilyn B. Young, *The Vietnam Wars, 1945-1990*, 1991; William Appleman Williams, *The Tragedy of American Diplomacy*, New Edition, 1988; and William Appleman Williams, *The Contours of American History*, New Edition, 1989 in *The Village Voice Literary Supplement*, 5 November 1991.

Copelman, Dina M. and Barbara Clark Smith, editors, "Excerpts from a Conference to Honor William Appleman Williams," *Radical History Review*, 50(Spring 1991):39-70.

Dee, Ivan R., "Revisionism Revisited," in Lloyd C. Gardner, editor, *Redefining the Past: Essays in Diplomatic History in Honor of William Appleman Williams*, Corvallis, Oregon State University Press, 1986.

Gardner, Lloyd, editor, *Redefining the Past: Essays in Diplomatic History in Honor of William Appleman Williams*, Corvallis, Oregon State University Press, 1986.

Genovese, Eugene, "William Appleman Williams on Marx and America," *Studies on the Left*, 6 (January-February 1966):70-86.

Hess, Gary R., "After the Tumult: The Wisconsin School's Tribute to William Appleman Williams," *Diplomatic History*, 12 (Fall 1988): 483-499.

Lasch, Christopher, "William Appleman Williams on American History," *Marxist Perspectives*, 2 (Fall 1978):118-126.

Livingston, James, "Farewell to Intellectual Godfather William Appleman Williams," *In These Times* (28 March–3 April 1990).

Marina, William, "William Appleman Williams," *Dictionary of Literary Biography*, vol. 17, *Twentieth Century Historians*, Detroit, Gale Research Company, 1983.

Meeropol, Michael, "Cold War Revisionism," in Mari Jo Buhle, Paul Buhle, and Dan Georgakas, editors, *Encyclopedia of the American Left*, New York, Garland, 1990.

Meeropol, Michael, "William Appleman Williams's Historiography," and Comments by James P. O'Brien, *Radical America*, 6 (August 1970):29-53.

Melanson, Richard A., "The Social and Political Thought of William Appleman Williams," *Western Political Quarterly*, 31(September 1978):392-409.

Melanson, Richard A., *Writing History and Making Policy: The Cold War, Vietnam and Revisionism*, Lanham, Maryland, University Presses of America, 1983.

Mommsen, Wolfgang J., *Theories of Imperialism*, translated by P. S. Falla, Chicago, University of Chicago Press, 1982.

Mosse, George, "New Left Intellectuals/New Left Politics," in Paul Buhle, editor, *History and the New Left: Madison, Wisconsin, 1950-1970*, Philadelphia, Temple University Press, 1990.

Noble, David W., *The End of American History*, Minneapolis, University of Minnesota Press, 1985.

Noble, David W., "William Appleman Williams and the Crisis of Public History," in Lloyd C. Gardner, editor, *Redefining the Past: Essays in Diplomatic History in Honor of William Appleman Williams*, Corvallis, Oregon State University Press, 1986.

Novick, Peter, *That Nobel Dream: The "Objectivity Question" and the American Historical Profession*, New York, Cambridge University Press, 1988.

Perkins, Bradford, "*The Tragedy of American Diplomacy*: Twenty-Five Years Later," *Reviews in American History*, 12 (March 1984):1-18. Reprinted in Lloyd C. Gardner, editor, *Redefining the Past: Essays in Diplomatic History in Honor of William Appleman Williams*, Corvallis, Oregon State University Press, 1986, and in *The Tragedy of American Diplomacy*, Twenty-Fifth Anniversary Edition, New York, Norton, 1988.

Rice-Maximin, Edward, "William Appleman Williams," in Mari Jo Buhle, Paul Buhle, and Harvey J. Kaye, editors, *The American Radical*, New York, Routledge, 1994.

Said, Edward, *Culture and Imperialism*, New York, Knopf, 1993.

Schonberger, Howard, "William Appleman Williams," *Radical History Newsletter*, 62 (May 1990):1, 7-8.

Theoharis, Athan G., "Revisionism," in *Encyclopedia of American Foreign Policy*, volume 3, *Studies of the Principal Movements and Ideas*, New York, Charles Scribner's Sons, 1978.

Thompson, J. A., "William Appleman Williams and the 'American Empire'," *Journal of American Studies* (United Kingdom), 7 (April 1973):91-104.

Tyrrell, Ian, *The Absent Marx: Class Analysis and Liberal History in Twentieth Century America*, Westport, Connecticut, Greenwood Press, 1986.

Weiner, Jon, "Radical Historians and the Crisis in American History, 1949-1980," *Journal of American History*, 76 (September 1989):399-434.

INDEX

250; expansionism, 138, 245; imperi-
alism, 74, 92, 158, 174; New World
Order, 248; Pax Americana, xv
Encounter, 272n.69, 277n.130
Engels, Friedrich, 135

Faragher, John Mack, 245, 246
Farmer, Paul, 39, 41, 66
Farmers, 132, 168-172; Farmers
Alliance, 175
FBI, 27-29, 45, 72, 95, 115, 166, 183,
194, 228-229, 261n.2
Federalist Papers, 232
Ferrell, Robert H., 220
Fleming, D. F., 193
Foner, Eric, 288n.97
Forrestal, James, 188
Fortune Magazine, 71
Founding Fathers, 113, 125, 130, 152,
174
Foreign Affairs, 52, 78
Foreign Policy Bulletin, 114
Foreign Relations, Council on, 114,
188
Frankfurt School, 34-35, 40, 92, 109,
124, 154, 155, 161, 213
Free Speech Movement (Berkeley),
157
Freedom of Information Act, 227
Freud, Sigmund, 21, 76, 93, 122, 124,
134, 153-154, 196; Freudianism,
12; Neo-, 154
Friedan, Betty, *The Feminine
Mystique*, 177-178
Fromm, Erich, 21-22, 153-154;
Escape From Freedom, 21; *The Sane
Society*, 153
Frontier, 131, 134, 152, 237, 246
Fulbright, Senator J. William, 215

Gaddis, John Lewis, 240-242
Gardner, Lloyd, 106, 107, 116, 171,
191, 193, 240
Garrison, William Lloyd, 59
Genovese, Eugene, 155, 157, 163,
181, 198, 213, 232, 279n.30
Gerth, Hans, 40-41, 46, 85, 105
Gestalt psychology, 12
GIs, 46, 84; GI Bill, 44, 64, 207
Gilmor, Herb (and Charlotte), 25-26, 28

H.M.S. *Glenesslin*, 237-238
Goheen, Mitzi, 287n.84
Goldberg, Harvey, 42, 66-67, 79, 88-
91, 148-150, 156, 160, 164, 166,
277n.1, 278n.2, 280n.48
Gompers, Samuel, 58, 133, 138
Goodwyn, Laurence, *The Democratic
Promise*, 175-176
Gordon, Linda, 280n.38
Graebner, Norman, 187, 195
Griffith, D. W., 131
Guatemala, 142, 271n.51, 277n.130
Gumberg, Alexander, 49, 53, 65
Gutman, Herbert G., 39, 72, 123,
163, 223

Haas, Ernest, 56
Hacker, Andrew, 119
Haiti, xiv
Hakim, Eleanor, 118
Hall, Radclyff, *The Well of Loneliness*, 11
Hamilton, Alexander, 94
Handlin, Oscar, 136-137, 175, 187,
192, 193, 195, 204, 220, 272n.69
Harriman, Averell, 82
Harrington, Fred Harvey, 36-39, 41-
42, 44, 46, 51-53, 64-65, 67, 86-87,
92, 97, 105, 115, 116, 148, 159,
267nn.84,1, 271n.56; biography of
Nathaniel P. Banks, 37; Nancy
(wife), 38, 44
Harrington, Michael, 140, 172-173,
265n.65, 281n.60; *The Other
America*, 140
Hartz, Louis, 120-121; *The Liberal
Tradition in America*, 120
Hatfield, Senator Mark, 201, 226,
286n.61
Hawley, Ellis, 279n.27
Hay, John, 53, 92-93
Hayden, Tom, 140
Hayes, Woody, 67
Hegel, Georg Wilhelm, 40;
Phenomenology of the Mind, 126
Heilbroner, Robert, 155
Heller, Joseph, *Catch 22*, 23
Hemingway, Ernest, *For Whom the
Bell Tolls*, 23
Hesseltine, William Best, 37-39, 46,
58, 104-105, 140

Hill, Lewis, 281n.59
Hirsh, Elroy "Crazy Legs," 44
Hicks, John D., 37
Higham, John, 42, 125, 136-137
Historians/Histories: British radical, 22, 50-51, 78, 103, 222-223; Catholic, 56; Chinese, 224; conservative, 131, 136-137, 220; Eastern (U.S.), 36-37, 174, 239; German, 221-222; Italian, 223; Ivy League, 43, 125, 184, 230; Japanese, 54-55; Jewish, 272n.70; liberal, 91, 94-95, 211, 229; Marxist, 78, 79, 102, 103; New Left, 174, 186, 188, 191, 193-195, 212, 242, 275n.108; New Social, 123, 175, 206, 239; Popular Front, 120-121; Populist, 37, 167; anti-Populist, 272nn.69,70; Progressive, 37, 39, 70-71, 73, 77, 121, 123-125,187, 197, 211-212; anti-Progressive, 120; Radical, 130, 139, 230; Neo-Realist, 210, 247; Revisionist, 56, 124, 206, 211, 220; Revisionist (diplomatic), 56, 247; Revisionist (Cold War), 57, 181, 193-196, 240-241, 267n.77; Revisionist (German), 192; Post-Revisionist, 223, 140-141; Socialist, 286n.56; West (U.S.),123-124, 245-247; Williams's "WPA" proposal for, 226-227; Women's, 187, 198, 205-206, 227, 242, 286n.54
Hobbes, Thomas, 106, 124
Hobson, John A., *Towards a Lasting Peace,* 92
Hoffman, Stanley, 240
Hofstadter, Richard, 36, 39, 88-89, 120-122, 124, 131, 167-168, 273n.74; *Age of Reform,* 121, 122; *American Political Tradition,* 120-121; *Progressive Historians,* 187
Hogan, Michael J., 133. 247
Homosexuals, 11, 63-64, 66, 74, 76-77, 105, 149; Gay Liberation Movement, 167;*The Lost Sex* (Lundberg/Farnham), 76
Horkheimer, Max, 34, 40, 124, 154, 170, 279n.18
Hook, Sidney, 72

Hoover, Herbert, xii, 9, 34, 83, 91, 94-95, 107, 126, 134, 142, 153, 182, 185, 201, 207, 209-210
Hoover, J. Edgar, 188
Horowitz, David, 193-194, 211, 288n.91; *Free World Colossus,* 211
The House I Live In (film), 25, 256n.58
How Green Was My Valley (film), 12
Howe, Irving, 84, 140, 145, 147, 170
HUAC, 71-72, 101, 104, 115-116, 271n.56. *See also* Communists; McCarthyism
Huberman, Leo, 78
Hughes, H. Stuart, 188-189
Hughes, J. R. T., 172
Humphrey, Hubert, 166, 192

Indiana Magazine of History, 56
Intercollegiate Review, 193
Ions, Edmund, 174
Iran-Contra Affair, 229, 235, 244
IRS (Internal Revenue Service), 101, 116
Isolationism, 94
Israel, 234
IWW (Industrial Workers of the World, "Wobblies"), 6, 67

Jackson, Andrew, 124, 126, 131, 209
Jackson, Senator Henry "Scoop," 233
Jacoby, Russell, *The Last Intellectuals,* 264n.50
James, C. L. R., 17, 138
James, Daniel, *Red Design on the Americas,* 277n.130
Jay, John, 130
Jefferson, Thomas, 106, 124, 126, 128, 130, 152
Jensen, Iowa Congressman Ben J., 18
Jensen, Merrill, 39, 79, 105, 130, 135
Jews, 7, 20, 26, 43, 102, 105, 148, 173
John Birch Society, 73, 117
Johnson, Lyndon Baines, 26, 157-159, 184-186; War on Poverty, 140
Journal of American History, 195
Judis, John, 286n.56

Kaplan, Amy, xiv
Kaplan, Lawrence S., 220